The law of Evidence, by Lord Chief Baron Gilbert. Considerably Enlarged by Capel Lofft, ... To Which is Prefixed, Some Account of the Author; and his Argument in a Case of Homicide in Ireland. Vol. I. of 4

THE

L A W

OF

E V I D E N C E,

BY

Sir Geoffrey

Lord Chief Baron GILBERT.

CONSIDERABLY ENLARGED

By C A P E L L O F F T,

BARRISTER AT LAW

TO WHICH IS PREFIXED,

Some ACCOUNT of the AUTHOR; and his ARGUMENT in a Cafe
of HOMICIDE in IRELAND.

VOL. I.

—DUBLIN—

PRINTED FOR P BYRNE, J. MOORE, W. JONES, AND J. RICE,

1795.

Rec, Dec. 11, 1889,

ADVERTISEMENT.

THE work, of which a part is now offered to the Public, has long poffeffed, in the original ftate of it, the fanction of a defervedly great name. It is much to be regretted that it's learned Author did not live to complete his own plan · and even if he had, the lapfe of fo many years, and the variety of important queftions relative to EVIDENCE which has been difcuffed fince his death would have rendered fome confiderable additions very material. To give this extenfive title of *Jurifprudence* as fully and fyftematically as poffible, has been the endeavour of the prefent editor. Profeffional men will difcern clearly, that no little time and refearch muft have been neceffary for executing fuch a defign in any degree fuitably. Much time has accordingly been employed, and interruptions have occurred which have fufpended the progrefs of the work A more particular explanation of thefe will not be defired, if the Profeffion fhall fee reafon to believe, that not much of voluntary inattention can be imputable The editor would certainly have wifhed to have publifhed the whole, (agreeably to the expectations which he entertained), at a period earlier from the commencement of the undertaking than his already paffed, but not having found it poffi-

ble,

ble, he has been induced by the requeſt of the Proprietors, of whoſe candour and patience during ſo long a delay he is very ſenſible, to publiſh two Volumes: which comprize the principal diviſions of the ſubject The remainder he hopes to finiſh ſo that it may be ready for publication by the end of the winter. To the completion of the work, a full *Index* of the *Principal Matters* and a Synoptical Table of *Caſes* is reſerved.

London, 16th *July,* 1791,

ALPHABETICAL

INDEX

OF

CASES

CONTAINED IN

THE FIRST VOLUME.

Thofe printed in Italics *are leading Cafes.*

Cavendifh

THE INDEX.

THE INDEX.

End of the Alphabetical Cafes to VOL I

PREFACE:

CONTAINING

An EXPLANATION of the PLAN

OF THE

PRESENT WORK;

WITH

SOME ACCOUNT

OF THE

LORD CHIEF BARON *GILBERT*,

IT is the Fate of the Law, that although, when it is ftudied in the juft extent, it is capable of exciting the beft faculties of the human mind, whatever their native force or cultivation, to a moft vigorous, ufeful, and honourable exertion, ftill the Celebrity acquired by it is confined within the fame Limits which bound the municipal Inftitutions eftablifhed in the Country of its refpective Profeffors And even in thefe, while the Labours of the Lawyer are eftimated in proportion to their national Utility, the Judgment of their Value refting in the Profeffion itfelf, the public admiration and Curiofity hardly furvive a few Years and the Memory of any circumftances not directly included in the profeffional Hiftory of the perfon foon fades and vanifhes; however eminent the ftation, and however great and confpicuous the Abilities while in other Profeffions and Employments, equal, or even inferior Talents may render the Poffeffor of them illuftrious in every civilized Nation , and give an Intereft and Permanency to the minuteft Particulars refpecting his Perfon, his Family, and his private Life How much oftener has *Martial* been remembered than *Ulpian* or

Papinian !

Papirian! With what frequency will the Name of *Gay* occur to our Posterity, if compared with that of *Coke!* How does the exactness of our Intelligence with regard to *Swift* strike us when contracted with our scanty Information respecting Sir *Matthew Hale!* In the military Profession, whether by Sea or Land, the Trophy beams with diffusive splendor. In the elegant and captivating Arts of Painting, Sculpture, and Music, the public Ear catches with eagerness every slight Memorial of a favoured Artist. In the grave and retired Studies of Theology and Medicine the biographical information of persons eminent in either will be found less defective than of persons proportionably remarkable for their application and knowledge in the Law

Of this Difference, in prejudice of the Law, when compared with any other liberal pursuit, a Difference mortifying indeed, if Fame were the best Reward of human Actions, THE AUTHOR OF THE LAW OF EVIDENCE is a complete Example At the distance of sixty-two years from his Death, though he filled a distinguished station, both in *Ireland* and *England*, with Abilities adequate to the greatest, my private Researches, public Enquiries, and the obliging aid of others, leave me still uninformed of the immediate Progenitors of the Lord Chief Baron *Gilbert* though, from the Arms upon his Tomb-stone at *Bath*, a Consanguinity may be conjectured between our Author and *John Gilbert*, of *Woodford*, in *Essex*; to whom, in 1609, part of the same Arms was confirmed.

Neither the *General Biography* nor the *British* contain his Name: however evidently most worthy to have graced both. And by the inadvertence of his Contemporaries we are left ignorant of the Place of his Birth, his Education, and of every thing, a single Essay excepted, which does not fall within the Line of his Profession. It does not appear that he was a *Graduate* in either *University* yet his education we may justly infer to have been liberal His Improvement in general Knowledge in the great branches of *liberal* and *useful* Learning is strongly indicated in such of his *Remains* as have been already published.

The Date of his Birth must be referred to 1674, as appears on a comparison of his Age and the Year of his Death in the *Epitaph* subjoined to this Account, and is confirmed by Lord RAYMOND The Year of the Birth is always expedient to be inserted in monumental Inscriptions, as well as the age and date of the Death, since thus, if a numeral Error (the most frequent of all mistakes, and of which there is a signal Example in the Epitaph of that admirable Poet, *Spenser;* happens to be committed in any one, the other two will ascertain afcertain how it is to be rectified· and for want of this, had not his eminent Contemporary eftablifhed the Age of GILBERT, in concurrence with the Infcription at *Bath* and other cotemporary Evidence, the Proof derived from the *Latin Epitaph* might have been regarded as doubtful in fome degree, though the Care manifefted by his Executors would have much reduced the probability of fuch error He was confequently about fourteen at the time of the glorious Revolution ; of an Age,

Ut fupere et quæ fit poffet cognofcere Virtus—

And it feems to have made a fuitable Impreffion· what his fentiments were of the Reign which rendered that Event neceffary will be feen, in fome meafure, in the Work now publifhed, what his Principles of legal Certainty and conftitutional Freedom, may be collected from the Tenor of his Works.

In 1715, if his *Epitaph* be correct, but in the year preceding, if a late curious and ufeful Publication * be exact in this particular, + he became one of the Judges of the King's BENCH in IRELAND, ‡ and before the end of that year, in which both agree, he was promoted to the Rank of CHIEF BARON of the EXCHEQUER, which he held till the early part of the year 1722, when he was called to ENGLAND, and fucceeded by *Barnard Hale*, Efq He was confequently nearly thirty-nine or forty when he was made a JUDGE, and continued fuch in different Courts about feven years in *Ireland*, and nearly five in *England* In which Station, during the Engagements of public Duty, and the trying Conflict he fuftained part of the time, moft of his Works, numerous and of deep Inveftigation as they are, feem to have been compofed

We are now brought to a Period when, during the Ferment of the Conteft, one Party would have thought no Apology fufficient, the other, perhaps, no Encomium adequate. We fhall offer neither, but ftate the Facts

marginal notes: Epitaph *Beatfon's Poll Index, II.* p 218 *Id* B P I 220,

---

* For want of Dates to the Cafes in the COURT of EXCHEQUER of IRELAND, preferved in the Folio Edition of 1742, I am not enabled to afcertain this point from thence as I expected to have done, *(margin:* DWYER's Cafe.*)*

‡ It fhould feem that during this Time a Cafe was folemnly argued before that Court on a fpecial Verdict on a Queftion of Homicide· we have unfortunately no more than the introductory Part of the Argument of GILBERT the Date of the Fact on which the Verdict was founded is Jan 1724, in the Folio Reports But this feems manifeftly a Miftake for 1714 The Argument being curious, it will be fubjoined by way of Appendix

When

When our *Author* was about the Age of forty-four, and had spent about four years in *Ireland*, the situation of that Country and of the Government and Policy of *England* engaged him in a very arduous Contest. This was in the *fifth* of *G. I.* and the occasion, a Contest of *Privilege* between the ultimate judicial Tribunal of each. From the time of Sir MOLYNEUX's justly celebrated Tract, the just Terms of Connection between the two Countries could not well fail of being investigated with increasing Attention. It could hardly then be expected that the Claim of the BRITISH HOUSE of LORDS to decide in the last Resort on Questions of real property in IRELAND, exclusively of the IRISH HOUSE of LORDS, on *Appeal* from the subordinate Jurisdictions in IRELAND, could prevail without a struggle. This accordingly happened, and a Deduction of the several Facts in the Order of Time may perhaps give the clearest Idea of the Case.

In the year 1703, 2 *An.* the *Irish House of Lords* had resolved, *Nemine contradicente*, in the following Terms on the Petition of *Edward*, Earl of *Meath*, and *Cecilia* Countess of *Meath*, his Wife.

That by the ancient known Laws and Statutes of this Kingdom her Majesty hath an undoubted Jurisdiction and Prerogative of judging in this her HIGH COURT OF PARLIAMENT *in all Appeals and Causes within her Majesty's* REALM *of* IRELAND.

That the Determinations and Judgments of this High Court of Parliament *are final and conclusive, and cannot be reversed or set aside by any other Court whatsoever.*

That if any Subject or Resiant within this Kingdom shall hereafter presume to remove any Cause determined in this High Court of Parliament to any other Court, such Person or Persons shall be deemed Betrayers of her Majesty's Prerogative and Jurisdiction, and the undoubted ancient Right and Privileges of this Honourable House and of the Rights and Liberties of the Subjects of this Kingdom.

That if any Subject or Resiant within this Kingdom shall presume to put in execution any Order from any other Court contrary to the Judgment and Determination of this High Court of Parliament, such Person or Persons shall be deemed Betrayers of her Majesty's Prerogative and Jurisdiction, and the undoubted ancient Rights and Liberties of this House, and of the Rights and Liberties of the Subjects of this Kingdom.

In Steine, Cler' Parliamentor'

About three years after these Resolutions GILBERT became one of the Barons of the Exchequer in Ireland, and Letoe the Court lesses Chief Baron of that Court

In

PREFACE.

In confequence of an *Appeal* received from the *Chancery Side* of the *Irifh Court of Exchequer*, in the Cafe of *Annefley* and *Sherlock*, early in the year 1717, the *Britifh Houfe of Lords* interpofed their Order in thefe Words

D'e Jov.s, 6to Februaru, 1717—*Upon Report from the Committee of the whole Houfe, to whom it was referred to confider by what Methods the Order of this Houfe, for the reftoring Poffeffion to* Maurice Annefley, *Efq of the Eftate in* Ireland, *whereof h. was difpoffeffed pending his Appeal* in this Houfe *may be moft properly enforced and exerted*, it is ordered by the Lords Spiritual and Temporal in Parliament affembled, *that the* Barons of the Court of Exchequer in *Ireland do caufe the faid* Maurice Annefley, *Efq to be forthwith* reftored to the Poffeffion of the Lands of which he was difpoffeffed pending his Appeal, *which was received by this Houfe the 8th Day of* June *laft*

Die Jovis 6to Februaru, 1717—Ordered by the Lords Spiritual and Temporal in Parliament affembled, *That the* Lord Chancellor *do tranfmit the Order of this Houfe* to the Barons of the Exchequer in *Ireland, which requires th m to caufe* Poffeffion to be forthwith delivered to *Maurice Annefl y*, Efq. *of the Lands of which* he was difpoffeffed pending his Appeal in this Houfe, *commanding the* Barons of the Exchequer *at the fame time to return to this Houfe, as foon as they can, an Account of what fhall be done therein*

William Cowper, Cler' Parliamentor'.

By an official Letter from the *Lord Chancellor* COWPER the Order of the *Houfe of Lords of Great Britain* was accordingly tranfmitted to the *Barons* of the *Exchequer in Ireland*

And on the 19th of *February*, 1717, the CHIEF BARON of the Court of EXCHEQUER in IRELAND produced in Court the faid Letter of the LORD CHANCELLOR of GREAT BRITAIN, with the Refolution and Order before ftated of the *Britifh Houfe of Lords*, and thereupon the *Lord Chief Baron* and the *other Barons* ordered an *Injunction* for the reftoring the faid *Maurice Annefley* to Poffeffion of the Lands of which he was difpoffeffed pending his faid *Appeal* in the *Houfe of Lords of Great Britain* the Order iffued in the Name of the *Chancellor, Treafurer, and Barons of the Exchequer,* commanding the Sheriff to reftore Poffeffion accordingly

And *Mark Annefley*, his Attorney, Agent, Solicitor, or Counfel, was ordered by the Court to attend the Chief Remembrancer or his Deputy with the Names of the Lands of which he had been fo difpoffeffed, and the County or Counties in which they lay.

On

Ibid.
Report of the
Lords Commit-
tees for Courts of
Justice, in Ire-
land, 15 Mar
1717

On the 15th of *March* the *Injunction* was ferved: the regularity of which, and to the Fact of there remaining any Right of Poffeffion in *Anneſley* of the Lands on which it was to operate, independent of the great Queſtion of *Privilege*, ſome Objections are ſtated by the *Committee* of the *Iriſh Houſe of Lords* but *Alexander Burrowes*, the then *High Sheriff* of the County of *Kildare*, in which the Lands lay, refuſed to execute it

P. 191 Nᵒ 2
Order of the
Houſe of Lords
of Ireland
thereon,
13 Oct. 1717

On the 13th of *October*, 1717, an *Order* was made by the Houſe of Lords of *Ireland* in hæc verba

Die Jovis tertio Die Octobris, 1717 — *Whereas by the Report made from the Lords Committees appointed to conſider the propereſt Method for the reliewing of Heſter Sherlock, Widow, &c purſuant to what was ordered and adjudged by this Houſe on the 19th Day of June*, 1716, *in a Cauſe wherein the ſaid Heſter Sherlock, Widow, was Appellant, and Maurice and John Anneſley, Eſqrs. were Reſpondents, as alſo upon the Reſolutions agreed to this Day by this Houſe, it appears that the Sum of One Thouſand Five Hundred and Seven Pounds Fourteen Shillings and Eight Pence Farthing was due to Heſter Sherlock, the Appellant, upon the 19th Day of February,* 1716, *on account of the Principal and Intereſt of the Portion of Edward Sherlock, decreed unto the ſaid Appellant, as Adminiſtratrix to the ſaid Edward, by this Houſe, on the 19th Day of June,* 1716, *and that the Lands of* Little Rath, *Bodingſtown,* Darr, *and* Mullenafooky *in the Barony of Naas, and County of Kildare, are chargeable with and liable to the Payment of the ſaid Sum, it is thereupon ordered by the Lords Spiritual and Temporal in Parliament aſſembled, that the High Sheriff of the County of Kildare, do forthwith* PUT *the ſaid Heſter Sherlock* INTO THE POSSESSION *of the ſaid Lands of* Little Rath, *Bodingſtown,* Darr, *and* Mullenafooky, *ſubject to the ſaid Sum of One Thouſand Five Hundred and Seven Pounds Fourteen Shillings and Eight Pence Farthing: to be held by her the ſaid Heſter until ſuch Time as ſhe ſhall receive the ſaid Sum chargeable upon the ſaid Lands as aforeſaid: and this ſhall be a ſufficient Warrant in that behalf*

To *Charles Nuttal*, Eſq *High Sheriff*
of the County of *Kildare*

On the 23d of *January*, 1718, it was ordered by the *Peers of Great Britain in Parliament aſſembled* in hæc verba:

Orders of the
Houſe of Lords
of Great Bri-
tain 23 Ja-
nuary, reinforc-
ing former or-
ders Orders.

Anneſley v *Sherlock, Die Veneris,* 23 *Januarii,* 1718 — *UPON REPORT from the Lords Committees appointed to inquire into the Reaſon of the Delay in not obeying the Orders of this Houſe relating to the Appeal of Maurice Anneſley, Eſq and how the ſame may more properly be inforced, it is ordered by*
the

the Lords Spiritual and Temporal in Parliament assembled, that the *Barons of the Court of Exchequer in* Ireland *be and are hereby directed to proceed by the most speedy and effectual Methods to cause Possession of the Estate of the said* Maurice Annesley, *as required by the Order of this House* of the 6th of February last, *to be restored to him*

William Cowper, Cler' Parliamentor'.

Annesley v Sherlock, Die Veneris, 23 Januarii, 1718 — ORDERED, by the Lords Spiritual and Temporal in Parliament assembled, *that the* Barons of the Court of Exchequer in Ireland *do cause the Respondent* Hester Sherlock *to account before them upon Oath for the Rents and Profits of the Estate in Question, which she has made or received since her gaining Possession thereof* by the Orders of the House of Lords in *Ireland, and to answer and pay the same to the Appellant* Maurice Annesley, *Esq without Prejudice to the Right, in case of an Appeal to be brought by either Party from the Decree of the* Court of Exchequer in IRELAND

William Cowper, Cler' Parliamentor'.

Annesley v Sherlock, Die Veneris, 23 Januarii, 1718 — ORDERED, by the Lords Spiritual and Temporal in Parliament assembled, *that the* LORD HIGH CHANCELLOR *of* GREAT BRITAIN *do transmit the two Orders, made this Day on the behalf of* Maurice Annesley, *Esq to the* BARONS *of the* COURT *of* EXCHEQUER *in* IRELAND, *commanding them at the same time to return, as soon as they can, an Account of what shall be done therein*

William Cowper, Cler' Parliamentor'.

By an official Letter, dated 27 Jan *inclosing Copies of the said Orders, the* Lord Chancellor PARKER *transmitted to the Barons of the Exchequer this renewed Signification of the Resolution of the British House of Lords on the Subject of this memorable Contest* and concluded—*Your Lordship will immediately communicate this to the rest of the Barons, and return, as soon as you can, an Account of what shall be done by yourself and the rest of the Barons in pursuance of your* * *Lordship's said Orders*

Letter of the Lord Chancellor of G B signifying the same to the Barons of the Exchequer in Ireland 27 Jan 1718 Qu their P

On the 13th of *May*, 1718, on the Complaint of *Maurice Annesley, an Order was made, fining the Sheriff forty shillings, unless he should return the Injunction in four days, and the Fine was increased by subsequent Motions to 77l*

Order of the Irish Exchequer

On the 7th of *July*, 1718, the then High Sheriff for the County of Kildare, after several *intermediate Motions, made a special Return to the Injunction, setting forth the Resolves and Order of the* IRISH

Further Proceedings of the Barons of the Exchequer in Ireland thereon, 7 July, 1718

IRISH HOUSE OF LORDS *above cited*, of the 11th of February, 1703, and the 19th of June 1716, and concluding, *that by virtue of the said Order he had put Hester Sherlock into full, quiet, and peaceable possession of all the Towns and Lands aforesaid, and that the said Hester from thenceforth continued in the same Possession of the premises aforesaid, according to the Tenor and Effect of the aforesaid Order by Reason of which Resolves and Order he did not in prejudice and Lesion of the PRIVILEGES of PARLIAMENT* by the Laws and Statutes of the Realm of IRELAND provided, *to restore the said Maurice Annesley, Esq to the Possession of the several Towns and Lands of* Little Rath, Darr. *and* Mullenasooky

On the 7th of July the Fines were reduced by the BARONS Pocklington and St Leger in consequence of the Return of the Injunction. but on the same day the *Officer of the Exchequer,* the *Attorney* for Mrs *Sherlock,* and the former Deputy Chief Remembrancer were directed to attend at the House of the LORD CHIEF BARON. when, in the presence of the *Chief* and of the other *Barons,* the *Injunction* and *Return* was read and the *Barons* declared that it was no *Return.* the *Attorney* for Mrs *Sherlock* prayed that the Fine might be respited to the next Term, or opportunity given to the *Officer* to justify his *Return,* which was refused The *Officer* was ordered to *take back* the Money which he had paid to the Box for taking off the *Fines,* and the Fines were estreated

Further Proceedings of the Sheriff, 7 Nov 1718
On the 7th of *November* an ATTACHMENT issued against the Sheriff, returnable before the *Chancellor, Treasurer,* and *Barons,* on the *Octave* of *Hilary,* and was renewed the 30th of January following But the *Sheriff,* by reason of the said *Attachments,* absconding, was not present when he ought to have come on his *Accounts* and was upon that Account *jacob* the *Barons* 1200*l* and upward

On the REPORT of the *Lords Committees,* comprising these and other particulars, the PEERS of IRELAND resolved, *it was said,*

That *Alexander Burrowes, Esq late High Sheriff of the County of Kildare, in not obeying the* Injunction *issued forth out of her Majesty's Court of Exchequer, dated the 22d of February,* 1717, *in the Cause between* Annesley *and* Sherlock, *has behaved himself with Integrity and Courage, and with due Respect to the* ORDERS *and Resolutions of* THIS HOUSE

Votes of Committees omitted Lords Committee Report Barons
That the Fines imposed (on the said late High Sheriff) *for not obeying the said Writ of Injunction be taken off without Fees.*
That the Fines imposed (on the said late High Sheriff) *for not attending to give over his Accounts, amounting to* 1200*l* and upwards, be

taken

taken off when he shall have made a just Account, without other Fees than such as are usual on passing Sheriff's Account

That the LORD CHIEF BARON and the other Barons *had due Notice of the* ORDER *of this* HOUSE *of the* 3d *of* October, 1717, *in the Cause of* Sherlock *and* Annesley

Resolved, *that* JEFFRAY GILBERT, *Esq* LORD CHIEF BARON *of his Majesty's* COURT *of* EXCHEQUER, *in the Proceedings in the Cause between* Sherlock *and* Annesley, *as also against* Alexander Burrowes, *Esq late* High Sheriff *of the County of* Kildare, *has acted in direct Violation of the* ORDERS *and Resolutions of this House*

Resolved, *that* JEFFRAY GILBERT, *Esq* LORD CHIEF BARON *of his Majesty's* COURT *of* EXCHEQUER, *in the Proceedings in the Cause between* Sherlock *and* Annesley, *as also against* Alexander Burrowes, *Esq late* High Sheriff *of the County of* Kildare, *has acted in manifest Derogation to and Diminution of the King's Prerogative of finally judging in his High Court of Parliament in* IRELAND, *as also of the Rights and Privileges of this Kingdom, and of the* PARLIAMENT *thereof*

The same Resolves with these two last passed against the *two other* BARONS

Resolved on the Question, Nem con *that it is the Duty of the* BARONS *of the* EXCHEQUER, *where* there is any Wrong or Prejudice done to the King, in Matters lying before them, *to inform the* KING *or the Chief Governor or Governors of the Kingdom, or the Council*

Resolved, *that the Case of* Sherlock *and* Annesley, *as it lately lay before the* BARONS *of the* EXCHEQUER, *being Matter not only of Law but of State, ought to have been laid before the* King *the Chief Governor or Governors of this Kingdom, or the Council of the same it so nearly concerning his Majesty's Prerogative and the Interest of the* WHOLE KINGDOM *

Dissentient.

Doneraile

Jo *Meath,*	*Midd'eton,* CANC
Welbore, Ki'dare,	*William,* Derry
Henry, *Killala and* Achonry,	
Timo *Kilmore and* Ardagh.	

---

* This seems to have Allusion to the latter part of the oath of a Baron of the Exchequer.—' Whereas ye may know any Wrong or Prejudice to be done to the King, ye shall put and do all your Power and Diligence that to redress and if ye may not do it yet shall tell it to the King, or to them of his Council which may make relation to the King, if ye may not come to him, to the King's Majesty's Lieutenant, or other Chief Governor or Governors of this Realm for the time being

Resolved,

Refolved, *that* JEFFRAY GILBERT, *Efq* LORD CHIEF
BARON *of the* COURT *of* EXCHEQUER, John Pocklington,
Efq and Sir John St Leger, Knt *Barons of the fame, in
their Proceedings in the Caufe between* Sherlock *and* Annefley,
and againft Alexander Burrowes, *Efq late* Sheriff *of the County of* Kildare, *have acted* contrary *to Law and to the eftablifhed Practice of the* King's Courts

Diffentient.

Doneraple

John Meath
Welbore Kildare
Henry Killala *and* Achonry
Timo Kilmore *and* Ardagh,

Middleton CANC
William Derry

Refolved, *that* JEFFRAY GILBERT, *Efq* LORD CHIEF
BARON *of the* COURT *of* EXCHEQUER, *having taken upon
him to put in Execution a pretended* Order *from another* Court,
contrary to the final Judgment of this HIGH COURT *of* PAR-
LIAMENT, *in the Caufe between* Sherlock *and* Annefley, *is a
Betrayer of his Majefty's Prerogative, and the ancient undoubted
Rights and Privileges of* THIS HOUSE, *and of the Rights and
Liberties of the Subjects of this Kingdom.*

Diffentient

Doneraple.

John Meath,
Welbore Kildare,
Henry Killala *and* Achonry,
Timo Kildare *and* Ardagh

Middleton CANC
William Derry,

The fame Refolve againft each of the two *other* BARONS.

Finally, the Houfe refolved and ordered, *in hæc verba*
ORDERED, by the LORDS Spiritual and Temporal in PAR-
LIAMENT affembled, *that the Right Honourable* JEFFRAY
GILBERT, *Efq* LORD CHIEF BARON *of the* COURT *of*
EXCHEQUER, *fhall for the faid Offences,* be taken into the
Cuftody *of the Gentleman Ufher of the Black Rod attending this*
HOUSE.

Diffentient.

Fitzwilliams

Jo Meath,
Welbore Kildare,
Henry Killala *and* Achonry,
Timo Kilmore *and* Ardagh

Middleton CANC.
Donerayle,
William Derry.

And

And the same ORDER passed, with the same Peers *dissentient*, against the two *other* BARONS The BRITISH HOUSE of LORDS, on the contrary, *approved* the Proceedings of the BARONS of the IRISH EXCHEQUER, *recommended* them to the royal favour as having been unjustly censured and illegally imprisoned for having done their Duty, and that a BILL be brought into PARLIAMENT for *securing the Dependence of* IRELAND *on the* CROWN *of* GREAT BRITAIN *

Afterwards, in the next year, the PARLIAMENT of GREAT BRITAIN declared their sense of this Claim of Jurisdiction by the HOUSE of LORDS in IRELAND by a *Statute* † often quoted in the Commencement of the unhappy Contest, in which the Government of this Country engaged against the AMERICAN COLONIES It is of a tremendous Conciseness the whole Act consisting of these two sentences:

An ACT *for the better securing the* Dependency *of* IRELAND *upon the* CROWN *of* GREAT BRITAIN

WHEREAS *the* HOUSE *of* LORDS *of* IRELAND *have of late, against* Law, *assumed to themselves a Power and Jurisdiction to examine, correct, and amend the Decrees of the Courts of Justice in the* KINGDOM *of* IRELAND: *therefore, for the better securing of the Dependency of* IRELAND *upon the* CROWN *of* GREAT BRITAIN, *may it please your Most Excellent* Majesty, *that it may be declared, and be it declared by the King's Most Excellent Majesty, by and with the Advice and Consent of the Lords Spiritual and Temporal and Commons in this present* PARLIAMENT *assembled, and by the Authority of the same, that the said Kingdom of* IRELAND *hath been, is, and of Right ought to be subordinate unto and dependent upon the Imperial* CROWN *of* GREAT BRITAIN, *as being inseparably united and annexed thereunto and that the King's Majesty, by and with the Advice and Consent of the Lords Spiritual and Temporal and Commons of* GREAT BRITAIN *in* PARLIAMENT *assembled, had, hath, and of* Right *ought to have full Power and Authority to make* LAWS *and* STATUTES *of sufficient Force and Validity to bind the* KINGDOM *and* PEOPLE *of* IRELAND

And be it further declared and enacted by the Authority aforesaid, that the HOUSE *of* LORDS *of* IRELAND *have not, nor of Right ought to have any Jurisdiction to judge of, affirm, or reverse any* JUDGMENT, *Sentence, or Decree, given or made in any Court within the said Kingdom: and that all Proceedings before the said* HOUSE *of* LORDS *upon any such Judgment, Sentence, or Decree, are, and are hereby declared to be utterly* NULL *and* VOID *to all Intents and Purposes whatsoever*

Mr.

* Ayres C V.
of E & J St.
Introd lxxiv,
et seq

1719.

† It received the
Royal Assent on
the 7th Apr
1720.
Ayres's C V.
lxxv.

xxiv

C. V. lxxii.

Mr. *Ayres* has a fpirited Remark on this Statute · *we are left in the dark to judge on what grounds that auguſt aſſembly were induced to believe a power exerted without controul* (he fpeaks of the power of judicature in the IRISH HOUSE of PEERS) *did not give a* RIGHT *A foreigner, unacquainted with the caſes which actuated that parliament, would imagine this a very extraordinary doctrine*

The PARLIAMENT of GREAT BRITAIN at length thought

22 G. III. c. 53

fo and repealed the ACT which had negatived the independent *legiſlative*, and the *judicial* Claims of the IRISH PARLIAMENT and Doubts being entertained whether the *Repeal* of an Act, which expreſſed itſelf in the *declaratory* ſtyle, would not leave room for the Claim of an *excluſive* Juriſdiction as of *Common Law*, independent of ſuch Statute fo

23 G. III. c. 28

repealed, another ACT paſſed, which with a wife ſimplicity removes all ſhadow of future Controverfy on this Queſtion. It is in theſe Words

WHEREAS by an ACT of the laſt Seſſion of this preſent PARLIAMENT, intitled, *an* ACT *to repeal an Act made in the Sixth Year of the Reign of his late Majeſty King George the Firſt*, intitled, *An Act for the better ſecuring the Dependency of the Kingdom of* IRELAND *upon the* CROWN *of* GREAT BRITAIN, *it was enacted, that the ſaid laſt mentioned Act, and all Matters and Things therein contained, ſhould be repealed* And whereas Doubts have ariſen *whether the Proviſions of the ſaid Act are ſufficient to ſecure to the* PEOPLE *of* IRELAND *the Rights claimed by them to be bound only by Laws enacted by his Majeſty and the Parliament of that* KINGDOM *in all Caſes whatever, and to have all* ACTIONS *and* SUITS *at* LAW *or in* EQUITY, *which may be inſtituted in that* KINGDOM, *decided in his Majeſty's* COURTS *therein* FINALLY, AND WITHOUT APPEAL *from thence* THEREFORE, *for removing all Doubts reſpecting the ſame,* May it pleaſe your Majeſty, that it may be DECLARED and enacted, *and be it declared and enacted by the* KING'S *Moſt Excellent Majeſty, by and with the Advice and Conſent of the* LORDS *Spiritual and Temporal and* COMMONS *in this preſent* PARLIAMENT *aſſembled, and by the Authority of the ſaire,* that *the ſaid* Right claimed by the PEOPLE *of* IRELAND *to be bound only by Laws enacted by his Majeſty and the Parliament of that* KINGDOM *in all Caſes whatever, and to have all* ACTIONS *and* SUITS *at* LAW *or in* EQUITY, *which may be inſtituted in that* KINGDOM, *decided in his Majeſty's* COURTS *therein* FINALLY, AND WITHOUT APPEAL *from thence, ſhall be, and it is hereby declared to be eſtabliſhed and aſcertained for ever, and ſhall at no Time hereafter be queſtioned or queſtioned.*

And

And be it further enacted, by the Authority aforesaid, that no Writ of ERROR *or* APPEAL *shall be received or adjudged, or any other Proceeding be had by or in any of his Majesty's Courts in this* KINGDOM, *in any Action or Suit at Law or in Equity, instituted in any of his Majesty's Courts in the Kingdom of* IRELAND *and that all such Writs, Appeals, or Proceedings, shall be, and they are hereby declared* NULL *and* VOID *to all Intents and Purposes and that all Records, Transcripts of Records, or Proceedings, which have been transmitted from* IRELAND *to* GREAT BRITAIN *by Virtue of any Writ of Error or Appeal, and upon which no Judgment has been given or Decree pronounced before the First Day of* June, *One Thousand Seven Hundred and Eighty-two, shall, upon Application made, by or in behalf of the Party in whose Favour Judgment was given or decree pronounced in* IRELAND, *be delivered to such Party or any Person by him authorised to apply for and receive the same*

The Conduct of our AUTHOR while this great Question was depending, could not be more fairly stated than by vouching the authentic public Documents of the time, nor could the Opinions of the LEGISLATURE on this subject at different periods be more satisfactorily expressed than by *Transcripts* of the Statutes respecting this long agitated Point of JURISDICTION For what time the LORD CHIEF BARON and his *Brethren* of that BENCH continued under *Imprisonment*, and the Proceedings of one of the *great* COURTS of COMMON LAW consequently suspended, appears not as yet While the Contest was recent, it was perhaps deemed inexpedient, by entering more particularly into the circumstances, to stir the sparks of a lately stifled Flame, and this may account for the total silence of the Epitaph But now, when all Causes of Dissension between the Sister Kingdoms on this subject (and, we may reasonably believe, on any other) are happily eradicated, some Observations may be calmly interposed on the Deportment of GILBERT and of the *other* BARONS in this important Transaction

The *Jurisdiction* exercised in ENGLAND was not a *Novelty* as APPEALS from the KING's BENCH in IRELAND to the KING's BENCH in ENGLAND were received, APPEALS from the *Equity Side* of the EXCHEQUER to the BRITISH HOUSE of LORDS stood upon the same Ground of *Analogy*, and had a less revolting Appearance The very able Advocate of the Rights of the IRISH NATION, whom we have already quoted, seems to acknowledge that the ultimate *judicial* Authority was a Question on which a Difference of Opinion might admit of a much fairer Account than the far more important Question of the independent *legislative* Authority.

With

V Rep. of the
Lords Commit.
P 192.

With regard to the fubordinate and collateral circumftances, fuch as its being objected that the Chief Baron had
granted the injunction, the COPIES of the ORDER of the
HOUSE of PEERS of GREAT BRITAIN, authenticated by
the CHANCELLOR, being produced and read in COURT,
without *Affidavit* of their being *figned* or *examined*, there appears nothing in this repugnant to the known *Principles* and
Rules of *Evidence* in like Cafes, as will be feen in the Work
itfelf to which this Account is prefixed

The Eftreat of the Fines, and the Order to take back the
Money, which had been paid on the fuppofed compounding
of them, contains fome circumftances of which an explanation were much to be defired It is difficult to imagine,
under the fentiments entertained by the CHIEF BARON and
his *Brethren*, how the Fines came to be reduced, unlefs
there was fome furprize upon the Court by fome evafive
Manœuvre On any other fuppofition an Incongruity in
the Proceedings of the fame Judges on the fame day, and
on a plain point, muft be admitted, which is utterly unintelli-
gible, not to fay, incredible

Thus much, from the Intelligence hitherto found attainable, concerning the CHIEF BARON during his Refidence
in a public Character in IRELAND More is greatly to be
defired and more, in this Age of liberal communication
on literary fubjects, may perhaps hereafter be obtained It
appears, I think, by the ftyle of the laft ORDER of the
IRISH HOUSE of LORDS, that he he was a *Privy Counfellor* of that Kingdom and it is noticed in his EPITAPH, that
a Tender was made to him of the GREAT SEAL, which
he declining, returned to his Country, and was firft called
to the Degree of an *Englifh Serjeant at Law*,† preparatory,
according to ancient Ufage, to his taking his feat as one of
the *Barons* of the *Exchequer*,‖ in which he fucceeded Sir
James Mortague and having remained in that ftation for

† 31 Mar
1722 B P J
P 440 Ap-
pointed 2.
May, 1722
B P J I
P 422
‖ He took his
feat June 9,
1722
Exch 113

---

† *A Paper of the Time, dated* Tuefday. June 12, 1722, *communicated by* Mr NICHOLS, *fays that he was called on* Thurfday
the 8th, *with* ALEXANDER DENTON, *Efq to the Bar of the*
COURT *of* COMMON PLEAS. *with only fuch Ceremonies as are
ufed at a private Call The Gentleman called with him afterwards,
with exemplary Candour, prefided as Judge at the Trial of Mr.*
ELWALL, *at the* STAFFORD ASSIZES, *for a fuppofed blafphemous
Libel, confifting in the Affertion of the divine* UNITY *I do not
pretend to afcertain the particular fentiments of either of thefe refpe?-
able Judges on this Point Good Men are wont to be friendly to the
ights of Confcience, whatever their particular Creed*

thirty years,* on the 7th of *January*, 1724, he was appoint- *B P J 411.
... e of the COMMISSIONERS of the GREAT SEAL in
the room of Lord MACCLESFIELD and never was that
Commission more refpectably filled, his Colleagues being Sir
Joseph Jekyll and Sir *Robert Raymond* the GREAT SEAL
continued in Commiffion till the 1ft of *June* in the year fuc-
ceeding, when Sir *Peter King* was conftituted LORD KEEPER,
and on the fame day Sir JEFFRAY GILBERT became, on the
Appointment of Sir *Rovert Eyre* to the *Chief Juftice fhip* of *1 June, 1725.*
the *Common Pleas,* LORD CHIEF BARON; which Office he *Ibid 419*
filled for *one* Year and lefs than *five* Months, when he deceaf- *Bunb 199*
ed at *Bath*, at an Age which may be called early, if compar- *14 Oct 1726.*
ed with the Multitude and the laborious Extent of his known
and remaining Works Five * Months before his Deceafe *12 May, 1726.*
he became a FELLOW of the ROYAL SOCIETY Thinking
it probable that his Talents and Learning might have acquired him this Diftinction, which has always been efteemed an
Ornament to the moft exalted ftation, I requefted a Friend,
who is a Member of that Society, to afcertain whether my
Conjecture were verified by Fact That it is fo, I confider
as a Difcovery alike honourable to that illuftrious Body and
to the party *elected*

Unexpectedly (confidering the doubtful Prefervation of
fugitive Papers after more than fixty years have expired)
a *contemporary Teftimony* * to this great Character has been * Commun-
obtained
cated alfo by
As the moft full and fatisfactory which perhaps we can now Mr NICHOLS.
hope, it is here tranfcribed.

" *London, Oct 12* We have an Account from *Bath*, that The Weekly
yefterday fe'nnight, after a long Indifpofition, † died there, Journal, or
in the fifty fecond Year of his Age, Sir *Jeffray Gilbert*, the Britifh
Knight, Lord Chief Baron of his Majefty's Court of *Exche-* Gazetteer
Saturday,
quer at *Weftminfter* " Oct 22, 1726

It then proceeds to ftate his feveral Appointments commencing with that of a Judge in the King's Bench in *Ireland*,
which it dates in 1715, and concluding with his promotion
to the Office of Chief Baron of the Exchequer in *England*,
before the Commiffion of the Great Seal (in which he was one
of the Lords Commiffioners) was determined ‖

---

† *We find him in* Eafter *Term, in the year in which he died, continuing to fit as Chief Baron It is uncertain whether his illnefs* Quilter v Muf-
permitted him to be in Court in the Trinity *Term His Reports are* fen line, T. P.
continued no lower than the Eafter *Term.* 12 G 1
‖ *This fee is a Miftake of the Editor of the Journal for the* Gilb 228 --
Commiffion determined at the time when he became Chief Baron 30
V p xiv

It

It then proceeds with his Character.

" He filled up every Station of Life with the greatest Integrity and most untainted Honour and discharged the Duties
of his Profession to the general satisfaction of all that had
any opportunity of observing his Conduct Nor did his speed-
dy Advancement from one Post to another procure him the
Envy even of the Gentlemen of the Long Robe, who con-
stantly paid him the Regard that is due to the greatest Merit
when he was alive, and by whom the Loss of him is now as
generally regretted The Skill and Experience he had in the
Laws of his Country, and the uncommon Penetration he
discovered in the Decision of such Causes of Equity as came
before him, were not more known in *Westminster Hall* than
his unwearied Pursuit of mathematical Studies (when his Affairs would permit) as well as his fine Taste of the more polite
Parts of Learning were to Men of the most exalted Genius
in either We are satisfied our Readers will not be displeas-
ed at the imperfect Account we have endeavoured to give of
this great Man, being persuaded his Character is so well
established, that it will not be reckoned amongst those extra-
vagant Encomiums which are bestowed with a liberal hand on
every common occasion "

It then notices some of the Legatees in his Will, and mentions the Attendance on his Funeral, thus

' We hear that he left his valuable Manuscripts to *Charles
Clarke*, Esq of *Lincoln's Inn*, and Mr *Perrot*,† his Clerk,
200 l Mr *Townsend*, Examiner, 200 l the said Gentleman's
Son, to whom his Lordship was Godfather, 100 l Mr *Mon-
crieff*, Train bearer 100 l M *Palmer*, his Marshal, 50 l he

† Seeming to a left the Bulk of his Share to Sir *John Norris*, and Sir *John
Correspond *Farmer*, of Such † Bart
Settles †
called a super   " On *Monday* next the Corpse was interred in a Vault
em, to Sent to that Purpose within the Abbey Church at *Bath*
Correct on Th The Pall being supported by the Lord *William Pawlett*, Lord
centre of Cav Bar *Cornwallis* Sir *Henry Ashhurst*, Bart Sir *John Austin*, Bart.
I 3   *the Cecil or*, Esq and *Daniel Pulteney*, Esq and Sir *Henry
The *Farrer*, Bart attended as Chief Mourner We hear a
I

+ It appeared to re der I examined the Will in the Commons,
to be Deventur and accordingly it stands, in the official Copy but
the Form of the Seal is doubtful As with a simplicity worthy
of the rest of his Character, GILBERT has not mentioned
in of his Will any Designation of Title or Office, he has been
silent with regard to the employments which any of his Legatees held
under in Its seems here to observe, that after his Death
the circumstances of their relation to his service, in his public Character, are not noted

very handsome Monument is designed to be erected to his Memory "

This, as we have seen, there was; and laudable is the attention of his Executors. But a nobler and more durable Monument, now impossible to be erected, would have been a complete Account of his Life and Writings

Of his WORKS, which have been *printed* with his Name, a List is subjoined Chronological Order, with regard to their Publication, is perhaps now impracticable The *List* is extracted from WORRAL's BIBLIOTHECA LEGUM

1 GILBERT's (Lord C B) CASES † *in Law and Equity:* with two Treatises one on the Action of Debt, the other, on the Constitution of *England*   8vo. 1730. 6s.

2 ————— REPORTS of Cases in Equity and Exchequer, from the 4th of Q *Anne* to the 12th of *G I* * To which are added some SELECT CASES *in Equity in the Court of Exchequer in* IRELAND, with many additional Notes and References   Fo 1734 7s. 1742 16s.

3 LAW of *Uses and Trusts* collected and digested in proper Order from the Books of Reports. together with a Treatise of Dower.   1734, 1741, the same, 6s.

4 TREATISE *of Tenures ·* containing, 1 The Original, Nature, Use, and Effect of Feudal or Common Law Tenures. 2 Customary or Copyhold Tenures, Customs, Duty to their Lords, &c   3d Ed 8vo. 1757 5 s.

5 LAW of *Devises, last Wills, and Revocations* To which are added Choice Precedents of last Wills Third Edition, revised, corrected, and improved   1730 2 s. 1756 3 s 8 o 1773 5s.

6 TREATISE *of* EJECTMENTS   1734 or 1741, the same, 5 s. Ditto To which are added Select Precedents, &c Second Edition, with Additions, by *Charles Runnington*, Esq,   8vo 1781 6s.

- LAW *and Practice of* Distress *and* Replevins *delineated:* wherein the whole Law under those Heads

---

| *These are Cases in 12 & 13 A* *Anno* 1713 In 1715 we out our Author one of the Judges of B R in IRELAND, if therefore really taken by him, it must have been shortly before he left ENGLAND There are one or two important Cases, and so well reported as not to be unworthy of him but in general, they are loose Notes very badly edited

‡ *The Lord Chief Baron died in the Vacation of* Trin 12 G I. which was the last year of that Reign

is confidered, with many References to the
beft Authorities. to which is added an
Appendix of *Englifh* Precedents in Replevin

2o Ed Svo.
1-2o 5s

8 LAW *of Executions*: to which are added, the Hiftory
and Practice of the Court of King's Bench,
and fome Cafes touching Wills of Lands
and Goods.

8-o 1763 6s
1758 3s 6d

9 TREATISE *of* RENTS.
10 ———— *of the* COURT *of* EXCHEQUER: in which
the Revenue of the Crown and the Manner
of receiving and accounting for the feveral

8vo 1743 5s

Branches of them are clearly explained
Before printed (in part only) under the
Title of *An hiftorical View of the Prac-*
tice of the Exchequer

8vo 1758 2s

11 HISTORY *and* PRACTICE *of* CIVIL ACTIONS *in the*
Court of Common Pleas being an hiftorical
Account of the Parts and Order of judicial Proceedings, with an Introduction on
the Conftitution of *England*

1737 2s
1761 3s

Third Edition, corrected, with Notes
and References

8vo 1779 5s
1758 6s

12 HISTORY of the High Court of Chancery, printed
from a correct manufcript Copy.

2o Ed 1s 6s,
1-6s

13 LAW of EVIDENCE
Ditto, with Additions, and a complete Table.

8-o 1777 4s
Ditto.
Pr...

14 ABSTRACT *of Mr* LOCKE'S *Effay on human Under-*
ftanding

In MANUSCRIPT

15 HISTORY *of the Feud* In the Collection of FRANCIS
HARGRAVE, Efq

Others afcribed to him on Probability, but without direct
Proof

16 TREATISE *of* REMAINDERS MS §
17 The Title LEASES, in BACON'S ABRIDGEMENT, is
believed to be from GILBERT

§ Of this I know thus much that it is held in high Eftimation
by the Gentlemen acknowledged to be among the moft competent to
judge of the merits of a Work developing the moft intricate of all
the branches of the Profeffion

Thus

Thus the moſt extenſive and intricate Subjects received, from the diligence and ſagacity of this great Man ample Diſcuſſion and approved Illuſtration If Teſtimonies are now ſubjoined, it is not for the purpoſe of adding Authority, but as pleaſing examples how willingly eminent Deſert is commended by the deſerving or, in the Words of the *Roman Orator*, who might well aſſert what his own Character and Writings exemplified, *Neminem qui ſuis virtutibus confidat alienæ invidere.*

TESTIMONIES.

In a Caſe, which was eſteemed a nice Queſtion, and as ſuch ordered to be ſolemnly argued, the Court ſaid, that many Caſes had been cited on both ſides, but that they founded their Determination upon Lord Chief Baron GIL-BERT's *Law of Diſtreſſes and Replevins*, ſo 231, 2; that it would be abſurd to grant a *return' habend'* where there was no *Avowry*.

Cutfield v. Coney Hil 31 G II, Wilſ. 83

In a very important Cauſe Mr *Peckham* adduced the Authority of GILBERT, in theſe Terms:

I ſhall only cite a few paſſages from *Lord Chief Baron* GILBERT's *Hiſtory of the Common Pleas*, which are deciſive upon this part of the Argument In p 40, ſpeaking of the ORDER of pleading, he ſays, " *The Defendant firſt pleads to the JURISDICTION of the Court*, ſecondly, *to the PERSON of the Plaintiff*, and, thirdly, *to the COUNT or Declaration. By this order of pleading, each ſubſequent Plea admits the former. As when he pleads to the perſon of the Plaintiff, he admits the Juriſdiction of the Court, for it wou'd be nugatory to plead any thing in that Court which has no Juriſdiction in the Caſe When he pleads to the Count or Declaration, he allows that the party is able to come into that Court to impead him, and he may be there properly impleaded* He lays it down in a ſubſequent part of this Treatiſe (p 148) as a poſitive Rule of Law, that if a Defendant pleads to the Juriſdiction of that Court, he muſt do it *inſtanter* on his appearance, for if he imparls, he owns the Juriſdiction of the Court by craving leave of the Court for time to plead in, and the Court ſhall never be ouſted of its Juriſdiction after Imparlance When I find this Doctrine in our old Law Books, when I ſee it ratified in modern times, and ſtamped with the Authority of COKE, HALE, HOLT, and GILBERT, I am warranted in ſaying that Governor *Moſtyn* cannot now agitate the Queſtion of Juriſdiction "

Fabrigas and Moſtyn H St. T. X, 192.

The AUTHOR of the COMMENTARIES has quoted three of GILBERT's Works with diſtinguiſhed Notice

III Comm.
c 10 p. 179.
N L

Of his TENURES, *as well explaining the Principles of the particular Cases mentioned by* Littleton, B. III 6.

Of his HISTORY of the COMMON PLEAS thus.

Ibid. c 18
p 272 N.

BOOKS *of Practice, as they are called, are all pretty much on a level in point of composition and solid instruction, so that that which bears the latest Edition is usually the best,* But GILBERT's HISTORY *and* PRACTICE *of the* COURT *of* COMMON PLEAS *is a book of a very different stamp. and though* (*like the rest of his Posthumous Works*) *it has suffered most grossly by ignorant or careless transcribers, yet it has traced out the reason of many parts of our modern practice from the feudal institutions, and the primitive construction of our Courts, in a most clear and ingenious manner*

Ibid. c. 23.
p 367.

Of his LAW *of* EVIDENCE thus —*The Nature of my present Design will not permit me to enter into the numberless niceties and distinctions of what is or is not* LEGAL EVIDENCE *to a* JURY: *this is admirably well performed in* LORD CHIEF BARON GILBERT s excellent Treatise of EVIDENCE *a work which it is impossible to abstract or abridge without losing some beauty and destroying the chain of the whole*

From Dr Falconer I learn that the Place of GILBERT's *Interment is on the north side of the centre Aisle of the* Parish Church of *St Peter and St Paul, commonly called the Abbey Church,* BATH, *and near the Door of the Choir* It simply expresses the *Day and Year of his Death, his Age and the Station in which he died* and refers to his MONUMENT in the TEMPLE CHURCH The stone is a blue slate even with the floor There is no *side Monument*. Over the Inscription are the *Arms, three Roses on a Chevron* (no Colours expressed). —CREST, *a Squirrel in profile, sitting on a twisted Cord, his Head turned to the dexter side* Beneath the Crest, a *Knight's Helmet* The Arms are on a Shield encompassed with *Palm Branches, as usual in the old Monuments*

The EPITAPH is in *Roman Characters,* arranged in the order printed underneath

SR JEFFRAY GILBERT KT
LORD CHIEF BARON
OF HIS MAJESTY's COURT
OF EXCHEQUER
OB 14 OCT. AD 1726 ÆT 52
A MONUMENT
ERECTED TO HIS MEMORY
IN THE TEMPLE CHURCH
IN LONDON.

Phillips

Philips Gybbon, Efq one of the Executors of the Lord Gent Mag. Aug 1788. p 699. Chief Baron was born 11 Oct 1678, confequently about four years later than the LORD CHIEF BARON whom he long furvived: being elected Member of Parliament for *Rye* in 1707, and in every fucceffive Parliament till 1741 To the Father of this Gentleman Sir *Matthew Hale* prefented a Copy of MS Notes on *Coke upon Littleton* B. L 149.

I have examined the WILL in the COMMONS: which is remarkably concife, fimple, and characteriftic

It remains to fay fomething of the TREATISE *now republifhed*, and of the *Plan* of the Publication Of the *firft Edition* I have not been able to obtain a fight . though it would have much gratified me to difcover what *Alterations* may have been afterwards made Some there have been certainly by the *Memorandum* at the end of the *fourth Edition*, † and it mentions *many Additions*, what thofe were, except *marginal Notes* and *References*, is at prefent uncertain In this Publication they are carefully diftinguifhed The Work, therefore, of the *original Author* will not be injured by unacknowledged Infertions of mine the chief Liberty I have taken is by *Tranfpofition* which will be fpecified by a TABLE of the correfpondent Pages in this Edition compared with the laft which has preceded it And here it may be proper to explain my motive for thefe variations in the Arrangement After the Death of an Author, his Works left unfinifhed moft ufually fuffer much and there feems reafon to regret that, by fome derangement probably of the *original Papers*, that full and perfpicuous order which the very eminent Author of this juftly celebrated Tract feems clearly to have defigned, fhould have been much broken the great Divifion of EVIDENCE into *written* and *unwritten*, and of its *Subject Matter*, according to the Diftribution of the *Roman furifts*, into CAUSES of CONTRACT, of TORT, and of DELICT, appear manifeftly marked It is alfo apparent that *Sections* were intended. though fuch and fimilar Divifions have not been hitherto marked in the printed Copies, in fo far as I am yet informed It has therefore been my endeavour to *reftore* the Difpofition of the Subject, and to fill the Outline. And at the fame time, for convenience, and the only ornament a fubject of ftrict Reafoning, blended with Authorities of municipal Law, can admit, the Indication of fome regular Order, the Treatife in its prefent enlarged State is divided into BOOKS, SECTIONS, CHAPTERS, TITLES, and *Paragraphs* and it was thought

† On account of Alterations in this Edition moft of the Pages are thrown back three Numbers.

the

the prefixing of a *General* ANALYSIS might be fervneable
to many, and even pleasing to some It has been in this
attempted to exhibit a SYSTEMATIC IDEA And upon this
Part of the Undertaking I cannot avoid expressing my obligations to the COMMENTARIES on the LAWS of ENG-
LAND, and to a Tract of Sir WILLIAM JONES (particularly
mentioned in the *Notes* to this Edition), beautifully arrang-
ing a very extensive Species of Contract, to which *Evidence*
applies with much Delicacy of Distinction. I have not
neglected to avail myself largely, in the latter Part, of the
full and correct REPORTS of Sir MICHAEL FOSTER, and
of his *admirable* DISCOURSES on the principal subjects of
the CROWN LAW I may possibly be thought to have
been too circumstantial, for a general and elementary Work,
in the Statement of *Cases* but it will be recollected that
they are generally Cases of Nicety and Importance that
the Attention of the Student is apt to be divided to a fa-
tiguing or discouraging degree by turning from one Book to
another, in order to attain that complete information which
is necessary *where every particular weighs something in the scale
of* EVIDENCE: and that perhaps in Books of Law, as
much as in any other, the Opinion of HUME will be justi-
fied,—that every Work should, as far as may be, include
within itself whatever is essential to its illustration, and not
refer any part of its Contents to be explained by the Writings of others where it can properly be avoided I may
add, that GILBERT had set the Example. the Case in the
fourth Edition relative to the manner of laying an *Assumpsit*
occupying near *twenty* Pages, which is a larger proportion
of the whole than any single Case will be found to occupy
in this

At the same time that I have amply consulted the great
Authority of Sir M Foster, I have cautiously gleaned from
the STATE TRIALS what seemed most material to the subject

There will be found *References* to such modern Cases as
appeared to illustrate the *Theory* and *Practice* of the LAW
of EVIDENCE

With regard to the *general Design* of the Original, in respect to the Choice of the Subject and its Extent, it may
be sufficient to observe that the LAW of EVIDENCE in its
fullest Acceptation pervades the SYSTEM of JURISPRU-
DENCE that perhaps no circumstance in the frame of our
legal Polity does more honour to the Wisdom and Equity of
our own municipal Institutions than the *Principles* and *Rules*
concerning *Evidence* none is more connected with the sublime Principles of moral and political Science, and the
Knowledge

Knowledge of human Nature, none more interesting to the Gentleman and the Scholar, from its Analogy to the Rules of the most civilized and greatest of the Nations of Antiquity, more awakening to the inquisitive mind, wishing to understand the sources of our Establishment, (a with much to be cultivated in our ingenuous Youth) or more important to every one who partakes of our CONSTITUTION, as a Government of LAWS administered on *fixed Principles*

The Rev Dr DISNEY will give me leave to acknowledge the first intimations I received relative to the *successive public Appointments* held by GILBERT and to Mr HARGRAVE (to whom every one engaged in researches on the *Law* and *legal Antiquities* of ENGLAND must feel his share of obligation) I am indebted for the perusal of an earlier *Law of Evidence*, with manuscript Notes, interleaved: and a Manuscript in *four Volumes* of GILBERT's LAW OF EVIDENCE (purchased by that Gentleman, at a considerable expence, with other manuscript Tracts said to have been written by our Author) This Manuscript appears to have been copied by an *Amanuensis*, and has literal Errors, some of which have been transferred into the printed Edition which I used, || and have been corrected in this, The Manuscript came into my hands when I had made a progress of about 590 Pages in this Edition What use has been made of it, and of the *other Law* of *Evidence*, ¶ will appear by the References to each in the Margin

|| The Fourth.

In the mention of Books, which have been consulted with a View to the Work now offered to the public, I had nearly overpassed THE THEORY OF EVIDENCE,† printed in 1761, of which the Author confesses himself greatly indebted to two *Manuscript* Treatises, written by different hands upon the same subject. yet, however, flatters himself that he has some Merit in not having slavishly copied after, either; but endeavoured, with Freedom, to correct their Errors and supply their Defects

This Work came too late into my hands to be of Use. except the *Analytical Index* at the End of it, which is drawn upon an ingenious Plan, and which (enlarged and improved) will be subjoined.

However, nothing of any consequence, I believe, has been lost. The chief part of it being a *Compendium* (and not an ill one) of GILBERT's LAW OF EVIDENCE, which had been in Print,—one *English* Edition at least, if not two,—

¶ Ascribed to NELSON. See the BIBLIOTHECA LEGUM. Of this there is an Edition in 1717, and a second in 1735.
† It consists of 128 *Octavo Pages*, exclusive of the *Index*.

before

before the Publication of this *Theory*   And almoſt every
thing it contains having been adopted into the preſent Work;
either from the LAW of NISI PRIUS, or from my own
Reſearches

The liberal Spirit of Communication, which does honour
to the preſent Age, has induced Gentlemen to whom I was
unknown to oblige me by hints reſpecting the Life of GIL-
BERT. The RECORDER of DURHAM† will allow me to
intimate how much I am obliged by his polite Attention to
my general Letter of Enquiry publiſhed in the *Gentleman's
Magazine*   I have ſimilar Thanks to return to another Gentleman, the preſent Proprietor of the Chief Baron's Eſtate
in KENT.

In this Edition the very numerous References of the laſt
preceding are reprinted, with ſome few Omiſſions; which
the Reader may be inclined to believe have been made generally for ſome ſufficient reaſons: ſome erroneous or miſ-
printed ones in that and other Books are corrected · and
much pains has been taken that thoſe References which are
in this might be accurate

I ſhall eſteem myſelf much obliged by the correction of
any Errors, of whatever kind which may have been incurred in a Work, of which the Labour is much better known
to me than the ſucceſs-in the Execution can be eſtimated.
To the Profeſſion,—whoſe Cenſure, being founded in Knowledge, will be juſt and candid,—I commit it: aſſured only
of this, that it has been my earneſt endeavour to render it
not unſerviceable to them, nor altogether unworthy of the
original AUTHOR.

                                                        C L.

Triſten ball, near BURY SUFFOLK.
        10th Nov 1788

        † WILLIAM AMBLER, *Eſq.*

ARGUMENT

ON

THE DISTINCTION

BETWEEN

MANSLAUGHTER AND MURTHER,

DEDUCED BY

An INVESTIGATION of our ANCIENT LAW:

Being the INTRODUCTORY PART

Of an OPINION delivered by *JEFFRAY GILBERT*,
Efq. then one of the JUDGES of the COURT of
KING's BENCH in *IRELAND*.

In *DWYER's* Case;

ON

A SPECIAL VERDICT.

PREFACE

TO THE

FOURTH EDITION.

As the former Editions of this Work met with great Succefs from the Public, the Editor is encouraged to publifh a Fourth, which has been carefully corrected throughout, with the Addition of many References to the beft Authorities. The Reader is defired to take notice that *Siderfin* is referred to as it was publifhed, not according to the Time the Cafes reported therein were taken, and of the following Abbreviations made ufe of in the Citations, *viz.* 2 Kel. *Mr. Juftice Kelynge's in King's Bench, &c.* 1764. St. Tri. *State Trials.* 2 Jones, *Sir Thomas Jones's Reports.* R. S. L. *Reading on the Statute*

PREFACE.

Statute Law. H. H. P. C. *Hales's Hiſtoria Placitorum Coronæ.*

This Fourth Edition is improved with Extracts from the Reports of Sir *James Burrow*, Serjeants *Wilſon* and *Sayer*, and other eminent Law Writers, who have favoured the Public with their judicious Collections, ſince the Publication of the Third Edition of this beſt Piece of all the learned Author's many valuable forenſic Performances.

ARGU-

ARGUMENT, &c.

Rex v. Dwyer.

DWYER was indicted for MURTHER, and on the Sta- GILBERT's
tute of *ftabbing* And on each Indictment a SPECIAL REPORTS,
VERDICT was found, *viz* 2d Ed. 1742.

That on the 17th of *January*, 1714,* DWYER met * So it fhould
THOMAS ROSS, deceafed, on *Effex Bridge*, with his *Wife* clearly be, tho
and two *Children* that *Dwyer* joftled one of the *Children* printed 1724
with his horfe he rode upon; that *Rofs* coming up to *Dwyer*, count of GIL-
and having hold of his Bridle ferzed him, that *Dwyer* im- BERT prefixed.
mediately drew his fword, and *wounded* ROSS, and lighted
down, that *Margaret*, ROSS's Wife, interpofed to prevent
farther Mifchief, faving, fhe had rather he would abufe
her than her Hufband; that *Dwyer* then returned to
his Horfe; and the fword wanting the fcabbard, one of the
Crowd reached it towards him, and the faid *Margaret* fnatch-
ed the fcabbard, and broke it, and *threw* it at *Dwyer*;
DWYER then mounted his Horfe, and fheathed his fword;
and other *angry Words* then paffing between *Rofs* and *Dwyer*,
DWYER, in a Paffion, difmounted again, and returns to
Rofs with his *drawn fword* in his hands, and that *Rofs* endeavoured to feize fomebody's ftick, as well to defend himfelf as to offend *Dwyer*, but that he *could not*; that DWYER,
with his *fword* LIFTED UP, *attacked* ROSS, affaulted and
BEAT him with it that *Rofs* and *Dwyer* clofed, and mutually gave and received feveral Blows, in which fcuffle *Dwyer*
ftabbed *Rofs* with his *fword*, on the left Pap, an Inch wide,
and three Inches deep, of which he *died*

In introducing of his OPINION on this fpecial Verdict,
the enfuing ARGUMENT was delivered by GILBERT:

To

To consider this Case § we must settle the *Difference* between MURTHER and *Manslaughter*; and whether, as this Case is circumstanced, it belongs to the *one* or the *other* Species of Crimes " And in order to this, it will be of " use to enquire in what manner, and by what degrees, the " Distinction between *Murther* and *Manslaughter* was intro- " duced and established "

(margin: CAPITAL CRIMES under the ancient Saxon Law commutable.)

By the ancient *Saxon Laws* all Crimes were capable of *Commutation* by pecuniary Payments; for they thought that under the *Christian Institution* no Person ought to die for any offence " to which Death was not expresly annexed by the " Law of *Moses* · nor even for those in the *first* instance, " unless with *one* or *two* exceptions of signal Crimes " and therefore the Laws of King *Ina*,† which are the first we have in *Lambard's* Code of *Saxon* Laws, appoint proper *Penalties* but no Compensation was for a *malicious* MUR-THER †

(margin: † Obiit 727 P C Prasiley's Court)

*(margin: * Oout 900)*

The Laws of King ALFRED * began with a *Preface* reciting the several *Mosaic* Institutions and expressly, after mentioning that the *Christian* Law was more mild, the Words are, *ubi vero propagato Dei Evangelio plurima Nationes atque adeo Argu verbo Dei fidem adjunxerant, nonulli per orbem terrarum cætus atque etiam in Anglia Episcoporum, aliorumque clar simorum satentum conventus agebantur. atque hi, divinâ edocti miseratione, cuique jam* PRIMUM PECCANTI *pœnam imperabant pecuniariam, ejusque (absque omni divinæ offensionis concitat one) exigendæ minus magistratui (dotâ prius veniâ) desit rehart· * PRODITORI *tantummodo, ac* DOMINI DESERTORII *hanc mitiorem pœram haud infligendam existimarunt quippe qui ejusmodi viro minime parcendum censuerunt tum quod Deus contemptores sui omni miseratione indignos voluit; tum quod Christi aliorum qui in mortem obtulerunt non est omnino misertus Dominum vero præ cæteris colendum sta uit*

(margin: APXAION, 21 2)

(margin: Exception of TREASON)

(margin: Pote us cxc... ... ...)

(margin: For sæ Kel R p.)

§ *With this may be compared* Steadman's *Case, which seems to resemble this, though less favourably circumstanced for the Prisoner, and which after solemn Argument was ruled* Manslaughter*, and on the other hand* Mawgridge's *Case, which was ruled* Murther*, that being strong Evidence in that Case of a destructive intention from the first*

(margin: T Comm IV p 14)

† *The Term* MURTHER *was anciently equivalent to* HOMICIDE, *in whatever circumstances, of which the* Justification *was not evident and full, and therefore did not, ex vi termini, imply Malice pretpense, as in our present Acceptation of it, there was then therefore no Tautology in that Addition, though there may now seem to be*

‡ *The Dom ni desertori, in the sentiment and language of those Times, I apprehend to mean an* Apostate, *they imagining themselves intitled and obliged to undertake the Defence of Religion by the secular Arm*

By

By this it appears that the *Law* which mentions *De Proditione Dominorum*, in which there is appointed an Estimate LL. *Alured* 4; for the *King's* head, and the heads of other *Lords*, and the P. 23, 4. Penalty of *Death* in case it were not paid, was in those Times thought a new Punishment, which they did not think fit to inflict for heinous offences, as HIGH TREASON against their PRINCE and *Petty Treason* against their *Lords*, without making a *Preface* to reconcile such Proceedings to the Law of God.

But to punish *Theft* or other Crimes with *Death* was esteemed directly opposite to the religious Opinions of those Times as appears by what the *Canonists* have observed on the Laws of *Frederic* the Emperor, who established that a Thief that stole *five shillings* should be hanged *Proles Fre-* *Julius Clauf.* *derici Imperatoris qui statuit in illâ Lege quod fur quinque soli-* *Sententiam.* *dorum suspenderetur, et sic quod homo ad Dei imaginem creatus* *Lib* 529 *propter bona occideretur, et alii Reges successores qui secuti sunt hanc Legem, eorumque Ministri, non regnaverunt super Terram, et male v iam finierunt, nec generatio eorum ad tertium gradum pervenit.*

But in *Alfred's* Law, in the TEXT DE HOMICIDIO, it ap- LL. *Alured*:26. pears that only a *pecuniary* Punishment was appointed for that offence, and in those Days was levied only by Imprisonment. unless in the Case before mentioned of *High Treason* and *Petty Treason*, where the Non-payment was punished with *Death* It is not very hard to conceive how the Kingdom was maintained by *pecuniary Mulcts* only. for in those days every Man was put in the *Decenna*, and if found wandering three days out of the *Decennary*, he was taken up and imprisoned, and he was presently to abjure the Kingdom, or else he lay at the Mercy of every one that would lay hands on him And if any Offence was committed in any of the *Decenraries*, if the Party was brought to answer, he was obliged to pay his Fine for the offence, * or he was *imprisoned* for ever. if he fled, the *Tything* was answerable for his *Mulct* or *Fine* to the King So that by this Dis-

---

* *Besides the Fine to the injured Party as a private Satisfaction* L XLVIII. *or Composition, there was a Mulct to the State See the LECTURES* P 359, 60 *on HISTORY and POLITICS by a Master-hand But here, on a sub-* P 349, 357. *ject of such importance and extent, it may be expected that some* 35ᵗ *Points may require to be reconsidered of such, it seems to me, there are instances in the recommendation of certain Modes of Punishment for atrocious Crimes not compatible with the calm dignity of the Laws, nor with that certainty of Punishment which has the most steady operation in preventing Crimes for, agreeably to the clear and found Maxim expressed in another Page of that eminently useful Work,* Great Severity ought to be avoided in the Sanction of Laws. The Severity hinders the Execution

cipline

cipline Men were put under a Neceſſity of being innocent, or paving a grievous Fine, or being totally deprived of the Converſation of Mankind And the laying " of" the Fine on the *Tything*, in caſe the Offender fled, made it the Intereſt of every Man to bring the Offender to Light, and made it exceeding difficult to conceal a *Theft* or a *Murther* And theſe Fines ſet by Law were the *Vitæ Majores* for the Party was taken and impriſoned, and not to be ſet at Liberty without paving theſe Fines for his Redemption, which were therefore called a Ranſom But the pecuniary Puniſhment, *e re natâ*, on offences were called *Vitæ minores*, or *Amercia-men's*, or *Miſericordiæ* becauſe they were referred to the Mercy of the Court, and not impoſed by preciſe Laws, but theſe becoming afterwards exorbitant were affeered *per Judicium Parium* And though the Fines are now impoſed arbitrarily, yet being impoſed by the Court, they are ſuppoſed to be according to the Law and Precedents in the like Caſe

Thus ſtood the Law till the time of *Canutus*, ‖ who, as *Lambard* gives an Account, conſtituted a particular Species of Crimes, *viz* he who inſidiouſly killed a *Dane*, by lying in wait, ſhould not pay any Price, but was certainly to die, unleſs he defended himſelf by his *Ordeal*, &c MURDRA *quidem inventa fuerant et conſtituta in diebus* Canuti, Dani *Regis, qui poſt acquiſitam* Angliam *et pacificatam*, rogatu Baaonum Anglorum *rem ſit in* Daniam *exercitum ſuum* Ipſi *vero* Ba-rones *extiterunt* Fidejuſſores *quatenus quotiquot in Terrâ ſecum relinqueret firmam Pacem per omnia haberent* Veruntamen *ſi quis* Anglicum *aliquem eorum int rfece it* ſi ſe ſuper hoc de-fendere non poſſit Juicio Dei, *ſcilicet* Aquâ vel Ferro, *fieret de eo Juſtim Si autem aufuceret, ſolveretur, ut ſupra dictum eſt* The Fine, by the foregoing Law, was forty-ſix Marks of which the King had forty, and the Relations of the deceaſed the Reſidue, if the Murtherer could not be brought to Juſtice

BRACTON gives the ſame Account of the Original of this Species of Crime And it appears that *William* the Conqueror revived this Law for the Security of his *Normans* as appears by the Laws of *William* the *Conqueror*, and by the Laws of *H* I And it ſeems, from the Time of *Canutus*, the Law began to inflict *capital* Puniſhments SANE quidem *teſtor exciſones et incendia, aperte* Comp *a*ones, Cædes ma-*riſ*ſ* e, D.mino *s*nquae Proditiones *ſunt* Jure humano inexpia-*bil*a " So that now they began to admit the Diſtinction between

---

Marginal notes (left column):

SHARP's *Congr.* COURTS, 17—20.

Or Wíte, Wíte, *Sax* Fine, or Mulct.

‖ Obiit 1036.

Death for Dane murder by Canute, Kel 121

A marginal note partly illegible

L 53 ⁊ 170

L 75 p 265
* T D
iore ſ Canute
ta is when
as s v on
other a crime
C ir a.

between Crimes * expiable *Jure divino*, which all Crimes, how heinous foever, are, and Crimes expiable *Jure humano*. The not attending to this diftinction was the original of their impofing *pecuniary Mulcts* in their former Laws, and henceforth they began to think it no offence, againft Chriftianity to inflict *capital Punifhments* for fome offences. Howbeit, in the Cafe of Theft, there was great Latitude left in the Punifhment, even to BRACTON's Time *Pro parvo enim Latrocinio vel pro parvâ re nullus Chriftianus Morti tradendus· fed alio modo fic caftigatur, ne facilitatis venia † aliis præbeat materiam delinquendi; et ne maleficia maneant impunita· et ideo fecundum rei qualitatem furatæ et valorem, fi Fur convictus fuerit vel Morti tradatur aut Regnum abjuret, vel Patriam, Comitat', Burgum, vel villam; aut caftigetur, et fic caftigatus dimittatur* **[margin: THEFT, to an Amount reputed great in thofe Days, CAPITAL in the time of BRACTON † ſ Ne Venia Facilitas]**

In the intermediate Times " between this and" *William* I it appears that the offence of *Theft* was punifhed with a pecuniary Mulct only, and indeed it feems, that as long as the *Decennary* Law continued in its full force, there feemed no neceffity of punifhing Theft with *Death*, becaufe there was no means of concealing the things that were *ftolen* But when, by the Inundation of People, the *Decennaries* were diffolved, it was neceffary, in cafe of *Theft*, to proceed to greater feverities **[margin: Lamb. 160.]**

And as the Law of *Murther* began in *Canutus*, fo alfo now the *Diftinction* began between *Murther* and *Manflaughter* The Law runs thus. *Si quis alium præmeditatus trucidarit palam, perempti cognatorum in poteftatem dator fin cædis infimuletur tantummodo, atque in excufatione afferendâ ceciderit, Epifcopum penes efto ejus rei Judicium* **[margin: Rife of the Diftinction between Murther and Manflaughter, and of Benefit of Clergy.]**

Hence it came to pafs that the Laws relating to *Homicide* were reduced into Form by the *Clergy*, and conftituted on the Plan of the *Mofaic Law*, for the Clergy ftill taught that the Life of a Man could not be taken away but as warranted by the Laws of GOD; and therefore the Law of *Deuteronomy* * became the *Pattern* of our Laws in the Cafe of *Manflaughter*. **[margin: * XIX.]**

---

* *Compare this with the Crimes marked with* Text Letter *in the* Abftract of Penal Statutes *annexed to the pofthumous Work of my reverend Friend on the* Conftruction and Polity of Prifons. *I find my Idea of the proper Limits of* capital Punifhment *nearly correfpondent with this* Enumeration *See alfo the* Analyfis. C. L

Though *neceffary to proceed to greater feverities than Fine, the humane and learned Author does not fay it was neceffary to make Larceny and other offences punifhable with Death, in the kind and circumftances of offence fo punifhable in his Time, and to which there has been great addition fince.*

Hence

In the Matter, that is, έπα ιλο ζυαρμ in the Fact

Hence it is, that in this Law of *Canutus*, in cafe of *apparent Homicide*, the Murtherer was put in the power of the
Relations of the deceafed † and from hence the Appeal ftill
continues to the next of kin, who was the Avenger of Blood
according to the *Jewifh* Law

And the *Appeal* of the *next* of *Kind*

From hence alfo came the Refolution, that the Avenger
of Blood muft make *frefh Purfuit* after the offender and it
was a good Plea in *Abatement* to the *Appeal*, that the Heir
had not made frefh Purfuit which was plainly according to
the *Mofaic* Pattern, which permits the *Avenger of Blood* to
purfue the offender, and to flay him, if he overtook him before he got to the *City* of *Refuge* But with us the Avenger
of Blood was not permitted to carve out his *own* Revenge, as
with them becaufe that part of the inftitution which permits
the Avenger of Blood to flay the offender, *Lege Talionis*, was
thought to be merely *political*, and permitted to the *Jews*
merely for the *Hardefs* of their Hearts: and was therefore

Mark v v 28

thought to be abrogated by the *Chriftian Inftitution*, which
feems to have abolifhed the *Lex Talionis*

* 6 E I Aⁿⁿᵒ 1278

And by the Statute of *Gloucefter* * it is provided they
fhould not plead in Abatement the want of frefh Suit, if it
was commenced within the *Year* and the *Day* From hence,
Murtherers being negligently profecuted by the Relations,

‖ 3 H VII. c. 1 Aⁿⁿᵒ 1486

the Statute ‖ was made that they proceed at the King's fuit
within the Year and the Day, but then the *Auterfois acquit*
or *condemned* fhould be no Bar to the *Appeal*

Ecclefiaftical Interpretation of the Mofaic Law

From the *Mofaic* Law came likewife the Diftinction between *Murther* and *Manflaughter* though the *Ecclefiaftical*
Interpretation carried the Diftinction much farther than the
Mofaic Law for by that, *whofo killeth his Neighbour, that he
hated not of time paft, as when a Man goeth into a Wood, and
the Head of his Axe flippeth off and killeth his Neighbour there,
he fhall flee to the City of Refuge, that the Avenger of Blood
revenge not him, inafmuch as he hated him not in time paft but if
any Man hate his Neighbour, and he in wait for him, and rife up
againft him, and fmite him that he die, and " fleeth into one of
" the Cities of Refuge,"* ‖ he was not to be received

Deut. 21

Intead the Jews interpreted the Diftinction that was made
in thefe feveral Laws to be " between" *voluntary* and " ca-
" fual" Homicide but by the *Interpretation* that was put
upon this Law by the *Clergy* of *England* they diftinguifhed it
into *Murther* and *Manflaughter* and they deemed him to be
a *Murtherer*, that in times paft had conceived Hatred againft

---

† For the King could pardon where the fuit is in the name of the
Crown but not an Appeal

‖ This is nearly, though not abfolutely a literal Quotation.

his

his Neighbour, and laid in wait for him, and him to be guilty only of *Manslaughter*, who, on a *sudden Provocation*, had committed *Homicide* The *intermediate* species of offence is not taken notice of in *Deuteronomy* † for there the *Examples* are taken of the *highest* and *lowest* offence · the first from *lying in wait* and *preconceived Malice*, and the other from *killing a Man with the Helm of his Axe against his Will* But this killing on a *sudden Provocation* being not taken notice of there, the *Christian Clergy* placed it with the mildest. *The Mosaic Law instances only in casual and voluntary Homicide.*

It appears likewise by the Laws of *Canutus*, that the *Bishop* was to judge of the Truth of the Fact, who, in ancient Times, sat with the *Sheriff* or *Earl* of the County in the *Torn*, or *Criminal Court* and if they judged it to be *Homicide*, he took him into the *Protection* of the *Church* *Of the Jurisdiction of the Bishop*

But in the *Norman* Times, this Jurisdiction in the *Temporal* Courts was taken away from the Bishops, both by the *Law* of the *Conqueror* and the *Canon* of *Toledo*, which ordains, that *his qui in sacris ordinibus constituti sunt in* Judiciis *Sanguinis adjutare non licet* And from henceforward the *Bishop* did not preside over the *Proofs* in *criminal* Cases in the *Courts* of *Justice* * and when the *Criminals* began to fly to the Church as to a *Sanctuary* and there the *Bishops* having inquired into the Crime, if they thought it *Homicide*, they would not deliver him up if it was MURTHER, they *some times* delivered him up to the *secular* Power · and this they vindicated upon the Pattern of the *Jewish* Law And to prevent this it was one of the Constitutions of *Clarendon*, that if any one " fled to" the Church, or any privileged Place, he must either come *ad standum recto vel quod cognoscat maleficium propter quod se teneat in Ecclesia* and if he did so, he had liberty to *abjure* the Realm, and go into *Banishment* BRACTON spends a whole Chapter to consider how this Law could be executed, and whether, in case they would not deliver up the Malefactor, they could enter the Church, and violate the sanctuary And he determines they could not because this would be *horribile*, *nefandum* but he says, that the *spiritual* and *temporal* Powers ought to aid each other: and adds farther, that whoever carried *sustenance* to the of-

How the bishop came to be excluded in capital causes from sitting in judgment.

Const Clarend. c 11 11 H II IV Comm. 264, 5

Abjuration of the Realm admitted in favour of those who had taken Sanctuary

---

† *It instances, however, in such a manner as to leave an implied Medium between deliberate purpose from previous Hatred and mere Accident*

* *They retire (with a Protest, saving their Right) before the* Question *is put of* guilty, *or not* guilty), *in the* HOUSE *of* PEERS *in* Parliament, *in capital Cases*

fender

ferder fhould be put out of the King's Protection ‡ And thus the Laicks were brought under the King's Protection and the civil Power; which punifhed all *voluntary* Murther with Death, and excepted the *involuntary*, according to the true fenfe of the *Mofaic* Law

Li. Canti. ut fupra

After which the Clergy challenged the Privilege not to be tried themfelves by any *temporal* Jurifdiction: and therefore the Punifhmen's of *Murther* and *Theft* by Death (as to *Ecclefiaftics*) were brought in by the King's Laws

Struggle between the Clergy and the Laity

The *Ecclefiaftics* alfo challenged an Exemption from *all fecular* Power, even in Cafes of *High Treafon* Thus the *Quære* of the *Canonift*—Nunquid Clericus *committens Crimen* LÆSÆ MAJESTATIS *poſſit puniri per Principem aut Judicem fecularem cum fit temporaliter fubditus?* Refp *de Jure loquendo*, QUOD NON Clericus *enim non dicitur proprie committens Crimen læfæ Majeftatis*, cum fit, NON VERE SUBDITUS; *tamen* DE FACTO *Principes feculares plures fervant contrarium:* but he refolves the Clergy were to be *degraded*, before they were punifhed (though it were *High Treafon*) by the *fecular* Arm

Benefit of Clergy gradually excluded in TREASON

But they came to this *Temper* in *England*, that for TREASON the *Benefit* of *Clergy* fhould not be allowed, on the *Canonift's* Notion, that they were not fubject to the King · and therefore, in the Cafe of the Bifhop of *Carlifle*, ar-

---

THUCYD Decad·1, 1731. L I p 86

‡ A fimilar Expedient was ufed againſt PAUSANIAS, when, dreading an Impeachment, he fled to the Temple of Minerva Chalciœcos. They would not force him from thence. but fhut up the Entrance by placing a ponderous ftone againſt it Λεγεται δε αυτον μελλοντα ξυλληφθησεσθαι . προς το Ιερον της Χαλκιοικου χωρησαι δρομω και προκαταφυγειν Ηδη εγγυς, το τεμενος Και εις οις οικημα μεγα ο ην του Ιερου εισελθων, ινα μη υπαιθριος ταλαιπωροιη, κουχαζεν Το παραυτικα μεν υϛερησαν τη δ'αξα, μελιζ δε τουτο τουις οικημαιος τον οροφον αφειλον, και τας θυρας, ινδον οντα τηρησαντες αυτον, και απολαβοντες εισω απωκοδομησαν πετ·καθειρξαντες εξεπολιορκησαν ΛΙΜΩ Και μ λλοντος αυτα αποψυχειν, αϛιν γ εχ εν τω οικημαιι εξαγουσιν εκ του Ιερου ετι εμπνουν οντα Και εξαχθεις απεθανε παραχρημα

It is remarkable that in this Narrative there is nothing of the Abruptnefs or Obfcurity, and little, if any thing, of the Harfhnef. of Style and Compofition obferved in the general Manner of this great Hiftorian Allowing for the Difference of Dialect, the Paffage more refembles Herodotus Diodorus Siculus, Plutarch, and Nepos, relate this Event with fome difference The firft makes the Mother of Paufanias to have ftopped the Entrance of the Temple, and with this Nepos agrees Plutarch eſcribes it to the Father. Aaven trious Embellifhments, when the Event became remote, and the original fimplicity ceaſed to fatify

Nepo. L B 16 § p 84.

---

ra gned

raigned for *Treafon*, this pretended Liberty of the Church was over-ruled by the Judges; but in the Cafe of a *Murder*, though it was to be punifhed by Death by the Laws of GOD, and the Flight of a *Levite* to the City of Refuge was not permitted (for the *Mofaic* Law had conftituted the Cities of Refuge to be the Towns of the *Levites*), it was never to be abufed for the Protection of a Murtherer; yet the *Clergy* claimed, even in *this* Cafe, an *Exemption* from the *fecular* Laws

" Thus then of TREASON "

But in all other Cafes of HOMICIDE and *Theft*, the *ecclefiaftical* Jurifdiction was readily allowed, and if they challenged any *ecclefiaftical* perfon, accufed before the *fecular* Judge of any of thefe offences, he was delivered to the *Ordinary*, who was to judge *de Corrigibilitate*, and if he adjudged him *corrigibile*, he appointed him a proper *Penance*, and after the performance of fuch *Penance* he was *affoiled*, but if the offender was judged *incorrigibile*, he was degraded

When this was fettled, the Difpute arofe, *who fhould be Judge?* and the *Canonifts* fay, *Quod* Probatio *et* Cognitio num aliquis fit Clericus *debet*' ecclefiafticæ Jurifdictioni—*debet fieri coram* Judice ecclefiaftico, *et non coram* Judice feculari Though in *Lindw.* (which gives us many of our Inftitutions) it is faid, Clericus *contra quem procedet* Judex fecularis *pro aliquo delicto exhibet coram ipfo Judice* feculari *Jura fua et inftrumenta: et iis vifis Judex eum remittet ad fuum Judicem* ecclefiafticum, *ubi fcil*' &c

The *Clergy* extended this Privilege to all that had *primam Tonfuram*; as the *Clerk* that fet the *Pfalm*, the *Door-keeper*, the *Exorcift*, the *Subdeacon*, the *Reader* and they being Judges who were *Ecclefiaftics*, it was thought proper to reftrain them within Bounds; and therefore the *Temporal* and *Ecclefiaftical* Power joined in making the *Reading* before the *Secular* and the *Spiritual* Judge as the *Teft* of their being *Ecclefiaftics*, fince no man could be prefumed to be an *Ecclefiaftic* that could not read, and therefore the *Reading was* before the *fecular* Judge, but the *Atteftation* that he could read was by the *Ordinary* *This Privilege extended by the Clergy to all any way employed in the offices of the Church* *Hence derived the TEST, num legat ut Clericus*

But before he was tried whether he was an Ecclefiaftic, he was tried for the *Fact* for if he was found guilty of MURTHER by *Inqueft*, the *Ordinary* could not claim him; becaufe, as has been faid, all *Ecclefiaftics* in that Cafe fuffered *Death*. *Trial for the Fact to precede Trial of ecclefiaftics.*

Anciently

Anciently when any Ecclefiaftic was indicted or appealed of any Crime fhort of *Treafon* againft the King, the *Ordinary* might challenge him, but if the *Ordinary* did not challenge him, he was to be tried as any other *temporal* Perfon

C 2 3 E L
Anno 1275
Purgation in-
troduced in
cafe of *Eccle-*
fiaftics,

But the *Statute* of *Weft* 1 provides, that fuch Perfons delivered to the *Ordinary* fhould not be difcharged without *Purgation* and this was made by Articles ex ibited againft the offender, and his Anfwer to them in the *Ecclefiaftical* Court If he was found guilty of MURTHER in that Court, they degraded him, but if he was guilty of *Homicide*, he made his *Purgation* by *Penance* or *Commutations* for Money, as the *Ordinary* thought expedient

But becaufe by the Delivery to the *Ordinary* the *King* loft the *Forfeiture* of his *Goods* and *Chattels*, and *Profits* of his *Land*, an *Inqueft* was taken, to know *qualis ordinario deliberari debeat?* This created a great Mifchief to the Prifoner for if he fubmitted to *plead*, he could not be claimed by the *Ordinary*, having fubjected himfelf, as a Layman, to the *fecular* Jurifdiction if he did not fubmit to plead, he loft his *Challenges* to the *Jury*, and the Inqueft of the *Jury*, though he had no Liberty to plead, paffed upon him, whereby his Goods and Chattels were forfeited

PRISOTT, *Chief Juftice* of the *Common Pleas* in *Henry* the VI th's Time, fet this on a better Foot founding himfelf on the 25 *E* III. which fays, that all *Clerks*, as well *fecular* as *religious*, from henceforth convicted before the *fecular* Juftices for other *Treafons* or *Felonies* than againft the King fhall from henceforth freely have and enjoy the Privileges of Holy Church, and fhall, without delay, be delivered up to the *Ordinary* demanding them

So that he allowed them to *plead* to the Felony, and after *Conviction* the *Ordinary* might demand them

How the De-
mand of *Clergy*
became re-
ftricted to *Man-*
flaughter and
other minor
Crimes.

This introduced the Liberty for the Prifoner to demand his Clergy, and if, on the Inqueft, he was found guilty of *Murther*, the Court did not admit fuch Demand from the Prifoner, becaufe he was to *die* by the Law of GOD and therefore in fuch Cafes the Court did not deliver him, unlefs the Ordinary did demand him, which, in fo heinous a Crime, was feldom done for Laymen, nor even for *Clerks* but Cafes of *Homicide* and *Theft* were looked upon as properly *corrigible* by the *Ordinary*, becaufe they were not guilty of *Death* by the Law of GOD and therefore they allowed any Perfon of Education that could *read*, the *Benefit* of *Clergy*, and the

Ordinary

Ordinary received such Persons to *Corrections* and *Purgation* by Money, because they were not offences which by the *Mosaic* Constitution were punishable with Death

But the meaner Persons, not educated in Learning, and *who had no Money to make Commutation*, were generally given up to the *Temporal* Law.

There were several intermediate Statutes, by which they endeavoured to abridge this *Privilege* of the Clergy · the first was de *Bigamis*,† which was, that the *Bishop* of *Rome* having made a Constitution that all Persons *twice married* should be excluded from *Clerks Privilge*,—that such Persons when convicted should not be delivered as *Clerks*, whether they were *Bigamists* before or after that Constitution after this Statute, when *Felons* arraigned challenged their Clergy, the Prosecutors, upon shewing that they were *Bigamists*, ousted them of this *Privilege* To defeat the Effect of this Statute, they procured another, that *Bigamy* should be tried by the *Bishop*, and not by the *Temporal* Law The Statutes of *Clarendon*,† that forbid the taking sanctuary whereby to avoid the *secular* Justice, were also enervated by *Articuli Cleri* † for if a Clerk fly to the *Sanctuary*, he should not be compelled to *abjure* the Realm. so that the Churches and privileged Places continued a sanctuary for the Clerks themselves

It has been likewise resolved, that if a Clerk had *confessed* the Felony, and became an *Approver*, he should not be delivered to the Ordinary, because by such Confession he had submitted to the *secular* Jurisdiction

But the *Ecclesiastics* pretended that such Confessions were *coram non Judice*, though it had been otherwise resolved in the *Temporal* Courts, as Lord *Coke* observes, but the Statute of *Articuli Cleri* enacts, that he shall enjoy his Privilege, *notwithstanding his* CONFESSION

And now the Law, amongst *Ecclesiastics*, stood on this threefold Division

First, *if a Clerk was convicted of* TREASON, *he was never delivered to the Ordinary*, for that would have given up the Prerogative of the King.

Secondly, *in the Case of* MURTHER, *he was delivered to the Ordinary, if demanded*, but then it was in order to be *a. graded*, and for no other Purpose, for in a Crime punished by the Law of GOD with *Death*, he was not permitted to make any *Purgation*, but such *Degradation* was taken in the Nature of the *Death* and *Destruction of the Clerk* and therefore he was not put to *Death*, they did not intend he should be *twice* punished for the same offence : and BRACTON says,

Clericus,

† 4 E I
Anno 1276

† *Temp*. H II.
A D 1164
V₁ IV Comm.
422
C 15
† 2 E II
Anno 1315.
II Inst p 599.
Ed 4

C 16

Recapitulation

Clericus, si de Crimine convictus degradatur, non sequitur alia Pœra pro UNO peccato,—delicto,—vel pluribus ante degradationem perpetratis

Thirdly, *if* the *Clerk* were *convicted* of any *Felony* except MURTHER, *he might then demand the Benefit of Clergy*; and so they permitted any Person to do that could *read*; and such Person was permitted to make *Purgation* before his *Ordinary*; and, if he *purged* himself, he was *acquitted.*

But if the Clerk *confessed* the Fact, he was delivered to the *Ordinary, absque Purgatione*. for he, having *confessed* the Fact, could not deny it afterwards before the *Ordinary*

To understand the Reasons of these Distinctions, we must consider what is formerly laid down· that in Case of *Blood* by the *Common Law*, the *Ecclesiastical Court* had *no Jurisdiction*: and therefore, when the Clerk was *convicted*, he could not be delivered to the Ecclesiastical Court to make *Purgation*, because they had no Cognizance of the Cause; but he was delivered to them *absque Purgatione*, in order to be *degraded* by them And the *Sentence* of the *Common Law* was, *deliberetur Ord nario, absque Purgatione.*—Fleta *Si criminaliter agatur versus Clericum, quamvis Clericus respondere noluerit in Foro seculari, Judex tamen Ecclesiasticus cognitionem habere non potuerit nec regiam auferre Jurisdictionem, licet habere debeat Judicii Executionem. in Causa enim sanguinis non poterit Ecclesiasticus Judex cognoscere neque judicare, nisi irregularitatem committat, et quamvis neminem valeat Morti condemnare, degradare tamen potuerit crimine convict' et perpetuâ Carceris inclusione custodire* Upon such Delivery the *Ordinary* not only *degraded* him, but put him in *prison* till he obtained the *King's Pardon.*

But if the *Ordinary* demanded him for a Clerk that was not so, he lost his *Temporality*; because it was *impeaching the Temporal Jurisdiction*

But in all Cases, except *Treason* and *Murther*, the *clerk* might himself demand his *Privilege*: and then he was delivered to the *Ordinary* without any Restriction· and by this Law of the Church he was to purge himself of that Crime by his own *Oath* confirmed with *twelve* Compurgators, *six* of which were *lay* and the other *six* CLERKS and if he failed in his Purgation. he was punished as if he had been convicted, or had confessed the Crime

When he failed in his Purgation, the *Ordinary* judged if he "were" *corrigible* or *incorrigible*. if the former, they imposed *Penance*, and on his Performance or *Commutation*, he was *assoiled*, if the latter, he was *deprived* and *imprisoned.*

By

By the *Canon Law*, if the Criminal was *notorious*, † they proceeded to sentence *absque Purgatione* —*super* notorio *nulli erit induenda Purgatio* sc *tantum Condemnationis promulganda sententia* · *cum patrati sceleris Evidentia neque Accusationis clamore indigeat*

Lay persons offending a second Time excluded Clergy, on what Principles.

The *Temporal Court* taking notice of the *Canon Law*, and likewise that the *Ordinary* could not take notice of the Judgment of their Court, when a Person became infamous by a *second* offence, they were wont to deliver him *absque Purgatione*; and therefore an *infamous* Thief was so delivered

And by the 4th of *H IV* it is enacted, that a *Clerk* that is a *Traitor* or *infamous* should be delivered to them *absque Purgatione*

Anno 1402.

But as the *Clergy* had *notoriously abused* their Privilege, it is enacted that none but Persons in Orders shall have the Benefit of their Clergy above *once*. and the "*Manslaughter*" shall be marked with an M, and the *Felon* with an F. and that Persons in Orders demanding their Clergy, shall shew their Orders at a day given by the Court.

By the 28th of *H. VIII* and 32 *H VIII* Persons in Orders shall receive the Benefit of Clergy but once.

C 1 §3. Anno 1536.

" But this is held to have been virtually repealed by a " subsequent Statute "

V 23 H VIII. c. 1

By 18 *Eliz* the Persons admitted to the *Benefit of Clergy* shall not be delivered to the *Ordinary*, but enlarged out of Prison by the Justices

C 7. Anno 1576. Delivery to the Ordinary taken away.

---

† *That is, one who became so by the Proof of his persisting to offend, after having once had advantage of the Privilege in a former Conviction.*

" No

IV Comm.
c 28
IrifhSt. 11, 12,
& 13 J 1 c 3
§ 2
21 J I. c. 6.
Anno 1623

" " No Provifion had been made for the extenfion of a
" fimilar legal indulgence to that part of Society which is
" peculiarly intitled to Lenity till early in the *laft* Century
" when it was enacted, that *Women*, convicted of *fimple*
" *Larceny* under the value of *ten Shillings*, fhould, for the
" firft offence, be *burnt* in the hand, and farther punifhed
" by *whipping*, putting in the ftocks, imprifonment not ex-
" ceeding one Year

3 Car I c. 4.
16 Car I c. 4
3 & 4 W & M
c. 9

" This Act in *England*, *temporary* in its *commencement*, was
" continued, with others paffed in the fame feffion, by the
" two Statutes of the fubfequent Reign This was after-
" wards extended to *Women* guilty of any clergyable Felony,
" with liability to imprifonment not exceeding the Period
" affigned by the former Statute

4 & 5 W & M
c. 2,
1 St 9 A
c. 6 § 1.
8 St.
5 A c. 6
Anno 1707.

" At length this Privilege was fet more completely yet,
" on its true Ground, as a Benefit to be claimed by the ig-
" norant and illiterate, to whofe circumftances it was chiefly
" applicable, and who certainly have the faireft preten-
" fions to it The *Teft* by *reading* was accordingly *abolifhed*
" but when the exemption from capital Punifhment became
" thus extenfive, it was neceffary to qualify this indulgence,
" fo that it might not degenerate into a contrary extreme.
" and therefore, by the fame Statute, a difcretionary *Com-*
" *mitment* for any time, not lefs than fix Months nor ex-
" ceeding two Years, is provided

Vi infra, B III
Ch. VII T 7.
et 13

" But the Benefit, in its prefent Amplitude, does not
" extend to a perfon within the Statute of *ftabbing* who
" actually gave the ftab: and therefore it is neceffary to
" diftinguifh whether the offence in this Cafe be Mur-
" ther;—or *Homicide* by *ftabbing* within the purview of

---

* It is greatly to be regretted if the Remainder of this Argument
be irrecoverable - till it be retrieved, if that be yet poffible, I have
ventured to add a Supplement of what may be fuppofed the probable
import of the Argument It is needlefs to add that this fupplemental part pretends to no Authority, and being carefully diftinguifhed, it can miflead none It muft be acknowledged that the
Boundary which divides Manflaughter, on the Facts found in this
Cafe, from Murther, is fuch (if it be any) as demands to be
viewed with much fteadinefs and attention to render it difcernible
nor will I take on me to affirm that the opinion here hazarded was
that of the Chief Baron Yet a Conjecture may be founded on that
part of the Argument which remains, for if he had thought it either
within the Statute or Mariner at Common Law, it is difficult to
imagine that he would have entered fo copioufly into the Hiftory of
the Privilege of Clergy, a Privilege, on thefe fuppofitions, inappli
cable to the Cafe.

" the

" the Statute, (both which are excluded from Clergy) or
" whether it be Manslaughter, as at Common Law, not
" affected by the Statute, in which Case the Benefit of
" Clergy intervenes for the offender, if he has not already
" pleaded and received that Privilege for some other clergya-
" ble offence

" Whatever may be conjectured, no preceding Malice
" between these Parties is found by the special Verdict.

" After *Dwyer* had jostled against *Ross*'s Child on the
" Bridge, and *Ross* seized his Bridle, *Dwyer* was then guilty
" by drawing and wounding *Ross*, of such violence, as,
" independent of the Statute, would have been capital, had
" *Ross* then been slain, or had the Jury found that he died in
" consequence of *that* Wound   But the Verdict negatives
" such Conclusion by referring the Death of *Ross* to the
" Wound afterwards given

" It appears on this Record, that after an *Expostulation*
" from the *Wife* of the *deceased*, DWYER returned to his
" Horse, without any intention, so far as is expressed by the
" Verdict, of committing any farther violence   and the
" sword wanting the *scabbard*, this was reached to him by
" one of the *Crowd*, when unhappily *Margaret*, the Wife of
" the deceased, seizes and breaks the scabbard, and then
" throws it at *Dwyer*   He, however, remounts his Horse,
" and *sheathes* his sword in the *broken* scabbard, which seems
" to imply a Disposition, at that Moment, to command
" his rising Passion, and to restrain himself from again pro-
" ceeding to Extremities   But Wrath being thus rekindled,
" angry Words take place between him and *Ross*, and from
" this moment every circumstance is material to the forming
" of a Judgment on the legal Quality of the Case   The
" Jury find that he dismounted in a Passion, and returned to
" *Ross* with his *drawn sword* in his hand; that *Ross* endea-
" voured to defend himself by seizing the Stick of one
" of the Bye-standers, but could not   *Dwyer* then assaulted
" and BEAT him with the sword, using it consequently
" *not* as a sword, to thrust and stab, but as a Stick or Cudgel.
" The Jury farther find, that (in consequence of this As-
" sault, and the Resistance of *Ross* in his own Defence)
" they closed   *blows* were *mutually* received and given,
" and in the struggle *Dwyer* (then for the *first* time in
" *this* Conflict, and the former being ended seems not
" to affect the Case,) gave the *fatal Stab*, of which Ross
" died,

" From

" From the fuddenness of the Conflict, the Paffion on
" each fide, the Blows reciprocally given, and the other
" circumftances, it does not feem that at *Common Law* this
" killing would be other than *Manflaughter*; though Man-
" flaughter fo circumftanced as to deferve a ftrict Animadver-
" fion. The Point for confideration, if this be admitted,
" is, whether it is fuch a *ftabbing* as falls under the
" Statute

" The folution of this muft turn upon that Claufe of the
" Statute which relates to the ftabbing of any perfon not
" having then firft ftricken: and as this Statute does not
" create a new Felony, but readers Evidence conclufive
" againft the Prifoner, where the ftabbing is circumftanced
" as the Act expreffes, it has always in the *Englifh* Courts,
" where it exifted much earlier, been liberally conftrued
" in favour of Life. fo as not to hazard carrying a Pre-
" fumption of this kind farther than the manifeft and ne-
" ceffary intent of the Legiflature

" This is the known Rule of Conftruction in all Statutes
" which vary the Rules of the Common Law, particular-
" ly in criminal, and moft of all in capital Cafes: it is
" exemplified in the Interpretation which has been given
" to the former part of the Claufe now under confideration,
" not having then a weapon drawn " *Inftruments* of *Of-*
" *fence* have been conftrued to be weapons drawn, that
" are not within the ftrict grammatical import, or within
" the common intendment of thofe Words, becaufe they are
" within the general Reafon of the Exceptions to the Rule
" of Evidence introduced by the Statute

Jones (W)
340.
*Byart's Cafe.

" In the *Englifh* Courts there has been a Decifion on the
" Claufe upon which the prefent Queftion turns: the Judges
" there thought, one only excepted, that not having firft
" ftricken required that the party ftabbed fhould have ftruck
" firft, fhould have given the firft blow in the Affray.
" though it is obvious that if fuch were the meaning of the
" Ligiflature, it might have been naturally and unambigu-
" oufly expreffed without an inverfion of the order of the

Richardfon Vi.
Hot. fimiliter
Show. 668.

" words The Judge who differed thought therefore that
" it meant, not having *ftruck* before the mortal wound
" given And this feems to be the fenfe moft agreeable
" to the Principles of Interpretation applied to Statutes
" which affect Life, and at the fame time moft confonant
" to the order and apparent import of the expreffions ufed
" in the Act.

" It

" It is obvious that if the firſt-mentioned of theſe Con-
" ſtructions be adopted (independent of the firſt Conflict)
" the Priſoner is not within the Benefit, for it is found that
" he gave the *firſt* Aſſault but if the ſecond (which ſeems
" to be the true Conſtruction) be admitted, he is, for the
" *deceaſed* has ſtricken *before* the mortal Wound given

" If this Reaſoning be juſt, it follows that the Priſoner,
" on the Verdict before the Court, is guilty only of MAN-
" SLAUGHTER but any finding of a *thruſt* made by *Dwyer* _{placeholder} 2 Ld Raym.
" in the commencement of *this Conflict*, or of a Quarrel 1488, 9
" *ſought* by him, would have clearly ſet this Caſe within the Poſt D II
" legal Definition of MURTHER." † C V § 3.
Kel 6

† *The Caſe in* Skinner *has much reſemblance to this and there* Keate's Caſe
HOLT *inclined ſtrongly to the Conſtruction of* Richardſon, *which* Skinn 666, &
FOSTER *alſo favours, but he thought, though not within the Statute,* M 8 W III
it was Murther at COMMON LAW. *But there being Doubts whether
the Verdict were not incomplete, and a* venire de novo *neceſſary,
no Judgment was given poſſibly, on farther Conſideration, it might
have been thought doubtful whether the killing were* Murther at
Common Law, *if the firſt ſtriking with the ſword was a Blow, as
the Word ſeems to imply, and not a Thruſt a Blow not likely to
kill, nor with that intent given, but rather to intimidate However
that Caſe was ſtronger againſt the Defendant, upon the ſpecial finding, than the preſent.*

VOL. I.

OF

E V I D E N C E

IN GENERAL

WRITTEN AND UNWRITTEN.

AND PARTICULARLY

In CIVIL ACTIONS real and mixed;

AND

In PERSONAL FOUNDED ON CONTRACT.

THE LAW O

*E*VIDENCE, in it. DEGREES, is $\begin{cases} 1 & \text{CERTAIN} \\ 2 & \text{PROBABLE} \end{cases}$

𝕭

In its CONSTRUC- $\begin{cases} 1 & \text{STRICT} \\ 2 & \text{AMPLE.} \end{cases}$
TION.

ℭ

In it. FORM. $\begin{cases} 1 & \text{WRITTEN} \\ 2 & \text{UNWRITTEN.} \end{cases}$

𝕯

In its MODE of re- $\begin{cases} 1 & \text{ORDINARY.} \\ 2. & \text{EXTRAORDINARY} \end{cases}$
cept in and inquiry

𝕰

In : OBJECTS. $\begin{cases} 1 & \text{CIVIL} \\ 2 & \text{CRIMINAL} \\ 3 & \text{CONTRACTS} \end{cases}$
          2. TORTS $\begin{cases} 1 & \text{Public} \\ 2. & \text{Private} \end{cases}$

𝕱

In its DESIGN and $\begin{cases} 1 & \text{PREVIOUS} \\ 2 & \text{DECISIVE} \end{cases}$
limitation of purpose

𝕲

In 's general DI-
RECTION $\begin{cases} 1 & \text{The COURT} \end{cases}$

II *UNWRITTEN.* $\begin{cases} \end{cases}$
1 *Positive* (cæteris paribus)
  strength than negative testim
2 *Circumstantial error may*
  ral Truth
3 *The single evidence on an a*
  insufficient in capital cases,
4 *The single evidence of any*
  very clear and certain, to h
  in criminal cases
5 *Great crimes are proportio*
  bable, and require the strong
6. *The probability or general*
  that a witness speaks truth,
  parent cause to the contrary
  strength, generally, in crim
  civil cases

GENERAL RULE; applicable to written and unw
The best Evidence in kind is always required, which
stances before the court presume

ℭ

FORM of EVIDENCE

I *WRITTEN* $\begin{cases} 1 & \text{Public} \\ 2 & \text{Private} \end{cases}$

       PUBLIC $\begin{cases} 1 & \text{RECORD} \\ 2 & \text{Inferio} \end{cases}$

$\begin{cases} \end{cases}$ 1 PUBLIC ACT OF PARLIAM
  dence of itself
2 JUDICIAL PROCEEDINGS
  having authority to fine and in
$\begin{cases} 1 & \text{Writ} \end{cases}$

L Y S I S
OF
F EVIDENCE.

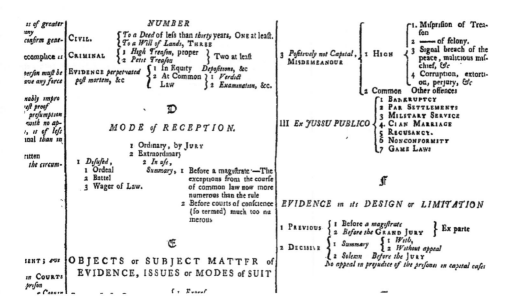

is of greater
tony
confirm gene-

CIVIL.

NUMBER

{ To a *Deed* of less than *thirty years*, ONE at least.
{ To a *Will* of *Lands*, THREE

ccomplice is   CRIMINAL   { 1 *High Treason*, proper } Two at least
{ 2 *Petit Treason*

person must be   EVIDENCE *perpetuated*   { 1 In Equity   *Depositions*, &c
have any force   *post mortem*, &c   { 2 At Common } 1 *Verdict*
{ Law } 2 *Examination*, &c.

nably impro
est proof
presumption
with no ap-
-, is of less
inal than in

℗

ritten
the circum-

MODE of RECEPTION.

1 Ordinary, by JURY
2 Extraordinary
1 *Disused*,   2 *In use*,
1 Ordeal   *Summary*, 1 Before a magistrate ·—The
2 Battel   exceptions from the course
3 Wager of Law.   of common law now more
numerous than the rule
2 Before courts of conscience
(fo termed) much too nu
merous

℃

IENT; ovs   OBJECTS or SUBJECT MATTER of
in COURTS   EVIDENCE, ISSUES or MODES of SUIT
prison
° C   { 1 *Exprefs*

3 *Positively not Capital*,   1 HIGH
MISDEMEANOUR

{ 1. Misprision of Trea-
fon
2 —— of felony.
3 Signal breach of the
peace, malicious mis-
chief, &c
4 Corruption, extorti-
on, perjury, &c
2 Common   Other offences

III *Ex* JUSSU PUBLICO

{ 1 BANKRUPTCY
2 PAR SETTLEMENTS
3 MILITARY SERVICE
4 CLAN MARRIAGE
5 RECUSANCY.
6 NONCONFORMITY
7 GAME LAWS

℉

EVIDENCE *in its* DESIGN *or* LIMITATION

1 PREVIOUS   { 1 Before a *magistrate*   } Ex parte
{ 2 *Before the* GRAND JURY

2 DECISIVE   { 1 *Summary*   { 1 *With*,
{ { 2 *Without appeal*
{ 2 *Solemn*   *Before the* JURY
No appeal *in prejudice of the prisoner in capital cases*

Ʊ

In its PLACE before
COURTS of JU
RISDICTION

- 1 GENERAL
- 2 LIMITED
- 3 SINGULAR
- 4 CONCURRENT
  ORIGINAL,
  SECONDARY

Я

DEGREES of EVIDENCE

CERTAINTY, *intuitive*, or *absolute*; is simple, and cannot be defined.

I DEMONSTRATION *Moral*—LEGAL CERTAINTY

II. PROBABILITY
- 1 Extraordinary —— Violent presumption of facts
- 2 Ordinary
  - Or certainty to a common intent.
- 3 Weak
  - Inconclusive
  - Evanescent

I LEGAL CERTAINTY is
- 1 MATTER *of* RECORD
- 2 Voluntary, deliberate CONFESSION in open COURT
- 3 CONCLUSION *of* LAW by necessary inference
- 4. CONCLUSION *of* FACT by full Proof.

II PRESUMPTION is
- 1 Of FACT.
  - 1 Violent.
  - 2 Probable
    - Repellable
- 2 Of LAW; necessary
  - Not repellable

PROOFS

Order
- 1 Original
- 2 Meine
- 3 Final.

Strength.
- 1 Direct
- 2. Circumstantial, independent, accumulative, which are required to convict or discharge from a contract certain
- 2 Probable, ordinary; sufficient to acquit or discharge from an uncertain contract.

Ⴚ

---

1 RECORD
- 1 Ev of itself in the Court to which it belongs
  - judicial
    - 1 Pleas
    - 2 Judgments
    - 1 Sv
    - 2 Of
- 3 PATENTS, &c
- 4. Particular ACTS of PARLIA
  Copy examined, or under Gr

- 1. CHANCERY PROCEEDINGS, Ev agt parties
- 2 ACTS of inferior COURTS law, not being of record
- 3 ECCLESIASTICAL PROCE
- 4. ACTS of certain other Co the REALM, not being law, so far as not of recor
- 5 DEEDS enrolled *Inspexin*
- 6 REGISTERS, &c *Copy*
- 7 ACTS of foreign countries fied

PRIVATE.
Primary, or Evidence in th
- 8 DEEDS not enrolled
  To be proved by witnesses.
  Rasure, interlineation, &c.

Inferior.
- 1 Real
  - Feoffment
  - Grant, &c.
- 2 Personal, or Mixed
  - 1 Annuity
  - 2 Bond.

- 9 WILLS,
  - 1 Formal
  - 2. Nuncupative
  - 1 Real, of Land
    - 1 Revoca
    - 2 Republ
  - 2 Personal, or testamentary Dispo sition
    - Con

- 10 Agreements, not under
- 11 Notes.
  Secondary or Evidence in d
- 12 Voluntary affidavits
- 13 Letters, &c.
- 14 Tradesmen's books, car
  supplemental.

II UNWRITTEN
- 1. Witnesses
- 2 Without witnesses.
  - 1. K
  - 2. F.

1. WITNESSES.
- 1. Quality
- 2 Number.

orn, ⎫ ...es ⎫ another
fice ⎰ ⎰ court

Founded, I. IN CONTRACTU { 2 Implied
    { 1 Ex injuria { Private wrong A*iv*
        privata { 1 Public wrong
II IN MALEFICIO { 2 Ex Delicto { 1 Indictment
           { 2 Information
           { 3 Impeachment.

MENT
{
1 Bills
2 Answers
3 Depositions
of common

EDINGS
URTS within
of common
d
ius

duly certi-

'first instance

{ 1. Single.
{ 2 With
  condition
1 L { 1 Ori
tion { ginal.
ication

Eccles ⎫ Pro-
Court ⎰ bate

eal.

fed of better

'oborative, or

nowledge of
-ors
it singulier.

        1 MALA IN SE
        2 Mala prohibita

CAUSES { I CIVIL
      { II CRIMINAL } General
      { III EX JUSSU PUBLICO, operating or particular
         CLASSES

I CIVIL { 1 Of right { 1 Real
      { 2 Of possession { 2 Personal
            { 3 Mixed

Founded in CON- { 1 Express { 1 Debt, Specialy, &c
  TRACT { 2 Implied { 2 Sale, exchange, &c

ASSUMPSIT
           { 1 Debt
1 Special { 2 Bailment, special
      { 3 Hiring, &c
        1 PUBLIC
        1 Undertaking of public TRUST
        2 Penalty, under statute.
          2 PRIVATE Contract uncertain.
        1 Service Quantum meruit
        2 Value Quantum valebat
        3 Money expended Per culia imperfe
2 GENERAL { 4 Money had and received Redhionita indebit
        5 BAILMENT { 1 Mandate or commission gratur sui } Man-
                          } datum
           2 Loan of hire Locatum
              1 Of things Rei
              2 Of work and labour Operis faciundi
              3 Of conve- { Mercium ve { 1 Public
                 ance { hendarum { 2 Private
           3 Loan of use Commodatum
           4 Pledge Pgnus
           5 Deposit Depositum

Founded on { 1 TRESPASS on the CASE P
FORT { 2 DISSEISIN R
     { 3 Ejectment M
     { 4 Waste M
     { 5 Trespass of Cl Fregit M
     { 6 Trover P
     { 7 Detinue P
     { 8 Trespass vi et armis { 1 Direct
                  { 2 Consequential
                    Inclusive

ANCIPITES, { 1 Assault, &c
having com- { 2 Slander { Gen
mon remedy {   { Spec

Ⓖ

EVIDENCE in its GENERAL DIRECTION

1 En pais { 1 Things real, lying in livery
     { 2 Criminal
     { 3 Personal, not of specialty

To be given in evidence to the JURY on the General Issue { 1 All specially general, & no. per se manifesta
        { 2 Or to be certified
        { 3 Or of the jurisdiction

2 Hors du pais { 1 Real, lying in grant
        { 2 Personal, of specialty

To the Court { En fait singulier { 1 Inspection
              { 2 Certificate
        { En Loi { 1 Pleadable
                       { 2 Record

PLEAS

1 GENERAL { 1 In public criminal suits
     { 2 In personal actions founded on specialty of form, or specialty of exemption
     { 3 In civil, where the deed is collateral to the title

2 SPECIAL { 1 In civil actions founded on specialty
     { 2 In personal actions founded on special claim, or defensible and r par icular justification

1 Dilatory { 1 To jurisdiction
     { 2 To ability { Death, infancy, coverture, outlawry, &c
     { 3 Abatement { 1 To writ { Defect, or
                 { 2 To court { Error

2 In bar to the action { 1 Release
       { 2 Justification
       { 3 Exemption { 1 By common law
                   { 2 By Statute
       { 4 Estoppel

Ⓗ

EVIDENCE as applied to JURISPRUDENCE

1. GENERAL { At Common Law { 1 KING'S BENCH
                      { 2 COMMON PLEAS
                      { 3 EXCHEQUER
                      { 4 CHANCERY, law sid
        { In Equity { 1 CHANCERY
                { 2 EXCHEQUER

2 Limited { County court
      Borough Courts,
      Manerial, &c

CERTAINTY, intuitive, or absolute; is simple, and cannot be defined.

I *DEMONSTRATION* Moral—LEGAL CERTAINTY.

II. PROBABILITY
- 1. Extraordinary —— Violent presumption of facts
- 2 Ordinary { Or certainty to a common intent
- 3 Weak { Inconclusive. Evanescent

I LEGAL CERTAINTY is
- 1 MATTER of RECORD.
- 2 Voluntary, deliberate CONFESSION in open COURT
- 3 CONCLUSION of LAW by necessary inference
- 4. CONCLUSION of FACT by full Proof

II PRESUMPTION is {
- 1 Of FACT { 1 Violent; 2 Probable { Repellable
- 2 Of LAW, necessary { Not repellable

PROOFS

Order { 1 Original. 2 Meine 3 Final

Strength. {
- 1 Direct
- 2. Circumstantial, independent, accumulative, *which are required to convict or discharge from a contract certain;*
- 2 Probable, ordinary; *sufficient to acquit or discharge from an uncertain contract.*

B

CONSTRUCTION of EVIDENCE

1. WRITTEN.
1. Words are to be understood according to their subject matter
2 A legal intent, sufficiently expressed, is in all cases to prevail.
3 The intent to be collected from the whole instrument taken together; or the whole system where complex
4 Antiquity of an instrument, well ascertained, is a presumption of validity
5 General certainty is to be preferred to particular convenience
6 General certainty is best secured by adhering to settled rules of interpretation
7 Matters of record are more strictly to be construed than matters en pais
8 Unfavourable contracts are to be strictly limited; favourable, to be liberally expounded.
9. Penal statutes admit of no extension
10 Remedial acts are to be taken largely in advancement of the relief
11 Acts of ademption or inhibition of general right are to be rigorously confined within their necessary sense
12 Summary and extraordinary jurisdictions must be kept within the letter of their authority
13 Revolutions of legal acts are not to be presumed
14 The COMMON LAW is never to be superseded unless in direct terms, or by in... cation

---

Inferior. {
6. REGISTERS, &c Copy.
7 ACTS of foreign countries c... fied

PRIVATE
Primary, or Evidence in the fir...
8 DEEDS not enrolled.
To be proved by witnesses Rasure, interlineation, &c
- 1. Real. { Feoffment Grant, &c.
- 2 Personal, or Mixed. { 1 Annuity. 2 Bond.

9. WILLS;
1 Formal
2. Nuncupative {
- 1 Real; of Land { Com I. 1. Revocation 2 Republication
- 2 Personal, or testamentary Disposition { Ecc Cou

10 Agreements, not under seal
11 Notes.
Secondary, or Evidence in default
12 Voluntary affidavits
13 Letters, &c.
14 Tradesmen's books, corroborative supplemental.

II. UNWRITTEN {
- 1. Witnesses
- 2 Without witnesses { 1 Known judicial 2 Fait

I WITNESSES { 1 Quality, 2 Number

I QUALITY {
- 1 Of Credit.
- 2 Of Competency
- 3 Neither of credit nor of compe...

I. Of CREDIT.
1 Persons of known and... character
2 Persons swearing against manifest interest
3 Not impeached in reputation contradicted by circumstance
4 Of preponderating character verisimilitude

II. Of COMPETENCY, or admissible.
1 Persons without direct improbable bias
2 Of doubtful character
3 Convict, but not attainted

III. Neither of CREDIT, nor ADMISSIBLE
1 Children, not having years of discernment of right or wrong.
2. Idiots, and insane { Propter de... pravitate... ni...
3 Persons directly interested. { Rei suae; ter luci numus
4 Persons legally infamous. { Propt... am
5 Persons excommunicated. { In c... Que... cep... min... cep...
6 Persons not on oath.
7 Under professional confidence { Propter infam...

(This sheet to face the Intro...

TRACT.   1 & 2 Implied 2. Sale, exchange, &c.

ASSUMPSIT

1. Special.
- 1 Debt
- 2 Bailment, special.
- 3 Hiring, &c

2. GENERAL.
- 1 PUBLIC
  - 1 Undertaking of public TRUST.
  - 2 Penalty, under statute
- 2. PRIVATE Contract uncertain.
  - 1 Service Quantum meruit
  - 2 Value. Quantum valebat
  - 3 Money expended Pe unæ impensæ.
  - 4 Money had and received Redhibitis indebitis.
- BAILMENT
  - 1 Mandate or commission gratuitous { Mandatum
  - 2 Loan of hire Locatum
    - 1 Of things Rei
    - 2 Of work and labour. Operis faciundi
    - 3 Of convey- { Mercium ve { 1 Public.
      ance { vehendarum { 2 Private
  - 3 Loan of use Commodatum
  - 4 Pledge Pignus
  - 5 Deposit Depositum

Founded on TORT
- 1 TRESPASS on the Case P
- 2 DISSEISIN   R
- 3 Ejectment   M
- 4 WASTE   M
- 5 Trespass of Cl Fregit M
- 6 Trover   P
- 7 Detinue   P
- 8 Trespass vi et armis { 1 Direct
                         { 2 Consequential Inclusive

ANCIPITES, having common remedy by public or private suit.
- 1 Assault, &c
- 2 Slander { Gen { Spec
- 3 Deceit { 1 Fraudulent conveyance.
          { 2 Other fraudulent dealings

II. CRIMINAL

1. CAPITAL
- 1 CAPITAL on the first offence, or without clergy.
- 2 Capital on the second offence, either identical, or of the same class, clergyable.

TREASON.
- Proper { Direct
         { Constructive.
- Improper { 1 Coinage.
           { 2 Petit Treason, murder of master, or mistress, or ecclesiastical superior

Other FELONY.

1 Capital ex JURE NATURALI primario aut hypothetico
- 1 MURDER
- 2 STUPRUM, vi patratum
- 3 CRIMEN innominandum
- 4 Burning of houses inhabited
- 5 Wilful sinking of ships, manned, &c
- 6 Robbery, with danger offered to life
- 7 House breaking (when inhabited) in the night, with like danger.

In the first instance
About ONE HUNDRED and SEVENTY other GENERA, and nearly Three Hundred and Thirty species of OFFENCES reduced to enumeration

2. Capital by STATUTE

In the second instance
Above EIGHTY GENERA species undetermined

---

1. GENERAL.
- 1 In personal actions founded on specialty of form, or specialty of exemption
- 2 In civil, where the deed is collateral to the title.

2. SPECIAL.
- 1 In civil actions founded on specialty
- 2 In personal actions founded on special claim, or defensible under particular justification

1. Dilatory
- 1 To jurisdiction
- 2 To ability { Death, infancy, coverture, outlawry, &c.
- 3 Abatement. { 1 To writ { Defect, or
              { 2 To court { Error.

2 In bar to the action
- 1 Release
- 2 Justification.
- 3 Exemption. { 1 By common law
              { 2 By Statute.
- 4 Estoppel.

H

EVIDENCE as applied to JURISPRUDENCE

1. GENERAL.
- At COMMON LAW
  - 1 KING'S BENCH
  - 2 COMMON PLEAS
  - 3 EXCHEQUER
  - 4 CHANCERY, law side
- In EQUITY
  - 1 CHANCERY
  - 2 EXCHEQUER

2. Limited
- County court
- Borough Courts,
- Manorial, &c

- 1 CHANCERY, in cases of mere equity
- 2 COMMON PLEAS in real actions
- 3 KING'S BENCH, on the high writs of prerogative, &c
- 4 PARLIAMENT, on impeachment.
- 5 Commons, on elections.
- 6 Lords, on questions of right of peerage.
- 7 Admiralty, on maritime causes

4. Concurrent
- 1 Ecclesiastical
- 2 Admiralty, &c.

5. Original
- Each of the GREAT COMMON LAW COURTS in their several jurisdiction

6 Secondary.
- 1 In the same court.
  - 1 New trial
  - 2 Attaint
  - 3 Appeal of murder, &c
- 2 To different courts
  - Writ of error or appeal
  - 1 From Common Pleas, to King's Bench The same from inferior Courts of Record
  - 2 From Exchequer side of Chancery and Exchequer
  - Appeal to House of Lords
  - 3 From common law side of Chancery, to King's Bench
  - 4 Of Exchequer, to the House of Lords
  - 5 From B R by bill to Exchequer
  - 6 On original, to the House of Lord.

THE

LAW

OF

EVIDENCE.

INTRODUCTION.

THE Subject to be confidered is Legal Evidence, " in the full comprehenfion of the Term, as it re-" lates, either to the Court, or *(a)* to the Jury '" and by what Rules of Probability it ought to be weighed.

In the firft place, it has been obferved by a † very learned † Locke. Man, that there are feveral Degrees from perfect Certainty and Demonstration, quite down to *Improbability* and unlikelinefs; even to the Confines of impoffibility · and there are feveral acts of the Mind proportioned to thefe Degrees of Evidence; which may be called the Degrees of Assent, from full Assurance and Confidence quite down to *Conjecture, Doubt, Diftruft,* and *Difbelief*

Now, what is to be done in all Trials, is to range all Matters in the Scale of " Proof," or " Verifimilitude " where direct Proof cannot be had according to the mea-" fure of Probability, which the fubject to be decided " requires or admits by the Rules of Law ." and then, " as to the Evidence of the Fact, to allow each par-" ticular its abfolute and relative Force " fo " that the" weight " fhall fall" where the caufe ought to preponderate and thereby to make the moft exact Discernment of Right.

(a) Locke, B IV Ch 15 §2 See the Philosophical Principles of Evidence *beautifully unfolded, with admirable deductions both fpeculative and practical, in the* IVth Dissertation *of* Dr. Price. *See alfo,* Watts's Logic, P 2 c 2 §8 *See alfo* Hartley's Theory *of the* Human Mind, *edited by* Dr Priestley, Ch 3 §2 Prop 38, 9, 40 *and* Wilkins Nat Rel Ch 1 3
†‡† *The Words between inverted commas in this Page are added to form a full and diftinct Divifion of the Subject · and it is generally to be underftood where they occur, that they denote Additions or Alterations*

Vol. I.   B   Now

Now to " underſtand LEGAL CERTAINTY, and even" to come to the true Knowledge of the Nature of *Probability* itſelf, it is neceſſary to look a little higher and ſee, " in general," what CERTAINTY is, and whence it ariſes

* Of CERTAINTY
1 *Intuitive*
2 *Demonſtrative*

ALL CERTAINTY IS A CLEAR AND DISTINCT PERCEPTION and ALL CLEAR AND DISTINCT PERCEPTIONS DEPEND UPON A MAN'S OWN PROPER SENSES Thus, this in the firſt place is certain, and that which we cannot doubt of if we would, that one Perception or Idea is not another, that what belongs to one man does not belong to another. and when Perceptions are thus diſtinguiſhed upon the firſt View, it is called SELF EVIDENCE, or INTUITIVE KNOWLEDGE (b)

Of demonſtrative, or deductive Certainty

There are ſome other Things whoſe Agreement or Difference is not known on the View · and then we compare them by the MEANS of ſome THIRD Matter; by which we come to meaſure their Agreement, Diſagreement, or Relation

As if the Queſtion be, whether certain Land be the Land of *I S* or of *I N* and a RECORD be produced whereby the Land appears to be transferred from *I S* to *I N*; now when we ſhew any ſuch third Perception that doth neceſſarily infer the Relation in Queſtion, this is called KNOWLEDGE by DEMONSTRATION (c) The Way of KNOWLEDGE by NECESSARY INFERENCE is certainly the higheſt and cleareſt that Man is capable of in his Way of Reaſoning and therefore always to be ſought when it may be had

The Difference between DEMONSTRATION and PROBABILITY.

DEMONSTRATION is always converſant about permanent Things, which being conſtantly obvious to our Senſes do afford to them a very clear and diſtinct * Comparison. but

(b) *Eſſ on* H U B IV C 2
(c) *This can only be ſg rarirely applied to Queſtions of* JURISPRUDENCE *and admit of no higher proofs than thoſe of the* THIRD *order or* VERY HIGH *and convincing* PROBABILITY, *at the moſt yet there are points which being not* LEGALLY CONTROVERTIBLE *are* FORENSICALLY DEMONSTRABLE † *Thus* NO AVERMENT *be agreeable againſt a* RECORD, *Evidence by* RECORD *is the* HIGHEST *Evidence · and therefore analogically* DEMONSTRATIVE
† *Ild Doctridge, b L.* 196 ·

transient

tranfient Things, that cannot always occur to our Senfes, are more obfcure , becaufe they have no conftant being, but muft be retrieved by Memory and Recollection

Now moft of the Bufinefs of CIVIL LIFE fubfifts on Actions of Men that are tranfient Things, and therefore often times are not capable of ftrict Demonftration, which, as I faid, is founded on the View of our Senfes and therefore the Rights of Men muft be determined by PROBABILITY

Now, as all DEMONSTRATION is founded on the View of a Man's own proper Senfes by a Gradation of clear and diftinct-Preceptions, fo all PROBABILITY is founded upon Views " partially, or in fome degree," obfcure and indiftinct, or upon Report from the Sight of others.

Now, this, in the firft place, is very plain, —that when we cannot fee or hear any thing ourfelves, and yet are obliged to make a judgment of it, we muft fee and hear by Report from others which is one ftep farther from Demonftration, which is founded upon the View of our own Senfes. And yet there is that Faith and Credit to be given to the Honefty and Integrity of credible and difinterefted Witneffes attefting any Fact, under the folemnities and obligations of Religion, and the Dangers and Perils of Perjury, that the Mind equally acquiefces therein as on a Knowledge by Demonftration ; for it cannot have any more reafon to be doubted than if we ourfelves had heard and feen it *(d)* and this is the " Bafis of the reliance to be " placed in Decifions upon folemn Trial, and of the fatis-" factory refult of legal Evidence "

CHAP I.

The beft Evidence to be had which the nature of the Fact fuppofes

The FIRST, therefore, and moft SIGNAL RULE in Relation to EVIDENCE is this—that A Man muft * PRODUCE THE UTMOST EVIDENCE THAT THE NATURE OF THE FACT is capable of *(e)* For the Defign of the Law is to

B 2   ·come

Per Holt
6 Mod 225,
248 Ld Raym.
154,746,1292,
1371 2 Vern
471, 591, 603,
Ch Pr 50, 64,
116 10 Mod
8 Str 526,
1122 fee alfo
Carth 79, 80,
142, 181, 220,
225, 265, 346,
Skin. 15, 24,
82, 174, 205,
431, 579, 584,
623, 4
* P 4

(*d*) *The Principles of our confidence in teftimony are fuch as may well fupport the high perfuafion it is capable of conveying for truth itfelf is fo congenial to the Mind that it may always be taken for certain, even a bad man will not violate the natural attachment to it from an abftract preference to falfehood , 2, in legal cafes, it is not only fpeculative but practical truth muft be infringed , and 3, it is not only the injury to a fellow man, but generally the hazard of detection which is indefinitely great, and the confequent immediate difgrace and temporal evils fuperadded to the influence of religion, and all the awful anticipations of futurity*

(*e*) *So in the cafe of Ludlam on Demife of Hunt, Queftion arofe, whether a Copy of a Will on which the title turned could be*
produced

639, 40, 672
3 Salk. 85,
6, 7   2 Salk.
690   7 Mod
192   Ld
Raym 730,
734, 5 1292
Str 161 Barnard K. B
243 Vez. 505

come to *legal* Demonstration in Matters of Right; and there can be no Demonstration of a Fact without the best Evidence that the nature of the Thing is capable of less Evidence doth create but opinion and surmise, and does not leave a Man the entire satisfaction that arises from Demonstration: for IF IT BE PLAINLY SEEN, IN THE NATURE OF THE TRANSACTION, THAT THERE IS SOME MORE EVIDENENCE THAT DOTH NOT APPEAR, THE VERY NOT PRODUCING IT IS A PRESUMPTION THAT IT WOULD HAVE DETECTED SOMETHING MORE THAN APPEARS ALREADY.

EXPLANATION: *limiting the Sense of this Rule to its just Construction*

When we say the Law requires the highest Evidence that the Nature of the Thing is capable of, it is not to be understood that in every Matter there must be all that Force and Attestation that, by ANY POSSIBILITY, might have been gathered to prove it, and that nothing under the highest Assurance possible should have been given in Evidence to prove any Matter in Question. To strain the Rule to that Height, would be to create an endless Charge and Perplexity; for there are almost infinite degrees of *possible Evidence*, one under the other, and if nothing but Matters of the highest Assurance might be given in Evidence, the way of Illustration of Right " *would rarely attain the End*" As, for instance, no verbal Contract could be proved, because a written Contract carries with it a greater Credibility, and consequently the unwritten Contract would not be the greatest Assurance that the Nature of the Thing is capable of so a Contract attested by two Witnesses gains more Credit than a Contract attested but by one; and * therefore, by the same Argument one Witness would be no good Proof of a Contract

But the true meaning of the Rule of Law that requires the greatest Evidence that the Nature of the Thing is

* P   5

produced from a Register of the Ecclesiastical Court Lord Mansfield said—the cafe is clear—a man by losing the Evidence of his Title, shall not lose his estate the Rule in all cases holds to take the legal Evidence which the case, rebus sic stantibus, *according to such real circumstances will admit 'if you cannot prove a Deed by producing it, you may produce the counter part; if you cannot produce the counterpart you may produce a copy, even if you cannot prove it to be a true Copy; but you must prove it cy prés, as the Case will admit, if a copy cannot be produced you may go into parol Evidence c, the Date* Mic 1: G III B R—C l.

Evidentia est plenissima, quam res recipiat, Probatio

capable

capable of, is this: THAT NO SUCH EVIDENCE fhall bè brought as, *ex Natura rei* fuppofes ftill greater Evidence behind in the party's own poffeffion and power: for fuch Evidence is altogether infufficient, and proves nothing it, *even as before intimated,* carries a prefumption contrary to the intent for which it was produced for, if the other greater Evidence did not make againft the party, why did he not produce it to the Court ? As if a Man offers a Copy of a Deed or Will, where he ought to produce the original : and therefore the Proof of a Copy in this Cafe is no Evidence, and cannot poffibly weigh any thing in a Court of Juftice.

CHAP II .

THE DIVISION of EVIDENCE into WRITTEN and UN-WRITTEN

Now, to underftand the true THEORY of Evidence we muft confider two Things

FIRST, of the feveral " KINDS" of TESTIMONY

SECONDLY, the FORCE of TESTIMONY to prove the Matter which is alledged

FIRST, of the feveral " KINDS" of TESTIMONY: and that is again TWOFOLD,

1 WRITTEN

2 UNWRITTEN

In the firft place we are to confider, which of thefe two is to be preferred in the SCALE of PROBABILITY, when they ftand in oppofition to each other

* CICERO, in his declaiming for *Archias* the Poet, gives * P 6. a handfome Turn in favour of the UNWRITTEN EVIDENCE , pleading there for the Freedom of the Poet when the Tables of the Enfranchifement were loft and it is to this fenfe. *(f)* " But here you demand the Production " of the Archives of HIRACIFA which it is " known to us all, perifhed in the Italian War Ridicu- " lous! to have no Reply to the Evidence in our Poffeffion , " and to demand that which it is impoffible we fhould

(f) *I have taken the Paffage rather higher than as before quoted and have varied the tranflation The original is thus , " Hic tu tabula defideras* Heraclienfium *publicas , quas* Italico Bello, *incenfo tabular o, interiiffe fcimus omnes Eft ridiculum, ad ea quæ habemus nihil dicere , quærere quæ habere non poffumus , et de hominum memoriâ tacere, literarum memoriam flagitare et cum habeas ampliffimi Viri religionem, integerrimi municipis jusjurandum ; ea quæ depravari nullo modo poffunt repudiare , tabulas, quas idem dicis folere corrumpi, defiderare."* § III.

" have

" have ! to difregard the recent information of men , and
" to infift on the authority of Regifters ! and when you
" have the illuftrious fanction of a Man of the firft eminence
" and honour, the uncorruptible teftimony of a free City,
" to require proof from Tables which yourfelf acknowledge
" to be often corrupted "

But the Balance of Probability is certainly on the other
fide : for the Teftimony of an honeft Man, however fortified with the folemnities of an Oath, is yet liable to the
imperfections of Memory and as the Remembrances of
Things fail and go off, Men are apt to entertain Opinions
in their ftead. and therefore the Argument turns the other
way in moft Cafes , for Contracts reduced to writing, are
the moft certain and deliberate Acts of the Mind, and are
more advantageofly fecured from all corruption by the
forms and folemnities of the Law, than they poffibly could
have been if retained in Memory only from * hence therefore we fhall begin with the WRITTEN EVIDENCE , that
has the FIRST place in the Difcourfes of PROOF *and* Probability

P 7

SECTION II.

Of WRITTEN EVIDENCE

WRITTEN EVIDENCE *is again twofold* .

1 PUBLIC
2 Private, *between Party and Party.*
FIRST, PUBLIC, and that is alfo twofold .
1 RECORDS
2 MATTERS *of inferior Nature*

And firft of RECORDS .—Thefe are the Memorials of the
LEGISLATURE and of the KING's COURTS of JUSTICE,
and are authentic beyond all manner of Contradiction
They are (if a Man may be permitted a fimile from another fcience) the proper DIAGRAMS for the Demonftration of Right and they do conftantly preferve the Memory of the Matter, that it is ever permanent and obvious
to the View, and to be feen at any time in all the certainty
of Demonftration *('g)* inafmuch as the RECORD, as is obferved

<hr>

(g) We have already intimated that proper demonftration *is only
of abftract Truths which are perceived by the underftanding to be the
certain refult of fimple, determinate, neceffary, ideas* Hypothetical,
or forenfic Demonftration *hath alfo been confidered there is yet another, appropriate to our fubject, which is the* popular, *or* civil *this
is capable of infinitely approximating to rigorous certainty fo as that
the*

served elsewhere, can never be * proved PER NOTIORA, for * P. 8.
a Demonstration is only appealing to a Man's own *clear*
Conceptions, which can never be done with more conviction than when you draw the consequence from what is
already *concessum* and, consequently there can be no greater
Demonstration to a COURT of JUSTICE, than an Appeal
to its own transactions†

RECORDS *not being removeable, a* COPY *shall be received in
Evidence*

But RECORDS, being the Precedents of the Demonstra-
tions of Justice, to which every man has a common Right
to have recourse, cannot be transferred from place to place,
to serve a private purpose and therefore they have a common Repository, from whence they ought not to be removed but by the authority of some other Court, and this
is in the Treasury of WESTMINSTER And this piece of
Law is plainly agreeable to the Maxims of Reason and Justice for if one man might demand a Record to serve his
own occasions, by the same Reason any other person might
demand it, but both could not possibly possess it at the same
time in different places; and therefore it must be kept in one
certain place, in common for them both. Besides, these Records, by being daily removed, would be in great danger
of being lost. and, consequently, it is on all hands convenient that these monuments of Justice should be fixed in a
certain place, and that they should not be transferred from
thence but by Public Authority from superior Justice   * P 9
    10 Co 92, 3
    * The COPIES of RECORDS *(h)* must be allowed in Ch. R 15
Evidence, for since you cannot have the Original, the best Co Litt 225
    Evidence

*the difference between them shall become evanescent It is then synoni-
mous to* Moral Demonstration, *which is the Basis of* ethical *and
political science though political indeed be properly a branch of* ETHIC,
as true Jurisprudence, *of* POLITIC
    † *Monumenta publica potiora sunt testibus* D 22 3 10
    (h) Of TRIAL BY RECORD *the underwritten passage is taken
from the* COMMENTARIES.
    " *This is only used in one particular instance and that is where
a Matter of* RECORD *is* PLEADED *in any Action as a* Fine, *a*
Judgment, *or the like, and the opposite party pleads* NUL TIEL RE-
CORD, *that there is no such matter of Record existing upon this issue
is tendered and joined in the following form* " and this he prays may
be enquired of by the Record," *and the other* " doth the like," *and
hereupon the party pleading the Record has a day given him to* " bring
forth the Record by him in pleading alledged, or else he shall be
condemned," *and on his failure his antagonist shall have judgment*
    10

a d 226 2 2-7
b Cro Car.
209 441, 2.
Cro Jac. 70,
103, 109, 292,
317, 360
Bulſt. 154, 5
Plᵗ Comm. 80
2 85 2 148
b 222 2 Dy
29 pl 199
200 2 5 Co
75 a.
Palm 857
R. Rep 332.
2 R Rep 172,
191
Evidence you can have of them is a true copy, and the rule of
Evidence commands no farther than to produce the beſt that
the Nature of the Thing is capable of for to tie men up to
the Original that is fixed to a Place, and cannot be had, is
totally to difcard their Evidence, but it were very hard
and injurious to remove from Evidence the beſt and moſt authentic Teſtimony, becauſe it is fo guarded and confined by
the Law that it cannot be had or produced itſelf For then the
Rules of Law and Right would be the Authors of * Injury;
which is the higheſt Abfurdity. For in many Cafes, Juſtice
muſt fail without proof from the Records, when themſelves
cannot be had at the Trial.

Mod Rep 226 Doct Pl 215 Saund, 9, 10 Mod. 8, 42, 3 74, 108, 9 126 292, 507, &c
515, &c 518   12 Mod 3, 24. 394, 41-, 494, 500, 579 8 Mod 75, 322   9 Mod 66
2 Vern 471, 591, 603 Ch Pr 166 Eq Abr 228 Ld Raym 153, 4 746 2d Ld Raym
763, 967, 1126, 1536 Str 401, 526 2 Sir 1122, 1186, 1198, 1241 St Tr 44. Lang-
horn's Tr 3 Lev 387, 8 S G c. 25 § 2
* P 10.

A COPY *of a* COPY, *not* EVIDENCE

2 Bac Abr
308 Skin 174.
584 By ſt. 20
But a Copy of a Copy is no Evidence for the Rule demands the beſt Evidence that the Nature of the Thing ad-

*to recover The Trial therefore of this iſſue is MERELY BY THE
RECORD for, as SIR EDWARD COKE obferves, a Record or Enrollment is a Matter of fo high a Nature and importeth in itſelf fuch
abſolute verity, that if it be pleaded there is no fuch Record it ſhall
not receive any Trial by Witnefs, Jury or otherwife, but only by itſelf
Thus Titles of Nobility, as whether earl or no earl, baron or no baron,
ſhall be tried by the King's Writ or Patent only, which is matter of
Record Alfo in cafe of an alien, whether alien friend or enemy, ſhall
be tried by the league or treaty between his fovereign and ours, for
every league or treaty is of Record And alfo, whether a Manor be
held in ancien defefne or not ſhall be tried by the Record of Do
mefday - the King's Exchequer COMM B III Ch 22 § I But
this goes to the cafe where the Record is triable PER CURIAM under
the PLEADINGS and in this inſtance, on the Iſſue of NUL TIEL
RECORD, the RECORD ITSELF muſt be produced, if it be a Record
of the fame Court, and if it be a Record of another Court, then an
exemplification muſt be brought in fub pede figilli This will be hereafter noticed (p) but it feemed proper to be anticipated here
  But the Cafe where a COPY of a Record ſhall be given in Evidence as above intimated in the text, is where the Record is a collateral Matter, the Inducement and NOT the GIST of the Action
for then it is not traverfable, but muſt be given in Evidence to
the Jury or the Proof of a Declaration For nothing can be of
itſelf traverfable that does not make a full end of the Matter, and
this it cannot do if Fact be joined with it in fuch cafe therefore, the
Iſſue therefore muſt be upon the Fact, and tried by a Jury, and the Record may be given in Evidence to fupport the fact - and wherever a
Record is offered to a Jury, the Copy is Evidence. L N P 230
                                                              mits,*

mits ; and a Copy of a Copy cannot be the beſt Evidence · ᴳ II.
for the farther off a thing lies from the firſt original Truth,
ſo much the weaker muſt the Evidence be : and therefore
they muſt give a true Copy in Evidence , which is to reduce
it to its firſt and beſt Certainty   Beſides, when you give a
Copy of a Copy in Evidence, there muſt be a Chaſm in
your Evidence . for, if you have the firſt Copy, and, by
oath or otherwiſe, prove that a true Copy, then the ſecond
Copy is altogether idle and inſignificant ; if you have only
the ſecond Copy, then it cannot appear that the firſt was a
true Copy, becauſe it is not there to be ſworn to, and by
conſequence it is not proved in Court · and then it is no Evidence and, conſequently, the tranſcript of that which is in
itſelf not Evidence cannot be Evidence

(margin) ᴳ II. c 14 § 14. Copies of let-ters of attor-ney, &c re-lating to prize-money made in evidence

Hence it is, that in an Ejectment upon an *Elegit* you muſt
prove, not only the Judgment, and by the Judgment Roll
that the Elegit iſſued and was returned ; but you muſt prove
the writ of Elegit by a true Copy thereof , and the inquiſition
thereon becauſe the * Notice of the Judgment Roll is no *
more than that the party did elect ſuch Execution to iſſue ,
and it is the Elegit and Inquiſition upon it, that carves out
the Term and gives the Title of Entry ſo that the Judgment Roll is no more than a Memorandum that was iſſued
and returned , and the Copy thereof is no Evidence, being
but a Copy of that which is but a Copy or Memorandum of
the Thing itſelf   *Sed quære*, becauſe *Holt* was of a different
opinion ; and was for allowing the Entry of the Roll to be
good Evidence, that an Elegit had iſſued . for a Notice on
the Roll of the being and Return of the *Elegit*, is as good
Evidence that ſuch *Elegit* was, as a Copy thereof

(margin) Kent, Tr Aſſ. 1709 per Tra-cey, Wilſon and Wycherley.   * P. 11.

SECTION III

Of the highest legal Records.

Acts of Parliament
1 Public, or General
2 Private, or Particular

The firſt ſort of Records are, Acts of Parliament
(1) theſe are the Memorials of the LEGISLATURE and
therefore

(1) *I have taken the Liberty to omit the Diſtinctions and inſtances of the Lord Chief Baron as they are not ſtated with his uſual
perſpicuity, being apparently* Memoranda *for a farther illuſtration ;
and in their place, I have ſubſtituted the explanation given in the
Commentaries which will be found free from the obſcurity in the principles, and from error n the inſtance·   It is thus ,*

" Statutes

therefore they are the higheſt and moſt abſolute Proof. And they either relate to the KINGDOM in GENERAL, and then they are called GENERAL ACTS of PARLIAMENT; or only to the concerns of private perſons, and are thence called *particular*, or PRIVATE Acts

* P 12
Salk 566
10 Mod 216
126 181
Keb 2 Jenk.
Cont 280
pl 5

* OF GENERAL ACTS.

Printed Statute Book

Of GENERAL ACTS of PARLIAMENT the Printed Statute Book is Evidence : " or rather is allowed to be uſed for " the recollection and better vouching of that which reſts on " its own ſtrength and legal Notoriety ." for it is not that the printed

" STATUTES *are either* GENERAL *or* ſpecial ; PUBLIC *or* private *A General or Public Act is an univerſal Rule that regards the* WHOLE COMMUNITY, *ſpecial or private Acts are rather Exceptions than Rules, being thoſe which only operate upon particular perſons and private concerns Thus, to ſhew the Diſtinction, the ſt 13 Eliz c. 10 to prevent ſpiritual Perſons from making Leaſes for longer terms than twenty one years or three Lives is a Public Act, it be ing a Rule preſcribed to the whole body of ſpiritual Perſons in the Na..on . but an Act to enable the Biſhop of Cheſter, to make a Leaſe to A B for ſixty years i. an except on to this Rule , it concerns only the parties, and the Biſhop's ſucceſſors , and is therefore a private Act.*" INTROD § 3

For the farther illuſtration of this it may be remarked, that the Act of Toleration, though in Larwood's Caſe it was a private Act, was by a great Authority, afterwards conſidered as a PUBLIC *one and on th is ground, that the diſtinction between a particular and a general ſtatute reſts upon the point of notoriety and univerſality Now the Diſſenters were a body of people well known in the Kingdom and even mentioned in ſeveral Acts of Parliament , and had public ſtatutes enacted againſt them before the Toleration Act , and therefore it ſhould in all reaſon be conſidered as a Public Act Eſpecially as it virtually affects all perſons in the kingdom, ſetting them at liberty and giving them a legal right to become Non-conformiſts if they are ſo diſpoſed And the preamble of the Act mentions another conſideration which is of the moſt public Nature "Foraſmuch as ſome eaſe to ſcrupulous Conſciences in the exerciſe of Religion may be an effectual means to unite their Majeſties Proteſtant ſubjects in intereſt and affection"—Now is it poſſible to conceive that this can be a private Act ?* APPENDIX *to Dr* FURNEAUX's Letters

May it not farther be concluded that the ACTS *for the* REVERSAL *of the* ATTAINDER *of Ld* RUSSEL *and of* SYDNEY *are notwith- ſtanding the ir form and their apparent termination in the individual Caſes, properly* PUBLIC ACTS , *being* DECLARATORY *of the Common* RIGHT *of every Perſon in like Caſes, and of* PRINCIPLES *of the moſt general importance in the* CONSTITUTION *of our* CRIMINAL LAW ? *as much therefore Public as the Act for the Reverſal of the Judgment againſt* HAMPDEN *in the Caſe of Ship Money, which is rightly printed among the Public Acts and to this Vindication*

printed Statutes are the perfect and authentic Copy of the Re- _{Hale's Hift.} C L. 15, 6
cords themfelves, " fince" there is no abfolute Affurance of Style 462
their Exactnefs but every perfon is fuppofed to apprehend and ^{Str 446} 3 R S L 90.
know the LAW which he is bound to obferve, " and which
" the CONSTITUTION regards as the Act of his Confent, See a remark
" either by general or approved Ufage, or under full and on this, Bl 117. the Public Acts
" fair Reprefentation," and therefore the printed Statutes of this Reign
are allowed to be Evidence, becaufe they are the Hints of compofe *feven*
that which is fuppofed to be lodged in every Man's mind of the *fourteen* volumes in
already. *Ruffhead's* Edi-
tion of the Acts
of *five* centu-
ries, verging to
a *fixth* com-
plete

Private Acts.

Printed Statute Book not to be read.

IN PRIVATE ACTS the printed Statute Book is not Evidence, though reduced into the fame Volume with the general Statutes; but the party ought to have a Copy compared with the Parliament Roll for private Statutes do not
concern the Kingdom in general, and therefore no Man is
underftood to be poffeffed of them, as they are of thofe
General Laws which are fet up as the Regulation of their
own actions and confequently the * private Statutes are * P. 13
no intimation to what is already known, but they are the
Rules and Decrees that relate to the private Fortune of this
or that particular Man, which no one elfe is obliged to underftand or take notice of, as Matter of Evidence. and they
ought therefore to be proved with the fame punctuality as
the Copies of all other Records. for they are not confidered
as already in the Minds of the People

But my *Lord Chief Juftice* PARKER allowed the printed
Statute Book to be Evidence in the Cafe of the COLLEGE 10 Mod 353
of PHYSICIANS and *Dr Weft*· of the Truth of a private But this mat-
Act of Parliament, touching the Inftitutions of the College. dence does not
" And this probably from the Notoriety of the Eftablifhment: appear there
" according to which it has been held, that a private Act ^{Ld Raym} 472.
" of Parliament in print for a purpofe which though
" fpecial, affects an extenfive diftrict, may be given in Evi-
" dence, as the Act for *Bedford Levels*, for rebuilding *Ti-*
" *verton*, &c not only becaufe they gain fome authority
" by being printed by the King's Printer, but befides, (and

cation of the Memories of thefe heroic Men and of our Laws, by the
Voice of Parliament, ought equally to have been And thus is well
exprelfed what characterizes a public Act in thefe words of GILBERT,
" If the Point of Law be never fo fpecial, yet if it relates equally
to all it is a GENERAL LAW "

" chiefly

" chiefly it may be prefumed) becaufe from the Notoriety
" of the fubject they cannot be fuppofed to be unknown in
" the Vicinage On like principles, printed Copies of
" other things have been admitted in Evidence, when of a
" public Nature , without being compared with the Ori-
" ginal: as the printed Proclamation for Peace was admit-
" ted to be read without being examined by the Record in

† L N P
P. VI. Ch. I
215-6

" Chancery †

SECTION IV

Of PLEADING, or giving in EVIDENCE, ACTS of PARLIAMENT.

✻ P 14.

A GENERAL ACT of PARLIAMENT is taken Notice ✻ of
by the Judges or Jury without being pleaded, for the Reafon already given

Fob 227
4 Co 76 a.
Nov 12,
Dct Pl 336
Plcwd. 65 2
6. a.
Cro I 112
5 Co. 2

" But, converfely, on the fame Account," a particular
Act of Parliament is not tal en notice of by the Court, without
being pleaded : for the Court cannot judge of particular Laws
which do not concern the whole Kingdom, unlefs that Law
be exhibited to the Court for they are obliged by their
oath to judge fecundum Leges & Confuetudines Angliæ, and therefore they cannot be obliged, ex officio, to take Notice of a
particular Law; becaufe it is not Lex Angliæ, a Law relating to the whole Kingdom : therefore, like all other private Matters, it muft be brought before them to judge
thereon.

But a private Act of Parliament, or any other private
Record, may be brought before the Jury, if it relate to the
Iffue in Queftion, though it be not pleaded for the Jury
are to find the Truth of the Fact in Queftion, according to
the Evidence brought before them , and therefore if the
private Act brought before them doth evince the Truth of
the Matter in Queftion, it is as proper Evidence to the purpofe as any Record or Evidence whatfoever.

✻ P 15

Now, fince fuch Records are moft authentic, it is the
moft proper fort of Evidence the Error in this ✻ Matter was
founded upon the old Notion, that the Jury could not find
an Act of Parliament, or other Matter of Record· which
is falfe , for the Allegata to the Jury, fays Hobart, are every
thing that is " alledged and proveable, which makes to the
" Iffue "

2 R Acr 683
W Jones 320

If an Action or Information be brought on a penal Statute,
and there is another ftatute which difcharges and exempts
the Defendant from the Penalty, this ought to be PLEADED,
and cannot be given in Evidence on the General Iffue for
the

the General Iſſue is but a denial of the Plaintiff's Declaration, and the Plaintiff hath proved him guilty when he hath
proved him within the Law upon which he hath founded
his Declaration, ſo that the Plaintiff hath performed what
he hath undertaken. but if the defendant would exempt
himſelf from the Charge of the Plaintiff, he ſhould not have
denied the Declaration; but have ſhewn the Law which
diſcharges him

Another Difference is taken where there is a ſaving Proviſo " and this is to be diſtinguiſhed. for where the ſaving
" in the Proviſo is MATTER of FACT" it may be given
in Evidence on the GENERAL ISSUE, becauſe if the Party * P 16.
be within the Proviſo, he is not guilty * on the body of
the Act on which the Action is founded, and if an Action of
Debt be brought againſt a ſpiritual perſon for taking a Farm,
the Defendant pleads " that he was not poſſeſſed of or
held the Farm contrary to the Form of the Statute" Upon
this Iſſue joined, the Defendant may give in Evidence that
it was for the maintenance of his Houſe according to the
Proviſo of the Statute

But where it was in a POINT of LAW it muſt be pleaded
" as a ſpecial exemption" Thus upon an Information of
the 5 and 6 E VI † againſt Ingroſſing, the Defendant can- † c 14
not give in Evidence a Licence of three Juſtices of the
Peace according to the Proviſo in the Statute " in ſupport
of the General Iſſue " becauſe whether there be a ſufficient Authority is a Point of Law, and cannot be given in
Evidence without pleading it.

And generally, Public no leſs than private Statutes ought to
be pleaded when they make void legal ſolemnities, " or take
' away the compulſion to the performance of a Contract "
For in this caſe the conſtruction of the Law is not that ſolemn
Contracts ſhall be deemed perfect Nullities, but that they
are voidable " on Principles of public ſecurity and Peace"
by the parties prejudiced by thoſe Contracts, when " they
" ſhall duly challenge that privilege of Exemption which
" the Law ſuffers them to claim, duely challenge it, in
" reſpect, at leaſt, of legal Forms and ſolemnities, ſo that
" under the General Iſſue the Plaintiff may not be ſurpriz-
' ed by Evidence, which from the courſe of the Proceed-
" ings he is not prepared to encounter on equal Terms"
And farther, another Reaſon of this Conſtruction ariſeth
from the Rule, that, " Any * one may renounce a Right ⚹ P 1-
' introduced for his own Benefit " Quilibet renuntiare poteſt
Juri pro ſe introducto Where any perſon has benefit by a Law,
he may renounce that Benefit if he will, and refuſe to take
advantage of it " Now a man who by pleading generally,
" denies the Fact of the exiſtence of a Contract virtually,
" by

" by fo doing relinquifhes a Right of claiming privilege to
" avoid the Contract Thus on Action of Affumpfit for a
" fimple Contract Debt, a Man pleads *not Guilty*, which is
" denying the exiftence of fuch Debt or undertaking, he
" fhall not give in Evidence that he did not undertake *within*
" *Six Years*, for this fpecial circumftance fupports not his
" Plea; fince that was a Denial, generally, of the under-
" taking; this a fubfequent Matter foreign to the Under-
" taking which confeffes and avoids it · within this exemp-
" tion therefore he muft bring himfelf by *pleading* it, and
" thus enabling the Plaintiff to go to Iffue on the real point
" on which the Defence is grounded "

" And farther," as what Solemnities fhall conftitute a legal
Contract is Matter of Law, " fo and much more is it"
how the effect of thofe Solemnities fhall be defeated and
deftroyed by " legal Exceptions " and therefore when any
Action is founded upon a folemn Contract " or when any
" Contract apparently in force is to be fuperfeded by legal
" Limitations as in the firft inftance the Specialty of the
" Contract is" offered to the Court that it may appear
whether legally made, " fo for its Avoidance the fpecial
" Claim of Exemption by Matter of Law fhould be of-
" fered to the Court that it may appear if it be legally"
defeated Both certainly muft " be referred" to the
fame Judicature

Therefore you cannot give the Act touching ufurious Contracts in Evidence on the General Iffue, nor will notice be
taken of it without pleading, but, though a General Law,
* P. 18. it ought to be pleaded So of a * Fine made VOID by the
ftatute of *Weftminfter* 2 *c* 1 " for" it is conftrued voidable
only " on pleading.

So of a Recovery by a Wife with a fecond Hufband
made void by 11 H VIII but conftrued voidable only " in
like manner "

So the 23 H VI *a* 10 of Sheriffs Bonds cannot be
given in Evidence on the General Iffue, but ought to be
pleaded

SECTION V.

COPIES *of* MINUTES *of* JOURNALS *of* THE HOUSE *of* LORDS

" It is here proper to mention thofe Records which ap-
" pertain to the higheft Judicature eftablifhed by the CON-
" STITUTION. In a Cafe where a Copy of the Minute
" Book of the HOUSE of LORDS was offered in Evidence,
" and

" and objection made to the receiving of it as fuch; Lord
" *Mansfield* expreffed himfelf to this effect, " The Mi-
" nutes of the Judgment are the folemn Judgment
" itfelf ." Not a Word is added upon the Journals And
" a Copy of them may certainly be read in Evidence: for
" the inconvenience would be endlefs if the Journals of the
" Houfe of Lords were carried all over the Kingdom.
" Formerly a doubt was entertained whether the Minutes
" of the House of Commons were *admiffible* ; becaufe it   † Cowp 17
" is *not* a Court of Record, but " thofe" of the Houst   Jones v Ran-
" of Lords have always-been admitted even in Criminal   dall, Hil 14
" Cafes †."   Geo 3

*SECTION VI.   *P. 19.

" We are now to fpeak of the" Copies of all other
Records. and they are twofold.
     1. Under Seal
     2 *Not under Seal*   10 Mod 125, 6
First, *under* Seal : And thefe are called by a particular
Name, Exemplifications, and are of better Credit than
any fworn Copy   For the Courts of Justice that put
their Seals to the Copy, are fuppofed more capable to examine and more exact and critical in their examinations, than
any other perfon is or can be   and there is more Credit to
be given to their Seal than to the Teftimony of any private
perfon.

Exemplifications are twofold

     1. *Under the* Broad Seal
     2 *Under the* Seal *of the* Court
Under the Broad Seal, Exemplifications are of   Sid 145, 6
themfelves Records of the greateft Validity: and to   Hard 118.
which the Jury ought to give Credit under Penalty of an   Pl Com 411 a.
Attaint. for there is more Faith due to the moft folemn
Atteftations of Public Authority than to any other Tranf-   3 Inft 15 6
actions whatfoever   and therefore a Falfification in this   25 E 3 St 5 c 2 v Mic-
Cafe is High Treafon   roir, c 1 § 6

When a Record is exemplified under the Great Seal   P 28
it muft be, either a Record of the Court of Chancery,
* or be fent for into the Chancery,—which is the Centre   3 Inft 173
of all the Courts, by a Certiorari, and from thence   * P 20.
the fubjects receive a Copy under the Atteftation of the
Great Seal   For in the firft Diftribution of the Courts, the
Chancery held the Seal from whence Authority iffued to
all Proceedings   and thofe Proceedings cannot be copied
         under

under the Great Seal unlefs they come into the Court where that Seal is lodged.

3 Inft. 173   When any Record is exemplified, the whole muft be exemplified; for the Conftruction muft be, from the view of the whole Matter taken together.

Under SEAL of the COURT.

The fecond fort of Copies under Seal are the EXEMPLIFICATIONS under the SEAL of the Court and thefe are of higher Credit than a fworn Copy, for the reafons formerly given *(k)*

" EXEMPLIFICATIONS *and inftruments* quæ fibi ipfa faciant
" Fidem *to be delivered to the Jury to take out with them* "

Sa 145
Harc 118
P' Com 411
a.   Thefe EXEMPLIFICATIONS, and all other under Seal, fhall be delivered to the Jury to be carried with them, but fworn Copies fhall not, for we have fhewn in " THE COURT OF CHANCERY," that the invention of Sealing was firft advanced inftead of Coins * themfelves,

* P 27.   and that from thence it began to be made ufe of by way of Atteftation; and from the Example of the King it began to be ufed in all the Courts of Juftice for the Atteftation of their Tranfactions, and from the fame Example it began to be ufed by private Lords of Manors for the Authenticating of their Grants, and for Tickets inftead of Pieces of Money; and from hence Impreffions were devifed with diftinctions of Arms and of Families, and thefe were perfectly known in the Neighbourhood, and therefore are always delivered to the view of the Jury, and the Jury are allowed to carry them away with them as the Acts of the moft remarkable Solemnity, that the moft folemn

Sid 145   Acts may make the laft Impreffion

But the Chirograph of a Fine, a fworn Copy, or any other Writing, though it may be given in Evidence, yet it fhall not be delivered to the Jury. for thefe have no intrinfic Credit in themfelves, and the Jury of themfelves are not fuppofed to take notice of them —they have no Credit but what they derive from fomething elfe—*viz* from the Oath of the Perfon who attefts them, or from fome prefumption in their favour fo that they receive their Credit from fome Acts in Court, but do not carry it along with them, and therefore cannot be removed out of Court with
the

L P N 227   *(l) Yet an Exemplification of a private Deed fhall not be admitted in Evidence where in the Cuftody of the party though under the Broad Seal for being in private Cuftody and not in that of the Law, they are fubject to rafures and interlineations, and ought to be produced themfelves as the beft Evidence of the Contract It is to the Exemplifications of a Record that this high Credit is given* the Jury. But things *under Seal* are fuppofed to have an intrinfic Credit from the Impreffion of the Signature · and are fuppofed to be known to the Jury in fome meafure, and therefore are very conveniently lodged in their poffeffion to difcern of them But of writings * that are not under Seal, * P. 22. the Jury can make no difcernment of their own : their Credit muft totally arife from fome Act in Court, and therefore they cannot be put in the Power of the Jury.

Of Seals Public *and Private.*

But here the Diftinction is to be made between SEALS of Public and Seals of Private CREDIT . for Seals of Public Credit are full Evidence of themfelves without any oath made but Seals of Private Credit are no Evidence, but by an Oath concurring to their Credibility

Seals of Public Credit are the Seals of the King and of the Public COURTS of JUSTICE time out of Mind · Now thefe Courts make a part of the Law and Conftitution of the Kingdom, and have their fanction in that immemorial Ufage that is the foundation of the Common Law ; " And" the Seals of thefe Courts are part of the Conftitution of the Courts themfelves · and by confequence, the Courts and the Seals of the Courts are fuppofed to be known to every body : fince they are equally entitled to that fuppofal as any other Cuftom or Law whatfoever.

So the Seal of a Court created by Act of Parliament is of full Credit, without farther Atteftation for the Act of Parliament is of the fame Notoriety, " prefumptively," as the Common Law : and therefore * the Court and the Seals, * P 23. thereby created are fuppofed " to be univerfally known

But the Seals of private Courts or of private Perfons are not full Evidence by themfelves without an Oath fupporting their Credibility · for it is not poffible to fuppofe thefe Seals to be univerfally known · and confequently, they ought to be attefted by fomething elfe ,—by the Oath of fome one who has Knowledge of them , for what is not of itfelf known muft be made known *aliunde* And when the Seals are thus attefted they ought to be delivered in to the Jury becaufe though part of their Credit arifes from the Oath that gives an Account of their Sealing, yet another part of their Credit arifes from a Diftinction of their own Impreffion , for, as I faid, antiently every Family had its own proper Seal as it is now in Corporations , and by this they diftinguifh their manner of contracting one from another , and by falfe Impreffions of their Seals they difcover a Counterfeit Contract , and therefore it was not the Oath

Margin notes:
Sid 146
Hardr 118, 9.
Pl Com 411.
a Bur R 147
Say R 298
A Commiffion under the Exchequer Seal, (though of Inftruction not of entitling,) is Evidence though not conclufive, yet, however, admiffible

Sid 146.

but the Impreffion of the Seal accompanying it, that made up the complete Credit of the Inftrument *(l)*

* P 24

But fince in all private Contracts the Diftinction of Sealing is worn out of ufe, and men ufually feal with any Impreffion that comes to hand, to be fure tnere * muft be Evidence of putting the Seal, becaufe at this day, little can be difcovered from the bare Impreffion " and" fince the Witneffes Names are inferted in the Contract, unlefs they appear to prove the Contract, there is not the utmoft Evidence that the Nature of the Thing " fuppofes " for their not appearing is a Prefumption that they never were privy to any fuch Tranfaction But of this hereafter.

SECTION VII.

COPIES *not under Seal*

The SECOND Sort of COPIES are thofe that are *not under Seal* and thefe are of two Sorts
    1 *Sworn Copies.*
    2 *Office Copies*

FIRST, SWORN COPIES thefe muft be of the Record, brought into Court on Parchment and not of a Judgment on Paper figned by the Mafter, though upon fuch Judgment you may take out Execution for it does not become a permanent Matter till it be delivered into Court, and there fixed as *Memoranda* or Rolls of that Court, and until it be a Roll of that Court it is transferable any where, and fo doth not come under the Reafon *(m)* of Law that permits us to give a Copy in Evidence

3 Inft 173

When a Man gives in Evidence the Sworn Copy of a Record he muft give the whole Copy of the Record in Evidence for the precedent and fubfequent Words and fentence may vary the whole Senfe and import of the thing

~ P 25

produced, and give it another Face * and therefore fo much at leaft ought to be produced as concerns the Matter in Queftion

(l) 8 Ed 1 Henry *de* Perpoint *came into the Chancery of* Lincoln, *and publickly declared he had loft his Seal, protefting that if any In ftrument were found fal d therewith after that time, the fant fhould be of ro value or effect, which Proteftation was regiftered at* *ceraingly* FULLER'S Worth Nottinghamfhire

(m) It is with reference chiefly to this and fimilar Cafe, where a General Rule refults from Principles that it is faid " Ceffante Ra ' tione Legis, ipfa Lex ceffat " for to pofitive Inftitutions, the Maxim does not apply

2. OFFICE

2 OFFICE COPIES

Here the Difference is to be taken between a Copy authenticated by a Perfon trufted to that purpofe, for there that Copy is Evidence, and a Copy given out by the Officer of the Court that is not trufted tó that purpofe, for that is not Evidence without proving it actually examined

The Reafon of the Difference is,—that where the Law hath appointed any perfon for any purpofe, the Law muft truft him, fo far as he acts under the Authority that the Law hath lodged in him, otherwife it would be to give Credit to him and another Officer at the fame time

Therefore the *Chirograph* of a *Fine* is Evidence to all perfons of fuch Fine, for the *Chirographer* is appointed to give out Copies between the parties, of thofe Agreements that are lodged of Record and therefore his Copy muft be admitted as Evidence without Difpute

So where a Deed is *enrolled*, the Endorfement of that *Enrollment* is Evidence, without farther proof of the Deed, becaufe the Officer is entrufted to authenticate fuch Deeds by Enrollment and when fuch Officer endorfeth that he hath done it purfuant to the Law, then the Law, which entrufted him with the Authority of doing it, ought to give Credit to what he has done

Where CUSTODY *only, and where Power of authenticating*
COPIES

* But if an Officer of the Court, who is not entrufted for that purpofe makes out a Copy, they ought to prove it examined the Reafon is, becaufe being no part of his Office he is but a private Man and a private Man's mere writing or word ought not to be credited without his Oath †

Therefore it is not enough to give in Evidence a Copy of a Judgment, though it be endorfed to have been examined by the Clerk of the Treafury, becaufe it is not part of the neceffary Office of fuch Clerk for he is only entrufted to keep the Records for the Benefit of all Mens Perufal, and not to make out Copies of them

So if the Deed enrolled be loft, and the Clerk of the Affize makes out a Copy of the Enrollment only, this is no Evidence, without proving it examined becaufe the Clerk is intrufted to authenticate the Deed itfelf by Enrollment, and not to give out Copies of the Enrollment of that Deed

Where a *Fine* with *Proclamations* is to be a Barr to a Stranger, there the Proclamations muft be examined from

Pl Com 11c

10 A c. 18, 8 G 2 c. 6. § 21

＊ P 26.

Chutel and Pound, H Aff 1700

† *In teftimonio non creditur nifi jurato.*

C 2

the

* P. 27. the Roll for the *Chirographer* is authorized by the Common Law to make out Copies to the parties of the Fine itself: yet is not appointed by the Statute to * Copy the Proclamations, and therefore his Endorsement on the Back of the Fine is not binding.

SECTION VIII.

Of LOST RECORDS

Ventr 257
Styl. Pr Reg 25
Mod 117
Salk. 285

Where a RECORD is *loft*, a COPY of it may be given in Evidence without swearing a true Copy, for the Record is in the Custody of the Law and not of the Party, and therefore if loft, there ought to be no Injury arising to the Party's private Right and consequently if it be loft, the Copy must be admitted without swearing the examination concerning it, since there is nothing with which the Copy can be compared, and therefore it must be presumed true without examination

Mod 117
Gavis D.g 252

But in such Cases as these, the Instruments must be according to the Rules required by the Civil Law; they must be *vetuflate Temporis*, *Judiciaria Cognitione*, *roborata*

Vent. 257

So the Copy of the Decree of Tythes *(n)* in *London* has been often given in Evidence without proving it a true Copy, because the Original is loft

Ind

So a Recovery of Lands in Antient Demefne was given in Evidence where the Original was loft, and Poffeffion had gone a long time according to the Recovery

SECTION IX.

Of THE MANNER
in which
A RECORD IS EVIDENCE

* P 28

Having thus shewn HOW the RECORD is to be given * in Evidence by proving a Copy, we must next see in WHAT MANNER and in what CASES they ought to be EVIDENCE.

And here, in the first place, it regularly appears that where the Record is PLEADED and appears in the Allegations it must be tried on the Iffue NUL TIEL RECORD, but where the Iffue is upon Fact, the Record may be given in Evidence to support that Fact

Sic 1, c, 6

But out of this Rule there is " an apparent Exception " which " indeed is rather a part of the Rule " itself fully " ftated" that where the Record is *Inducement* and not the

(n) In the Reign of H VIII it was about a Century old when it was of this Je. red Authority.

GIST

GIST of the Action, there it is not of itself traversable; and therefore " though it be upon the pleadings, yet stand- " ing as an Allegation not conclusive, it is SUBSTANTIALLY NOT PLEADED" and therefore must be given in Evidence on the Proof of the Action.

When the Issue is NUL TIEL RECORD, the Record if of another Court, must be exemplified by bringing it in SUB PEDE SIGILLI of that Court, but where offered to a Jury, any of the beforementioned Copies are Evidence

" Where a Record is collateral to the Issue, you must " first prove all the circumstances necessary to give operation " to the Record as between the parties" Thus, to a RE- COVERY, it is essential that there be a TENANT to the PRÆCIPE " the person thus sued must * be seized of the " Freehold, and in a modern Recovery this seizin must be " proved "

" But" where a Recovery is antient, † you need not prove any Seizin in the Tenant to the *Præcipe*, for in an ancient Recovery the Presumption is for the Recoveror; " who" shall be supposed seized at the time of the Reco- very, since he hath been seized ever since

' And now by the statute 14 G II c 20 § 4 " con- " formably to the spirit of the common Law, if the Re- " covery itself do not appear to be entered, or be not re- " gularly entered on the Record, yet the Deed to make a " Tenant to the Præcipe, and to declare the Uses of " a Recovery shall after a Possession of TWENTY Years, " be *sufficient Evidence* in behalf of a Purchasor for " valuable Consideration.

" And notwithstanding the *legal* Freehold be vested in " Lessees, those entitled to the next freehold in remainder ' or reversion may make a *good Tenant to the Præcipe*, and " the Deed or fine creating such Tenant, though subsequent " to the Judgment of Recovery, yet, if one of the " same Term, shall be valid "

And therefore the Act, Tenant for Life, the Remainder in fee, and he in the Remainder in fee, suffers a Common Recovery with *single* Voucher, and the * Recovery is an- tient, " and it was objected that Part of the Lands were " leased off for Life, and that for those Lands there could " be no Tenant to the Præcipe" but in Regard the Pos- session had followed for so long a time, the Court said, they would presume a surrender

" Tenant for Life merely, cannot suffer a Recovery to " affect the Entail And further," if Tenant for Life, and

Margin notes:
Style 22.
Sid 145
* P. 29
Vent 257.
2 Str 1129
1185 1267
* P. 30.
Moor 256 pl
402
1 R Abr 395.
Pig of Rec 36.

† *Ex Diuturnitate Temporis omnia præsumuntur solenni'er acta*

the

the Remainder-man in Tail, join in a common Recovery
with SINGLE VOUCHER, this will not bar the Entail for
in this Cafe the PRÆCIPE is brought againſt them both as
JOINT-TENANTS now he in Remainder hath no immediate Eſtate of Freehold in him, and " therefore" is not
Tenant to the PRÆCIPE and " confequently" is not bound
by the Recovery had againſt the Tenant for Life, unleſs he
come in upon the AID PRAYER, thorgh the Remainder is
turned to a Right by fuch Recovery

2 R Aor 396   But if there be Tenant for Life, the Remainder in Tail
" and the Præcipe be brought againſt the Tenant for Life
" (or a Tenant of the Freehold otherwiſe made for the oc-
" caſion, by the ſaid Tenant for Life,) and he vouches the
" Tenant in Tail, who vouches over the Common Vouchee,
" then on the DOUBLE VOUCHER" he in Remainder is
barred, becauſe he is as properly called in as Vouchee as if
he had been called in en PRAYER of AID of Tenant for
Life · and when he takes up the Defence and makes Default, then he muſt be barred by the Judgment for want of
Title appearing ; for when any perſon is properly in Court

* P 31.   and doth not defend his Title, he is as * properly barred as
he which hath no Title at all, and when Tenant in Tail is
barred for want of Title, the Iſſue can never after recover
in his *Formedon* (o)

Comm 2 c   " So in a FINE, if it be pleaded, and the Defendant in
21   " his Replication alledge, that *partes finis nil habuerunt*, that
" it was levied by thoſe who had no intereſt in the Eſtate,
" this will be good to bar the operation of the Fine, if it be
" by Common Law, but not ſo if it be a Fine with Pro
" clamations under the ſtatute, for that ſhall bind the Parties
" and all who claim under them, and ſhall alſo, if no Claim
" be made within five years, bind STRANGERS With
" theſe exceptions, that if they had not a preſent Right at
" the time levied, or were under impediment of ſuing ſuch
" Right when the Fine was levied by reaſon of coverture,
" abſence beyond Sea, infanity, or impriſonment, the Non
" Claim ſhall be computed only from the accruer of the
" Right or Removal of the Impediment "

(o) Smyth z Clifford, E 27 G III T R 738 A *Tenant
for Life, Remainder to B for Life, Remainder to firſt,* &c *Sons of
B in tail A and B by leaſe and releaſe n ake a Tenant to the
præcipe, and ſuffer a recovery to bar B's Remainder in tail, ſubſequent
i th entail or his Sons This is no forfeiture of the Eſtate of A or
B, the prior Entail is not deveſted by it, and it is a good Recovery
t bar the Entail of B*

S IX *Title* 2
OF VERDICTS

IF A VERDICT BE HAD ON THE SAME POINT, AND BETWEEN THE SAME PARTIES, IT MAY BE GIVEN IN EVIDENCE, though the Trial was not had for the same Lands.

The Verdict ought to be between the same Parties, becaufe otherwife a Man would be bound by a Decifion when he had not Liberty to crofs examine and nothing can be more contrary to natural Juftice than that any fhould be injured by any determination he was not at Liberty to controvert, for that is to * fet up a Decifion unexamined, fo far " as refpects the Parties," in prejudice of a Caufe that is under Examination Befides, one that is not party to the Trial has no Redrefs for the Injury if the Verdict were falfe, for he can not have an ATTAINT, and therefore ought not to be injured by the Verdict

Lewes and Clerges, Term Pafch 1700

* P 32.

But it is not neceffary that the Verdict fhould relate to the *fame Land* for the verdict is only fet up to prove the point in Queftion, and if the verdict be upon the fame Queftion, then it is no doubt a good Evidence

Ibid Stri 308 2 Str 1151 Carth 79,181 5 Mod 386, 2 Jones 221 2 Mod 142

CASES *illuftrative of the preceding Principle*

In an Action of Trefpafs the INDICTMENT for the fame Trefpafs and Verdict " thereupon" fhall not be given in Evidence, if the Indictment " were not otherwife proved than" by the Party's own oath for if the Party's oath be no Evidence in his own Caufe (as we fhall hereafter fhew that it is not) then can not the verdict be any Evidence that is founded only on the Party's own Oath, for what cannot be Evidence directly, cannot be made Evidence, by any fuch Circuity But where the Verdict on the Indictment is founded on other Evidence, befides the Party's own oath, there, that Verdict may be given in Evidence for there, this Verdict feems to be under the fame General Rule with all others, and there the Judgment of twelve Men on the Fact " hath" fway in the determination of the fame Fact, whether the verdict be on Indictment or Action But yet it may be objected, that the Fact might find Credit from the Party's own Oath which ought not to fupport the Action and fince the Evidence is fo intermixed that it doth not * appear on what it was founded, 'the Verdict can not be produced in corroboration of the Evidence on the Action

2 Sid 325.

Ex Rel, Mr Phibbs. 1700

* P 33

It

It is true, this doth in part take off the force of fuch Evidence: for, as where a Verdict is produced in Evidence, it may be anfwered, that if it did not arife from the Merits of the Caufe, but from fome formal Defect in the Proof, and that makes it no Evidence towards gaining the point in Queftion, fo a Verdict may be diminifhed in point of Authority, by fhewing that it was in part founded on the Oath of the party interefted in the Action, and the Jury are to refpect it no farther than as they prefume it given and fupported by the Credit of other Teftimony not concerned in the Caufe

Yet others have faid, the Verdict given on the Indictment cannot be given in Evidence · becaufe, on that Profecution, there is no liberty left to the Party to attaint *(k)* the Jury, as he hath power to do when injured in a Civil Action therefore *quære*

* P. 34 * Where there is an ACQUITTAL, A VERDICT in a Criminal Cafe, where the Matter was capital, is not to be given in Evidence in a Civil Cafe; as where the Father was acquitted on an Indictment for having two Wives, this could not be given in Evidence in a Civil Cafe, where the Validity of the fecond Marriage was controverted, the Reafon feems to be, becaufe much lefs Evidence is neceffary to maintain the Action than to attaint the Criminal, and therefore, the Acquittal was no Argument that the Fact was not true

---

(k) The modern Remedy for a Verdict againſt Evidence being more comprehenſive, more eaſy beyond comparſion in the mode, and not accompanied with thoſe dreadful conſequences of hazarding the perjury of a ſecond or the utter ignominy and deſtruction of the former Jury, on a Point which can rarely be ſuppoſed ſuſceptible of ſatisfactory Proof, the old Law of ATTAINTS *is fallen into total Diſuſe It will however be noticed in it's place as to the Evidence to be received on it. The Jury on whom this awful Inveſtigation was devolved, conſiſted of* twenty four *It ſeems to have been thought, that an Attaint would lie in criminal Caſes at the ſuit of the Crown but the later, and as one ſhould think, evidently the more conſtitutional opinion is, that as it cannot be proſecuted at the ſuit of the Sufferer by the Verdict, ſo neither is the Prerogative armed with this tremendous Inſtrument but that it is confined wholly to* CIVIL *Caſes But againſt the malice or corruption which may affect a Verdict, there is another courſe of proceeding Criminally to be mentioned in its place though happily, in our times, occaſions have not ariſen on which it has been called into exertion This relates to the Crime of* TWO *or more of the Jurors, without their fellows being privy to the Offence . and is by Indictment of* CONSPIRACY

r Rights of
Jur- and at-
ed in the Cafe
rf the Dear of
S. Sept, f
11, 12

" The

" The Acquittal afcertains no Fact ; and therefore can- L. N P 245.
" not tend to negative the firft Marriage, or eftablifh the
" fecond "

If a Verdict be given againft the Defendant on the fame Tr Aff 1701.
Point, though another party were Plaintiff, yet in fome
Cafes it may be given in Evidence: as if there be Trial of
Title between *A* Leffee of *E*, and *B*. and afterwards there
be a trial of the fame Title between *C* Leffee of *E* and *B* ;
C may give the Verdict found againft *B* in Evidence on the
Trial between him and *B*. for this was the Senfe of a former
Jury on the Fact. *(l)*

If there be *(m)* " feveral" Ejectments brought againft feve- * P 35.
ral perfons, " though for Lands under the fame Title," if
there be a Verdict againft one, that Verdict can not be given 3 Mod 141.
in Evidence againft the reft. for it is the party againft whom Lord Raym.
the Verdict is given that can have relief by Attaint, in as 1292 Vern
much as the Refidue are not prejudiced, and thefe parties 413 Ch Pr
fhall not be injured by a Verdict, they had not a power to 319 339
controvert " This muft be underftood of Ejectments in Gilb R 2.
" the ftricteft Senfe, againft parties that have or might have Str 1151
" prefumeably an actual Intereft to defend in the Term Carth 79 181.
" created. 2 Jones 221

" For now in Ejectment, when ufed as it is generally, as 2 Mod 1, 2.
" an expeditious Form for Trial of the Right, the Court

---

*(l) It will be remarked that the Evidence of a former Verdict is -
generally (except where it is directly conclufive) cautioufly to be
received by a Jury who are to decide on their own Confcience and
not upon that of other Men If there was clear and full Proof to
guide the Opinion of the former Jury, another Jury will be fatisfied
by like Proof, if the Evidence before was doubtful in its Nature,
no Verdict will render it otherwife, while the Facts remain the fame
Perhaps there is among men in general too great pronenefs to be prejudicated in Matters of fact, and even in points of Confcience by
the Notions or Determinations of others, who may have been antecedently fo prejudicated themfelves, inftead of attending to their moft
folemn Duty when called by the Nature of the Subject to ufe their
own On the whole, though the Verdict of one Jury may be Evidence to another, and that Evidence may vary in its real force, yet
generally it feems to be Evidence merely admiffible it is wifely
limited by Law within very narrow bounds In proof of an antient Cuftom it is very ftrong See DOUGLAS Introd Conteft.
ELECT 21.*

*(m) It has been neceffary to correct the firft Paragraph in this
page, by inferting the Limitations which appear to be contained in
the Cafe of Locke v. Norborne. Mic. 3. J. II. 1687. 3 Mod. 141*

" will

" will take notice who the real party is and not let the Rule
" of Evidence, refpecting a Verdict between the Parties on
" the fame Queftion, be defeated by fuch a change as merely
" the Subftitution of a fictitious Name, when the real Parties
" are the fame, and the queftion remains unaltered For a
" Fiction operates only for the purpose for which the Law
" adopts it

I o Howard
and Lady
Inchiquin,
3-62

" This Principle of Evidence may be otherwife deduced
" and illuftrated, thus " if *A, Termor* for Years recover
againft *B* the Reverfioner might give fuch Verdict in Evidence for it is fit the Reverfioner fhould make ufe of the
Verdict, and have benefit by it, fince he had been difpoffeffed by the Verdict if it had gone againft the Termor, and
his Reverfion would have been turned to a naked Right
and *B* has no prejudice, becaufe he had Liberty to crofs-
examine the Witneffes or to attaint the Jury, " or to have
" obtained a New Trial "

± P 36

But if there be a Recovery againft *Tenant* for Life * by
Verd ct; this is no Evidence againft the Reverfioner for
the Tenant for Life is feized in his own Right, " *ut de*
" *libero tenemento*," and the Poffeffion is properly his own
and he is at Liberty to pray in aid of the Reverfioner, or
not; and the Reverfioner cannot poffibly controvert the
Matter where no Aid was prayed, for he had no permiffion

1 N P 252
Sec. 22

to intereft himfelf in the Controverfy " But if he had
" come in on Aid Prayer, then the verdict had been Evi-
" dence againft him Since Perfons under a derivative
" Title, confequently come within the Spirit of the Rule

2 R Ab- C8o

" And accordingly," if a Verdict were given againft *I S*
and *I S* alien to *I N*, the Verdict againft *I S* may be
given in Evidence againft *I N* for the Alienation of *I S*
can not put *I N* in a better Condition than *I S* was for
the Subftitute of *I S* can but fucceed in his place, and at
the time of the Alienation, the Verdict might have been
given in Evidence againft *I S*

Rufworth v
Cou ee of
Peny role and
C r r
nura 472

But if *A.* prefer a Bill againft *B* and *B* exhibit his Bill
in the fame Matter againft *A* and *C*, and a Trial at Law
is directed, *C* cannot give in Evidence the Depofitions in a
Caufe between *A* and *B*, but it muft be tried entirely *ut
Res nova*, " for the Reafon already given "

" We have feen that an ACQUITTAL on a criminal Pro
' fecution, can not be Evidence on a civil Suit where the
" Fact charged becomes material to be proved but a CON-
' VICTION may, where the Point to be fupported by it
" comes in fuch a kind as to be cognizable at the Common
" Law " Thus, if a man have two Wives, and be thereof

± P 37

convicted, and die " this * in an Ejectment would be

CONCLUSIVE

" CONCLUSIVE Evidence, when the Title turned on the
" Validity of the Marriage " but if a man be convict of
Bigamy, and die, and the second Wife claim Dower, and
the Heir plead *ne unques accouple en loyal Matrimonie*, the
Verdict and Conviction can not now be given in Evidence ;
but in this Case the Writ must go to the Bishop for " now
" the point" is of ecclefiaftical Jurifdiction, and is not to be
decided at common Law

But the Verdict may be made an Exhibit before the
Bishop as Proof " of the Bigamy, and the ecclefiaftical
" Court would give Credit to it as decisive , being the
" Judgment of a competent Jurifdiction as the Court of
" Common Law would to the Spiritual Court upon a De-
" cision of theirs on a Matter within their Cognizance
" But of this, more hereafter

" The Record of a Conviction in a Civil Caufe, cannot Caf Temp
" be given in Evidence on a criminal Profecution "   Hardw 312.

T I T. III.

WHERE,EVIDENCE *of a* VERDICT *is good, though not between
Parties, on account of the General Nature of the Queftion*

On an antient Verdict, where the CUSTOM of Tithing
is fet out, whether it might be given in Evidence againft another Parifhioner that was not party to the Verdict, " was
" doubted " but Lands in Queftion * " was doubted but * P 38
" by the better Opinion," it might be given in Evidence Per Opin
becaufe it appeared to be antient, and becaufe there can be I. Dod in the
no other Proofs but of this fort of what was then thought Cafe of the
to be the Cuftom.   Vicar of
                                                            Rolvend
And fo *as it feems* a fpecial Verdict between other Parties Carth 181
ftating a Pedigree is Evidence to prove a Defcent   L N P 233
" And a Verdict, with the Evidence given, in an Action v infra *Un-*
" brought by the Carrier for Goods delivered to him to be *written Evi-*
" carried, fhall be Evidence on an Action by the Owner *dence* Tit
" againft the Carrier for the fame Goods for it is ftrong L N P 243
" Proof againft him that he had the Plaintiff's Goods   Per Holt 14
" But a VERDICT will not be admitted in Evidence with- W 3 atGuild-
" out likewife producing a Copy of the Judgment founded was the *laft* of
" upon it   becaufe, otherwife the Judgment may have W the Public
" been arrefted or a New Trial granted but on an Iffue lower than the
" directed out of Chancery, it being not ufual to enter a 13th
" Judgment in fuch Cafe, the DECREE is equally Proof Montgomerie
" that the Verdict is fatisfactory and ftands in force." v Clarke,
                                                          1745, before
" It has been held," that in an Information by the At- the Delegates
torney General for the King, when the Jury are ready to L N P 234.
give

give their Verdict, the Attorney General may withdraw a Juror: for " that" it is the part of the PREROGATIVE, and in the room of the *Non-suit* of the subject, for the King cannot be *Non-suit* being always in Court and, " farther," this " Distinction prevails" on the general Reason of the King's Employment for * the Public Safety and therefore, if he hath failed in any point of Proof, so that Disadvantage may be expected from the Verdict, it shall be at his Election, whether he will receive the Verdict or not, and in a second Information, none of the first Jury shall be admitted to give in Evidence that they were agreed in their Verdict: for thereby, " if it were permitted," the King might be " indi-" rectly" dispossessed of the Benefit of his Prerogative.

But if the King alien the Estate on which the Trial was had, so that it comes into private hands; there, on a second Trial between private persons, the agreement of the Jury may be given in Evidence: for the *Prerogative* is annexed to the *Crown*, and cannot extend to any private person, and therefore, they take the Estate with the Disadvantage of a Verdict against them

" But a Verdict cannot be thus avoided in criminal " Cases: for there the Party must consent to the with-" drawing of a Juror· since he is in Character and Esti-" mation so highly interested: and hath a Right, if he so " prefer, to entitle himself to a solemn Acquittal by his " Peers † (*n*)

" As a Verdict can not be given in Evidence without " the Record, so neither can an Agreement of the Jury to " have found for the Defendant be given in * Evidence, in the " Case just stated, against the King's Alienee, without a Re-" cord of the Proceedings on the first Information.".

SECTION X.

Of WRITS.

See farther Cr. i fere-at r T t Ap-judi.

" We have now treated of legislative Records; of judi-" cial Records, either as the Acts of the Parties solemnized " by the Court, or as the Sentence of Law, on Trial " the next species of Record requiring Consideration, are

---

† *Quod fieri vetatur per directum, vetatur etiam per obliquum*
† Lex Communis ita Regis Prærogativam circumscripsit ut ne cujus hæredita tem famamve lædat

Case of Alex-noch and Ci Kinloch, Post 16
(*n*) *And in favor of the Defendant in* HIGH TREASON, *where a Jury was sworn and charged with the Issue, and the Indictment opened, before Evidence given, a Juror was withdrawn by Consent of the Attorney General, in order that the Defendants might plead to the Jurisdiction.*

" WRITS,

" WRITS, *Prerogative,* or Judicial The Prerogative are
" either, of RIGHT, as 1 the WRIT of ELECTION to
" PARLIAMENT in behalf of the COMMON WEAL; 2 the
" writ of MANDAMUS; or, 3. EX GRATIA, of which
" fomething is to be faid hereafter."

WRITS *judicial, are either*
1. *Original*
2. *Of mefne Procefs.*
3 *Of Execution*

" WRITS *original* iffue out of CHANCERY, and are the
" Foundation of the fuit."

WHEN a Writ out of Court is only *Inducement* to the
Action, the taking out of the Writ may be proved without
any Copy of it, becaufe poffibly it might be not returned,
and then it is no Record, and therefore the Copy of it is
not required, but where a Writ itfelf is the GIST of the
Action, you muft have a Copy from the Record, in as
much as you are to have the uttermoft Evidence the thing
is capable of.

" A WRIT of MESNE PROCESS is that which iffues to
" fupport the fuit from its Commencement to its ultimate
" Conclufion

" Of this Nature the Principal is the *Capias ad refponden-*
" *dum,* to bring a party into Court by Arreft to anfwer to
" the fuit

" * The Bailiff on mefne Procefs cannot juftify breaking * P. 41.
" open the OUTER Door of an Houfe to execute the Writ; Cowp 1—9
" but he may the INNER, if obftructed   Lee and Ganfel
                                          Hil 14 G III
" Where an Houfe is divided into feveral Tenements, 1774
" and the entrance to each is by a feparate outer Door,
" each partakes feparately of this privilege

" Chambers in the Inns of Court, and in Colleges, are
" within the Rule.

" Or if a perfon be lawfully arrefted, out of an Houfe, Com III p
" and efcape, the Officer may juftify breaking open an 288.
" Houfe to retake him.

" A fworn Officer may arreft within his Precinct without Burn, Title
" fhewing his warrant; (o) but he ought to apprize the Arreft 109
" party of his Authority in general Terms, that he may
" know it is not unlawful violence.

" An arreft (unlefs by fubmiffion of the party) is not by
" words only without corporal feizure; but for this, the Blatch v Ar-
" flighteft touching fuffices. and this feizure need not be by cher
                                                              Cowp. 65

(o) *Otherwife of a Diftrefs Warrant by a Juftice of the Peace
ly the St 27 G II. c. 20 for that muft be fhewn, if required, and
a Copy permitted to be taken.*

" the

" the hand of the Bailiff, if it be by his authority, and he
" at hand, though not in fight

Com III 289 " Perfons attending on Procefs on a Court of Record are
Bl. Rep 1113 " privileged from Arreft in going, attending, and returning,
" and this being in furtherance of Juftice is liberally con-
" ftrued, fo that a flight delay or a fmall deviation from the
" road defeats not the privilege

* P 42 " * And in this Cafe the Court will generally extend its
" relief in the fulleft manner, by releafing the party fo ar-
" refted out of Cuftody, and not merely punifhing the Offi-
" cer for the trefpafs or the Contempt

Cowp 9 " But in other Cafes generally it is in the Difcretion of
" the Court, on the circumftances, to pronounce the Procefs
" void by the undue execution of it, or fimply to leave the
" party to his remedy for the Trefpafs

Com III 289 " All perfons are exempt from Arreft on Sundays, except
" for Treafon, Felony, or breach of the Peace

" The Members of either Houfe of Parliament are ex-
" empt, except in the inftances above fpecified

V B Rep " And EMBASSADORS and their menial fervants by the
49 9 " Law of NATIONS fo that againft thefe the Arreft is
" utterly void, in like manner as againft Members of Parli
" ament, the perfon of the Reprefentative of an indepen-
" dent Community being entitled, while he comporteth
" himfelf as fuch, to inviolable Security

" And of Privileges annexed to public Functions the
" Court taketh Notice, † without their being fpecially
" pleaded "

Fenwick v
Fenwick.
Bl. 758

Yet, as to the Mode of Proof, a Member of the HOUSE
of COMMONS, moving to be difcharged on PRIVILEGE,
was obliged to give in *Evidence* the *Return* of the Writ of
Election

* P 43 * In an Action of Trefpafs againft a Bailiff for taking
L. N P 234 Goods in EXECUTION, " if it be brought by the Party
1 Rol m 733 " againft whom the Writ iffued, it is fufficient for the Offi
" cer to give in Evidence the writ of *fieri facias*, without
" fhewing a Copy of the Judgment but if the Plaintiff
" be not the party againft whom the Writ iffued, but claim
" the Goods by a prior Execution (or Sale), that was frau-

---

† *And formerly, their fervants, but Parliament made a wife and
liberal furrender of this and many other Privileges to public Convenience, by* 10 G III c 50 4 G III c 33

† *In Lord Banbury's Cafe, it not appearing he had ever fat in
Parliament as a Peer by Virtue of a Writ of Summons, the Court
refufed to take Notice of the Privilege on Motion Silk 512 V
Com m 400, where fee the Diftinction between a Call by Writ and
by Patent of Peerage*

" dulent.

" dulent, there the Officer muſt not only prove the Writ,
" but a Copy of the Judgment For, in the firſt Caſe, by
" proving that he took the Goods in obedience to a Writ
" iſſued againſt the Plaintiff, he has proved himſelf guilty
" of no Treſpaſs but in the other Caſe, they are not the
" Goods of the Party againſt whom the Writ iſſued; and
" therefore the Officer is not juſtified by the Writ in taking
" them, unleſs he can bring the Caſe within 13 Eliz., for
" which purpoſe it is neceſſary to ſhew a Judgment "

In Debt againſt the Executor, the Defendant pleads that
the Teſtator was taken in *Execution* by a *Capias ad ſatisfacien-
dum*, and found, that he was taken in Execution on an *Alias
Capias* this is well enough for an *Alias* is but renewing
the ſame *Capias*, and doth not differ from it in ſubſtance,
but in circumſtance only, as being the ſecond Proceſs of
the *ſame Nature* but if they had found that he had been
taken in Execution by a *Capias pro Fine*, or a *Capias utlaga-
tum*, this had * not maintained the Plea ˙ becauſe they are not * P. 44.
the ſame ſort of Execution with the *Ca ſa (p)* but in their
Nature diſtinct and when the Jury finds that the party was
taken in Execution upon the *Alias Capias*, it ſhall be intended
upon the *ſame* judgment, without any Averment, becauſe
the Doubt exhibited to the Court ſhall not be intended to be
quite foreign to the Matter, but ariſing out of it. and
therefore it muſt be intended an *Alias Capias* on the ſame
Judgment, for it is out of Controverſy that a *Capias* upon
another Judgment could not poſſibly maintain the Plea

" Upon *plene adminiſtravit*, upon Return of a *devaſtavit by
" the Sheriff*," (q) the Execution executed cannot be given in Per Holt

---

(p) *It is ſtriking to conſider, notwithſtanding the Prolixity of the
Law is in ſome caſes ſo much cenſured, what a formiaable Brevity
there is in other thus a Fi ſa ſhall deprive a Man of all his perſonal property, a Ca ſa conſign him to a priſon, frequently for life
(and theſe awful exertions of Authority are as compendiouſly pro-* Com B IV
nounced as they are written), and a Suſp per Coll againſt a Name Ch 32
in the Convicts Calendar ſhall be a Warrant on a capital Felony to L N P 142
deprive him ignominiouſly of life itſelf Tremendous, but not exem- Ca K B 411
plary Conciſeneſs ! It is now indeed in Engliſh, and at length, let Salk. 310
*him be hanged by the neck, but ſtill how juſtly is it with a mark
of melancholy ſurprize,* " that the execution of a man, the moſt
" important and terrible taſk of any, ſhall depend upon a mar-
" ginal note " *In London indeed it is more ſolemnly by a diſtinct
airant*

(q) *For explanation of this it may be proper to remark, that if* " Ex-
" ecutor ſuffer Judgment by Default, it amounts in law to a
" Confeſſion of aſſets ſufficient to pay the Debt and therefore
" if the Sheriff on a Fi ſa do not find Goods of the Teſtator,
" he returns a *devaſtavit*."

Evidence without the Judgment; becaufe there appears no Authority for fuch Execution without the Judgment for where the Execution is of Record, and the Authority for fuch Execution is alfo of Record, they muft both appear to the Jury; otherwife they have not the uttermoft Evidence of the Fact in Queftion

* P 45.   * " *Where the* TIME *of fuing out the* ORIGINAL *muft be fhewn*

" If the Plaintiff, on *Non affumpfit infra fex annos,* does
L. N. P 149 " not bring the Commencement of the Action on the
" Pleadings, fo that it be admitted by the Defendant, he
" muft *prove* the taking out of the Original
" As a LATITAT fued out in the Vacation is by fiction
" of Law referred to the firft Day of the preceding Term,
" the Defendant may avoid being concluded by the fictitious
" Relation, by pleading in his *Rejoinder* the real † Day on
See alfo Burr " which the Writ iffued
Mansf—1243 - " If the Plaintiff would take Advantage of fuch Procefs,
L N P 151 " he muft fhew that he has continued the Writ to the time
" of the Action brought, and muft fet forth that the firft
" Writ was returned for if the Defendant plead *Non af-*
" *fumpfit within fix years before the exhibiting of the Bill,* and
" iffue be taken thereupon, he cannot give the Latitat in
" Evidence, *for the Latitat may be only Procefs to bring the*
" *Defendant into Court,* and may as fuch be fued out before
" the Caufe of Action accrues
L. N P 187 " On an Action againft the Hundred to recover Da-
" mages for a Robbery, the Plaintiff muft, under the 27
" Eliz produce a *Copy* of the *Original,* to fhew that he
" has commenced his Action *within the year,* and alfo that
" the Oath of the *Robbery* was within twenty Days before
" the *Tefte* "

* P. 46.   * " *Who muft fhew the* RETURN *of the* WRIT.

" Where an Officer and another join in the fame Juftifi-
L. N P 23 " cation, if it be not fufficient for the Officer, neither is it
" fufficient for the other, and whenever an Officer juftifies
" an imprifonment under a Writ which he fhould return,
" (and all *mefne* Procefs ought to be returned) ne muft fhew
" that the writ was returned but it is otherwife in the
" Cafe of a *fubordinate* Officer, for he is only to execute
" t'e Sheriff's warrant

† F &c femper infra Æquitatis limites fubfiftit propter quam in-
ducta eft
Fictio contra Juris Veritatem n hil operatur.

In

In an Action brought by an Attorney for his Fees, it is Silby v sufficient to prove the Return of the Writ by a Warrant Hinckly Tr Aff 1701. made by the Coroners. for the Writ may not be returned per Gould of Record, and then the Warrant is sufficient to prove a Title to his Fees

" We have obferved already that there is alfo another " Species of Records, which are thofe of PRIVILEGE, or " EX GRATIA, and thefe are PATENTS, 1 of *Honour*; 2 " of *Improvement*; 3. of *Pardon*. They iffue under the " *Great Seal.*

CHAP III.

WRITTEN EVIDENCE NOT *of* RECORD.

" Before we enter on the Confideration of other Evidence " under this head, it appears proper to mention feparately " the Journals of the HOUSE OF COMMONS

" Thefe, though not of Record, yet from the Dignity of " the great Affembly to which they belong, * and the uni- * P. 47. " verfal Notoriety which the Law prefumes of their Tranf- " actions, appear to be equivalent to Records in the Prin- " ciples and Mode of Proof by which Evidence of them " may be received This hath been intimated already in re- " ference to the Proceedings of the other Houfe: but it " merited to be feparately noticed, and for that reafon it is " here mentioned."

SECTION II.

WRITTEN EVIDENCE *inferior to* RECORD.

1 PUBLIC

The Things that do ftand fecond in point of PROBABILITY are all PUBLIC Matters that are *not of Record*

The public Matters that are not of Record, and ftand next in Authority to Records, do all come under this gene- ral Definition· they muft be fuch Matters as have an Evi- dence in themfelves, and that do not expect an Illuftration from any other Thing: fuch are the Copies of Court Rolls and TRANSACTIONS in CHANCERY, and the like and the Copies of fuch Matters may be given in Evidence, in 'as much as there is a plain and coherent proof: for the Matters *themfelves* are fuppofed to be felf-evident, and, by confe- quence, when your Copy of them is produced * upon Oath, * P 48. you have a full proof. becaufe you have proved upon Oath a Matter which, when proved, would carry its own light with it

VOL I.   D   But

But here it will be objected that this is not the utmost Evidence that the Nature of the Thing is capable of, for these Testimonies themselves must needs be better than Copies of them

To this the Answer is, that the Copy upon oath is, " in " such instances," reckoned as an equivalent to the Thing itself. " since" the testimony itself must not be rigorously required, because these Matters, lying for public satisfaction, every Man has a Right to their Evidence. and in several places they cannot be at the same time, and therefore the Things themselves cannot be demanded, but only Copies of them

THE FIRST sort of " these" TESTIMONIES that are not of Record, are, the PROCEEDINGS of the COURT of CHANCERY on the *English* side

The Reason why the Proceedings in Chancery, and the Rolls of the Court, are not Records, is this, because they are not the Precedents of Justice. for the * Proceedings in Chancery are founded only on the Circumstances of each private Case, and they cannot be rules to any other, and the judgment there, is *secundum æquum et bonum*, and not *secundum leges et consuetudines* and the Reason why any Record is of Authority is, because it is declarative of the sense of the Law, and is a Memorial of what is the Law of the Nation. Now Chancery Proceedings are no Memorial of the Law of *England*; because the Chancellor is not bound to proceed according to Law *(q)*

* P. 49

SECTION III

Of BILLS in CHANCERY

The *Bill* in *Chancery* is Evidence against the Complainant for the Allegations of every Man's Bill shall be supposed to be true, nor shall it be supposed to be preferred by the Counsel or Solicitor without Privity of the party, and there-

Co Ca 64, 5
En Au. 227
r t
Net Co. R
102

S e the
1 ASCRED
1 LLG ship
(all Rep
r1 L.
Question
takes
from the
Prosecution
has rest
to his not

(q) The Reason here given for Chancery Proceedings on the Equity side not being Records, might lead into great Error as to the Nature of the Jurisdiction of that Court, in its present improved state, to which it has been gradually matured by the progressive Extent of its Practice, with the legal Knowledge and other eminent Qualifications of those who have successively presided in it. Chancery differs from the Court of Common Law rather in the Forms of Process, the Modes of Investigation and the subjects of its interference than in the Certainty of Principles and Adherence to settled Rules. Stare decisis, so far as justly may be done, is, for the public Security and Freedom, a governing Maxim on each side of the Hall

fore

fore is Evidence as to the Confeſſion and Admittance of
the Truth of any Faſt by the Party himſelf· and. if the
Counſel hath mingled in it what is not true, the party may
have his Aſtion but where a Bill is exhibited, and there
are no Proceedings upon it, then it cannot be given in Evidence , unleſs they prove a Privity in the party. for a Man
may file a Bill in another's Name to rob him of his Evidence by a ſham Confeſſion and therefore a Bill filed without any Proceedings, hath not the Force of an Evidence
for no man can ſuppoſe the party did himſelf file the Bill
* without any proceedings, to bring his Adverſary to anſwer **＊ P. 50**
ſuch Bill; " this" is of no uſe to the party, and therefore
muſt be ſuppoſed rather to be filed by a Stranger to do him
an Injury (p)

　　This " has been" accounted to ſtand, in point of Cre- **2 Sid 221.**
dibility, in the ſame circumſtances as a Confeſſion by Letter **Keb 780.**
under the party's hand, where no one ſaw the party write
it " but this, though urged by the Counſel, does not ap-
" pear to have been ſo taken by the Court and" it ſeems
the Allegation in a Court of Juſtice, that amounts to a
Confeſſion of any Faſt, ought to have more Weight and
Authority with it than any private owning

　　" But a mere general ſuggeſtion of Faſts, in order to a
" Diſcovery, ſhall not be read in Evidence. for this is no
" more than ſurmiſe of the Counſel, in order to come at
" Faſts otherwiſe of a Faſt ſtated in the Bill, on which **L N P 235,6.**
" the Plaintiff founds his prayer for relief."

SECTION IV.

ANSWER.

　　And if the *Bill* be Evidence againſt the Complainant, **Godb. 326**
much more is the *Anſwer* Evidence againſt the Defendant,
and carries higher Weight of Probability along with it , becauſe this is delivered in upon oath , and therefore over and
above the ſingle Confeſſion, it has an Authority from the
ſanſtion of an oath

　　* But when you read an Anſwer, the Confeſſion muſt be **＊ P 51**
all taken together , and you ſhall not take only what makes **Brockmans**
againſt him, and leave out what makes for him. for the **Caſe.**
Anſwer is read as the ſenſe of the Party himſelf; and if it **Tr Aſſ 1705**
2 Vern 194
288

　　(r) *The Caſe was this· a Parſon was ſued by his Patron on a* **5 Mod 10**
ſimoniacal Bond he preferred a Bill in Chancery to be relieved from **Ch Ca 154**
the Bond and it appearing there had been proceedings on the Bill, it **Keb R 780**
was reſolved it might be given in Evidence on an Ejeſtment brought **2 Sid 221**
to make void the Parſon's Living

is to be taken in this manner, you muft take it entire and unbroken

Tit II. Infants, &c

2 Ver. 71
3 Mod 259
Carth 70
3 P W 237
Anfr of
Femme Co-
verte 3 P W
258 Vern
60, 109, 10
L N P 23

An Infant's Anfwer by his Guardian fhall never be admitted in Evidence againft him on a Trial at Law, for the Law has that tendernefs for the Affairs of Infants, that it will not fuffer them to be prejudiced by the Guardian's oath, for the Authority the Law gives to the Guardian is for the Infant's Benefit, and not his Prejudice (s)

Anon H.I.
Vacat 1707
per Cowper

" So the Anfwer of a Truftee can in no Cafe be admitted " as Evidence againft *Ceftuy que* Truft "

A B II was brought by Creditors againft an Executor to have an Account of the perfonal Eftate, the Executor fets forth by *Anfwer*, that there was 1100*l* left by the Teftator in his hands; and that coming afterwards to make up his Accounts with the Teftator, he gave Bond for 1000*l* and

* P 52

the other 100*l*. was given * him as a Gift for his Trouble and Pains taken in the Teftator's bufinefs and there was no other Evidence in the Cafe that the 1100*l* was depofited but merely the Executor's own oath and it was argued that the Anfwer, though it was put in Iffue, fhould be allowed fince there is the fame Rule of Evidence in Equity as in Law. and that if a Man was fo honeft as to charge himfelf when he might have denied it, and no teftimony could have appeared, he ought to find Credit where he fwears in his own Difcharge.

But it was anfwered, 'and refolved by the Court, that when an Anfwer was put in Iffue, what was confeffed and admitted need not be proved; but it behoved the Defendant to make out by Proofs what was infifted upon by way of Avoidance and this Diftinction was held where the Defendant admits a Fact, and infifts on a *diftinct* Fact by way of Avoidance, there he ought to prove the Matter of his Defence, becaufe it may be probable that he admitted it out of Apprehenfion that it might be proved; and therefore fuch Admittance ought not to profit him fo far as to pafs for Truth whatever he fays in Avoidance but if it had been *one* Fact, as if the Defendant had faid the Teftator had given him 100*l* it ought to have been allowed, unlefs

* P 53

difproved, becaufe nothing of the * Fact charged is admitted, and the Plaintiff may difprove the whole Fact as

(s) Ἐις ΟΙΚΟΔΟΜΗΝ, ουκ ἐις ΚΑΘΑΙΡΕΣΙΝ.
Neque interdicto, neque cæteris in caufis, pupillo nocere debet res per *Tutorem* acta. v. D. 50 17 l. 198

fworn.

sworn, if he can do it It was " further" urged, that
here the Presumption was on the Defendant's side; because
a Bond was not taken for this sum as for the residue : the
Chancellor said, there was some Presumption in that, but
not enough to carry so large a sum without better Attestation

Par 2

ANSWER *Evidence on an* INFORMATION *for* PERJURY.

In an *Information* for *Perjury*, an *Answer* may be given in
Evidence without any Person to prove that the Defendant
swore it; for the Identity may be proved by many Things
out of the Answer itself· besides, the party is obliged to *sign*
his *Answer* and the Perjury may be further illustrated by a
Comparison of *Hands* , which, possibly, may be Evidence in
Concurrence with other Proofs that out of the Answer itself
evince the Identity of the Person

Par 3

Concerning the Proof by Comparison of Hands solely *in* Criminal
Cases ; *that it is* not *admissible , otherwise*, *in* Civil.

But that the *Comparison* of *Hands* ONLY *(t)* should be
Proof in a CRIMINAL Prosecution was never Law, but
only in the time of King *James*, and the Distinction has
ever been taken, that the *Comparison* of *Hands* is Evidence in
Civil, but not in Criminal Cases· the * Reason why the Com- * P 54.
parison of Hands is Evidence in *Civil* Matters is, because
Men are distinguished by their *Hand-writing* as well as by
faces for it is very seldom that the shape of their letters
agrees any more than the shape of their Bodies . therefore
the Comparison of Hands serves for a Distinction in *Civil*
Commerce , for the likeness does induce a Presumption that
they are the same, and the Presumption is Evidence till the

(t) *Preamble to the Act* 1 *W & M. for* REVERSING *the* AT-
TAINDER *of* ALGERNON SYDNEY , *reciting, among other Enor-
mities of that most illegal and sanguinary Process, that the "* Paper
" found in his Closet was not proved by any one Witness to
" have been written by him " *In order to give some possibility of
this important Act being better known than at present, it will be
added in the* APPENDIX. *At the same time I must here repeat my
Hope that it will one day be found in the Editions of the* PUBLIC
STATUTES *its proper* PLACE *It has been published lately, with
that for reversing the Attainder of Lord* RUSSEL, *by the* SOCIETY
for CONSTITUTIONAL INFORMATION

In Layer's *Case* * *Evidence was admitted of a Person "* who Hargrave's St.
" had often seen him write; *and in* Henley's *Case the like Evi-* Tr VI 279
dence admitted Both went to introductory Matter, and not *to the* 1, 2 Burr
overt acts *laid in the several Indictments*   Mansf 642

contrary

contrary appears for every Presumption that remains un-
contested hath the force of an Evidence, for light Proof
on the one side will outweigh the Defect of the Proof on
the other. but in Criminal Prosecutions the Presumption is in
Favour of the Defendant (for thus far is to be hoped of all
Mankind, that they are not guilty in such instances), and
the Penalty enhances the Presumption Now the *Comparison* of *Hands* is no more than a *Presumption founded only on
the Likeness which may easily fail*, because they are very subject to be counterfeited therefore when the Comparison of
the Hands is *the only Evidence* in a Criminal Prosecution,
there is no more than one Presumption against another,
which weighs nothing

P. 55   **Tit III.**

Second Answer *explanatory, to be read in Evidence*

In an *Information* for *Perjury*, the Perjury assigned was the
Defendant's *Answer*, " that he received no Money," and on
Exceptions for Insufficiency, the Defendant says, in a *second* Answer, " that he received no Money until such a
" day," (*u*) and on the Trial of the Information it was
held

(*u*) *It must be taken of course that the Day was material to the
Cause, so that* non receipt *till after such a day would come within
the sense, as to the Matter before the Court, of* non receiver *generally* Much more is it reasonable that such explanation should be
admitted on vivâ voce Evidence and when in cross-examining,
Counsel have impeached the Credit of a Witness on apparently contradictory testimony, Lord Mansfield has often said, " would you
" have the Witness perjured, because he will not be perjured, but
' corrects himself like an honest Man?" There was a late singular
instance where this explanation supported itself by all the circumstances imaginable, the absolute indifference of the fact to
the witness, the substantial Agreement between what he said, and
what he immediately explained himself to have meant to say,
the certainty of the party *examined*, that the fact was *known* to
the party *examining*, and to the *Court*, so as to preclude all idea
of a design to falsify The Case was this Captain *Shipley*, of
the *Alexarder and Margaret*, applied to the *Court of Admiralty
of the Borough of* Great Yarmouth to recover Anchors and
Cables which his Ship, by stress of weather, was obliged to leave
in *Yarmouth* Road, on paying the charge of salvage Mr *Hurry*,
as Agent to Captain *Shipley*, paid the Bill, but having an Objection to the charge of Cartage, summoned Mr *Watson* before
the Court of Requests, to answer for an Overcharge Mr *Watson an Attorney*, was Judge of the Court of Admiralty,
and Mr *Reynolds*, his partner, presided in the Court of Requests
The

held that nothing should be assigned for Perjury that was explained in the second Answer for the first Answer *shall* be charitably *expounded, according to what appears to be the party's sense in the second Answer*, for the Court would rather intend there was some oversight in the Draft, and that it was afterwards amended in the second Answer, than suppose the party to be guilty of manifest and corrupt Perjury

The Clerk of the Court administered the Oath to Mr. *Hurry,* according to the Practice, in order to his proving the Demand, and then asked him, *Is Mr* John Watson *indebted to you, Mr* Hurry, *in the sum of eleven shillings?* the sum demanded: he answered, *he is.* On the Question being repeated, and the Witness desired to recollect himself, he subjoined, " *as Agent to Mr* " Shipley" On this he was indicted for PERJURY before Sir *George Nares,* at the *Thetford* Assizes, *March,* 18, 1786, the Indictment charging him with having " falsely, corruptly, wil- " fully, and maliciously depofed, that the said *John Watson* was " indebted to him, the said *William Hurry,* in the sum of eleven " shillings, whereas in truth, and in fact, the said *John Watson* " was not indebted to him, the said *William Hurry,* in the afore- " said sum, nor in any other sum of Money whatever" The Case, as stated, appearing on the Trial, from the Evidence on the side of Profecution, the *Judge* rose, and said, " *It would be hard indeed if a man were not suffered to explain his own meaning; here is evidently an Indictment found on part of an Oath, when that which is most essential to its meaning is left out* " The Counsel on the other side, would have had the Cause go on but the Judge added, that it *could not —and that he hoped future prosecutors would take care from such an example to prefer indictments on juster Grounds* And then immediately turning to the Jury, repeated, that *this was Perjury, assigned on part only of an Oath, the most material part being purposely kept back That of course they must find the Defendant* Not Guilty This they did, by a Verdict warmly expressive of their Feeling

Afterwards, on an Action for a *malicious Profecution,* strengthened by Aggravated circumstances in the *subsequent* Conduct of the Profecutor, who had caused it to be advertized, *that the Perjury Cause went off in Consequence of a DEFECT in the Indictment, but that a fresh Bill would be preferred* Mr. *Erskine* manifested the powers of his Eloquence and Senfibility, and the JURY, which was a *Special* one, gave Damages of 3000l

On this Trial they proved the Advertisement, by the Evidence of a Copy delivered to the Printer by an Agent (for that Purpose) of the Profecutor, *Watson* who swore that he copied it from one received from *Watson* The Counsel for the Defendant, objected to this Evidence, but the Judge said, in common Cafes you are certainly right but in this, Mr *Watson* gave Mr *Locke* one Paper which was meant to be *multiplied* He employed Mr *Locke* as his AGENT He entrusted him with *Agency,* and *therefore* becomes answerable for his Acts The paragraph is admissible Evidence.

Proceedings in the Trial of *Hurry* and on the *Action* against *Watson.* NORWICH 1787

When

2 Sid 419   When a Man is sworn in Chancery to answer directly to his *Knowledge*, Perjury cannot be assigned on any thing which is not within his Knowledge, as upon his Belief, &c. for what he swears on his Belief is not within the Compass of his oath.

* P 56   * Tit. IV.

Difference *between* Answer *in Chancery and* Voluntary Affidavit.

Brockman's
Cafe, 1701
Str 35
P W. 675.

Analogous to this is a Man's own voluntary Affidavit; which may also be given in Evidence against him: but then the *Proceedings* muft be given in Evidence on which this Affidavit did arife. and the Reafon why the Proceedings muft alfo be given in Evidence is, to prove the *Identity* of the Perfon; for to prove an Affidavit fworn, is not fuffi-cient · for it may be fworn by Fraud and Contrivance, the perfon being perfonated by fomebody elfe and therefore, to bring home the Proof to the perfon, you muft prove the *occafion* of the fwearing, for it is not to be thought that a Man, without fome occafion or other, would make Affi-davit, " and if the Caufe and Circumftances be fuppreffed, " it infers Fraud in the party fuggefting the Affidavit in pre-" judice of the party charged to have made it."

* P 57   * " But, notwithftanding fome General Analogy," there is a very great Difference between the Evidence of an Anfwer, and that of a voluntary Affidavit.

Mic. T 1714,
in Canc inter
Roch and Rix,
Admin of
Howard et al

An Answer cannot be given in Evidence Generally, without producing the Bill : becaufe, without the Bill, there does not appear to be a Caufe depending : but if there be Proof by the proper Officer, that the Bill has been fearched for diligently in the Office, and cannot be found, the An-fwer " may, on circumftances otherwife inducing a Belief " that a Bill once really exifted, and that proceedings were " had upon it," be read without a fight, of the Bill and this Lord Chancellor *Broderick* allowed, though the Lofs of the Bill was not proved by the proper Officer, but by the Clerk only who wrote in the Office, and fwore he fearched carefully with the Officer, and could not find the

* P 58   Bill   * " And in this Connection with the Original Pro-" ceedings, there is Analogy between an Anfwer and a " Voluntary Affidavit.

Hill. Aſ 1700   " But," an *Anfwer* is *proved* by fhewing the Allegations in Court, *viz* by fhewing the Bill, which is the Charge, and the Anfwer which is, as it were, the Defence to the Bill, and this, in civil Cafes, fhall be *intended* to be fworn, becaufe

becaufe the Proceedings upon fuch Defence *are* upon Oath. Now, fince the Proceedings of any " fuperior" Court of Judicature, within the Kingdom are good Evidence in other Courts, " who will take notice of the Practice and general " Courfe of fuch Court," and the Proceedings in this Court are upon Oath, it follows of courfe, that in all *civil* Cafes the *Anfwer* is to be taken as an *Oath* without any farther Proof, but from the Proceedings in the Caufe

But a *Voluntary Affidavit* is not part of any Caufe in a Court of Juftice, and therefore it muft be *proved* to be *fworn*, for if you only prove it figned by the Party, * the Proof goes no farther than to fuppofe it as a Note or Letter: (and as fuch, you may give it in Evidence without more proof) for a Note or Letter is a bare Acknowledgment (v) under the hand of the Party; and this is no more unlefs you prove it to be fworn alfo, for it cannot be *prefumed* to be fworn, being not filed as an Oath in a Court of Juftice

Such are the Affidavits made before a Mafter in Chancery by the Vendor of the Eftate in fatisfaction of the Purchafer, that the Eftate is free from all charges and incumbrances

The *fecond* Difference between them is, that the *Copy* of an *Anfwer* may be given in Evidence; but the Copy of a Voluntary Affidavit cannot · " for the Reafon already " given," that an Anfwer is an Allegation in a *Court of Judicature,* and being Matter of *Public Credit,* the *Copies* of

Marginal references:
Vern 53. 413.
Lord Raym.
311 734.
* P 59.
2 Vern 471
547 555 591.
603 Ch Pre
59 116 212
3 Mod 36
9 Mod 66
11 Mod 210.
262
12 Mod 136.
231 305 310.
319 339 342
375 394 414.
494 500 521.
555 565 579.
607
3 Mod 116

(v) An Action of Covenant brought againft two, the Affidavit of one of them was given in Evidence as the *Acknowledgment* of them both becaufe the Acknowledgment of one of them, where they had a *joint* Intereft, was to be looked upon as a Truth relating to them both , and the Confideration of the Matter is to be left to the Jury, how far it is Evidence againft the other — Vicary's Cafe in the Exchequer

And *an Anfwer of the Mother concerning the illegitimacy of her Son, was ruled to be good Evidence admiffible to prove the Legitimacy after the Death of the Mother, and that it ought not to have been rejected* — Goodright on Demife of Stephens againft Mofs, E 17 G Il Cowp 591 4

It is favourable to public Manners and to legal Certainty, that fo little Credit is allowed to Voluntary Affidavits, where a Caufe is depending, there is proportionable weight in that Teftimony which the Law requires of the Parties. but in voluntary Affidavits, Rafhnefs, Paffion, latent Interefts, Fraud, have a dangerous fcope Villainy has much lefs to apprehend from but an Cenfure, and even perfons not abfolutely profligate, may be prefumed lefs careful of exact Truth, than if under the Solemnities of a judicial Examination And,

Qui facile, et ultro, et ex proclivi jurant us non temere credendum

it

it may be given in Evidence but a *Voluntary Affidavit* hath no Relation to any Court of Justice, and therefore is not entitled to public Credit, and being a private Matter, the Affidavit itself must be produced as the best Evidence

" And since weaker Evidence can not be introduced, " where stronger, under the same circumstances, would not " be admitted" the Voluntary Affidavit of a stranger, *can by no means be given in Evidence* , because the opposite party had not the Liberty to cross-examine. But of this in the next Section

‡ P. 60.

Sacheverill *and* Sacheverill,
5 Mar 1716,
before the Delegates
L N P 241
Mar and May,
A D a Bar
v No e to the
P ceeding

‡ " CASES indeed may exist where a voluntary Affidavit " shall be Evidence between Strangers but they are such, " where the Confession of the party making the Affidavit " would be Evidence Thus where a Widow came for Administration, the Marriage being contested, an Affidavit " of the Man himself was read So on an Issue directed " out of Chancery, to try the Legitimacy of the Plaintiff, " the Father's Oath before the Judges on a private Bill, " was allowed to be Evidence "

SECTION V

DEPOSITIONS

The *next* Thing is the *depositions* · and here we must, in the first place, consider in what rank they stand in point of Credibility And to enlighten this Matter, we must give an Account of their original use " now" they plainly come over to us from the *Civil* Law It is very plain, " that " under that Law," the parties exhibited their Interrogatories upon their several Allegations but that the Witnesses were privately examined upon these Interrogatories by the *same Judge* who tried the Cause so that the Course, anciently among the *Romans*, was very different from the modern pleadings of the *Chancery*, where the sense of the Witness is stated by the Examiner; on which the Chancellor is to Judge

That this which I have mentioned, was the antient Course of the *Civil* Law, is " evident" from the modern Epistle of *Adrian* to *Varus*, the Legate of *Cilicia* " You best may

‡ P 61

P 2.

5 § 3

" judge what Credit is to be allowed to Witnesses; * who, " and of what worth, of what Estimation they are who " of them appear to speak with Simplicity whether they " bring before you one premeditated Account, or, being " interrogated on the sudden, give probable Answers, with " that general consistency, that unpreparedness for literal

" and

" and minute exactnefs, which bears the native Character
" of Integrity and Truth " *(w)*

Now thefe Examinations were firft made privately: that
the Judge might, in the firft place, be poffeffed of the
" mere" Fact, and the fenfe of thefe Witneffes was after
taken in Writing, and then Publication paffed, that the
Judge might have all due Affiftance from the Obfervation of
the Advocate, if he had not fufficiently compared and
weighed the Examination —As the Trials of the *Civil* Law
thus ftood, when the Judges viewed the Behaviour of the
Witneffes, there is very little difference between this Trial
and that of the *Jury* · fave only that the *Trial by Jury* is
much more fpeedy, and the Evidence more entire, while
in the other way, the Judges take up the Evidence at one
time, and the Glofs at another, and fuch breaking of the
Evidence may be dangerous to a weak and lefs confidering
Judge befides, the Judge not being of the *Neighbourhood*,
cannot fo eafily diftinguifh the Credit of the Witneffes and
upon this account alfo, the *Trial by Jury* is preferable to
the Examination of the *Civil* Law, when under the beft
Regulations

⁂ And no doubt, in *our Chancery Proceedings*, the Witneffes ⁎ P 62
were formerly examined by the *Mafters*, who fat in Court

*(w) I have rendered this fine paffage freely and rather para-
phraftically, according to the import in which it ftrikes my mind   The
original is referved for its proper Place, as a Note with fimilar Extracts on unwritten Evidence*
*Thefe and other confiderations, eftablifh a ftriking preference for
this admirable Mode of Trial, even in* Civil *Cafes; in criminal,
a Title to our Confidence and unceafing care for its prefervation
in its full extent, without farther reduction of its Objects, and in
its purity and vigour, without any impairing of its conftitutional
Spirit, is yet more confpicuous, when Jurors are confidered under
their peculiar difcriminations, as indifferently chofen, liable to be
rejected, on exceptions duly made, by the Crown and by the Prifoner,
with a wife and humane Delicacy, on exception without Affignment* v Fortefcue de
of Caufe, to as great a Number as any fair purpofe can be fuppofed Laud L A
to require *to confift on Trial of a Foreigner of a moiety of* 625 30 p. 77
Foreigners and which is the Glory of the Inftitution, the Judg- 112 Gregor's
ment on the whole Matter of Law and Fact, not entrufted to one or Ed 1773
more of the Bench, but the fentence of Law, the fword of Juf- Montefquieu,
ce, fufpended over the accufed by an adamantine Chain, until the B XI 6ç
current Voice of this feparate and fo conftituted body of his De Lolme,
EQUALS *pronounce him,* Guilty *no conclufion of Law being poffible* 182 —4
to reach againft him, without their previous Confent and unani- 4th Ld 1623
mous Decifion on the Trial
⁎ 35 *in* Treafon, *and fince,* 22 H VIII c 14 *in* Felonies
of inferior Nature, 20
• *That the* Greek *Jurifts too, call* ΑΠΟ ΣΤΟΜΑΤΟΣ

to inform the Chancery of their Credibility; until Caufes
fo multiplied, that the Mafters were employed in other Affairs, and fo the Examination of Witneffes was left to Ex
aminers *out of Court*

Par 2
Comparative Value of Depofitions to immediate Vivâ Voce *Tef
timony*

Now fince this Practice has been ufed, no Doubt the
Credit of DEPOSITIONS, *cæteris paribus*, falls much below
tne Credibility of a prefent examination *Vivâ Voce* · for th
Examiners and Commiffioners in fuch Cafes, do often dref,
up fecret Examinations, and fet a quite Different Air upon
tnem from what they would feem, if the fame Teftimony
had been plainly delivered under the ftrict and open Examin
ation of the Judge af the Affizes.

Par 3
Comparative Value of Depofitions to hearfay Evidence.

But though the *Depofitions* do fall fhort of Examination,
V vâ Voce, yet they feem fuperior to what a Witnefs faid a
a former Trial for what is reduced to Writing, by an
Officer fworn to that purpofe, from the very Mouth of the
Witnefs, is of more Credit than what a ftander-by retains
in Memory, of the fame Oath for the Images of things
cccay in the Memory by the perpetual Change of Appear
ances· fo that we cannot be certain on a verbal Atteftation,
but that fome circumftances of the Fact may be loft in the
Recollection: but what is reduced to Writing continues
conftantly the fame

‡ P 65
¶ Raym 335

⁎ DEPOSITIONS before an Anfwer put in, are not admitted to be read, unlefs the Defendant appears to be in Con
tempt· for if a Caufe doth not appear to be depending, then
are the Depofitions confidered as *voluntary* Affidavits for
unlefs a fuit is fhewn to be commenced, it doth not appear
that the adverfe party had Liberty to crofs examine but if
the adverfe party had been in Contempt, then the Depo
fitions of the Witneffes fhould have been admitted, for then
it is the fault of the Objector, that he did not crofs examine
the Witneffes, fince he would not join in the Examination
of the Witneffes

When the Bill s difmiffed, the Rule as to the reading of
Depofitions is this, where the Bill is difmiffed, becaufe the
Matter is not proper for *Equity* to decree, yet the Depofi
tions of the Fact in the Caufe, may be read afterwards in
a new Caufe between the *fame* parties for though th·
Matter is not proper for Equity to decree, yet there was a
Caufe

Caufe properly before the Court, for it is proper for the Jurifdiction of Equity to confider how far the Law ought to be relaxed and moderated: and where there is a Caufe properly before the Court, howfoever that Caufe be decided, yet the Depofitions in that Caufe muft be Evidence, as well as in all others

* But if a Caufe in Equity be difmiffed for the irregu- * P 64 larity of the Complainant, the *Depofitions* in that Caufe can Ch Ca 175. never be read as where a Devifee, in a fuit pending by his Devifor, brings a Bill of *Revivor*, and feveral Depofitions are taken, and then the Caufe on a hearing is difmiffed, becaufe a *Devifee*, claiming as a *Purchafor* and not by *Reprefentation*, cannot bring a Bill of *Revivor (x)* In this Cafe, on a new original Bill exhibited, the Devifee cannot ufe the former depofitions for in the firft Caufe, miftaking the Bill that he ought to bring, there was no Complaint before the Court,—fince the Court does not allow any *Devifee* to complain in that manner, by Right of *Reprefentation*, and there being no Caufe regularly before the Court, there could be no depofitions in it

In *Crofs Caufes* in Equity, an Agreement was proved in one of the Caufes, and in that Caufe it was not fet forth in the Allegations of the Bill, nor in the Anfwer * in the other Caufe, the agreement was fet forth in the Bill, and not proved in the Caufe. an order was obtained before Publication, that the fame Depofitions fhould be read in both Caufes and by the better opinion this might be but fince the order was before Publication, in the fecond Caufe, the Defendant had * Liberty to crofs examine Witneffes, on * P 65 which particular he pleafed, and the fight of the Depofitions was to his Advantage

" For on the fame principles of Natural Juftice, on Hardr ut fupra, which the Rule at the COMMON LAW, refpecting VER- Atk Rep 445. DICTS in Evidence is founded " a DEPOSITION cannot 3 Atk 415 be given in Evidence againft any perfon that was not Party 2 Bac Abr to the fuit · and the Reafon is, that he had not Liberty to 314 crofs examine the Witneffes, and it is againft natural Juftice that a Man fhould be concluded in a Caufe to which he never was a Party.

(x) Wherever a fuit abates by Death, and the Intereft of the Pleadings in perfon whofe death has caufed the abatement, is tranfmitted the Court of to that reprefentative, the Law gives or afcertains as an heir, at Chanc p 46 an, executor or adminiftrator, fo that the title can not be difputed, at leaft in the Court of Chancery, but the perfon is one to be afcertained, the fuit may be continued by Bill of vivor merely

" And

" And confequently, on the other fide," a Man fhall *never take Advantage* of a depofition that was *not party* to the fuit: for if he cannot be prejudiced by the depofition, he fhall never receive any advantage from it: for this would create the greateft Mifchief that could be: for then a Man that never was party to the Chancery Proceedings, might ufe againft his Adverfary all the Depofitions that made againft him, and he, in his own Advantage, could not ufe the Depofitions that made for him; becaufe the other party not being concerned in the fuit, had not the Liberty to crofs examine, and therefore cannot be encountered with any Depofitions out of the Caufe.

" And" if a Witnefs be examined *de bene effe*, and before the coming in of the Anfwer, the Defendant * not being in Contempt, the Witnefs dies, yet his depofition fhall not be read. becaufe the oppofite party had not the power to crofs examine him and the Rule of the *Common Law* is ftrict to this, that no Evidence fhall be admitted but what is, or might be, under the Examination of both the Parties

" And to this muft be referred the Rule, before noticed, " that" a voluntary Affidavit can not poffibly be admitted as Evidence; unlefs between the Parties

Of Depofitions † as Evidence poft Mortem, v infra.

SECTION VI

SPIRITUAL COURT

" The SPIRITUAL COURT is fo called, becaufe it judges
" of *fecular* Matters on Account of their fuppofed reference
" to things *Spiritual* Of *Marriage*, as being formerly ac-
" counted a *Sacrament* of *Wills*, pro *Salute Animæ*, as
" was called, becaufe the Confcience and *Soul* of the te-
" ceafed was prefumed to be concerned in the difpofal of
" his effects, agreeabl, to the Precepts of *Holy Church* ar
" finalit, they were drawing *all temporal* Caufes within the
" Jurifdiction · becaufe to *difobey a Law*, was a *Sin*, and
" *Sin* was of *ecclefiaftical* Cognizance, becaufe, to perform
" a *Contract*, was a *moral* Duty recognized and confirmed

† But in fuch Cafes as thefe, the Way is to move the Court of Chancery that fuch a Witnefs's Depofitions fhould be read and f the Court fee caufe, they will order it, and fuch Order will bird the parties to affent to the reading of fuch Depofitions —though it doth not bind the Court of *Nifi Prius* —and it ir I ought juft, becaufe the Witneffes are examined by Officers of the Court who are fuppofed to favour neither party

" by *Religion* and wherever *Religion* was concerned, in the
" clearest points of Obligation, or * imagined to be con- * P 6;.
' cerned in Cases most diametrically the reverfe, the *Church*
" never neglected to avail herfelf of that powerful aid to
" enforce her domination. At length the Monftroufnefs
" and intolerable Excefs of the Evil became its Cure.
" The *Crown* found even its juft Authority on the point of
" being annihilated, by thofe whom it had protected and
" advanced as the inftruments of abfolute Sovereignty, the
" *Barons*, with manly Spirit, vindicated the COMMON LAW
" of the LAND, and the rifing Strength of the Common-
" alty matured itfelf for that exertion of its Might, which
" was to break the Yoke of Civil and of religious Defpotifm.
" *Sed in longum tamen ævum manferunt, hodieque manent Veftigia.*
" The Practice of thefe Courts is analogous to that of the
" *Civil* Law."

Of PROCEEDINGS in THE SPIRITUAL COURT.

TIT II

* P 68.

" The Chief Matters now of ufual Cognizance in the 2 Mod 231.
" Spiritual or Ecclefiaftical Court, are" CAUSES MATRI- 2 Str 900, 1.
MONIAL, and CAUSES TESTAMENTARY How thefe Eq Abr 227
Courts gained the Jurifdiction in Caufes *Teftamentary*, which Ch Pre 59
were originally of *temporal* Conuzance, has been already 64 116 212
 10 Mod 42, 3,
tranfiently fuggefted, and beyond this general intimation is 4 74 108, 9.
not here to be confidered, farther than is neceffary to 126 Vern 53
determine the Weight of Credibility to be given to their 413 2 Vern
 471 591 547-
fentences 555 603
 Fitzgib 197
* The way of authenticating *Teftaments* by the *Civil* Law, Lord Raym
was this The *Teftator* and his Witneffes fubfcribed the Will, 734 89, 936
bound it up, and fealed it with their Seals which, after the 68 P W R
 414, 5 6 Mod. ,
Deceafe of the Teftator was opened in the prefence of the 9 Mod 66
Prætor, and he delivered Copies of the Will, and kept 11 Mod 210
the Original in " the" Public Treafury · and hence it is, 12 Gilb Eq R
that the *Spiritual* Court keeps the *Original* will, and gives 2 230 12 Mod
 24 85 136
 215 231 305
 310 319 339
(*i*) The Probate *of Wills* did *originally belong to the temporal* 342 343 375
Courts and every Legatee had a proper Remedy to recover their
Legacies in thofe Courts And Glanville *tells us,* " *there is a writ* Swinburne,
which lies at Common Law to demand a Legacy Linwood, who B VI § 11
was Dean of the Arches, and wrote about the Beginning of the * L.VII 6 7
Reign of H VI *confeffes, that the Probate of Wills did not belong*
to the ordinary de jure, but only by Cuftom And Archbifhop Parker,
publifhed a Book 1573, *wherein he writes,* Teftamenti probandi au-
thoritatem Epifcopi non habebant, nec Adminiftrationis poteftatem cuique delegare potuerunt

 the

394. 414. 494. the PROBATE which is but a Copy of the Will under their
500 521 555   Seals.
565 579 607
Str 95 162   " But this accounts for the Form only for the Cause
308 Barnard.   " or Pretence of entertaining Jurisdiction, it was thus "
K B 243   Originally, among the *Germans*, the Goods, as well as the
2 Str 960.   *Feud* itself, belonged to the Lord: afterwards it was thought
1151 1242   fit hat the Feudary should dispose of them ; and then the
2 R Abr 679   Will was proved in the *County* Courts, before the *Alderman*
Wilf. R. K. B (ealdenmon, *Senior*) and *Bishop*, and if any Man died in-
124, 5 Caf.   testate, they were distributed among his Children but after
Temp. Hard   the Conquest, † the Probate of the Will, and the Commif-
12   fion of Administration was indulged to the *Bishop*, who
Granville   never had it in the times of the Empire, under Pretence,
Sharpe's Con- that Provision would be better made for the Souls of the de
gregational   ceafed · but if they exceeded their Commiffion, they had
Courts 60, &c. plainly no Authority · and therefore they muft confine them-
2 Ed 1786   felves to the Bequeft of the *perfonal* Eftate   * for the *Feud*
                was not *devifable* until the 32 H VIII. for reafons mentioned
≠ P. 69.   in another Place.

Tit III.

On *Will of* Lands, *Probate not Evidence.*

Roll'sAbr 673   Therefore if a Man devife Lands by Force of the Statute
                of Wills, or by Cuftom, the *Probate* of the Will in the
                Spiritual Court can not be given in Evidence for all their
                Proceedings, fo far as they relate to Lands are plainly *coram*
                non Judice, for they have no power to authenticate any fuch
                Devife , and therefore, a Copy produced under their Seals,
                is no Evidence of a true Copy.

R Abr 6-8   But the *Probate* of the Will is good Evidence as to the
                perfonal Eftate: (and *indeed, ordinarily the only Evidence*) and
                they are the Records of that Court , and therefore a Copy
                of them, under the *Seal* of that Court, muft be good Evi
                dence · and this is ftill the more reafonable, becaufe it is the
                Ufe of that Court to preferve the *original* Will, and only to
                give back to the party the *Copy*, under the Seal of the
                Court *& infra, of concurrent Jurifdictions.*

Co I · 180   ; *Conq-eft is taken by our Jurifts in a peculiar Serfe not as for*
                fub,ugation by Arms, but, " quod quis conquifivit *aliter quam juft*
                haereditario fibi obtentam " as we fay Purchafe, *not fimply for buy*
                ing, but for any legal Mode of Acquifition, otherwife than by D
                fcent or Reprefentat on And as obferved by Mr Hargrave, *in h.*
                execller· Notes on Coke's Littleton *the Divifion would be more ac*
                curate into Eftates by Act of Law and Eftates by Act of the Party

                                                                    " D

" But it was held, that" where a Perfon in Ejectment *Polhill and Pol-*
would prove the *Relation* of Father and Son, by his Fa- *hill, Hil 1701.*
ther's Will, he muft have the *Original* Will, and not the
Probate only · for where the Original is in being, the Copy
is no Evidence ; and the Probate is no more than a true
Copy, under the Seal of the Court, * of a private Inftru- * P. 70.
ment , and the Law, which feeks the beft Evidence, will
not allow of a Copy only : befides, this is not proved to be a *Polhill and Pol-*
true Copy. for the Seal doth not prove the *Truth* of the *hill, Hil 1701.*
Copy, unlefs the Suit related to the *perfonal* Eftate only

" Yet though the Probate be *not* Evidence in the in- L N P 246.
" ftance above cited for the Reafon given, it feemeth that"
the *Leiger Book is* Evidence in fuch a Cafe Becaufe *thefe* are
not confidered merely as *Copies* . they are the *Rolls* of the
Court· and though the Law doth not allow thefe Rolls to
prove a *Devife* of *Lands*, yet when the Will is only to prove
a *Relation*, the Rolls of the Spiritual Court, that hath
Authority to enroll *all* Wills, are fufficient Proof: for if
there be fuch a Teftament, as appears by the Rolls of that
Court, the Relation is proved " now" that there is fuch
a Teftament doth not appear by a Copy " of the Court,
" but by the very Roll of the Court, which is an Original "
However, the Copy of the Leiger was not allowed to be
read in this Cafe ; becaufe the Common Practice had prevailed otherwife : " yet the Opinion of my Lord *Holt*, who
" would have admitted it, appears to be the better Opinion ,"
and the Common Practice feems to be founded in a miftake
that the *Leiger Book* is a Copy, whereas the *Leiger Book* is
a *Roll* of the *Prerogative* Court; and fince the Original
would be read * as a Roll of the Court without farther At- * P. 71.
teftation, it feems fit the Copy fhould be read L N P 246.

" And where the Probate is Evidence and conclufive Evi- T Raym 404.
" dence, as of perfonal Eftate it is, where it appears the 6 Lev 235.
" Act of the proper Court having Jurifdiction," the adverfe 2 Keb 337
party may give in Evidence that the Probate was *forged*, 343 641
becaufe fuch Evidence fheweth that the Spiritual Court hath Comyns 150.
given no Judgment " that their fuppofed Act is indeed not Lord Raym
" their Act ." and fo there is no Reafon for the Temporal 261 Str 481.
Court to be concluded , for a forged Probate is none at all P W R 388.

" But that the Will was forged on which the Probate was Noel v Well*,
" granted, you cannot give in Evidence: for upon that, the 2 Sid 359
" proper Jurifdiction has already decided. 1 Str 481

R v Vincent
Lev 235
2 Keb 337.
343 641
Comyns 150
Ld Raym 262
P W R 388.

T I T. IV.

R E G I S T E R.

riu Aff 1702.
Sid 71
Godolph 145
Noy 146
Brownl 20

* P. 72

2 R. Abr 115
pl 11 Cro
Eliz. 4 *
Moor 45*
Salk 28
12 Mod 56
Cacolph 164.

2 Str 1703

THE REGISTER of Marriages, Chriftenings and " Bu-
" rials," is good Evidence, or a Copy of it   The Regifter began in the 30th of H VIII by the Inftigation of
Lord *Cromwell*, who at that time was vefted * with all the
Authority that the Pope's Legates formerly had, under the
Title of Vicar General to the King. and all Wills that were
above the Value of two hundred Pounds were to be proved
in that Court   And therefore, it ferved his purpofe to fet
on foot a Regiftry of all perfons that were chriftened and
buried---and when a Book was appointed by Public Authority,
it muft be a Public Evidence · this was afterwards confirmed
by the Injunction of Edw. VI and the particular manner of
Regiftering appointed   as that the Regiftering fhould be in
the Prefence of the Parfon and Churchwardens on Sunday
and that the Book fhould be kept locked in the Church, to
which the Vicar and Churchwardens are to have Keys.

L. N. P 247.

" Though it appear in Evidence that the Regifter was
" made from a Day-Book, kept by the Minifter for that pur-
" pofe, yet the Day-Book will not be admitted to contradict
" the Evidence in the Regifter. e g —to prove a Child bafe
" born, where no Notice is taken of it in the Regifter, which
" would therefore be Evidence to prove him legitimate "

Sid. 71, 2

An Indictment for entering a falfe Marriage in the Regifter Book † and the Defendant fined 200 Marks   for
fince the Regifter is Public Evidence, it muft be guarded
by the Law, that it be not counterfeited

* P 73

* S E C T I O N VII

ROLLS of COURT BARON

Hill. Aff 1701

The *Court Polls* are Evidence, or Copies thereof, for
they are the public Rolls by which the Inheritance of every
Tenant is preferved   and they are the Rolls of the Manor
Court, which was anciently a Court of Juftice relating to
all Property within the Diftrict

Jones & Per,
Ant. per Tra-
ctr, 705

" But" if *Copyhold Rolls* make mention of a furrender to
the Ufe of the Tenant's laft Will, and then admit *A.* as De
vifee to the Will, this was ruled to be no Evidence of the
feifin or Title of *A* without the Will itfelf   becaufe the

† This was no a Felony without Clergy by the ftatute 26 G 9. II
· 33 § 16

Land doth not pass by the surrender without the Will; and therefore the Will must be shewn as the best Evidence of *A*'s Possession and Title

T I T II

Public Books, Surveys, &c (z)

If the Question be whether a certain Manor be *ancient Demesne* or not, the Trial shall be by *Domesday Book*, which shall be *inspected* by the *Court*. Ancient Demesnes are the Socage Tenures that were in the hands of *Edward* the *Confessor*, and which *William* the Conqueror, in Honour of him, endowed with several Privileges   *Domesday Book* was a *Terrier*, or *Survey* of * the King's Lands, which was made in * the time of the Conqueror, and which ascertains the particular Manors which had this Privilege.

* P 74.

To know whether any thing be done in or out of the *Ports*, there lies in the *Exchequer* a particular survey of the King's *Ports*, which ascertains their extent.

T I T. III.

Ancient Memorials *and Acts of particular* Jurisdictions

An old *Terrier* or *survey* of a Manor, whether *Ecclesiastical* or *Temporal*, may be given in Evidencee, for " sometimes" there can be no other way of ascertaining old Tenures or *Boundaries*

" But a Terrier of Glebe is not Evidence for the Parson, L N. P 248.
" unless signed by the Churchwardens as well as by the
" Parson   nor then, *or at least barely admissible*, if they be
" of his nomination, and though it be signed by them,
" yet it seems to deserve very little Credit, unless it be like-

(z) *The Court of* B R *refused a Rule moved by the Attorney* Blackst Rep
General against the Vice Chancellor of Oxford, *to produce the Sta-* 37, 46 E 22.
tutes of the University, in order to prove a Misdemeanour against C. 11
the Vice-chancellor.

The Evidence of a *neighbouring* Manor shall not in general be admitted to shew the Customs of another Manor, because each is go
verned by its own   But this is not so universal as not to be va-
ried in some instances   for in the *Mine Countries* the Courts of
Law have admitted Evidence with regard to Profits of Mines, &c
out of *other* Manors, where they are similar, to explain the Cus- 2Tr Atk 198,
tom of the Manor in Question   Per *Hardw Ch. v N. of the 4th* P 78
Ed of this Work.

" wife

" wife figned by the fubftantial 'nhabitants: but, in al
" Cafes, t is ftrong Evidence againft the Parfon.

" ROLLS or *ancient* Books in the *Heralds'* Office are Evi-
" dence to prove a *Pedigree,* and fo *Epitaphs,* &c but an
" *Extract* of a Pedigree, proved to be taken out of *Records*
" fhall not · becaufe fuch Extract is not the beft Evidence
L. N P 248 " in the Nature of the Thing, as a Copy of fuch Records
" m ght be had "

* P. 75 * An old *Map* of Lands allowed Evidence.

Yates & Har- " *Camden's Britannia* would not be Evidence to prove a
rs, Hil Aff. " *particular* Cuftom . but a general Hiftory may be given
1702 " in Evidence to prove a Matter relative to the Kingdom
" in general. As in the Cafe of *Neal* and *Jay,* Chronicles
L. N P at fu- " were admitted to prove that King *Philip* did not take the
pra. " *Style* in the *Dead* at that time , Charles V. of *Spain,* not
" having furrendered."

An *Inventory,* taken by a Sheriff on an Execution, is Evidence between ftrangers to prove the Quantity and Value of
the Goods , for the Law, entrufting him with the Execution, muft truft him throughout

The Regifter of the *Navy Office,* with proof of the Me-
Ibid 249 thod there ufed, to return all perfons dead with the Mark
Palm. 427 *Dd,* is fufficient Evidence of a Death

The POPE's *Licence* without the King's, has been held
* P. 76 good Evidence of an Impropriation becaufe * anciently
the Pope was held to have a Difpofition of all fpiritual Be-
nefices with the Concurrence of the Patron, without any
leave from the Prince of the Country; and thefe ancient
Matters muft be admitted according to the Error of the
times in which they were tranfacted

Palm 38. " Yet" a Pope's Bull is no Evidence on a general Prefcription to be difcharged of Tythes. becaufe that fhews that
there was no time or Memory of Things to the contrary,
fo that the Bull itfelf doth contradict fuch Prefcription

L N P 248 But the Pope's Bull vas Evidence on a fpiritual Prefcrip-
31 h VIII tion, when you only fay the lands belorged to fuch a Mo
c 13 § 21 naftery as was difcharged of Tythe at the time of the Diffo-
lution , for then they continue difcharged by Act of Parlia
ment.

* P 77 * PART II.

Of WRITTEN EVIDENCE, *private.*

CHAPTER I

, I DEEDS

We now come, in the fecond Place to that which
is only *private* Evidence between Party and Party : and that
is alfo twofold

I. DEED

1 DEEDS.
2 Matters of inferior Nature

SECTION II.

Of DEEDS.

And here the general Rule is, that when any person *claims* by a *Deed* in the *Pleadings*, there he ought to make a *Profert* of it to the *Court*, and when he would prove any *Fact* in *Issue* by a Deed, " there, he ought to give it in Evidence to " the *Jury* " in both Cases the Deeds themselves must be shewn

A DEED consists of three parts.
  1 Of SEALING by the Parties,
  2 Of Delivery to the Party to whom the Deed is made,
  3. Of a Right transferred, or Obligation created

TIT II

I Of SEALING

The SEAL was very ancient in the *Roman* and *Grecian* Governments and from them it came to the *Northern* * Na- * P. 78. tions, who anciently passed all Manner of Right by the actual Tradition of the Thing itself: the *Seal* followed, from the Invention of Coins, and is a Derivation from the same Convenience for as Coins were invented as Tickets to facilitate the Exchange of all manner of Commodities, so when Coin was wanting, or not ready for payment, Tickets were given by Impression in Wax, and these passed instead of the Coin itself. and these Impressions were made with great Distinction, for they contained the Arms or some notorious Symbol of the Person contracting now when such Distinctions were taken up, and found of use, they were at last required in authenticating of all manner of written Contracts; and from hence the Law grew, that there could be no solemn Contract without the Distinction of the Seal.

(a) But now any impression on the Paper amounts to sealing, if Sheppard's made with that intent And a Deed by a Corporation shall be good, Touchstone though not with their common seal unless where certain Acts (ex- Hilliard's Ed clusively) are limited to the sanction of a certain seal, as the GREAT 55 SEAL, &c And where the seal is torn off, &c Evidence may be L N P. 268 given to a Jury how it happened, &c in Relief of Accidents Unless perhaps where the Issue is directly upon the Deed as on NON EST FACTUM SIGNING now seems necessary as well as sealing (in most cases) since 29 Car II which is the more reasonable as the seals now annexed to Deeds are no longer symbols of the Parties. v. Comm B II Ch. 20.

2. Of DELIVERY.

2 *The Delivery* was always a folemn Sign ufed by the *Northern* Nations in transferring of Right and as they anciently delivered the Thing itfelf, and by that Delivery made the Alienation ; fo when *Contracts* * took the place of Things themfelves that were to be delivered, they annexed the folemnity to the Contract, and the Contract was completed by Delivery · and from thence it became neceffary that a Delivery fhould be made in all Contracts

* P. 79

3 *Right transferred, or Obligation created*

Thirdly, in every Contract there muft be fome Right transferred. and to whom , to fhew what Obligation was created, and to whom; and the fenfe and fignification of the words muft be expounded by Law, fince it is the province of the Law to determine the forms and folemnities and operation of all manner of Contracts: for the operation and effect of a Contract cannot be determined but by the Rules of Law that are appointed as the meafures of transferring Right, and of creating Obligations, and without fuch ftated Rules in every fociety, no man could be certain of any Property, for then the fenfe of the Contract muft be at the Mercy of the Judge or Jury, who might conftrue or refine on it at pleafure.

T I T III

PROFERT of DEEDS

There muft therefore be a PROFERT made of all folemn Contracts in any Action *founded* on fuch Contracts

* Firft, for the fecurity of the fubject, that what Right is transferred, or Obligation created, might be judged according to the Rules of Law

* P. 80

Secondly, becaufe all Allegations in a Court of Juftice muft fet forth the Thing demanded now the Thing demanded cannot be fet forth without the Inftrument fhewn upon which the Demand arifes , for fince the Demand is by the Inftrument, there can be no Demand at all, without fhewing that from which it arifes

RULES *concerning* PROFERT of DEEDS.

Co Litt. 226

Therefore *Parties* to a Deed cannot found any Claim without *fhewing* it to the *Court*.

267

Nor can *Privies in Eftate* take any Advantage of a Deed

10 Rep 92

without fhewing it.

As

As if there be Tenant for Life, Remainder in Fee, and Ibid 93 there be a Releafe to him in Remainder, Tenant for Life cannot take Advantage of it without fhewing the Deed for fince the Right paffed merely *by* the Deed, to fay that any Perfon releafed without + Deed will not be a good Plea

* Profert *of Deeds* Collateral *not neceffary*   * P 81.

" But, on the other hand," when a Man fhews a Title in himfelf, every Thing collateral to that Title fhall be intended, whether it be fhewn or not for though the Law requires an Exactnefs in the Derivation of the Title, yet when that Title is fhewn, the Law will prefume all collateral circumftances in favour of Right. for when lawful Conveyances, which are made with Care and Confideration, do appear, it would create too great Nicety to require an Exactnefs in the fhewing of every collateral Matter, and would tend to the intangling of Right with too many difficulties and therefore by the Benignity of Juftice they fhall be *intended* + befides a Matter collateral to a Title is what doth not enter into the Effence of a Title, but arifes *alrunde* , fo that there muft be a good Derivation of your Right without it

As when a Man declares of a Grant or Feoffment of a Co Litt 310 Manor, the *Attornment* fhall be *interded* for when a Title is Cro. El 401 fhewn to a Manor, Attornment of the Tenant, which is *collateral* to the Title, fhall be " prefumed" till the contrary is fhewn on the other fide

So in *Trefpafs,* the Defendant conveys the Houfe in which, &c by Feoffment from *T S* and juftifies * *Damage* * P 82 *prafint* · the Plaintiff replies, that *T S* before the Feoffment, made a Leafe to *T N* who affigned to him , the De- 6 Co 38
Cro Ja 102 fendant rejoins, that the Leafe was made on Condition that if *T N* affigned over without Licence by Deed from *T S.* that then *T S* fhould re-enter ; the Plaintiff fur-rejoins that *T S did* give Licence by Deed, without any *Profert* of the Deed , and yet his fur-rejoinder was good , becaufe the Plaintiff's Title was by Affignment of the Leafe from *T N* , and confequently the Licence from *T S* is but a Matter *collateral* to the Affignment , and by confequence the Deed muft be intended to be well and legally made, though it be not fhewn to the *Court*

† *De non apparentibus et non exiftentibus eadem eft Ratio.*
‡ *Lex non vult fupervacua neque nimis fubt lia Infinitum in Lege reprobatur*
   Ubi Jus al quod probatur, omnia ex eo legitime confequentia prafimantur
   Stab.tur Præfumptions donec probetur in contrarium.

But.

Where not *truly* COLLATERAL *being neffary* ex provifione Legis

6 Co. 38

But when Matter " is faid to be" collateral to the Title, then there is another Difference to be confidered and that is, where the Deed is neceffary *ex provifione hominis*, and where it is neceffary *ex Inftitutione Legis* for where the Deed is neceffary *ex Inftitutione. Legis*, there you muft fhew it for it is repugnant that the Law fhould require a Deed, and not put you to fhew that Deed when it is made as if you are obliged to fhew the *Attornment* of a *Corporation*, there you muft fhew a *Deed*; in as much as *(b)* corporate Bodies, by the Rule of the Law, cannot act but by corporate Inftru-

*P 83.

ments ; for the Body confifts in * Agreement and Union, by Creation of Law, by Patents and Inftruments under Seal and there is no Act of the aggregate Body but in the fame manner , fo that there can be Attornment without a Deed, and the Law cannot allow the Attornment of fuch a Body without it, therefore no Attornment is fhewn, unlefs a Deed is fhewn alfo . " and in this and fimilar inftances, what " would otherwife have been collateral, becomes indeed a " part of the Title."

But when a Deed is neceffary *ex provifione hominis*, there, when it is collateral, as in the Cafe of the Licence before-mentioned, it needs not " to" be fhewn ✝ for the private Act of the parties fhall not controul the Judgment of the Law, that *interds* all fuch Matters without fhewing.

" And here it is proper to notice one leading and general Difference ; that of *Matter en pais*, and *Matter hors du pais*, of which the former is to the *Jury*, the latter to the *Court*.

Par 3.
Of MATTER.
1 *En Pais*
2 *Hors du Pais*

* P. 84

" Now *Matter en Pais*, and its *contradiftinctive*, are each " of them ancient and comprehenfive Terms in the Law " the former fignifying Acts to which no * *particular legal* " *folemnity* is required, and the latter, Acts of which *the* " *Conftitution and the Allegation* is fpecial the one being con-" fidered as Facts fimply tranfacted without profeffional

(*b*) It is fuppofed that the change, or rather reftitution of corpo-rate for corporeal, as it before ftood, cannot be doubted
See St 4 A c 16 whereby all *Attornments* of Tenants are taken away, N. 4 Ed. They appear now to be no longer of ufe except only to fave a manerial *Fine*
✝ *Res in se privatos acta publico Juri non intercedit.*

" Affiftance,

" Aſſiſtance, and cognizable by the Country from their Sim-
" plicity and public Notoriety, the other as ſolemn Com-
" pacts to be regularly framed by due Advice in the Profeſ-
" ſion, to be pleaded formally according to their Nature, and
" to be decided by the Judgment of the ſages of the Law.

" And hither is to be referred a grand Diviſion immedi-
" ately applicable to that branch of the Law of Evidence
" which is now before us · that is, of *Things* that lie *in Li-*
" *very*, and" Things that lie in *Grant* for Things in Livery
may be pleaded without Deed ; but for a Thing that lies in
Grant, regularly a Deed muſt be ſhewn.

Par 4
Of THINGS.

1. *In Livery*
2. *In Grant*

1ſt *Of Things in Livery* it is to be known, that Livery
was the ancient Conveyance, which was a ſolemn Delivery
of Land in *Sight* of the Inhabitants , and becauſe this was | Bef Right.
done *coram Paribus Curiæ*, and the Tenant ever after *reſted* | Bef reſided.
in the Poſſeſſion, it was reckoned the moſt notorious way
Conveyance . ✳ and ſince this was the ancient *Gothic* way, | ✳ P. 85.
and becauſe they reckoned it of itſelf moſt manifeſt, the ſolemnities of a Deed were not neceſſary

And therefore a Man may plead that *T S enfeoffed* him, | 2.R. Abr 682.
without ſaying *per Indenturam* ; and yet give the Indenture
in Evidence . becauſe the Indenture is not the *Feoffment*, but
the Feoffment is made by the *Livery* , and by that only the
party is inveſted with the *Feud* , and the Indenture is only *Evidence* of ſuch Feoffment

But if a Man plead that *T S* hath enfeoffed him *per Fait*, | Ibid.
( ) whether a Man may give a *parol* Feoffment in Evidence
hath been reaſonably doubted . becauſe he hath bound himſelf up to a Feoffment by *Deed* , and if the Jury have only
Evidence of a *parol* Feoffment, and yet find the Iſſue, the
Deed may be uſed by way of *Eſtoppel* ever after, where in
truth there was no ſuch Deed.

So a *Demiſe* may be made without Deed as well as a Feoff- | 2 R.Abr 682
ment for here the Party reſides in the Poſſeſſion , and therefore the old way of contracting governs this Caſe and
" therefore" a man may plead a Demiſe without Deed, and
give the ✳ Indenture in Evidence : for the Indenture may be | ✳ P. 86.
uſed as Evidence of a Contract that would be good whether

(c) So a Leaſe *not ſtamped permitted to be given in Evidence to* | v alſo Weakly
prove a Demiſe by parol *for ſo many years as the Stat* Car *allows* | ex Dim Yea
for though void to all intents and purpoſes as a Deed, it is good to ma- | v Bucknell,
nifeſt the general Right of the Claimant, as holding under a Demiſe | Cowp 473.
that would have been valid without Writing.

there

there were any Indenture or not · but if the Demife were
laid, *by Indenture*, it feemeth that they could not give a
parol Demife in Evidence.

Of Estoppels

Co Litt. 352 — Livery alfo is an *Eftoppel*, (d) and is by *Coke* an *Eftoppel en Pais* · becaufe it is a Fact a Man cannot impeach or
deny · and this, from the Notoriety of the Ceremony for
when Solemnities are fettled for transferring a legal Poffeffion, they ought to be held as facred by the Law. and therefore a man is concluded from deftroying that of which he
himfelf is the Author, or from impeaching that which is
held as facred in transferring all poffeffions

Fou 225
Litt. § 365. — Therefore if the Defendant pleads the *Livery* and *Seizin*
" from" the Plaintiff, the Plaintiff cannot reply, that the
Livery was conditional, without fhewing the Deed in a.
much as the Plaintiff is *eftopped* to defeat his own Livery, by
a naked Averment and parol Evidence only

✻ P. 87 — ✻ But the Jury are not *eftopped* on the general Iffue from
finding fuch a conditional Feoffment for the Jury are Men
of the Neighbourhood that are fuppofed to be prefent at the
folemnity · and they are fworn *ad Veritatem dicendam*, and
therefore they cannot be eftopped from finding the Truth of
the Matter, and, by confequence, may exhibit the Condition of the Feoffment.

Alteration *by the* Statute *of* Frauds

But fince the ufe of the folemnities before the Men of the
Country hath ceafed, by allowing fecret Liveries only in
Prefence of two Witneffes, therefore the *Statute of Frauds*
29 Car II   *and Perjuries* hath enacted, that no Leafes, Eftates, or In-
2 3 § 1   terefts of Freehold, or for a Term of Years or uncertain In-

---

Co. Litt. §667   (d) Estoppel, or Corclufion, *is where a Man's own Act or*
Comm III   *Acceptance ftoppeth or clofeth up his Mouth, to alledge or plead the*
308.   *Truth and it is either by Matter* EN PAIS, *or* HORS DU PAIS
Sect. 22   *Thus a Man,* Tenant for Years, *having leafed a Fine, is eftopped*
1 & W & M   *from faying, in order to recover fuch Lands, that he had no freehold,*
Co Litt. fupra   *a Man who has expended Money or an immoral Confideration fues to*
                 recover it by indebitatus affumpfit, *he is eftopped from faying the*
                 confideration was immoral for he was knowingly parted with it on fuch
                 confideration upon which he ought to lofe it thus again, where a Man
                 who has accepted Rent he is eftopped from faying the Payer was not his
                 Tenant But Acceptance of Rent, after Notice to quit, doe for oc-
Comp 243   cupation, *fubfequent to the time of the Notice, does not operate as an*
Dec et Dim   *Eftoppel or waivure of* Notice, *though it may of the penalty of doubl-*
Creered   *Rer. given by the* 4 G II
Eaton

terel

tereſt (not being Copyhold) ſhall be aſſigned, granted, or [1 R Abr 24.]
ſurrendered, unleſs it be deed or Note in Writing under the [a Lev. 227.]
hand of the Party, or his Agent, thereunto lawfully authorized in Writing, or by Act and Operation of Law

" Excepting Leaſes not exceeding the Term of three [§ 2.]
" years on a Rent reſerved of not leſs than two-thirds of
" the full value of the demiſed premiſſes "

So that by this Statute the Ceremony of Livery only is
not ſufficient to paſs Eſtates of Freehold, or Terms for
Years " greater than as above ſpecified " but it is not neceſſary to ſet forth ſuch Contract on the Pleadings· for they
are as before, *feoffavit et demiſit*

* A Man may plead a Condition to determine an Eſtate [* P 88.]
for Years without Deed: for this begins without any Livery, [Co Litt 225.]
and therefore the Party is not eſtopped by any notorious [Litt § 365.]
circumſtance from averring the Condition.

But where a Man ſets out a Feoffment, the other Party
may reply, that it was by Deed, and ſhew the Condition,
for then there is an Eſtoppel and ſo the Matter is in equal
Balance, and therefore muſt be determined according to
Truth.

Par 5

Of Things lying in GRANT

Secondly, of THINGS lying in GRANT: and theſe are [Comm B II.]
all Rights, as Fairs, Markets, Advowſons, " Titles" to [Ch 20 P 317]
Lands, where the owner is out of poſſeſſion. and theſe
being Rights, they cannot poſſibly paſs by Inveſtiture of the
Poſſeſſion, becauſe they cannot poſſibly be delivered over nor
" viſibly" poſſeſſed· and therefore they muſt paſs by the
ſecond Sort of " Conveyance," that holds the ſecond place
in ſolemnity· and that is, by *Grant* under the Hand and
Seal of the Party

Par. 6

Of Grant preſumed, or PRESCRIPTION

Now a perſon that claims any Thing by *Grant* muſt ſhew
his Deed from the Party that had the original Grant, or
otherwiſe he muſt preſcribe in the Thing he pretends to, and
the *Preſcription* being ſuppoſed immemorial, ſupplies the
place of a *Grant*

He alſo that has a *particular* Eſtate, by the Agreement of [10 Co 93.]
the Parties, muſt ſhew, not only his own Conveyance, but
the Deeds paramount for there can be " no Title to a Thing [* P 89]
in Agreement but by ſhewing ſuch Agreement, and the
particular Tenant ought to have the power of the Deeds, in

as

as much as he has no Title unlefs he can derive the Eftate that arifes in Agreement up to the firft original Grant.

Par 7.

10 Co. 95, 4.

Of particular Eftates by Act of Law.

But where any perfon claims any " fuch particular" Eftate by an Act of Law, there they may make their Claims without fhewing the Deeds as *Tenant* in *Dower* or by *Elegit* (*e*) or the Guardian in *Chivalry* may claim an Eftate in a Thing lying in Dower, without the Deed · for when the Law creates an Eftate, and yet doth not give the particular Tenant the property of the Deeds, it muft be allowed that the Eftate be defended without them , otherwife the Creation of the Eftate were altogether vain

So they may plead a Condition without fhewing the Deeds becaufe they claim an Eftate by the Act of the Law, and therefore are not eftopped by the Livery · fo that they may claim an Eftate, " defeafible or Condition," without a Deed · alfo they are not fuppofed to have the Deeds and Muniments

* P. 90.

of the * Eftate : and therefore, for the reafon formerly given, may do it without Deed

Co Litt.226 2
10 Co 93. 4.
Dr Leyfield's
Cafe.

But *Tenant* by the *Curtefy* cannot claim an Eftate lying in Grant without Deed " fhewn therefore, if there be a Re- " leafe made to his Wife, or Condition by the Wife, and " re-entry on Condition broken, he ought to produce it, " for he hath the power over fuch Deeds during his Life " he hath the property and Cuftody of them " in Right of " his Eftate · and this" cannot be divefted out of him dur- ing the continuance of his Eftate " and therefore the Law " prefumeth his poffeffion of fuch Deeds and Evidences, and " calleth on him to fhew them in manifeftation of his Title "

" And as" he cannot defeat an Eftate of Freehold with- out fhewing the Deed, fo neither can the Lord by *Efcheat* for the Act of Livery is an Eftoppel that runs with the Land, and bars all perfons to claim it by virtue of any Condition, without the Condition " be apparent" in a Deed for the Solemnity and Notoriety of the Act is that which makes it obligatory to all perfons ; fo that they cannot impeach it without fhewing a precedent Title equally notorious and fince in both Cafes the Cuftody of the Deeds refides with them they muft fhew the Condition

Wood, B 1'.
C 1
Comm II
Ch. 9

(*e*) The Eftate by *Elegit* entitles a Creditor, after Judgment to one half of the profits of the Lands, and all the Goods (*Oxen and Beafts of the Plough excepted*) until the Debt be fatisfied, o his fuing out the *Writ* of *Elegit within a year of the Judgment*

Tn

GENERAL RULE: *Parties or Privies shall shew a Deed, but not* STRANGERS

So that the GENERAL RULE is, that where any person *ought* to have the *Custody* of the Deeds, there when such person is compelled to shew his Title, he ought to make *Profert* of those Deeds to the Court for every man ought to keep his Deeds, and cannot take the Advantage of his own Negligence in losing them

Therefore, in the Case formerly put of Tenant for Life, the Remainder in Fee, and a Release to him in Remainder; Tenant for Life ought to 'make *Profert* of the Deed · for they have both parts of the same Feud, and therefore, Tenant for Life is supposed to be equally entitled to the Deeds as he in Remainder

But where a person is an utter *Stranger* to any Deed, there Co. Litt. 226. In Pleading he is not compelled to shew it. for where he is not Styl Reg 205. supposed in Law to have Custody of the Deeds, there he cannot be compelled in Pleading to shew such Deed to the Court · for that were to compel the Party to *impossibilities*, which were a very unequitable and unjust Law

* As if a Man mortgageth his Land, and the Mortgagee * P. 92. leaseth the Land for Years, reserving a Rent, and then the Condition is performed, the Mortgagor re-enters · the Lessee, in Bar of an Action of Debt, shall plead the Condition and Re-entry without shewing the Deed, for the Lessee was never, nor could be, entitled to the Custody of the Deed, and therefore it would be altogether unjust to compel him to produce it

So if a Man bring a *præcipe* against *A* he shall plead that he was only a Mortgagee, and that the Mortgage was performed, so that he hath no longer seisin of the Estate and this without shewing the Deed for, upon performance of the Condition, the property of the Deed was no longer in the Mortgagee, but it ought to be rebailed to the Mortgagor; and having no longer any Title to the, Deed, he may plead the Condition without shewing it

So in an Action of Waste, or in discharge of the Arrears 10 Co 94. of Rent, the Tenant pleads a Grant of the Lord with Attornment, he cannot shew the Grant, *Causa quâ supra*

In an Action of Debt upon a Bond, it is Matter of Substance to make PROFERT of the Deed: because this is the
Contract

* P 93.
Cro Ja. 32
2 Saund. 402
3 Keb 61

2 Str 1260, 1

* P 94

5 Co 74, 5

Contract on which the Court ought to found * their Judgment, and therefore it ought to be exhibited to the Court
" But where Plaintiff declared as Administrator without
" concluding, *et hic profert Curiæ Litt Administr* it was
" held a defect of Form against which advantage should not
" be taken on a *general* Demurrer."

And where a third Person claims under an Executor or Administrator, there (on the general Principle before stated)
PROFERT is not required

A Deed enrolled must be offered to the Court in pleading,
though the Deed be enrolled in the same Court in which the
Plea is depending. for this is no Record ; but a *Deed* recorded. for a Record must be the Act of the Court: or of " public Authority " and therefore the Decisions of Justice by
the Court that lie as Precedents for future Observation, and
LETTERS PATENT, which are the King's Acts " in his
" executive Capacity, and STATUTES which are the Acts
" of the entire Legislature in behalf of the whole Com-
" munity,' are RECORDS and of" the highest legal Authority : but a Deed enrolled is only the *private* Act of the
Party *authenticated* in Court and from thence this Difference
is drawn, that *Letters Patent*, enrolled in the same Court,
need not be *proffered* to the Court ; * but a Deed enrolled
must for all Records that are public Acts, and that lie for
the Direction of the Court in Matters of Judicature, must be
taken Notice of, and therefore, they need not refer to them
with a *prout patet per Recordam*, for the Court will take Notice
of the Course and Orders of the Court upon reference to
them but Deeds enrolled are no more than the private Act
of the Parties authenticated by the Court and they do not
lie for the Direction of the Court, but take hold of the Authority of it to give them Credit : and therefore, the Court
doth not take notice of them, unless they be *pleaded* " but
" of" the Letters Patent of *another* Court, the Court doth
not take notice, unless they be *offered*, for since they are
none of the Records which are directory to this Court of
Justice, it is not the office of the Court to take notice of them
and therefore it is the Duty of " the Parties who would
" take Advantage of them," to offer them as they do all
other Allegations

Since the TERM, to avoid the entering up of the several
Continuances of Business, is reckoned as *one continued Law
Day*, therefore, Deeds pleaded, shall be in the Custody of
the Law during the whole Term, being the Day wherein they
are pleaded ; and being then before the Court, any Body
may take Advantage of them but since they belong to the
Custody

Cuſtody of the Party, if the Deed be not denied, it ſhall go back to the Party after the Term is over, and then no Body can take advantage of it, without a new PROFERT, for then it is not before the Court

* And therefore, the Plaintiff, in the *King's Bench*, may, * P. 95. in his Replication, take advantage of the Condition of a Deed, becauſe it was " et prædictus A dicit"—as of the *same* Term · but he cannot, in his Replication in the *Common Pleas*, take advantage of a Deed, becauſe there they enter an *(f)* Imparlance to *another* Term

But where the Deed comes in, and is denied, it remains 5 Co 74, 5. in Court for ever becauſe that is the only point in Debate on which the Deciſion of the Court is founded, and therefore, like all other Deciſions, it muſt remain among the Records of the Court. and becauſe it is tied up to this Court, and is impoſſible to be removed, it ſhall be pleaded in another Court without ſhewing

Par 2.

Of Deeds taken away by the contrary Party.

As no party ſhall take Advantage of his own Negligence Co Litt 226. in not keeping his Deeds, which in all Caſes ought *fairly* to be produced to the Court, ſo his Adverſary ſhall not take any Advantage " by" violently detaining of them for the * P. 96. one by a violent taking away * of the Deeds, gives a juſt excuſe to the other for not having them at Command; and no man can ever make advantage of his own Injury and therefore, it is a good Plea for the party to ſay, that the other entered, and took away the Cheſt where the Deeds were

TIT. V

Of giving DEEDS in EVIDENCE to the Jury

SECONDLY, of giving *Deeds* in Evidence to the Jury and here the General Rule is, that where any Thing is to be proved, the *Deed itself* muſt be given in Evidence, and *not* the *Copy* of it and the Deed muſt be regularly proved by *one* Witneſs at leaſt " which latter requiſite belongs to our ſub-

(f) An IMPARLANCE *is a Licence to take time where the ſuit* Comm.III 20 *commences without ſpecial Original, ſo that the Defendant, by his delay of pleading, may not incur a* Diſcontinuance *And the Law preſumeth that he employs this time to* interparle or converſe *amicably with the Plaintiff for accommodation of the Difference In this Senſe ſome have underſtood the Fragment in the twelve Tables,* endo viam TAB I 7 *uſpaiceunt orato, and it is thought alluſion is made to it in the Goſpel* Luc XII 58.
" ſequent

" fequent Divifion; and will be more fully treated under
" the Head of UNWRITTEN TESTIMONY"

Firft, the *Deed* ought to be given in Evidence, and *not*
the *Copy* · for though in *Records* the Copy is admitted in
Evidence, yet the Law will not regularly allow it in *private*
Deeds for they are not within the fame Reafon as *Records*.
for a Record, " as before noticed," is fixed in a certain
place; and therefore the Original cannot be had; and by
confequence the Copy is not the beft Evidence

* P 97.

* But *Deeds* are only *private* Evidence, and not fixed or
confined to a certain place lodged in the Cuftody of the
Party, not of the Law · and therefore, muft be produced
in Evidence. the Law requiring the beft Evidence of which
the Nature of the Thing is capable: and the Deed is much
better Evidence than the Copy of it; for the Rozure and
Interlineation that might vacate the Deed; might appear in
the Deed itfelf and the very offering a Copy, carries a Prefumption as if the Original were defective, and therefore,
the Copy is not to be admitted. Befides, fince the Deeds are
in the Cuftody of the Party, the Deeds themfelves muft be
produced : " for it concerns him to make apparent thofe fe-
" curities of which he would take advantage. and a general
" loofe Allegation of his having" loft' or miflaid them,"
which is his own fault, he can not make any part of his Excufe.

T I T. VI.

But out of this General Rule, " for the Production of
" Deeds," there are fome Exceptions

1 *Deftruction by Accident.*

1ft. And that is, where they *prove* the Deeds themfelves
to be burned with Fire for the Proof of this Matter will
excufe the Deed from being produced to the Jury " but
" where the Deed, is the Ground of the Action, and it is
" therefore neceffary to be pleaded, * it may feem an actual
" Profert is neceffary and indifpenfable " for there is that
Convenience in keeping to known Rules, that they cannot
be broken, though they tend, " accidentally," to the Mifchief of particular perfons § and there can not be a more convenient Rule than that the *Caufe* of every complaint ought to
be fhewed to the *Court*, but the *Jury* muft go according to
the Evidence of the Fact

" And therefore, where Evidence is to be given of, a Deed
to a Jury" to prove the import of the Deed, that it was in

10 Co 52 b
93
Mod 4 9
11; S P b-
Hardw Ch
5 1 b Rep
214.

* P 98

2 S+ 1:55
1158
1 Mod 266.

§ Lex 10 1 , *vult pati privatum inconveniens quam publicum Malur.*
Ubi Res ipfa per fe cenfat, præfumptioni non eft Locus.

fuch

such an House, and that the House was burned, is the best ○ Evidence that can be had of such Deed, and gives reasonable Grounds to the Jury to find it.

2 *Suppreffion by the Party*

2 A *Copy* of a Deed is good Evidence where the Deed is in the Defendant's hands, and he will not produce it ∙ " and " if you cannot shew a Copy in such Case, you may give " inferior Evidence, the best in your power, to prove the " Contents " For when the Original is in the Defendant's hands, the Copy is the best Evidence ∙ for the Presumption that opposes the Copy is, because the Original Deed is, or ought to be, in the party's hands that would produce the Copy, now the Presumption is destroyed, where the Plaintiff * proves the Deed itself to have been in the hands of the * P. 99. Defendant, for then it can not be presumed that there was any better evidence, or that there was any Interlineation that obliged the Plaintiff to cover it, for if the Copy were not perfect and exact, it would be overthrown by the Defendant's producing the Original " The same observation will apply " to any inferior Evidence intimated above, when you can " not even produce a Copy, for no Evidence is slight against " him who suppresses what otherwise would have been " given

" But where you rely on a Paper as the Copy of a Deed, " that" Copy must be proved by a Witness who compared it with the Original for there is no proof of the Truth of the Copy, or that it hath any Relation to the Deed, unless there be some body to prove its comparison with the Original

Where the *Effect* or *Contents (g)* of a Deed are proved, and the Deed is afterwards given in Evidence, and they disagree, there the Deed itself shall control the other Evidence. So it is where the Jury on the special Verdict do collect the Contents, and yet afterwards do find the Deed, *in hæc Verba* ∙ the Court there, is not * to regard the Collection they have * P 100. made of the Substance of the Deed, but the Deed itself, for that Collection derives its Authority from the Deed, and

---

' *(g) In* Civil *Cafes, the Court will force parties to produce Evi-* Burr *dence which may prove against themfelves, or leave the Refufal to* Manef *do it (after proper Notice) as a ftrong Prefumption to the Jury* The M 10 Geo III. *Court will do it, in many Cafes, under particular circumftances by* 2489 *Rule before the Trial, efpecially, if the Party from whom the Pro-* *duction is wanted, applies for a Favour But in a* criminal *or* penal *Caufe, the Defendant is never forced to produce any Evidence, though* *be fhould hold it in his hands, in Court* Not of the form Ed cular

therefore muſt of itſelf fail and come to nothing, when it is oppoſite to the Deed of which it is a Collection.

3 Copy of Antient Deed where Original loſt.

Where the Poſſeſſion hath gone along with the Deed many Years, there a very old Copy of the Deed may be given in Evidence ; with Proof alſo that the Original is loſt and that is according to the Rule of the Civil Law, " if they be cor-
Former Ed
" roborated by Length of Time and judiciary Cognizance," ſi vetuſtate Temporis et judiciariâ Cognitione ſint roboratæ for Poſſeſſion could not be ſuppoſed to have gone along in the ſame manner, unleſs there had been originally ſuch a Deed, and ſo executed as the Copy mentions and the Copy can not be ſuppoſed to be only offered in Evidence to avoid ſight of the Original, ſince it is ſo antient, that the antiquity alone prevents all ſuſpicion of its being counterfeit , and the Antiquity is known from the Antientneſs of the Poſſeſſion

" And of very antient Deeds, the Original may be taken
" to be loſt on ſmall Evidence beyond the natural Probabi-
" lity of the Thing —otherwiſe of a modern Deed "

* P 101

* 4 Inſpeximus

5 Co 54 Sty
445 Keb 117
Salk 280.
4 The Inſpection of a Deed enrolled ſhall be given in Evidence : " for," where the Deed needs Enrollment, there the Enrollment is the ſign of the lawful Execution of ſuch Deed . and the Officer appointed to authenticate ſuch Deeds by Enrollment. is alſo empowered to take care of the fair-
Former Ed legally
neſs " or legibility" of ſuch Deeds and therefore, a Copy of ſuch Enrollment muſt be ſufficient . for when the Law hath appointed them to be made Public Acts, the Copy of them, " as of" all other Public Acts, ſhall be a ſufficient Atteſtation

The Recital of one Deed in another, is no Evidence of the Deed recited , though the Deed containing the Recital be well proved becauſe there ſtill wants an Atteſtation of the firſt Deed · but if the perſon, objecting to the Evidence of the recited Deed, claims under the perſon who executed the Deed, " containing the recital," this is Evidence againſt him of the Reality of the recited Deed· becauſe, he that claims under me, ſtands in my place ; and therefore, what is Evidence againſt me muſt be Evidence againſt him.

Thus, in the Caſe of Fitzgerald and Euſtace Euſtace the Plaintiff, claimed in Equity a Debt on the Defendant's Eſtate, by virtue of a power, reſerved in the Grandfather's Settle-
- P 102.
ment, on the Defendant's Father to charge * the Eſtate for payment of Debts and Younger Children's portions There, Defendant

Defendant objected that there were not proper parties; because the Grandfather had made a Mortgage purfuant to that power to one *Cox* who was not party to the Bill, and did not produce the Original Mortgage, but only an Affignment thereof to *Wybrants*, to which the Grandfather was party: yet the Court allowed it to be Evidence of the original Mortgage; becaufe the party claimed under the Grandfather, who was party to the Affignment

But where a Deed needs no Enrollment, there, though it be enrolled, the *Infpeximus* of fuch Enrollment is no Evidence becaufe, fince the Officer hath no Authority to enroll them, fuch Enrollment cannot make them Public Acts; and confequently can not entitle the Copy of them to be given in Evidence " for" fuch practices " might" be improved to very ill purpofes, " fince" then, if the Deed were doubtful, it were but to enroll it, and bring the Copy or Infpection of it in Evidence, and thereby avoid giving in Evidence a Deed that was in any way fufpicious

Infpeximus of antient Deed

But the *Infpeximus* on an antient Deed, may be given in Evidence, though the Deeds need no Enrollment: for an antient Deed may be eafily fuppofed to be worn out, or loft, and the offering " of" the *infpeximus* in Evidence, induces no fufpicion that the Deed is doubtful for it hath a Sanction from Antiquity, and if it had been ill executed, it muft be fuppofed to be detected when it was newly made.

* Tit. VII. *Affeftation* * P. 103.

As to the *fecond* part of the Rule, *the Deed muft be proved to the Jury by one Witnefs at leaft* for though the Deed be produced under Hand and Seal, and the hand of the party that executes the Deed be proved, yet this is no full proof of the Deed' for the *Delivery* is neceffary to the Effence of the Deed, and the Deed takes effect from the Delivery, fo that unlefs the Delivery be proved, there is no perfect Proof of the Deed, and there is no proof of the delivery but by a Witnefs who faw the Delivery.

Exceptions

But to this Rule there are feveral Exceptions

Deed a certain Number of Years old.

First, if a Deed be *forty* Years old, that Deed may be given in Evidence without any Proof of the Execution of it ·

for

for the Witnefs cannot be fuppofed to live above forty Years: and forty years is proof fufficient of a Prefcription for the Age of Man is no more than Sixty-Years, and a Man is fuppofed to be *(h) twenty* Years before he is of Age fufficient to underftand

(h) Thirty is the Rule now *eftablifhed and more agreeable to the expectation of the continuance of living teftimony*

At twelve, a perfon fhall be fworn in the County Court at fourteen, a male, and at twelve, a female is held capable of contracting Marriage and at the fame Age either may appoint Executors at eighteen, a man fhall be liable to ferve in the Militia ; at twenty-one perfons fhall have the difpofal of their real property at the fame age, by Statute, they fhall be permitted to marry without confent of Parents, Guardians, &c. at the fame Age a man may fit in Parliament but by a very brief Act of the Legiflature, none of the Defcendants of George the Second, *except the Iffue of Princeffes married into foreign Families, fhall be permitted to contract marriage without confent of the King, declared in Council entered in the Council Books, and fignified under the Great Seal with an Exception (of a very fingular Fabric) refpecting fuch Defcendants above the Age of* twenty-five. *And for the fole nmixing, or affifting at, fuch Marriage or matrimonial Contract, the Pains and Penalties of a Premunire are provided and fuch Marriage is pronounced* null and void to all intents and purpofes *fo that inftead of ite* Cæfaribus virtus advenit ante diem, *the Defcendants of this Friend to Liberty and to focial Happinefs, are to be four years later than all the other inhabitants of the Ifland before they are in* Parliamentary Judgment *capable of forming this firft and moft important of natural Contracts, by their own uninterdicted Choice and even then, this poffibility is fo checked and counterchecked, and finally liable to be negatived by an Addrefs of the two Houfes, as to be hardly a difference in their favour .* perpetual Celibacy, *in obedience to a fingle Mandate, would have been more confiftently enjoined in Terms than a nominal indulgence given of fo extraordinary a kind, on errorious the moft repugnant to manly Dignity, to feminine Delicacy, and to the Voice of Nature I know this Note is of a different kind from fuch as ufually have place in works of this fort but if it be poffible that an Attempt fhould be made to put this Act in Execution (and to objects, fhould they be only the male Defcendants, might amount, within a Century, to hundreds or even thoufands) a new fpecies of Evidence refpecting the Validity of Marriage, would emerge, each perhaps in its conftruction, but far otherwife in its Refult and in contefting the Validity of the Contract a difficulty might arife to which it can never be expedient that a legiflative Affembly fhould give caufe That* LAW †is a JUST SANCTION, *prefcribing* RIGHT *and forbidding* WRONG, *conveys to the Mind of the* COMMUNITY *an auguft Idea . but if any ordinance be paffed to which a contrary Defcription fhall apply, the folemnity of Form may be found inadequate to its fupport*

If

† Lex eft fanctio jufta, jubens honefta et prohibens contraria

Comm I e
15 il c 32
P 497

12 G II
c. 11 1772

underſtand the General Forms of contracting . ſo that after forty years, the Witneſs muſt be ſuppoſed to be dead and therefore, ſince no perſon living can be ſuppoſed to be co-eval with ſuch Deeds, they may be offered in Evidence without Proof.

* *Failure of Poſſeſſion*   * P 104.

But although the Deed be " of the Age mentioned," yet if Poſſeſſion hath not gone along with the Deed, they ought to give ſome account of the Deed becauſe the Preſumption fails where there is no Poſſeſſion , for it is no more than old Parchment, if they give no Account of its Execution

Aſſ 1702 per Haſſel.

2 *Raſure, or Interlineation*

" And" if there be any blemiſh in the Deed by Raſure or Interlineation, then it ought to be proved, though it be " of " the Age which otherwiſe would prove itſelf." if the Wit-neſſes be living, then they ought to prove it by the Witneſſes ; if dead, they ought to prove the hands of the Witneſſes " and of the party ." for " though" there muſt be (as is ſaid) a Preſumption in favour of the Deed when " it is beyond " the Period of probable Duration of living Teſtimony," yet that is encountered by another Preſumption from the Blemiſh-es of the Deed itſelf , and therefore, the Credit of the Deed ought to be reſtored by Proof of the Execution of it

3 *Fraud apparent*

So if the Deed imports Fraud , as where a Man conveys a Reverſion to one, and after conveys it to another, and the ſecond Purchaſer proves his Title , there the firſt Deed muſt be proved, " though of the * Age of preſumed authenticity " for the Preſumption of the Antiquity of the Deed is deſtroyed

Chattel and Pound, Hil Aſſ 1701 in Kent

* P. 105

If the Age of Man be computed by the number of years in which a Moiety remains of perſons born within a given Period, it might prob-ably be eſtimated at between thirty-one and thirty-two, according to a Table deduced by Dr PRICE *from Obſervations on the Bills of Mortality in* NORTHAMPTON *, by which it appears that leſs than half of a large given number ſurvive at thirty-two but at any Age between twenty-ſix and forty, though the probability of any one Witneſs being alive at the end of thirty years from the Atteſtation be againſt the event, the probability of one out of two living is for it.* MONTAIGNE *ſays, with his uſual ſtrength and vivacity* C'eſt un vice des loix meſmes, d'avoit cette fauce imagination elles ne veulent pas qu'un homme ſoit capable du maniement de ſes biens qu'il n'ait vingt & cinque ans, & à peine conſervera il juſque lors le maniement de ſa vie.

Eſſai I Ch 57

by

by an oppofite Prefumption 'for no man fhall be fuppofed to be guilty of fo a manifeft a Fraud. and therefore here alfo the Credit of the firft Deed muft be reftored by proving the Execution of it.

Tit. VIII

Where Livery *to be proved*

Roll Rep 192, 227
Cro Ja.

If a Deed of Feoffment be proved, and Poffeffion has gone along with the Deed, there Livery fhall be prefumed, though it be not proved: for when there has been Poffeffion in the manner that the Deed fets forth, it founds a very ftrong Prefumption that Poffeffion was " fo delivered ," for that there fhould be a Contract to transfer Poffeffion, and that Poffeffion fhould go according to that Contract, are fuch concurring circumftances as cannot be accounted for, unlefs the Poffeffion was transferred according to the Contract · and confequently, the Livery and feifin muft be fuppofed by the Jury

Pl. Comm.6,7

But if Poffeffion hath not gone along with the Deed, then the Livery upon the Feoffment muft be proved for fince the Livery is to give Poffeffion on the Deed, * where no Poffeffion is, the Prefumption is that there was no Livery · and confequently the Livery muft be proved to encounter that Prefumption.

* P 106.

Roll Rep 132.

But if the Jury find the Deed of Feoffment, and that Poffeffion hath gone along with the Deed, yet the Judges, upon fuch Finding, cannot adjudge it a good conveyance for the Jury are Judges of the Fact, and what is probable, and what improbable; the Court is only Judge of what is Law, and have nothing to do with any Probabilities of Fact therefore it is the Jury only that are to make the Conclufions and Deductions as to the Truth of the Fact; the Court cannot, if they are not drawn by neceffary confequence out of the Words of the Verdict for to the Court the Rule is, *De non apparentibus et non exiftent.bus eadem eft Ratio*. therefore they cannot conclude that there was a lawful conveyance, unlefs the Jury find the Delivery of the Deed

A Deed of Feoffment may be given in Evidence as a Releafe: for where the party is in poffeffion already, the Deed only will be a fufficient Contract to transfer a Right

Secondly, a Deed may be given in Evidence, on a Rule of Court, without proving fuch Deed

* P 107

2 Std. 269

* A Deed may be given in Evidence, " or taken as if " given in Evidence," on a Rule of Court, without proving fuch Deed: " as where the Rule is in Ejectment to con- " fefs Leafe, Entry, and Oufter." for the Confent of Parties

ties concerned muſt be ſufficient and concluding Evidence of the Truth of ſuch Faƈt.

Tit IX

Of the Effeƈt of Raſure, Interlineation, Breaking of Seals, &c.

We come now to give an Account where the Raſure and Interlineation, and where the breaking of the ſeal avoids the Deed.

As to Raſure, Interlineation, and Addition—

Formerly, if there were any Raſure or Interlineation the Judges determined, upon the *Profert* of the Deed and View of it, whether the Deed was good or not for the very Contrivance of ſolemn Contraƈts, ſuch as Deeds are, was founded on this, that the intent of the Parties is there manifeſtly ſettled in expreſs words, and notoriouſly authenticated: and there ſuch Contraƈts are totally referred to the Court, if the Truth of the ſolemnities, viz of the Seal and of the Delivery, be admitted , and therefore muſt be diſſolved by * a Contraƈt of equal ſolemnity · becauſe how they are to be deſtroyed and avoided muſt appear to the ſame Judges who are by law to determine of them " And thus" it came to paſs that if a Deed was raſed or interlined, they adjudged it a void Deed, becauſe it did not certainly appear to the Court that were the Judges of theſe ſolemn contraƈts, whether the mind of the party was contained in ſuch a mangled Contraƈt or not.

But as the Manner of conveyancing ſwelled from ſhort little Deeds to large and voluminous ones, ſo vaſt room was left to the Miſpriſions of the Clerks, that muſt be altered and amended, or with greater Labour and Expence of Time written over again · from thence the Court thought it neceſſary not to diſcharge the Deeds raſed or interlined, as void, upon the (1) Demurrer , but they referred to the Jury, upon the Iſſue of *Non eſt Faƈtum*, whether the Deed, thus raſed

10 Co 92.

* P 108.

Ibid

(1) To demur is to join iſſue in Law, by admitting the Faƈts as pleaded, and inſiſting that the charge is inſufficient, or the juſtification invalid, and thereon praying the Judgment of the Court There may too in civil caſes, though it very rarely happens, be, after Iſſue of Faƈt joined and Evidence given, a Demurrer to the Evidence: a d the party who huzards this, admits the whole Evidence of Faƈt againſt him as offered to the Jury, but denies the legal conſequences · if this happen, it withdraws the Matter from the cognizance of the Jury, and refers it to the Court, whence the Record iſſued, upon which the Cauſe went down to Trial.

V. Comm II c 21 Comm III. c 23. P 372.

and

and interlined, was the original Contract delivered by the Parties.

11 Co 27
2 Str. 1160

If a Deed (" as Bond, for inftance,") be altered by a ftranger without the Confent of the Obligee, in a point not material, this does not avoid the Deed, otherwife it is, if it be altered by a ftranger in a point material, for the Witneffes cannot prove it to be the * Act of the Party that fealed and

* P. 109.

delivered it, when there is any material difference from the fenfe of the Contract: but if the Contract doth contain the fenfe of the Parties, the Witneffes may well fwear it to be their Act, for an immaterial Alteration doth not change the Deed, and confequently the Witneffes may atteft that very Deed, without danger of Perjury

11 Co 27

But if the Deed be altered by the Party himfelf, though in a point not material, yet it will avoid the Deed for when the Party himfelf makes any Alteration in his own Deed, it difchargeth the Contract: (k) for the Contract had its whole Form from the Words of the Obligor, now when the Obligor undertakes to fupply it with new words, and to alter thofe the Party hath fixed upon, this is, according to the Rules of Law, which takes every man's Act moft ftrongly againft himfelf, a new Making and a new Framing of the Contract " by one Party without concurrence of the other " and for a Man to contract with himfelf is utterly void and ineffectual (k)

Another Reafon of this Interpretation of Law might be, " or at leaft a beneficial effect naturally refulting from it," to add a fanction to Deeds that Perfons + who had them in

* P 110.

their Cuftody might not alter them, for fear of deftroying their fecurities

11 Co 286

If there be feveral Covenants in the Deed, and one of them be altered, this deftroys the whole Deed for the Deed is but a Complication of all the Covenants, fo that the Deed, which is the whole, cannot be the fame, unlefs every Covenant of which it confifts be the fame alfo

2 R. Abr 29

All Interefts that pafs without Deeds would pafs though the Deed were afterwards interlined or altered (l) " for

(k) So where *Aumerle* had hid in his Bofom the engagement of confpiracy againft *Henry*, our Poet, who ranged civil Life for topics and characters, as well as vifible Nature and the World of Paffions for Defcription and Intereft, replies to a fuggeftion of the Mother of the Youth, that it might be a Bond for fupplying his expences againft the approaching Pageant,

————————bound to himfelf ?

Capell's Shakefpeare, 5 R II A v 5 I

What doth he with a Bond that he is bound to ?

(l) As to the Queftion of Alteration, many which were Mifdemeanours at Common Law are now capital FELONIES under the Statut Law relating Forgery, of which this intimation may fuffice at prefent

the

the Interest once vested did not thereby return back again, since the Deed is not absolutely necessary to the passing of the Interest, but is only *Evidence* that it was passed. but by the Statute it is in many of those Cases necessary to shew a Writing under the hand of the Parties " And where a " Demise under such Writing is necessary to support the " Claim, there the party claiming by the Deed must make " good his Claim by the very unaltered and perfect Deed on " which the Contract was founded; otherwise where such " Writing is used, not as a formal Instrument under which " Title is made, but as mere general proof of an Agree- " ment "

If there be Blanks left in an Obligation in places material, and filled up afterward by the Assent of the * Parties, yet the Obligation is void but if there is a Blank left in the Obliga- tion, and filled up afterward with something immaterial, this doth not avoid the Contract for where there is a material part of the Contract added after the sealing and Delivery, it is not the same Contract that was sealed and delivered; as if a Bond was made to *C* with a Blank left for Christian Names and Additions, which is afterward filled up by Assent of the Parties, yet this is a void Bond, but if any imma- terial part of the Contract be added after sealing and Deli- very, as if *A* with a Blank left after his Name, be bound to *B* and after *C* is added as a joint Obligor, this does not avoid the Bond, because this does not alter the Contract of *A* for he was bound to pay the whole Money without such Addition

Roll's Rep 39.
40
2 R Abr 29.
∗ P. 111.

Ventr 185.

2 Lev 35
2 Keb 372,
88,
Moor, 547,
619 Cro.
Eliz 627.

SEAL *broken off, &c.*

Where a Thing lies in *Livery*, a Deed formerly sealed may be given in Evidence, though the *Seal* be afterward torn off for the Interest passed by the Act of the Livery that invests the Party with the Possession, and the Deed is only an Evidence of transferring Possession. for by the Act of Livery the Possession passes; and the Deed without the seal, the Livery being indorsed, * is an Evidence of such Pos- session so if the Conveyance was made by Lease and Re- lease, the *Uses* were once executed by the Statute, and they do not return back again by cancelling the Deed

But if a Man shews a Title to a Thing lying in *Grant*, there he fails, if the Seal be torn off from his Deed: for a Man cannot shew a Title to a Thing lying in solemn Agree- ment but by solemn Agreement, and there can be no solemn Agreement " of this kind" without a seal so that " here" Possession alone is no good Title, since the Thing itself doth

not

Palm 403,
Mod 11
Ventr 14.
2 Keb 556.
2 Lev. 220.
2 Show 28.

∗ P. 112.

3 Bulf 79.
R R 188

not lie in Poffeffion but in Agreement: therefore a Man cannot claim a Title to a Water-courfe but by Deed and under Seal

2 Bulftr 246
2 R Abr.
28—30.

" For generally," where a Contract creates an Obligation, it cannot be pleaded if the Seal be taken off: for the feal is " an" effential part of the Deed· and without a feal it is no longer a deed, nor to be pleaded and given in Evidence as a Deed; unlefs in the Cafe above mentioned, where

* P. 113.

the intereft vefts though the Deed hath * no Continuance but where the Deed is neceffary to be fhewn, in order to acquire the Intereft, there it muft have the Effentials of a Deed

Ow 3
Co Fitz 120
5 Co 119, b
2 Bulf. 247.
Dy 59, pl. 12 3
Co Lit 283 a.
Doct Pl. 262
R R 29, 40.
2 R. Abr 29

2 Inf 675.

If an Obligation were fealed when pleaded, and after Iffue joined, the feal was torn off, yet fhall the plaintiff recover· becaufe the Deed proferred to the Court was in the Cuftody of the Law, and therefore the Law ought to defend it befides, the Truth of the Plea which is to be proved muft have relation to the time when Iffue was taken, and at the time of the Iffue it had the Effentials of a good Deed and therefore that is fufficient to maintain the Iffue

Alfo if the feal of a Deed be broken off in Court, it fhall be there enrolled for the benefit of the Parties becaufe where any thing is impaired under the Cuftody of the Law,† it fhall be reftored by the Benignity of the Law, as far as poffible.

1 oy 112.
2 R R 30, 40
5 Co 23. 1
Cro Eliz 546.
176
11 Co 28 b.

If there be a joint Contract or Obligation, and one of the Obligor's feals be broken off, it deftroys the Obligation becaufe they are both bound as one perfon, and if one be difcharged, the other cannot ftand obliged, becaufe they both make up but one Obligor

5 Co 23 1.
Cro Liz 546
R R p 4, 149
Cro Eliz 408,
546, 576
* P 114.
11 Co 28 b.
Lect, plac
260 261 3.
Mar 125
2 Saou 29.

But if two Perfons be bound feverally, there, if the feal of one of the Obligors be broken off, yet the Obligation continues in the other· becaufe there are * feveral Contractors and feveral Contracts; and therefore by deftroying the Obligation of one of them, the Obligation of the other is not taken away.

But if two Men are bound jointly and feverally, and the feal of one of them is torn off by the Obligee, this is a difcharge of the other for the manner of the Obligation is difcharged by the Act of the Obligee and therefore that (according to the rule of the Law, that conftrues every man's own Act moft ftrongly againft himfelf) a Difcharge of the Obligation itfelf· befides, fince both are jointly bound as one perfon, difcharging one of them is a difcharge of the whole, and a fatisfaction is fuppofed to be given for

† *Lex vult ut neminem fibi crediti pœniteat.*

the whole Debt: and when one man is difcharged, that concurs to make an Obligor, and the whole Debt is fatisfied, no Obligation can reft upon the other,

Of WILLS.

SECTION III.

" The *laft* Conveyance to which the Law annexes parti-
" cular folemnities is now to be inveftigated, with refpect to
" the Evidence that applies to it, and this is a WILL:
" which is firft to be confidered in itfelf; and after in its
" incidents of REVOCATION and of REPUBLICATION.

* TIT II.   ** P. 115.*

†WILL *defined*

" A WILL *is the laft legal Declaration of that which a Man*
" *will'eth to be done refpecting his Property after his Deceafe (m)*
                                          " WILLS

(m) Teftamentum eft Voluntatis noftræ jufta Sententia : de eo
quod quis mortem fuam fieri vult

The celebrated Statute of Weftminfter, 3 Quia Emptores Terrarum, *foon enabled the Clergy to fuggeft the expedient of devifing an Ufe under a precedent Feoffment. Succeffive Statutes were applied to obviate thefe Ufes fo far as they effected Alterations in Mortmain, of Land, or Profits, to the benefit of the Church But the Invention enabled individuals in fome degree to extend their pofthumous favour to their relations or friends. The ufe was a matter of confcience, of which the Ecclefiaftics prefiding in Chancery enforced the performance But when the great Statute for transferring the poffeffion executed the Ufe to the Land, it became, in contemplation of Law, the Land itfelf, and confequently, about five years after, it was found neceffary to enable Devifes of Land by Will*

In proving a Will according to the Statute of Frauds and Perjuries, if one Witnefs prove his own Atteftation, and that the other Witneffes were there prefent, and did atteft it, this is proof fufficient of fuch Will, without having all the Witneffes there to prove it for then it is proved by a Witnefs that the Will was executed according to the Method required by the Statute, unlefs they fhew fuch characters of Fraud as would make it neceffary to produce the reft —GILB It feems, however, that without fuggefting Fraud, the party by whom the Will is contefted is entitled to demand that the three Witneffes be feverally examined in Court upon the Trial, for each is the beft Evidence as to the Fact of his own Atteftation, and probably the remark refpecting the proof of the fubfcribing by the Evidence of one Witnefs only, which is inferted where it breaks the continuity of the Work, is not from G.lbert.

‖ Conditionem

D 28
18 Ed I 1290.
Swinb I p 48,
Comm II
c 18
Ma Charta,
c 36
9 H III 1225.
7 E I 13 E I.
before the Statute *Quia Emptores,* went againft *purchafa leafe* and reco-very 15 R II againft Ufes a full Century after the ftat. 23 H VIII againft Grants to lay hands and charges of heirs to fuperftitious Ufes And 9 Geo II limits the time and circum-ftances of Gifts *to charitable Ufes Anno* 1736 Such is the progrefs of legiflative precaution in a courfe of more than 500 years.

Wnght's Te-
nure s, 17², 3
Wyndham &
Chetwynd
4Burr 419,20
32 H VIII.
c. 1
34. H. VIII
c 5
[D 28 1 L
22 p 1

T C L 6 23. 1

*Wyndham and
Chetwynd,
Pl. 100.*

1 L II 10
§ 10

" WILLS were by Common Law before the Conquest,
" afterwards they were reſtricted to particular places, and
" about the time of the Reformation again revived by Sta-
" tute.

" A will

|| Conditionem teſtium tunc inſpicere debemus cum ſignarent;
non mortis tempore fi igitur tunc cum ſignarent tales fuerint ut
adhiberi poſſint, nihil nocet fi quid poſtea eis contingerit

† Teſtes, ſervi an liberi fuerint, non in hac cauſa tractari oportet
cum eo tempore quo teſtamentum ſignabatur, omnium conſenſu
liberorum loco habiti ſint, nec quiſquam eis uſque adhuc ſtatus
.controverſiam moverit.

The Statute 29 Car. II. was not meant to check the teſtamen
tary power over property, but only to guard againſt Fraud   In
Theory it ſeemed a ſtrong guard, in Practice it may be ſome
guard   But I believe more fair Wills have been deſtroyed for
want of obſerving its reſtrictions than fraudulent wills obſtructed
by its Caution   In all my experience at the Court of Dele
gates, I never knew a fraudulent Will, but what was legally at
teſted; and I have heard the ſame from many learned Civilians.
Courts of Juſtice ought therefore to lean rather againſt than in
ſupport of any too rigid Formalities   Lord *Manſfield, I muſt
here be permitted to notice a ſeeming inadvertence,* Animi ad majora
properantis, *where his Lordſhip reaſons generally on the Admiſſibility
of Witneſſes under the Roman Law, even where directly intereſted,
and adduces a Paſſage in the* Miloniana, *where* Cicero *and* Clodius
were the hæredes Ecti, *under the Will of* Cyrus *the Architect, and
the Argument infers they were alſo Witneſſes to the Will, — from theſe
words* Una fui. teſtamentum ſimul obſignavi cum Clodio,
teſtamentum autem palam fecerat, et illum hæredem et me
ſcripſerat. *But* Obſignare *is not the Act of the Witneſſes, as
ſimply* Signare; *it is the Act of the Heir, or of the Teſtator, or of
ſome Confidential Friend under his direction, ſealing up a cloſed
Will to prevent its being altered   And ſo* Paulus, *of the* Subſtitutio
pupillaris—in extrema pagina fieri debuit ut pars illa quam
diu Pupillus annos pubertatis egrediatur obſignata maneat, et
pars prior referetur

V. N. in Sueton 1691. p 100 *the Will ſeems to have been
ſealed, as the Book is repreſented in the* Apocalyptic Viſion, *where
the opening of each Seal is conſidered as ſucceſſively revealing the
Events, ſealed or latent in that Book of Fate , the* חעלבמה, *abſcon

dita or obſignata of the prophetic Series   And this obſignatio was
entirely different, as I apprehend, from the atteſting Signature of
the Teſtament, both in the Mode and intent , and perhaps generally
in the perſons by whom it was performed, the one being of Atteſta
tion ſimply, the other of* Cuſtody   *And, though, by the old Law,
the Real Heir or Deviſee general, might be a Witneſs, yet he was
exhorted not to abuſe this privilege of which, indeed, the Uſe could
hardly ever have been conſidered as very decorous.* Cicero, *we may
juſtly preſume, would not have uſed it   and from an Anecdote, reſpecting* Hortenſius *and* Craſſus *preſerved in the Offices, we have
reaſon to ſuppoſe, that perſons largely benefited, and particularly
general*

" A will may be either *real*, simply of Lands alone ; or
" *personal*, of such property alone as is included in the
" Personalty , or *mixed*, which conveys both species of In-
" terest ;

*general Devisees, were not usually called to witness a Will 'The
Anecdote gives one pain, particularly for Hortensius, so distinguished
by his Talents and by his Merit . but what was indeed very unbe-
coming, circumstanced as the Case was, had been flagitious, had
they been Witnesses, or their Names annexed as such in that instance.*
De Officiis,
III 18
L VII 7 § 2,
et 8 § 8, 9
See too, Valerius Maximus, *in the places to which the Margin refers
Had* Cicero *been a Witness, the words had been,* subscripsi , *or* sub-
scripsi et signavi *but not* obsignavi, *of this it seems one may be*
*very nearly certain The Translation of this passage, in the Select
Orations, published in 1741, is right*
Roßni Antiq.
VI 2

*It is curious, and not foreign to our Subject, to observe the succes-
sive Changes in the Solemnities of a* Roman *Testament first, in Peace
it was in the* Comitia calata *which were when the* Præco, *twice
in the Year, summoned the Citizens of* Rome *to hold an Assembly
for the purpose of giving Sanction, by their presence, to such Wills
as should be made before them, or, in* procinctu, *which was an
informal military Testament, indulged in time of War, to those who
were hazarding their Lives for the Republic and the first of these
assembles our Feoffments anciently, in the presence of the* Pares
Curiæ *Afterwards, a fictitious Bargain and Sale ; and it opera-
ted as a Surrender to Uses at the time declared, to vest in possession
after the Death of the Testator It was thus five Witnesses, Citizens of* Rome, *attended, the* Libripens, *or balance holder, who
either was or represented the Testator, and the* Emptor Familiæ,
or Purchaser these were the Actores Fabulæ Solemnis *The*
Emptor Familiæ, *who was in the Nature of an Executor, said,
I claim the Family (including in that Term, all the rights, real and
personal of the Testator, which can fall into Representation) , I
claim the Family of this Person, which I have purchased according
to the antient Law of Rome, with this Coin and balance. He
then struck the Balance with a piece of Copper Coin and this*
Ros Antiq.
VIII 6
emancipatio, *or Surrender to Uses, being performed in Virtue of the
supposed purchase, then followed the* Nuncupatio Testamenti, *or
Declaration of Uses according to the Will and then the Will was
produced in the presence of the five Witnesses And hence it was, that
the number of seven became requisite to authenticate a Will when
the* Tabulæ Testamenti *thus stated, came in the place of this fictitious and circuitous conveyance, which however was singular and
ingenious, and perhaps gave the hint to our common Recovery, and
the earlier invention of Fines as well as the more modern* Bargain
and Sale, *which for want of notoriety, is by Statute required to
be enrolled, and* Lease *and* Release, *by which first a Chattel Interest passes from the Tenant of the freehold to the Bargainor, and
then the Statute immediately annexes and vests the Possession to the
Use and he thus becoming Tenant in possession to Uses, the Release
completes the power by conveying an Interest of freehold to the possession, adequate to the purposes for which the Trust is created and
this without enrollment . for Chattel Interests were not held of sufficient*
Comm II 20
P 338, 9

" tereft; and, according to the Denomination of the higher
" Genus of Eftate, is liable to the Rules of a Will fimply
" real. A *perfonal* is either,

    1 *Formal*,
    2 *Nuncupative*.

" Firft, and chiefly, we are to treat of a *Will of Lands*

TIT. III.

Of a WILL of LANDS.

" In a Will are to be regarded,

    1 *The Act and Perfon of the Teftator*,
    2 *The Number and Competency of the Witneffes*,
    3. *The Intereft to be conveyed.*

1. The ACT and PERSON of the TESTATOR.

" All perfons may make a Will of Lands who are not
" incapacitated by fuch impediments as apply alfo to con-
" veyances *inter vivos* · 1 Want of difpofing *Mind*, as
" Infants, Ideots, infane perfons; 2. Want of difpofing
" *Power :*

    1 *By Crime; as Outlaws, attaint perfons, &c.*
    2. *By Birth; as Aliens.*
    3 *By Condition, as Femme Couverte.*

*P 116   * Par 2.

1. ACT of the TESTATOR

" The ACT of the TESTATOR is now to be obferved
" 1 And firft, it is neceffary that there be a SIGNING;
" but if the Will be in the *Hand-writing* of the Teftator,
" with his Name at the beginning of it, this is Evidence
" of a fufficient figning And farther, on account of cor-
" poral infirmity, the figning may be by the hand of an-
29 Car II. c. " other, in the prefence of the Teftator, and by his exprefs
3 9 5   " Directions

*ficient confideration to be fo protected by the Statute, or to be within
the danger againft which the notoriety of enrolment was provided
row this laft conveyance, originating in fo low a Chattel intereft as
a Leafe for a Year, converts itfelf by the fubfequent Releafe, into an
inftrument of equal efficacy with the bargain and fale · an Eftate
of equal Extent thus accompanying the legal poffeffion · and at the fame
time, the original imbecility of the Eftate was allowed to exempt it
from the purview of the Statute*

                                    " 2. Next

" 2 Next, either the *figning* muſt be in the *Preſence* of
" the *Witneſſes*, or the Teſtator muſt *acknowledge* the In-
" ſtrument in their preſence '

Par. 3.

2. Of *the* WITNESSES

" The next Point of Evidence is the WITNESSES.

1. *Number*

" The NUMBER of the Witneſſes, ſince the Statute, ne-   Lea v Libb.
" ceſſary to a Will, is THREE.   Carth 35.

2 *Preſence.*

" They muſt abſolutely ſubſcribe the Will in the preſence
" of the Teſtator. and this preſence hath never been carried   3 Mod '259.
" farther in Conſtruction than the Interpoſition of a *Win-*
" *dow*, through which the Witneſs and the Teſtator might
" be intended to ſee each other.
" But it is not neceſſary, though prudent, that the Wit-
" neſſes ſhould all ſubſcribe in the preſence of *each other* ·   3 Burr Manſf.
" nor that they know the Contents :   1775.
" Nor that they atteſt every Page, Folio, or Sheet · but
" it ſeems to be neceſſary that the whole Will, if conſiſting
" of ſeveral ſheets, ſhould be in the room at the time of
" Atteſtation.

* Par 4.   * P. 117.

3 Of the Credibility of Witneſſes

" There is nothing more diſtinguiſhed in Law and Reaſon   Bond v Sew-
" than the abſtract *Competency* of Witneſſes, which entitles   ell
"   3 Burr Manſf.
" them to be heard, and their *Credit*, on which the ſatis-   1773
" factory fulneſs of the proof depends   This Diſtinction   Mic 1765.
" will be hereafter noticed -more at large   however a neg-
" ligence of expreſſion in the Statute ſeems to have intro-
" duced, till within theſe few years it was diſpelled, ſome
" degree of obſcurity, not to ſay of confuſion, reſpecting
" this very plain and natural diſtinction
" The Statute directs " that all deviſes of Lands ſhall be   § 5
" atteſted and ſubſcribed, in the preſence of the Deviſor,
" by three or four credible Witneſſes   or elſe they ſhall be
" utterly void and of none effect "
" And this requiſite of three Witneſſes to the Will is   Attorney Gen
" indiſpenſable, nor will three to the Codicil ſatisfy it   nor   & Barnes
"   2 Vern 597.
" three partitively.   Lea & Libb.
                                                              3 Mod 262

" A

" As to Credibility, it may neither be uninteresting nor
" useless to consider, in the order of time, some of the
" most remarkable Cases which have arisen upon the Con-
" struction of this Clause

Carth. 514.
Hillyard v
Jennings.
Hil 11 W III
B R

¶ That it might
be good, in like
circumstances,
As to other De-
vises, see Baugh
and Holloway,
in Canc.
1 P W 557

*P 118

Str 1253
E 19 G II
Bl. 8—17
Hl. 20 G II

" The first Case I shall mention occurred in little more
" than twenty years after the Statute. Lands were devised
" to one of the Witnesses of the Will and there the Court
" could have no difficulty in deciding as they did, that
" quoad ‖ this Devise the Will was a void Will, being at-
" tested but by two Witnesses, since the Plaintiff, the Le-
" gatee, could not be Witness to establish an Estate de-
" vised to himself.

⚹ " The Case of Anstey and Dowsing arose seventy years
" after the Statute: in that Case the Testator devised
" an Estate in Tail to the Defendant, and charged his real
" and personal Estate with the payment of annuities and
" legacies of these was an annuity of 20l for life to
" Elizabeth, the Wife of John Hailes, to her separate use,
" and 10l each to the said John and his Wife, for Mourn-
" ing. John Hailes, the before-mentioned Legatee, was
" one of the Three subscribing Witnesses to the Will, and
" on an Ejectment brought by the Heir at Law to recover
" the devised premises, LEE, Chief Justice, and the whole
" Court were of opinion that this was not a good Attestation
" under the Statute, by reason of the interest in the said
" Witness John Hailes · and that consequently the Title
" of the Defendant under the Will could not be main-
" tained

" As to the History of this Cause, there is a rather un-
" usual difference in the Account of the Reporters Sir
" John Strange, who was of Counsel afterwards for the
" Defendant in Error, (the Plaintiff of Course in the ori-
" ginal Cause) has given the Judgment of B R pretty
" much at large, but no Account of the Arguments at the
" Bar. Sir William Blackstone is copious in relating the
" Arguments in Error in the Exchequer Chamber, but gives
" no Account of the Judgment, nor could give any, for
" the Parties came to a Compromise

⚹ P. 119

⚹ " In this Case, LEE, Chief Justice, relied much on
" the Rule of the Roman Law, which says, that" the Condition of Witnesses is to be regarded, such as it was at the
time of sealing; " and that of the Code, concerning the
" reputed Condition of Witnesses at the time of" sealing
" Of these, the first applies to a very plain point in fa-
" vour of testimony, that no subsequent change in the con-
" dition of the Witnesses shall defeat their Attestation; and
" the other seems to go so far as that the reputed freedom
" of

" of the Witnesses, in general Estimation, at the 'time of
" their attesting, shall supply the defect of an absolute legal
" freedom · a position which it may be difficult to support
" in principle ; unless on the ground, that there had been
" no direct Adjudication against their freedom ; but it shews
" a kind of anxiety to support the competency of Witnesses,
" so far as possible. Another reason distinguishes it from our
" Rule of Witnesses to a Will and this is to be observed in
" attending to the next Case ; by which this whole Doctrine
" has been admirably cleared, illustrated, and settled.

" For in *Wyndham* against *Chetwynd* the Case was this. On Bl 25—103
" an Issue out of Chancery, *devisavit, vel non*, on the Will Mic. 31 G II.
" of Mr *Chetwynd*, the Jury found a *special Verdict* that the Burr Manf.
" Testator died 17th of *May*, 1750, leaving the Will at- 414—30.
" tested by three Witnesses, to all of whom he was indebt-
" ed at the time of Attestation ; but who had been paid
" (except a small mistake in casting up as to two of them, who
" were Attornies and Partners) before the Trial of the Issue :
" that the real Estate was charged with payment of Debts
" and Legacies ; but that the personal was much more than
" sufficient for the discharge of all specialty and simple Con-
" tract Debts And whether these were *credible* Witnesses
" within the Statute was the point submitted to the Court.

" * Lord MANSFIELD, *Chief Justice*, in delivering the * P. 120.
" opinion of the Court, went fully into the Principles and
" Cases. He shewed that experience had not confirmed the
" expectation of preventing frauds concerning Wills by the
" multiplying of Witnesses and other Forms that the Com-
" petency to Attestation was to be maintained as much as a
" just Theory founded upon the Nature and Analogy of Evi-
" dence, and consistent with Adjudications, would allow,
" for the sake of giving effect to the last Disposal of Pro-
" perty. He remarked on the vague and general import
" of the word *credible* in the Statute, and evinced that
" such Witnesses as were competent at Common Law re-
" mained competent · that by Common Law Interest went
" against the Competency of a Witness on the pre-
" sumed Bias, but that an Interest of such a Nature as to be
" probably unknown to the Witness at the time of
" signing, an Interest satisfied or renounced before the Trial,
" was not within the Presumption

" That with respect to Decisions, a *Release* was allowed
" to take away the objection to Interest: that in the Case of
" *Hillyard* and *Jennings*, the Plaintiff was the substantial De-
" visee, and came to establish that Interest to himself which
" he had attested. That in the Case of *Anesly* and *Dowsing*,
" the Wife's Annuity could not be released · and it was the

" Interest of the Husband to establish it as a Provision for his
" Wife, for whom he was legally compellable to provide,
" and be ng to her separate use, the Defendant, the Devisee
" held in Trust for her , and her Annuity could only be ob-
" tained by establishing the Devise to him That in the ge-
" neral reasoning on the Case, LEE, *Chief Justice*, had in-
" deed adverted to a Doctrine of the *Roman* Law, as to the
" Period which was to fix the Competency but that the
" Witnesses under that Law had a" positive capacity " pre-

* P. 121. " scribed , that they be" free, Adults, " and possessed of
" other *Qualifications* " * that *this* was the *Condition* of the
" Witnesses to which the Law, in the *Digests* and the *Code*,
" referred : but that there is no such positive Condition in
" that Law or in the Law of *England*, excluding a Legatee
" or Creditor from being a Witness · that such when incom-
" petent are so on the general Principles of Interest in a
" Witness, and therefore, no farther than those Principles
" extend.

" That had the resort of the Witnesses been to the real
" Estate, it did not seem, in a case like this, their Compe-
" tency even then should have been impeached. however,
" that they had no occasion to resort to the real Estate,
" and had been already paid And that therefore, the
" Court was unanimously of Opinion, that the Will was

2 P. W. 258. " duly attested by three Witnesses.

A COPYHOLD is not within the Statute : for it passes by the
Surrender.

" By the Statute 25 G. II *Ch* 6 said to have been occa-
" sioned by the Case of *Ansley* and *Dowsing*, entitled, *An*
" *Act for putting an End to certain Doubts and Questions*, re-
" *lating to the Attestation of Wills and Codicils, concerning Real*
" *Estates in that part of* Great Britain *called* England, *and in*
" *his Majesty's* Colonies *and* Plantations *in* America," where
" Devisee or Legatee attests, the Devise, &c is void as to
" him ; and he shall be admitted a Witness to prove the
" Will

" Creditor shall be admitted a Witness ; notwithstanding

* P. 122. " the Land is charged with Debts
Lowe and Jo-
lisse, Pl 365 * " And a Will may be established by proof of Sanity, by
1 2 G III. " other Witnesses, though the subscribing Witnesses concur
" in endeavouring to impeach it · for they are conclusive
" only to the mere existence of the Instrument.

" The Act of the Testator, and of the Witnesses, being
" made known, it remains to speak of the Interest conveyed
" by a Will of Lands.

Par. 4.

3. Interest conveyed.

" Now this interest is most general, in as much as by Will Comm II 23.
" shall pass all such Estate as a Man" hath, in possession, re-
P 378
Brett and Rig-
" mainder or reversion †, at the time of making his Will den, Pl Comm.
" but after-purchased Lands require a" Republication 343, 4
" otherwise they will not pass by general Words of Devise, Cooke, Mic. 6
" such as" all my Lands or all my Estate. " for these ge-
Anne, B R
" neral expressions will be referred to the time of making the Sik 237
" Will. For Wills are considered as conveyances or dif-
4 Burr 1496.
" positions, less fettered in point of form, than Acts taking * By what ge-
neral words a
" effect *inter vivos* to pass the real Estate, and where the pass, and *contra*,
" Terms are general, it would be a foreign intendment to v Bl 200.—4.
" suppose any other Estate in contemplation of the Testator
" to pass, than such as he then had, either in possession or
" in right · and hence it is, and not upon the force of the
" word " having," that subsequent purchases are not in-
" cluded : for the word " having," is only a description of
" a general Case ; not a *Limitation* of the *power* to devise ;
" and it is of experience, * that if a man sufficiently declare * P. 123.
" his purpose to pass" after-purchased " Estates, such Es-
" tates shall pass.

T ɪ ᴛ. IV.

How a WILL shall be revoked

29 Car, II. c. 3.
§ 6

" No Revocation shall be good of a Will of Lands, nor
" any Clause thereof shall be revokable, otherwise than by
" some other *Will* or Codicil in Writing, or other Writing,
" declaring the same signed in the presence of three or four
" Witnesses, or by Burning, Cancelling, Tearing, or Ob-
" literating by the Testator, or in his presence, and by his
" direction and consent.

" But this does not extend to Revocations by *Act* of *Law*,
" as by Sale of the Lands devised, or *Forfeiture* · or by
" Marriage of a *Femme*, who was sole when she made the
" Will for this is revoked by the Act of marrying, which
" deprives her of the Disposal of her property : and such
" Will does not revive, in Case she outlive her Hus-
" band ; but remains revoked, unless renewed by repub-
" lication.

" And by intendment of Law, a Marriage with Issue hath Brown and
" been held a complete constructive Revocation of a Will Thompson,
" made before. 1701.

" But

v 1 P W 304.
2 Eq.Abr 413.
4 Bur Manf.
2171
|| Haines v.
Haines, 2 Vern.
441.
Anno 1702.

" But no deftruction by another fhall defeat the Will and
fruftrate the meaning of the Teftator, if the Contents can
be proved ||

" And *no Acts* of the *Party* fhall revoke a Will, if fuch
" Act be *deficient* in any of the requifites of the Statute

" Neither fhall any formal Act amount to a *Revocation,* if
" the *intent* to revoke the Inftrument (the *Animus revocandi*)
" accompany it not.

* P. 124.

* " And, leaft of all, fhall a *Change of Eftate* operate as
" a Revocation, where the difpofing Power over the Pro-
" perty remains, and the formal Change appears to have
" been made only to effectuate the fubftantial intent.—We
" will examine,

    1 *Formal erroneous Acts*
    2 *Incomplete difpofals to different purpofes.*
    3 *Change of Eftate.*

" Firft, therefore, to confider an erroneous deftruction
" of a Will, or a fubfequent contrary Will that can not
" take effect ·

Par. 2

1 *Erroneous cancelling, &c*

1 P W 345
2 10 Burtenfhaw
and Gilbert, E
14 G III
B R.
Goodright on
Dem of
Glazier, Hil.
10 G III
4 Burr 2512
15

" A Will remains good, though formally cancelled if it
" be in Evidence, that it was not the intent of the Teftator
" to cancel that Will As, if a Man, fick and infirm, hav-
" ing two Wills near him, fhould order a perfon to cancel
" his firft Will, who, by miftake, cancels his laft. Now
" here the laft Will is in force, and the firft cannot revive ·
" though if the fecond had been intentionally cancelled by
" the Teftator, this, *ipfo facto,* would have revived the firft,
" as a repealed Act of Parliament revives of Courfe by the
" Abrogation of the repealing Act

" So if the Teftator had accidentally thrown Ink upon the
" Will inftead of Sand, and defaced thereby the Signatures
" of the Witneffes

Par 3

2 *Of a Subfequent ineffective Will, or incomplete Difpofal.*

Eccleftone v
Speke,
3 Mod 258.

* P. 125

" On this, where it was ftated on a fpecial Verdict, that
" Lady *Anne Speke,* being feized in Fee, did, on the 12th
" day of *March* 1682, make her Will, and devifed the
" Lands to *John Petit* for Life , and * afterwards to *George*
" his Son, and his Heirs for ever · on condition of his tak-
" ing the name of *Speke*

" That,

" That, on the 25th of *December* 1685, she caused ano-
" ther Writing to be made, purporting to be her Will ; which
" was Signed, Sealed, and Published by her, in the presence
" of three Witnesses in the Chamber where she was,
" and where she continued while the Witnesses subscrib-
" ed their name in the Hall, and that she could not see them
" so Subscribing.

" That the Lessors of the Plaintiff are Heirs at Law, &c.

" And upon the first Argument, Judgment was given for
" the Defendant . for that the second Will must be a good
" Will in all circumstances, otherwise it would not revoke
" a former Will

" And this Doctrine needs little illustration : for if you I. 2. 17 10.
" cannot produce the instrument as a Will, you cannot shew *ex et autem sola*
" that the instrument which preceded it, valid in itself, was
" not the last Will. And to prove it was an ineffective Will,
" is to prove that it cannot stand in the way of the former.

" And, pursuant to this Principle, where a Man having Onions v.
" made his Will, after made a second, with change of Trus- Tyrer,
" tees, but not effective under the Statute of Frauds, and Ch Pre 459
" then cancels the Duplicate of the first, * this is no Revo- * P. 126.
" cation, for he meant his first to be void only on supposi-
" tion of his second being good : and this illustrates both the
" preceding Propositions

Par. 4

3. Of Change in Estate.

" And here the Rule already recited, may serve as a general Jenkinson v.
" Direction This Question of *constructive* Revocations by Watts, Tr 14
" *Change of Estate*, was largely discussed before the Lord G III.
" CHANCELLOR on a *Rehearing* from the *Rolls*.

" In this Case, Mr Watts made his Will, and devised a
" capital *Mansion House* and Estate in strict Settlement Af-
" terwards he contracts for the Manor of *Hunsworth*, in
" *Bucks*, to be purchased of the *Duke of Kingston* for 40,000*l*.
" and then by Codicil, he disposes of the Estate under Con-
" tract to the same Uses as those in the Will the Vendor
" having covenanted to convey to Trustees, subject to such
" Uses as the Purchaser should appoint

" Afterwards, by completing the purchase, he takes the
" legal Estate absolutely to himself, who had the equitable
" before, by virtue of the Contract, and the Trust to such
" Uses as by himself should be appointed The CHANCEL-
" LOR was of Opinion, that this taking of the *legal* Estate
" was no such change as should be construed a Revocation :
" it being substantially the *same* Estate, and taken in comple-
" tion

" tion of the *same purposes* which he had before declared
" by his Codicil. And the Prayer of the Petition was dif-
" missed.

* P. 127.
Swift and
Neale, 3 Burr
Manf 1488
Tr 4 G III.
1764.

" * And where it was held, that a Devisee by a Joint Ten-
" ant of his part and interest in the Estate which he jointly
" held, was not good, a partition having been made, after
" the Will, and prior to the Death of the Testator, this, though
" cited as an instance of a constructive Revocation, was not
" so, but was decided on very different Grounds, that the
" Estate of a Joint Tenant was before partition not devisable ;
" and that the subsequent event could not make it so . the
" Right of Survivorship, at the time of making the Will,
" being paramount to the power of devising.

Greenhill v
Greenhill,
2 Ve.n.679,80

" And in a Caf., in 1711, where the Testator articled for
" the Purchase of Lands, and afterwards made his Will, and
" after took the legal Estate to himself, by payment of the
" purchase Money and Entry, this was held a good Devise
" of the Lands so under Contract, and that the subsequent
" Change of the Estate, by Completion of the Purchase,
" was no Revocation

Clarke and Ux.
v Berkeley et
al. 2 Vern.
720

" So on the Marriage of a Daughter, to whom there was
" a conditional Devise of Lands, part of which Lands were
" settled by the Testator after making his said Will, on the
" Husband of his said Daughter.—So a *Mortgage*, shall be

Salk 158.

" only a Revocation *pro tanto.*

* P. 128

" * But where a person takes a different Estate, for purposes
" contrary to those of his Will, though such purposes never
" take effect, and the disposing power was only conditionally
" devested, yet this change of Estate, for the purpose of an
" intended new appointment, has been held a Revocation.

" So, where the Earl of *Lincoln* devised a mortgaged
" Estate, in default of Issue to his next Heir in the Honour,
" Sir *Francis Clinton* and afterwards, in contemplation of a

Earl of Lincoln
and Rolls, et al
Eq Ca Abr
412

" supposed future Marriage, by Lease and Release, took an
" Estate in Trust to himself and his Heirs, till the Marriage
" should take effect, and afterwards, in part to the use of
" the Marriage, and died without marrying, this was held
" a Revocation, and the Decree was accordingly affirmed in
" the House of Lords.

" For this, a satisfactory explanation may perhaps be
" given: for there was once a purpose incompatible with

Pollen and
Hubana, Mic.
1712

" the Will, and a change made in the Estate in order to the
" execution of such purpose But in a subsequent Case,
" after a general Devise in Tail, on condition of taking the
" Name of the Testator, with diverse remainders over, the
" Testator conveved a part of his Estate in Trust, to convey
" to such Uses as he, by Deed or Will, should appoint ; he
" died

" died without making any appointment, and without alter-
" ing his Will, and yet, even this was held a Revocation of
" the Will

" * But extreme Cafes of this kind, will, at moft, be un- * P. 129.
" derftood as being applicable to future Queftions, only when
" they fhall be abfolutely in point   Lord MANSFIELD has Burr Manf.
" obferved, that *conftructive Revocations contrary to the Inten-* 1491.
" *tion of the Teftator, ought not to be indulged: and that fome*
" *overftrained Refolutions of that fort, had brought a Scandal*
" *upon the Law*

" In a celebrated Cafe before Lord HARDWICKE †, there Parfons and
' was a Change of the Eftate by fuffering a Recovery. The Freeman,
" Chancellor after obferving, that Cafes of Revocation, by 9 Nov. 1751
" Act of Law, had gone farther, and extended to inftances
" of an alteration in the Eftate, far fhort of that before the
" Court, and after difcountenancing the idea, that a revoca-
" tion in Law would not be a revocation in Equity, for that
" it would be mifchievous, if revocations in Equity fhould
" not turn on the fame principles as of legal Eftates at Com-
" mon Law, proceeds to diftinguifh, that where the change
" of Eftate is for a particular purpofe only, there a Revoca-
" tion fhall not be intended farther than that purpofe requires,
" while the Eftate fubftantially remains as before · as when
" a Teftator mortgages, this is but a Security, and a revo-
" cation only *pro tanto* ; and as it would have been fubject to
" Redemption, in favor of the Heir, fo it fhall in favor of
" the Devifee.

" And had there been no more in this Cafe, but executing
" the equitable Eftate, by taking in the legal one, it had
" been no revocation, but the purpofe of this recovery was
" to vary and alter the power of appointing; and how can
" this be called a particular purpofe, which might operate
" over the whole inftrument, and ride over the whole
" Eftate

" * His Lordfhip concluded ;—and therefore, I am of Opi- * P. 130.
" nion, he took a new fee, under different qualifications,
" and fubject to be conveyed in different ways, and under
" very different circumftances: and that this can not be
" called a change, fo limited a particular purpofe, as that
" the Court can reftrain the revocation to it

† *The Subftance of this I copy from a Manufcript Collection of my*
Father   If from him, in purfuit of the fame profeffion, I may have
learnt one part of that beft paternal wifh, Virtutem verumque labo-
rem, *of the reft I fhall not be over folicitous.*

" From

Inferences

" From the whole, refult three Rules refpecting this fpe-
" cies of conftructive Revocation ; 1   That nothing is
" fuch, (while the difpofing power remains,) which is done
" with the defign of carrying into *execution* the intent of the
" Teftator, and would have been neceffary or expedient on
" the part of the Devifee, to complete and perfect the Eftate
" given by the Devife †—And this Rule hath been intima-
" ted already

" 2 That a partial change of Eftate, for a particular pur-
" pofe, fhall be (generally,) but a partial and proportionable
" change in the intereft devifed, and not a total Revocation.

" 3 That a change of the Eftate, which varies fubftan-
" tially the difpofing power, or which is made for a pur-
" pofe of indefinite Extent, fo that it can not be afcer-
" tained that any part of the originally devifed Intereft
" was without the fcope of it, fhall operate as an abfolute
" Revocation.

Tit V

Republication

" Republication, being the perfecting or renewal of
" a legal intent, once competently declared, is favourable in
" Law, as Revocation is unfavourable . and therefore is
" readily admitted

*P 131.
Roll's Abr.
618 8.*

" * And therefore, if a Man have Land in *D* and devife
" by his Will all his Land in *D* this will carry fuch land as he
" then had when he publifhed his Will, and not *other* Land
" in *D* but if after making and publifhing his Will, he pur-
" chafe other Lands in *D* and on Treaty for thofe Lands,
" he declares that he will not fell the new purchafed Lands,
" for that he means they fhall go to the Devifee of the reft
" (his Executor) under the Will, and after adds a Codicil,
" difpofing of perfonal property, and dieth, this is a fuf-
" ficient Republication to pafs the newly purchafed Lands
" in *D*

*Heylin v Hey-
lin, T 14 G III.
Cowp 130*

" And fo, Teftator makes his Will, and devifes his Lands
" freehold and copyhold . he after purchafes other Copy-

*Wild and
Aft on, et al
Mic 9 G II
in care
A S Co L
Doe on Dem
or Patent Davy,
Cowp 158*

† *So alfo a Devife for payment of Debts   Truft Term created for
that purpofe · and her Term with new Truftees and preference of Debts
by Spec alty   No Revocation of the former*

‖ *And, in another Cafe, where the Surrender was to fuch Ufes at
Tefta or fhould appoint, a Codicil, confirming the Will, excepting Al-
teras ons, was fufficient.*

" hold,

" hold, and furrenders it to the Ufe of his Will, declared or
" to be declared. This is an effectual Republication.

" No precife form of Words is neceffary to a Repub-
" lication. And a Codicil, not annexed to the Will, but on
" a different Paper, may, though the Will was not even be-
" fore the Teftator at the time, nor is republifhed by it in
" Terms, amount to a Republication, if it evidently adverts
" to the Will

" A Will once revoked, according to the Statute of Frauds,
" a Republication to revive it muft have all the Solemnities
" required by that Statute. †

Potter and Potter, 7 May, 1750 Str Mafter of the Rolls, Ch. L M S

T i t VI.

" * We are now to fpeak briefly of the Will of PERSÓN-
" ALTY · and as the Authentication of this Species of Will,
" is retained in a Court which borrows much of its Terms,
" Rules, and Modes of proceeding from the Civil Law, it
" is characterized by a Name which that Law gave to the
" whole Genus, *Teftament*, or teftamentary Difposition.

* P. 132.

Par 2.

Will of Perfona'ty, relatively confidered

" Thefe are to be noticed chiefly in refpect of their leading
" Analogies or Differences from a Will of Lands.

1 *Good without Witnefs, if written by Teftator.*

" And firft, if a Will of perfonalty be written by the
" Teftator, it will be valid without any fubfcribing Witnefs

Harris's Juftin L ll 11 § a.

2 *Valid without Executor.*

" Secondly, though the appointment of an Executor be
" neceffary to the full Idea of a Teftament, Bequefts lawfully
" made, fhall be fupported, though there be no Executor·

Swinborne, I. 6 p 2

† By this is meant, that it cannot be republifhed by an inftrument
figned by two Witneffes, or otherwife defective. But it may be republifhed, as already has been obferved, if the Teftator deftroy the Revocation But if the firft Will be deftroyed, then it fhall not revive
by the fimple deftruction of the Revocation Thus a man makes a
Will and Duplicate he after makes a fecond Will, and thereby re-
vokes all former Wills, and, at the fame time, cancels the former Will
in his Cuftody He then fends for an Attorney to make a third Will,
but dies before it could be completed After his Death, the fecond Will
is found cancelled. the firft is alfo found in the fame Paper, cancelled
but the Duplicate of the firft is found, uncancelled, among the Teftator's Deeds and Papers The cancelling the fecond, doth not, under
thefe circumftances, revive the firft.

Burtenfhaw v Gilbert, E 14 G III Cowp 49

" for

" for it is yet a laſt Will, though leſs ſolemn and leſs provi-
" dently guarded.

Legg and Legg,
Salk. 592 Mic.
8 W III.

3 Revoked by Marriage with Iſſue.

" Marriage with Birth of a Child, is a Revocation of a
" Will, which makes a general Diſpoſition of perſonalty.

* P. 133.   *** Par. 3.**

Of Ademption.

" To the head of conſtructive Revocations of Bequeſts,

Swinb. VII.
10. p 526. 21.
P. 530.

" are to be referred, Ademption and Satisfaction, which are
" Revocations pro tanto, on the implied intent.

" Firſt, if the ſame Sum be twice given in the ſame in-
" ſtrument to the ſame perſon, without any diſtinction of
" cauſe, or difference of expreſſion, the preſumption is, that
" it is only once given

" When a Will reſerves a power of adding a Codicil, and
" a Codicil is after added, and annexed to the Will, they
" are both as one inſtrument, and ſubject to the ſame
" conſtruction, as if the double Legacy had been in the
" Will only

" When a Codicil is made without ſuch reference to the
" Will, they are different inſtruments, and on the ſame Sum

Swinb p. 530.
D. 34. 4. 9

" given to the ſame perſon by each, the preſumption is for
" the Deviſee

" If an hundred Pounds be given to A by Will, and af-
" terwards fifty to A by the ſame Will, the preſumption is,
" that A ſhall take both.

" And where a ſmaller Sum (500l. was given by the Will,
" and after the Teſtatrix adds a Codicil to her Will, and
" gives an Annuity, expreſsly, over and above, of 12l for
" Life to the ſame perſon ; and afterwards a greater ſum by
" another codicil (1000l) to the ſame perſon, and ſays, in
" the laſt Bequeſt, " I add this Codicil to my Will," " * and

* P 134.

" there was a Year and two months between the Will and
" the laſt Codicil, the Maſter of the Rolls was of Opinion,
" that 1500l was due, over and above the Annuity. And

Patton and
Hooley, Bil
13 G III See
2 Vc Maſters and
Maſter, P W
421—4.
Cuthbert and
Peacock,
Salk. 155
Mic 6 Anne
per Cowper,
Canc.
Cranmer'.Caſe
12 Canc.

" the Chancellor, by his Decree, on a rehearing, confirmed
" the Judgment of the Maſter. Mr. Juſtice Aſton, and the
" Chief Baron Smyth aſſiſting.

" So if there are Aſſets to ſatisfy Debts and Legacies, with
" out preſuming a Legacy to go in Satisfaction of a Debt,
" it ſhall be preſumed a pure Benefit, where no intent appears
" to the contrary, and the Executors ſhall pay both.

" A Legacy given to A who dies before the Teſtator, is
" a lapſed Legacy : for the Bequeſt ſpeaks at the time of the
         " Teſtator's

" Teſtator's Death. But where he takes as a Truſtee, it ſhall
" not lapſe in prejudice of the Truſt.

" A Legacy given to one, if he live to the Age of
" Twenty-one, is a lapſed Legacy if he die before; but a
" Legacy, *payable* WHEN he ſhall attain the age of Twenty-
" one, veſts immediately if he ſurvive the Teſtator, and
" ſhall go over by Repreſentation to ſuch perſons as ſhall
" repreſentatively be entitled at the time when 'it becomes
" payable It is *debitum in præſenti, ſolvendum in futuro.*
" And the Diſtinction is, that when the time is annexed to
" the Legacy, it ſhall not be paid if the Legatee die before
" the time; for the time is the *condition*, on failure of which
" it never becomes due; but if the time is annexed to the
" *payment*, then the Legacy is abſolute, and *due* immediately
" if the Legatee ſurvive the Teſtator; though *payable* at
" a future Day And this ſenſible Diſtinction was adopt-
" ed into our principles of legal Conſtruction, in clear
" and preciſe terms, more than an hundred and eighty
" Years back.

* " It is remarkable, that *Wentworth*, where above cited,
" appears to treat this as a nice and doubtful Diſtinction: and
" ſo late as the year 1700, though admitted binding as a
" Precedent, it was treated with yet more ſeverity: and
" yet there is on its ſide *Analogy* to thoſe Laws, which go-
" vern, by voluntary Adoption, the other parts of the teſ-
" tamentary Law in *England*, it has *reaſon*, as a perſonal
" Bequeſt carries no certain preſumption of a ſubſtitutional
" benefit to an unknown repreſentative, if the Legatee, in
" immediate contemplation, die before the Teſtator, and
" a remote contemplation ought not to be intended; and it
" has *certainty*, being a clear and preciſe diviſion between
" ſuch Legacies as ſhall be deemed extinct, and ſuch as
" ſurvive. (n)

" A charge

Marginal notes: Salk. 508. per *Harcourt*, Canc 2 Eq C Abr. 296, 297. Eq. C 295. Br. Deviſe 27 Mic 3 Ja- B R Dyer 59. Office of Ex. 240 1 Ed. 1720. Swinb 535. VII. 23

* P. 135.

(n) *It ſeems not true that the diſtinction in the civil Law does
not go the whole length of coincidence with ours for although by
that Law, it appears at firſt as if a Legacy given at a very diſtant period, might veſt abſolutely in the Legatee : by the circumſtances taken together it ſeems ſufficiently diſtinct, that it is only
meant of a Legacy payable at ſuch remote Period that if the Legatee
ſurvive the Teſtator, the intereſt ſhall go over by repreſentation ;
this will beſt appear by quoting the ſeveral clauſes* ·* Si Dies appo
ſita legato non eſt, præſens debetur; aut confeſtim ad eum pertinet cui datum eſt . adjecta, quamvis longa ſit, ſi certa eſt, dies
(veluti, *Calendis Januarii centeſimis*) dies quidem legati ſtatim
cedit, ſed ante diem peti non poteſt.

D. 36. 2, 11, 2, 3.

" At

2 Vern. 498
Brown v Daw-
son, 1705 " A charge by two feveral Securities of 14*l* *per Ann.* to
" a Wife, in confideration of her giving up part of her
" Jointure; bequeft of 14*l per Ann* for Life, without no-
" ticing the charges, held a fatisfaction.

Par 4.

INTESTACY *as to part.*

" Nothing fhall pafs as bequeathed in general Terms,
" which belongs to a different Clafs, or does not appear to
" have been within the fcope of the intention of the Tefta-
" tor And therefore, where a Seaman made his Will
* P 136.
Cook v Oak-
ley, & al
P W 302
Hil 1715
per *T-e-r.* " abroad, and bequeathed to his Mother * his Gold Rings,
" Buttons, and Cheft of Cloaths, and to his Friend (who
" was on board with him) his red Box, Arrack, and
" all Things not before bequeathed, this was held reftricted
" to Things *ejufdem Generis,* and not to extend to Leafe-
" hold Intereft, which had been bequeathed him during his
" Abfence

Moore v
Magrath,
Hil. 14 G III.
Cowp 9 " For this is analogous to a *fweeping* Claufe, cuftoma-
" rily and fometimes incautioufly inferted in a Deed, which
" is taken with reference to preceding Claufes; and not fo
" as to pafs a confiderable property unnoticed in any other
" part of the Deed, not apparently under particular, or
" at leaft, general, contemplation to be fo conveyed.
" only that the prefumption of a total Difpofition of pro-
" perty is agreeable to the Nature of a Will, and not of
" a Deed

E. of Darling-
ton v Pulteney.
E. 15 Geo III.
Cowp 260 " A Power to be executed by DEED is not executed if
" by WILL at leaft unlefs in benefit of a Wife, Children,
" or Creditors

At fi incerta (quafi, *cum pubes erit, cum in familiam nupferit;
cum magiftratum inerit, cum aliquid* quod fcribendo comprehendere
fit commodum, *fecerit,)* nifi tempus conditione obtigit, neque
res pertinere, dies legati cedere poteft
Si Titio " *cum is annorum quatuordecim erit factus*" legatum
fuerit, et is ante quartum decimum annum decefferit, verum eft
ad hæredem ejus, legatum *non tranfire* quoniam non folum diem
fed et conditionem hoc legatum in fe continet; fi effectus effet annorum quatuordecim, qui autem in rerum natura non effet, annorum
quatuordecem non effe intelligeretur Nec intereft utrum fcri
batur si *annorum quatuorcæcem factus erit,* an ita, Titio " *CUM,*
&c.*" cum priore fcriptura per conditionem tempus demonftra
tur, fequenti per tempus conditio untrobique tamen eadem
conditio
V r-a-r Ho-
l-r hz!-A
368, 9 7° Suppleo vocem cum, &c quod interceditte videtur
Huberus quæftionem non contemnendam citat de *Archiguberno
Claffis Britannicæ;* antiquiffimo enimvero.

Par.

Par 3

NUNCUPATIVE WILL.

" Formerly, Wills were allowed with very little regard West's Case,
" to the mode and Solemnities of the *Devise*, and of courfe, Moor 177
" with lefs nicety ftill, as to a mere *bequeft* · a *Letter* has Swinb 49.
" been held a good Will of Lands: and *nuncupative* Wills,
" which are verbal Declarations of * intent, were good * P 137.
" even as to realty, and much more as to perfonalty, al Swinb I 12.
" moft as unreftrictedly as the *teftamentum in procinctu* among p 51 48
" the *Romans* · but it is now with us limited by the Statute,
" as it was inftituted by them, in favour of military perfons,
" by whom alone fuch nuncupative Wills can, to any con-
" fiderable amount be made, as before, were allowed in
" general: for in refpect of others, it is required, 1 That
" *no written Will of perfonalty fhall be revoked by a fubfequent* 29 Car II c.
" *nuncupative one, except the fame fhould be in the life-time of* 3 § 22.
" *the Teftator reduced to writing, and read over to him and ap-*
" *proved, and unlefs the fame be proved to have been fo done by*
" *the oath of three Witneffes at the leaft.*
" 2 *That no nuncupative Will fhall in any wife be good* § 19.
" *where the Eftate bequeathed exceeds* 30l *unlefs proved by*
" *three Witneffes prefent at the making thereof; and unlefs*
" *they or fome of them were fpecially required to bear Witnefs*
" *thereto by the Teftator himfelf, and unlefs it was made in his*
" *laft ficknefs, in his own habitation or dwelling-houfe, or where*
" *he had been previoufly refident ten days at the leaft, except he*
" *be furprized with ficknefs on a journey, or from home, and dies*
" *without return to his dwelling*
" * 3. *That no nuncupative Will fhall be proved by the Witneffes* * P 138.
" *after fix Months from the making, unlefs it were put in Writ-* § 20.
" *ing within fix Days.*
" Nor fhall a nuncupative Will be proved till fourteen § 21
" days after the death of the Teftator· nor till procefs hath
" firft iffued to the Widow or next of kin to conteft it, if
" they think proper.
" Thus nuncupative Wills in general are advanced to the
" rank of written Evidence, fo as to be proper to be men-
" tioned in this place

SECTION IV.

" We are now led to attend to the lefs folemn written
" Evidence And firft of AGREEMENTS *not under Seal* ·
" including in this term fuch feveral inftruments as the Law
" allows to take effect in this manner *inter vivos*; promiffory

Notes

" *Notes* and *Bills* of *Exchange* excepted, which are after to
" be treated under a diftinct head.

Tit. II.

" Thefe may be divided into

Agreements:

1. *Executory of* 1. *Real,*
     2 *Chattel Intereft,*
     3. *Perfonal.*

2. *Executed.*

* P. 139.   *** Par. 2.**

1. Of Agreements Real.

Bac. Abr. 67
Tit. Agr

" 1 Agreements *real, not under feal,* nor executed
" by *Livery,* are fuch Contracts ufually as are preparatory
" to a more folemn Mode of Tranfaction by Deed, as Ar-
" ticles in Confideration of an intended Marriage, or of a
" Purchafe.

" For thefe unlefs the Remedy which is fought lies fim-
" ply in *Damages,* which the Courts of Common Law may
" wholly and at once redrefs upon *Action on the Cafe,* in which
" the Jury will give damages according to the Proof, the
" general Redrefs is in the *Chancery.*

2 Vern. 215
Anno 1690

" Thus if the Anceftor feized in Fee hath agreed for the
" fale of Lands, and hath received part of the Purchafe
" Money, Equity will compel his heir to convey, and the
" Purchafe Money will go to the Executor.

" So a defective Conveyance to a younger Son will be

Bac. 68

" decreed to be completed by the Heir, 1. Where there is
" a Covenant for farther Affurance ,

" 2 Where there is Provifion made by the Father in his
" life-time for the Heir, or fuch provifion devolves on him
" by defcent from the Father

* P. 140.

* " But if Tenant in Tail agree to convey, and die before
" Fine or Recovery be levied, *Equity* will not oblige the

Cavendifh v
Worfley
hob 203
1 Chanc. Ca.
171

" iffue to fupply this Defect; unlefs fome Act be done by
" the Iffue which amounts to a conftructive Ratification of
" the Agreement · for Equity cannot fuperfede the ftatute *de*
" *Donis*; its province being to give liberal relief, but not
" againft Law.

Voluntary.

Voluntary.

" *Voluntary* Agreements reduced to Writing are good against
" those who have no higher than a voluntary Claim, and
" *Equity* will not relieve against them in favour of such, nor
" suffer them to be disturbed as between the parties; though
" it will as against *Creditors, Purchasers* for valuable conside-
" ration, (*o*) or younger Children

Par. 3.

2. Of Agreements relating to Chattels real.

" A lease for Years, to commence at a future Day, may
" be good without Seal · and an Agreement signed by the
" Parties for that purpose shall entitle to Damages at *Law*
" for non performance in *Equity.*

* Par. 4.   * P. 141.

3. Of AGREEMENTS *personal*

Promise of Marriage within the Statute of Frauds.

" It is proper, on all Accounts, to mention, first, *Agree-*
" *ments in consideration of Marriage*; and the rather, since
" by the Statute so frequently already cited, no Contract 29 Car. II. c.
" *in Consideration of Marriage* is suable, unless it be in Writ- 3 § 4
" ing, and signed by the party charged, or by his Au- 3 Lev 65, 6.
" thority   1 Str 34
" A Contract to marry, upon which an Action for
" breach of promise is founded, is generally proved by
" some Evidence in writing and when such a Contract
" has been duly in Evidence before the Court, Damages
" have been frequently recovered, either in a specific sum
" ascertained by the Contract, or more generally, where no
" sum has been stipulated, the Jury have awarded liberally
" according to the circumstances of the party and the other
" considerations of the Case. But it hath been long settled

(*o*) *Consideration* in Law is either good, *bona,* as of propinquity Comm II
or natural affection, or valuable, *æstimabilis,* the worth of which Ch 20, p. 296,
is estimated by a certain Rule of Justice, as for so much Money; 7
or on account of Marriage, a simply *good* Consideration, is not
available against *Creditors,* &c.

All *voluntary* Conveyances are void, as against Creditors or Pur- * 13 Eliz c 5.
chasers for consideration, by the two statutes of *Elizabeth*; or, 27 Eliz c 4.
perhaps, more accurately, at *Common Law* affirmed, explained,
and enforced by the Legislature.

" that

" that a Promife to marry is not a Contract *in confideration* of
" Marriage fo as to fubject the Proof of it to the Limita
" tions of the Statute.

" It is remarkable that *Levinz,* only *five* years after the
" Statute, feems to have had no Doubt that a Promife of
" Marriage *was* an Agreement in Confideration of Marriage
" within the ftatute: but the Cafe in *Levinz* has no report
" of the Judgment annexed · and the Cafe in *Strange,* al-
" ready cited in the Margin, is directly contrary though it
" makes a mifreference to the Book, the Note is probably
" correct, fhort as it is, as to the refolution of the Court of
" *Common Pleas*, which it ftates to have been, that fubfe-
*P. 142 " quent determinations * were againft the Cafe in *Levinz* and
" a modern Book of confiderable reputation affirms the Au-
L. N P. 280 " thority of the Cafe in *Strange.*

Par. 5.

Contract or Agreement in confideration *of Marriage, within the Statute*

Bawdes v.
Amhurft.
Ch Pre 402
Eq C. Abr 21.
" On a Treaty of Marriage the Lady's Father propofed
" to give 4 500*l.* Portion, and the Hufband was to fettle a
" or 500*l* per *Annum* Jointure   The Father and intended
" Hufband went to the Chambers of a Conveyancer, who
" heard the Propofals on both fides, took minutes, and or
" dered a fettlement to be drawn according to the Terms o'
" the Agreement the next day the Father fell fick, and
" died in two hours after; and the next Morning the Mar-
" riage was confummated.

" On a Bill brought to have a fpecific performance of the
" Agreement, the Lord *Chancellor* decreed it to be within the
" Statute: and faid, he knew no Cafe where an Agreement,
" though" written " by the Party himfelf, fhould bind, if
" not figned, or" in part executed " by him: and that thofe
" preparatory heads might have received feveral Alterations
" or Additions, or the Agreement might have entirely
" broke off.

*P 143   * Par. 6.

Notes or Bonds in reftraint of Marriage are void.

" But a Bond by which *A* engages that he will not marry
" any other Perfon but *B* on Penalty of 1000*l* though
" figned and fealed by the party, is held not a good Agree-
" ment, for it is not in confideration of Marriage, but ra-
" ther in reftraint of Marriage, fince *B* is not bound to ac-
                                                          " cept

" cept *A* for her hufband, and if the Bond were fupported,
" a party might be bound under fuch penalty as would
" amount to an abfolute prohibition of Marriage, which
" would be againft all Policy, Reafon, and natural Right
" Accordingly an Obligation under Seal to this purport
" having been fued, Lord *Mansfield* left it to the Jury, on an
" Action of Covenant, to find 1000*l* Damages, if they
" thought the Deed a good Deed

" On this two Motions were made, one for a *new Trial*,
" on the fuggeftion that the Damages ought to have been
" left at large to the Jury. but on this the Rule was dif-
" charged, for the Damages were afcertained by the
" parties, and muft be either none or entire, as liquidated by
' the Contract, but the Motion in Arreft of Judgment
" went on the Ground that there was no Obligation on
" which an Action * could be maintained what was plead-
" ed as fuch being void, as amounting in fubftance not to
" an engagement to marry the Plaintiff, but to be reftrained,
" if fhe fhould fo pleafe, fiom marrying any other Perfon
" And of this opinion was the whole Court, Judgment
" was accordingly arrefted, and the Exchequer Chamber
" confirmed the Decifion

" Upon this occafion, to fhew how far the principles of
" legal Policy had prevailed againft reftraints on Marriage,
" the Chief Juftice quoted a Cafe, than which it is indeed
" difficult to conceive a ftronger, and well may one be
" permitted to acknowledge, even independent of the inti-
" mations from that great Authority, that, juft and bene-
" ficial as the general Principle is, the determination in that
" particular inftance, went farther than Equity or public
" Convenience can eafily be imagined to require A Lady,
" who was near thirty, and not unapprized of the extent
" of her Engagement, for fhe was a Widow, freely and
" deliberately gave a Bond, which *fi non pertæfum thalami*
" *tædæque fuiffet*, it may be thought fhe would have declin-
" ed however, the generous Lady forfeited the Obligation
" (if it had * been forfeitable) by marrying, and joined in an
" Application with her Hufband, that the Bond, which was
" for 100*l* might be delivered up to be cancelled · there
" was a Counterbond in an equal fum, payable to her ex-
" ecutors, in cafe fhe fhould not marry a fecond time, and
" it was contended her Daughter by the firft Hufband might
" have had the Benefit of this that there was no furprize
" or inequality in the Contract, that fhe had expreffed her
" fubfequent as well as previous Approbation to it How-
" ever, the Bond was ordered to be delivered up And
" in referring to this Cafe, Lord *Mansfield* remarks, that

Catharine
Lowe v. New-
fham, Peers
L. 8 G III
4 Burr
Manfi 2225

* P 144

2 Vern 215
Baker & U,
v White & al'

* P 145

H   " reftraint

" reftraint, on a firft marriage, is contrary to the general In
" terefts of Society and the fettled Policy of the Law,
" but that the frequent Cuftoms of Copyholds feemed to
4 Burr Manff " intimate the reftraint on a fecond, was not equally fo held,
2233 " yet that the Bond was decreed to be delivered up
" Thefe were indeed both Obligations by fpecialty, and
" fo do not apply to this head, otherwife than *à fortiori*, and
" as they illuftrate the general principle by which written
" Agreements of this nature are decided
" Where, after Propofal by *Letter*, made and rejected,
" the Lady's Father *offered* a certain fum to be paid down
" which had been demanded on the other fide, and the
Skinn. 142, 3 " Marriage took place, this was held a good promife.

* P. 146.   ** Other Agreements.*

Par 7.

' *Agreements* by an *Executor* to anfwer out of his *own*
" Eflate, and generally, Agreements by fpecial Promife to
" anfwer for the debt, default, or mifcarriage of another,
" muft be proved in the fame manner as promifes in confide-
29 Car II c. " ration of Marriage, and cannot be fupported by *parol* Evi-
3 ut fupra " dence only.
§ 7
§ 2   " So of a Demife of a Term of Years exceeding three '
§ 3   " the fame of Affignment of Interefts, freehold or cufto-
§ 4. ut fupra " mary
" The fame is to be underftood of any Contract or Sale of
' Lands, Tenements, or Hereditaments, or any *Intereft* in
" or concerning them
Ventr 361,2 " The Affignment of a *Term* is clearly within this Claufe,
" and was fo refolved in the Court of King's Bench very
" foon after the Statute
[7, 8, 9 " All Declarations and Affignments of Truft by Act of
" the Party fall under the provifion of the Statute
" Any Agreement, which is not to be performed within
" a Year, muft alfo be in writing, and figned by the party
" cha.ged
S.h 280 " But where the Agreement depends for the time of its
L N P 280 " performance on a *contingency*, and may probably in the
" Nature of the Thing, and the prefumable expectation of
" the parties, be performed within the year, it is not within
7 T de 219, " the Statute †
in tul, and
fevera other curious Points, the Cafe of Simon and Metivier or Motivor, Tr 6 G III B R
3 ber 15-1, and more at large, 1 Bl 259

SECTION V

BILLS of EXCHANGE

" The Progrefs of thefe Confiderations on the Evidence
" applicable to written Agreements, not of fpecialty, has
" now brought us to *Bills of Exchange*, an Article of moft
" extenfive importance, particularly * in the commercial * P. 147,
" World, and of which the Limits and Nature of this Work
" will not permit a complete Detail "

T I T. II.

To underftand this Matter aright, we muft confider the
Nature of Bills of Exchange a little more extendedly from
their original

All Exchange is made either in Goods, or Money, or " on
" Credit," and may accordingly be termed

1 *Actual, or fimple,*
2 *Eftimative,*
3 *Pignorative.*

" The *firft* is of the earlieft Antiquity, and is ftill pre-
" ferved among thofe Nations which are, or have been re-
" pu ed, *favage.* It confifts in battering Goods for Goods,
" and in any Country would fupply the mere neceffaries of
" natural Life in a Country tolerably fruitful, and of due
" Extent, compared with its Population, it will anfwer a
" great part of the real and general conveniences, but when
" Arts and Luxury prevail, it is wholly inadequate to the
" artificial exigencies of Society Some Medium, *(p)* there-
" fore, which has a *conventional* value, muft be adopted, and
" this ought to be fomething eafily diftinguifhed, durable,
" capable of receiving a vifible fanction from the impreffed

(p) Here it may be allowed to quote a paffage from that great Mir- I 3 24. 2.
ror of Antiquity and Manners, the imperifhable Poems of HOMER, † Urfini Virgil.
if any thing not immediately divine may be allowed that Epithet It illuftr —38.
has frequently indeed been quoted by various writers, yet it will bear,
and merits to be ftill as often repeated

Νῆάς δ' εκ Λήμνοιο παρεςασαν ΟΙ ΝΟΝ ἀγυσαι   1Λ H 467,
Πολλὰς τὰς προέπκεν Ἰησονίδης Ευηος   9 472, 5
Ἔνθεν ἀρ' οινίζοντο καρηκομόωνtες Αχαιοι
Ἄλλοι μὲν χαλχῷ, ἄλλοιαδ' αἴθωνι σιδηρῳ,
Ἄλλοι δε ρινοῖς, αλμοι δ' ἀυτοῖσι βόεσσιν,
Ἄλλοι δ' ανδραπόδεσσι

† Think of a Poet of *twenty-feven Centuries,* who has defcended
to us probably without the lofs of a line.

H 2   " Authority

" Authority of the State, and likely to be received in pay-
" ment in other civilized focieties, though not at an equal

* P 148 " Eftimation as at home ; and * *portable,* fo that a fuffici-
" ent quantity for general prefent occafions may eafily accom-
" panv the perfon All thefe requifites fo far unite in a
" Metal, commonly accounted of the moft ordinary kind
" *(iron excepted,* from its wart of *malleability,* and *lead,* from

† What we " its extreme fofinefs,) that Copper † has been the Money
call *Brass* in " of moft Countries during the firft Period of civil fociety ,
tranfluting the
Ancients, par- " and *gold* Coin has been unknown, not only to the *Infancy,*
ticularly the ' but to the full *Manhood* of the greateft ftates
Pits, is *Copper,*
the native Me- " But when Commerce becomes extenfive, Nations (as
tal, not *Brafs,* " late Experience hath too largely inftructed moft of the
the factitious
one. See, ref- " chief Communities of modern times) will, firft, from
pecting thefe " the neceffity or obvious convenience of the thing, indulge
Metals, WAT-
son's CHEM " to individuals a farther and fecondary fubftitution , and
Ess Vol III " at length will tax the aggregate of the induftry, power,
IV " and real or prefumed refources of the ftate, in fupport of
" a FUND of CREDIT Hence BILLS of EXCHANGE,
" *Banks* incorporated for *local* purpofes and that amazing
" political Eftablifhment a NATIONAL BANK, which bears
" fuch complicated Relations to the Manners, the Confti-
" tution, the domeftic and external operations of a Com-
" munity.

Comm II " Bills of Exchange are faid to have been firft introduced
c 30 P 466 " in this Country by the *Jews* and *Lombards,* when banifhed
" from *Guienne,* and afterwards from *England,* and other
" Countries, about five Centuries from the prefent period.
" Yet it is afferted they are confiderably an earlier inven-
" tion, and that they had been introduced into the *Mogul*
" Empire in 1236 Be this as it may, it is comparatively

* P 149 " but of late, * fince they became an important branch of
" our Jurifprudence Our Reports are nearly filent con-
' cerning them till about the æra of the *Revolution* they
" were complimented by the *Legiflature* with an exemption
W & M " from ftamps in 1694, apparently from being thought fo
c 21 § 5 " convenient that no obftacles fhould be thrown in their way
" (Parliament has fince appeared to be of opinion that their
" convenience was an argument for fubjecting them to fuc-
" ceffive ftamps) and in 1698 a direct legiflative fupport was
9 & 10 W III " given to them Their Currency was enforced and extend
c 17 " ed by an Act paffed fix years after in the fubfequent Reign,
3 & 4 Ac 9 " and *promiffory Notes* payable to the party, or *Order,* which
s 2

*One is grieved to quote in the fame paffage an inftance of eafe and
plenty, from a more extended intercourfe than the firft ftate of Nations
admits of, and of oppreffive cruelty in the deteftable* SLAVE TRADE

" before

" before were not affignable, were made equivalent to in-
" land Bills of Exchange This Act (temporary in its firft
" appointment, and that a very brief period indeed) was
" foon made perpetual and from that time the medium of
" commercial intercourfe acquired ftability and univerfality,
" and our Books abounded in Cafes by which this grand Ar-
" ticle of mercantile Law has been progreffively formed into 7 A c. 25 §3.
" a SYSTEM.

TIT. III

What is a Bill of Exchange

" *A Bill of Exchange is an open Letter of Requeft from one*
" *perfon to another, defiring him to pay a fum named therein to*
" *the third perfon on his Account.*

*TIT. IV   * P. 150.

" In this are to be regarded,

    1 *The Bill,*
    2 *Its collateral incidents.*

    1 *Acceptance,*
    2 *Indorfement,*
    3 *Proteft*

Par 3

" It is effential to the *Bill* that it be *a promife to pay*, and
" therefore, if limited to a *fpecial, future, contingent Fund,*
" it will not maintain a Declaration in *Affumpfit*, as on a Bill
" of Exchange

ARGENTUM *fignatum eft Anno Urbis* DLXXXV Q_ Fabio *Confule
quinque annis ante primum bellum* Punicum AUREUS NUMMUS
poft annum LXII *percuffus eft quam argenteus*
Suppofing this Computation had been correct, and no Error of the Plin N H 33
Prefs or MSS, *it is probable that* CORRADUS, *in his whimfical but* c 3 1 3
elegant QUÆSTURA, *where he compares the Life of* CICERO *to a* p 240
feries of Medals, would have marked this coincidence , for it brings it Ed 1601
to the æra of the Birth of that illuftrious Roman according to Middleton, *the very year , though* Corradus *places it a year later, in* 648
*of the City, but the truth is, there is an Error of no lefs than a Cen-
tury , which the Syncronifm of a Period fo well marked as that of
the firft* Punic *War corrects we fhould therefore read the firft æra*
CCCCLXXXV, *and the fecond, confequently* DXLVII
*I do not know that fince the Conqueft we have any earlier gold
Coin than that ftruck by* Edward III *in* 1364, *on occafion of his vic-
tory by Sea againft the Spanifh Cruifers*

                             " Sir,

Dawes and
Wife against
Ea-Deloraine
Bl 2S-
Tr 11 Geo.III
C P.

" Sir,

" Seven Weeks after Date, pay Miss R 32l out of W. S's
" Money, as soon as you shall receive it.

" Plaintiff's counted, 1 on a Bill of Exchange, according
" to the Custom of Merchants.

" Per Curiam—" As this Count in the Declaration is found-
" ed on the Custom of Merchants, if the Bill in Question
" be not a Bill of Exchange, according to that Custom, no
" Action will lie on this Count : we deliver no opinion on
" the omission of the Words, " Value received" and " Order,"
" but confine ourselves to the latter objection, that the Bill
" is drawn payable out of a particular Fund, and upon an
" Event which is future and contingent, the Drawee's hav-
" ing received W. S 's Money.

* P. 151 * " A Bill of Exchange always implies a personal general
" Course of Negotiation

Par 3

Form of a BILL of EXCHANGE

" The usual Form of a Bill of Exchange is well known

" At fight, [or 6 : Days after fight, or : Days after
" Date,] please to pay to   of :   Merchant
"   the sum of :   and place the same to the Ac-
" count of
" But a Note, payable to   or Bearer, is negocia-
" ble , and so where it was, Pay to SHIP FORTUNE, or
" BEARER.

Gant v
Vaughan
T 4 Geo III
3 Bur Manff
1516 S C 1
Bl R 485

There were Two COUNTS.

1   On an Inland Bill of Exchange,
2   On indebitatus assumpsit

" The Note was lost, and payment stopped : this Action
" was brought by the Bearer, who purchased it, without
" Notice, for a valuable consideration

" The Opinion of the Court was that the Bill was NEGO-
" TIABLE

" That the Plaintiff was certainly entitled to recover on
" the second Count ; and the Court seems strongly to have
" intimated that even if it had stood on the first Count alone,
" the Action might still have been maintained.

* P. 152. " But the Bearer, to entitle himself, must have come
" by it honestly ; and when he has so come by it, whatever
" may be the merits between the Drawer and a third per-
                                                - " son,

" fon, he fhall never be fubjected to lofe what he hath pur-
" chafed in the Courfe of Trade for Confideration, and
" without Notice.

" So a Bank Bill, payable to *A* or Bearer, was givento *A* and 1 Salk. 126
" loft, a ftranger found and tranſferred it to *C* for valuable Mic 10 W III.
" confideration *Per* HOLT, *Chief Juftice*, *A* may have *Trover*
" againſt the ſtranger who found the Bill, for he had no Title,
" though payment to him would have indemnified the Bank.
" But *A* cannot maintain Trover againſt *C* by reaſon of
" the Courſe of Trade, which creates a property in the Af-
" ſignee or Bearer

" And thus a *Bank Note*, of which the Mail had been Miller v Race
" robbed, having been purchaſed, without knowledge of the Hil 31 G II
" Robery, for a valuable confideration, it was held *Trover* 1 Burr Manſ.
" would not lie againſt the *Purchaſer* , but that it was *Caſh* in 422
" his hands, who was entitled to it accordingly againſt all the
" World, this being neceſſary to the Freedom and Security
" of Commerce, and a juſt reſult from the very Nature of
" the ſubject in diſpute

* " And in this reſpect, there is no difference between *Bank* * P. 153.
" *Bills*, and other *Bills* of *Exchange* 3 Burr Manſf.
1524
" In the *principal* Caſe juſt cited, Notice is taken of ſome 3 Lev 299.
" early Opinions before this Point of Juriſprudence had been Horton v
" much agitated, evidently founded in miſtake. As that Cogge
" which ſuppoſes ſuch a Bill, might be paid to the Nominee Mic 3 W &
M C B
" of it, after it came into the hand of a perſon entitling
" himſelf as *Bearer*, without notice from the Bearer. A thing Nicholſon v.
Sedgewick
" plainly repugnant to the very Nature of theſe Tranſactions. 1 Lord Ramy.
180
" And a later Caſe, which ſuggeſts that the Action ought
" not to be brought in the Name of the *Bearer*, but in that of
" the *Payee*, particularly ſpecified in the Bill, in order to pre-
" vent a perſon claiming who came into poſſeſſion of a Bill
" without confideration, was obſerved to go on a *Petitio Prin-*
" *cipii*, that ſuch holder, would be entitled: whereas the 3 Burr Manſf.
" holder, who claims as Bearer, will be put to prove the con- 1521
" ſideration and the fairneſs of his poſſeſſion

" A Bill may be drawn (though *Engliſh* Bills of Exchange
" in *England*, ſeem not generally ſo to be) payable at *ſingle*, L N P 269
" double, or treble *Uſance* (or Credit), which is commonly at Buckley v
Campbell
" ſo many Months after Date but if a Plaintiff declare on Hil 7 A
" a foreign Bill bearing ſuch Uſance, he muſt aver in his Salk 131.
" Declaration what that Uſance is. 6 Mod. 30.

' A Bill is good if drawn, " *pay to me or order*," for the
" third perſon is as effectually included in it, as if it had
" been expreſſed in the uſual Terms.

Of

* Of ACCEPTANCE

Tit V

1

" An *Acceptance* is an *undertaking* to pay on the *Credit* of
" the *Drawer* (q)
" There are no precife words requifite to an Acceptance
" any thing will make one that gives a determinate Credit to
" the Bill

Par 2

L. V P 271
3 Bac Ab-.
612 Moll B II.
c. 10 § 20

An Acceptance may be *abfolute* or *conditional*

1 abfolute

" Thus," *leave the Bill with me and I will accept it to mor-*
row, this is an Acceptance; for it is giving Credit to the Bill,
and hindering the Proteft in the mean time.

2 *conditional*

(q) *The Cafe in* 6 Mod *furnifhes an opportunity of afcertaining,*
with reafonable probability, when inland Bills of Exchange began to
be confidered in our Law, and what idea was entertained of them at
their firft introduction to our Courts HOLT Ch Juft, *fays, I re-*
member when Actions on inland Bills of Exchange aid firft begin, it
was about thirty Years ago (this brings it to about 1670) *And*
there they laid a particular Cuftom between London *and* Briftol, *and*
it was an Act on againft the Acceptor The Defendant's Counfel
would put them to prove the Cuftom at which, Hale, *who tried it,*
laughed, and faid, they had a hopeful Cafe on it And in my Lord
North's *Cafe, it was faid, the Cuftom in that Cafe, was part of the*
Common Law of England *and the Actions fince became frequent as*
the Trade of the Nation did increafe —And the Notes in queftion, are
only an invention of the Goldfmith's *Company, who had a mind to*
make a Law to bind all thofe that did deal with them and furely,
to allow fuch Note to carry any Lien with it, were to turn a piece
of paper, which is, in Law, but Evidence of a parol Contract, into

- Mr ac Car II, a
1 Seffi-
Par 85.

a Specialty.
This Cafe feems to have manifefted, that the Court were very anxi-
ous to keep up the diftinction between promiffory Notes, though ex-
prefsly drawn negotiable, and Bills of Exchange , and that the Bills
of Exchange, at that time, were fuppofed not much to concern inland
commerce for a chief part of the prefs feems to be laid on their
hindering export at or of Money out of the Kingdom
The firft Cafe that has hitherto occurred to me, was in 1668, *and*
it fo well reported, and illuftrates fo much the Idea entertained at
that time, that I fhall quote it at large
In an action for 100l (on DEBT), *the Plaintiff declared, that*
by the Cuftom of England, *if a Merchant fend a Bill of Exchange*
to another Merchant, to pay Money to another Perfon, and the Bill be
accepted,

2 *conditional.*

But if the Merchant fay, leave the Bill with me, and I
will look over my Books and Accounts between the Drawer
and me, call to morrow, and accordingly the Bill fhall be
accepted: this is no complete Acceptance, becaufe it depends
upon the Balance of the Account, and on the Merchant having effects in his hands to anfwer it · fo that the Merchant
gives no abfolute Credit to the Bill, but the Deliverer was
willing to commit it to him, and to delay the Proteft till his
anfwer.

Moll B 2.
c 10. § 20
3Bac.Abr 610.
Str 648
Lord Raym.
444
2 Str 817
Barnard, K B.
87
2 Lord Raym.
1542
2 Str 955
" And Hard 136
2 Barn 120.
2 Str 1000

*accepted, that he who accepts the Bill, does thereby become chargeable
with the Sum therein contained, and that a certain Merchant drew
a Bill of Exchange upon the* Defendant, *payable to the* Plaintiff,
which Bill the Defendant *accepted* per quod Actio accrevit.
And upon nil debet *pleaded, a Verdict paffed for the* Plaintiff. *And
now it was moved in* Arreft of Judgment *by* Offley,

1 That the Declaration is naught.
2 That the Action of Debt lies not
For the firft, *he faid the* Declaration *was* naught, *becaufe the*
Plaintiff *declared,* per Confuetudinem Angliæ *becaufe the* Cuftom
of England *is the* Law *of* England,* which the Judges are bound to
take notice of *and that therefore, the* Confuetudo Angliæ, *ought to
have been omitted, and that it would have been naught, on a general
Demurrer* †
Secondly, *an Action of Debt lies not in this Cafe, becaufe there is
no Privity, nor any Contract, in Deed or in Law, between the* Y B 4 fo.18
Plaintiff *and* Defendant *and where thefe fail, Debt hath not*
Stevens pro Quer . *As to the firft Exception, it has been a Doubt
before, but it is now fettled to be good —And for the Second, it is a
Rule in Law, that where the Common Law, or any particular Cuftom creates a Duty,* Debt *lies for it*
Chief Baron *This is a Cafe of Weight and Concern for the future,
and deferves Confideration Declarations upon Bills of Exchange
have often varied, fometimes Declarations have been on the Cuftom
among Merchants only, without laying an exprefs Promife Afterwards
they came to declare upon an Affumpfit And after all, if an Action of
Debt will lie, it will be a fhort Cut, and pare off a long Recital.
For if Debt lies, a Man may declare upon a Bill of Exchange acquired in Debt, or in an indebitatus affumpfit for fo much Money.*
* Confuetudo Angliæ eft Lex Angliæ
† The Cafe of 2 H 4 was quoted in fupport of this Doctrine
but it does not fupport it, for there the Plaintiff counted on the
General Cuftom of the Realm, and the Defendant would have
had him fhew the Cuftom, and this the Court very fenfibly over-
ruled for the common Cuftom is the Common Law
‖ A Duty here is *a legal Liability in a fum certain* · fee this   * P 2 H IV 6
Principle accurately ftated in the *Law of Nifi Prius,* ‖ it will   ‖ P H C IV
be neceffary to fpeak of it more at large hereafter in treating of the   167
Action of Debt, &c

But

* P 155.
L N £ 272
Lumley v
Palmer
Sr 1000,

* " And this Acceptance is no otherwise neceſſary to be
" in Writing, than to charge the *Drawer* with *Damages* and
" *Coſts :* but an Action will lie againſt the Acceptor on a
" *paro'* Acceptance

" And, of Courſe, an Acceptance when in Writing is not
" neceſſary to be on the Bill itſelf, but may be by Letter or
" otherwiſe detached from the Bill.

" So

But for the Plaintiff's inſerting the Cuſtom of the Realm *into his
Declaration here, I hold that to be mere ſuperfluity and redundancy,
which does not vitiate the Declaration. And without doubt, if the*
Common Law, *or the Cuſtom of the Place, create a Duty,* DEBT
lies for it as in the Caſe of a Toll due *by* Cuſtom, 20 H. 7. 1. *But
the great Queſtion here is, whether or no, a Debt or Duty be hereby
raiſed. For if it be no more than a* collateral Engagement, *order,
or Promiſe,* DEBT *lies not   as in the Caſe that has been cited of Goods
delivered by A to B at the requeſt of C. which C promiſes to pay for,
if B. do not : for in that Caſe, a Debt or Duty doth not ariſe between A. and C, but a* collateral Obligation *only   In our Caſe,*

1 Show 317
L N p 273.

*the Acceptance of a Bill amounts clearly to a Promiſe to pay the
Money , but it may be a Queſtion, whether it amount to a Debt or
not , for if ſo, then it is aſſignable to the King or by* Commiſſioners
of Bankrupt   *And it were worth while to enquire what the Courſe
hath been among* Merchants *, or to direct an Iſſue for trial of the
Cuſtom among Merchants in this Caſe , for although we muſt take
notice in general, of the* Law of Merchants *, yet all their Cuſtoms
we cannot know but by Information.*

Precedents were ordered to be ſearched   and afterwards in Hil.
Term, *it was moved again   and ſhewn, that by the Opinion of* Chief
Juſtice, Debt *lay not, and all the Clerks in* Guildhall *certified, that
they had no Precedent in* London, *of Debt, in ſuch a Caſe   Afterwards (in the ſame manner) the Court declared their opinions, that
an Action of Debt would not lie upon a Bill of Exchange accepted
againſt the Acceptor · but that a* ſpecial Action on the Caſe *muſt
be brought againſt him   For that the Acceptance does not create a
Duty .—And this courſe of accepting Bills, being a general Cuſtom
amongſt all Traders, both within and without the Realm, and having every where that effect, as to make the* Acceptor *ſubject to pay
the Contents, the Court muſt take notice of that Cuſtom ; but the
Cuſtom does not extend ſo far as to create a Debt , only make the Acceptor* Onerabilis *for the Money*

*Here follows a remark (and a very reaſonable one   it ſeems), pro
bably made by the Reporter,* " *tho' Cuſtom may give an action of
debt as in* 20 H   7 *of* Toll   *and ſo in caſe of a Fine for a Copyhold "*

And it then concludes,

*Wherefore, and becauſe no Precedents could be produced, that
an Action of Debt had been brought upon an accepted Bill of Exchange . judgment was arreſted.*

The

" So a Draft on a third person by the *Drawee*, to pay
" and place to Account of *Drawer*, is an Acceptance.
" An Acceptance is good after the time of payment elapſ-
" ed, and amounts to a promiſe to pay, generally So an Ac-
" ceptance to pay at a longer Date than the Bill has to run
" It was before ſhewn, that an Acceptance might be con-
" ditional on a faƈt aſcertainable at the time . and ſo it may
" on a future *contingency* . and will be binding when the con-
" tingency takes place : as to pay, *when effeƈts come to 'hand*,
" or the like   But where the Plaintiffs were entreated to
" accept and draw on G they drew on G. who *does not accept* :
" this was held no implied Acceptance of the Plaintiffs.
                                        Par 3

*Moor v Withy
Tr 10 Cʒo III.
B R.
J ˆ ſon v.
Pigot
10 W III.
Salk 127
V alſo S. P.
Salk 129
ʒ Str 1153

Smith v Abbot.
Str 1152
Smith v Niſſen.
T Rep T
26 G III.*

The Doƈtrine of General Cuſtoms, *may illuſtrate what has been before intimated, concerning the Diſtinƈtion between* General *and* Special Aƈts *of* Parliament.
With regard to the Term Exchange, *there is another ſenſe of it properly relative to foreign Bills And in this ſenſe* Exchange *is a Reduƈtion of Coins or Denominations of Money from the Species of one Country to thoſe of another ; or in a Senſe more materially commercial,* Exchange is the relative Value of Specie *in the* Conversion of Bills, &c *into* Cash *payable in* another Country *And this greatly depends upon the abſolute Value. This relative Value is fixed by the current Courſe of Commerce, and the general Opinion and Conſent of Merchants . but is not fixable by a permanent Law of any State, being in its Nature ſubjeƈt to inceſſant Variations from innumerable circumſtances. In general where there is much Specie the Exchange is* low *where there is leſs, the Exchange, or relative Value between the two Countries, muſt be higher in that Country, which has the comparative deficiency of Specie.*
When Money in France, *for inſtance, yields Money of the ſame ſtandard and weight in* England, *the Exchange between theſe two Countries is ſaid to be at* Par. *when it yields more than* Par *it is* high, *when below, it is* low.
When an Exchange is below Par *from one Country to another, the former loſes as* Debtor *and* Buyer, *and gains as* Creditor *and* Seller. *Thus, let the Par be repreſented by* 100, *if the Exchange between* England *and* France *is at* 90, *then* England, *in purchaſing of* France *ſuffers a depreciation to that amount, but if ſhe ſell to* France, *ſhe will be to receive the difference as a balance in her favour.*
Or ſuppoſe as between France *and* Holland *in* 1774, *that the Par was* 54 *gros, for a French crown of three livres, and that the Exchange to* Holland *is below Par, namely at* 50, *let there be a Bill for* 5400 *gros, payable from* Holland *to* France, 108 *French Crowns will pay this and at* 54 *it would have been paid by* 100 *, the ſuppoſed abſolute Value and at* 60 *it would have been diſcharged by payment of* 90 *Crowns*
Now reverſe this . let France *have to pay to* Holland 108 *Crowns :* *at* 50, *ſhe muſt pay* 5,400 *Gros at* 54, *ſhe muſt pay* 5832 *and at* 60, *ſhe muſt pay* 6480. *This is not meant to ſtate the Mode of payment*

Vide Cyctor
laſt Ed Tit
Exchange

Par. 3.

Of partial Acceptance.

L. N. P. 270.

" An *Acceptance* may be also *partial*, and shall be good *pro*
" *tanto* for so much of the Value as the Acceptor consents
" to charge himself with responsibility So it may be other-
" wise

payment in Exchange, or of Computation between different Countries,
but to intimate the Nature of it.

Exchange *has a third mercantile sense, as it stands for the Com-*
mission which a Merchant receives for Money advanced payable by
Bill abroad, and this varies from 3 to 15 or more per Cent in dif-
ferent places and at different Periods

Of Policies of Insurance

Though Policies *of Insurance are properly, at least in general Mat-*
ters of Specialty, yet they have such a Connection, especially those
upon Ships, with mercantile Transactions, that they are proper to be
here mentioned

The Court *of Policies of Assurance, erected in the Year 1601,*
is a Jurisdiction which the Great Seal is empowered annually to create
by granting a Commission to the Judge of the Admiralty, the Recorder

Comm. III.
c. 6. p 74, 5

* 43 Eliz. c. 12

13 & 14 Car II
c. 23

of London, two Doctors of the Civil, two of the Common Law, and
eight Merchants : any three of which, one being a Civilian or a Bar-
rister, are thereby, and by the Statute of the third subsequent King,
empowered summarily to determine all causes concerning Policies of As-
surance in London, with an Appeal to Chancery by way of Bill

1 Show 396

But this power being held (perhaps by too restricted a Construction
derived from the Preamble solely, for the enacting Clause seems suf-
ficiently general) to be confined to Causes instituted by the assured, and
not by the Assurers , and it being certainly confined to such Policies of
Assurance as should be entered in the Assurance Office of the City of
London, no such Commission has lately issued , but Assurance Causes
have generally been determined by the Verdict of a Jury of Merchants,
and the Opinion of the Judges, in case of any legal Doubt, whereby
the Decision is more speedy, satisfactory, and final At the same time

15 & 16 Car II
§ 3, 4

the Author of the Commentaries remarks that it were to be wished that
some of the parliamentary powers invested in those Commissioners (espe-
cially for the examination of witnesses, either beyond seas, or speedily

Comm II
c. 30 p. 461

going out of the Kingdom) could be adopted in the Courts of Westmin-
ster, without requiring the Consent of Parties

19 Geo II
c. 37

To confine these Insurances to their proper object, the encouragement
of Commerce, and the security of fair Trade, a statute was passed
about the middle of the late Reign, by which all insurances, interest
or no interest, or without farther proof of the Interest than from the
Policy itself, or by way of gaming or wagering, or without benefit of
salvage to the insurer, shall be totally null and void, with an excep-
tion to privateers, and ships in the Spanish and Portuguese trade) and
that no reassurance be lawful, except the former insurer be insolvent,
a bankrupt or dead

An

"wife qualified · as part in *goods* and part in money   but he
"to whom the Bill is due, may refuse such Acceptance, and
"protest the Bill, so as to charge the Drawer.

V Sprat v.
Matthews.
P 16 G 1H.
T Rep.

* *Par.* 4.   * P 156.

Whose Acceptance shall bind another

If a Bill be drawn on two, or either of them, either
may accept the Bill and if one accept, it can not be protested for non-acceptance but the party accepting only, is
liable to the Action, because he only has given Credit to
the Bill.

But

And in general these being Contracts, the very essence of which
consisteth in the purest faith and integrity, they are vacated by any
the least shadow of fraud or concealment   at the same time being much
for the security and extension of trade, they are protected and encou-
raged both by Common Law, and by various Acts of Parliament.

And it was held, even before the Statute, that Insurance with-
out interest was relievable   Indeed there was a circumstance of
manifest Fraud in that Case, by using the Name of the first Sub-
scriber as a Decoy, which might be a part inducement, but the opi-
nion of the Court, as reported in the Book, is founded on the Extent
of the general Principle

The Case was   Thornborough and others came to the Insurance
Office, and bought a Policy on the Life of one Horwell, (in whose
Life they had no interest) for one Year, and the Policy ran, whe-
ther Interest or not Interest, and the Premium 5 per Cent,
Wittingham v.
Thornborough.
Ch Pre 20
Hil, 1690

They took this way to draw in subscribers   one Marwood, a noted
Merchant on the Exchange, and a leading Man in such Cases, to
subscribe first · but in case Horwell died within the year, Marwood
was to lose nothing   on the contrary, he was to share what should
be gained from the other subscribers

On the Credit of Marwood subscribing, several others, who had
enquired of him about the Life ensured, who was his neighbour, sub-
scribed likewise   Horwell lived about four Months, and then died

On Bill to be relieved against the Policy, this Matter was all
confessed by Answer   The Court decreed the Policy to be delivered
up, and the Premium to be repaid, the Plaintiffs deducting thereout
their Costs

The Court said, this way of insuring was first set up for the Be-
nefit of Trade, that when a Merchant happened to have a Loss, he
Preamble to
43 Eliz c 12
might not be undone by it, the Loss this way being borne by many, but
if such ill Practices were used, it would turn to the ruin of Trade,
instead of advancing it

And again, in another Case, the Court said, on the same general
Reason, Take it, that the Law is settled that if a Man has no Inter-
2 Vern 269
Goddart v
Garret
Yr 1692
est, and insures, the insurance is void, although it be expressed in
the Party, interested or not interested.

What

Molloy,
B II c 12,
§ 18.

But if a Bill be drawn on two " jointly, who are not " Partners," it feems that both muft accept it, otherwife it may be protefted " for their Credit is tendered by the " Drawer to the Payee jointly

If ten Merchants employ one Factor, and he draws a Bill upon them all, and one accepts it, it fhall only bind him, and not the reft, becaufe they are feparate in Intereft, one from the other.

Pinkey v Hall
Lord Raym
175 Mic
3 & 9 W III
S C Salk 126
very fhort but
clear

But in Cafe of two JOINT TRADERS, the *Acceptance* of the one will bind the other, becaufe they trade for a common Benefit, and therefore, where one of them gives Credit, it is the Act of both.

But

What Naval Infurance is.

V Bac Abr.
Tit MER-
CHANT
(1) 3 p 598

NAVAL INSURANCE is where, for a certain fum, a Perfon takes on himfelf the Rifque a SHIP and GOODS, or both, are to run in a certain Voyage

Skinn 411, 2
*Tomkynsand
Barnet

If a Man pay Money on a Policy of Infurance, fuppofing a Lofs where in reality there was no Lofs, either in Fact, the Ship being fafe, or in Law, the infurance being in fraud of the infurer, he fhall recover the Value on indebitatus affumpfit

|| 2 Vern 176.

|| *Where there is Infurance againft* Reftraint of Princes, *this intends fuch Reftraint as the party by a lawful and regular Conduct might have avoided. And therefore, where the enfured fhall navigate contrary to the Law of the Country, or where feizure is incurred by non payment of Cuftoms, he is not within the benefit of the Policy*

† M 1 J II.
b R Skinn
243

† *An Infurance until the Ship fhall have ended, and be difcharged her Voyage, is not fatisfied by her Arrival in Port merely.*

§ Skinn 327

§ *Infurance by T S for himfelf and fuch as fhould have Goods on board the Ship   Good as to fuch who might lawfully have goods on board*

* Bac Abr 3.
559

If a Ship is warranted to depart with Convoy, this muft be underftood not only departing the firft port with Convoy, but alfo a continuance with fuch Convoy, if poffible, during the Voyage *

But Evidence, that the Ship was fevered from her Convoy by ftrefs of Weathe, and all in, will render the Infurers liable, if no neglect

†Carth 216 7
Hil 3 W & M
B R S C
balk 443
3 Lev and
much beft
48 Mod 58
though at the
end there is a
tranfpofition,
for it fhould be,
if the Ship had
run from the

appears of endeavour to rejoin the Convoy ‡

Regularly, a Lofs by Deviation, either directly or confequentially happening is not within the benefit of the Policy, which protects only in and during the Voyage

But to go out of the courfe for the purpofe of joining Convoy at the ufual place of rendezvous for Convoy, is no Deviation

So got back to repair, having fprung a leak in the Voyage, or for the purpofe of avoiding an Enemy, or for any other purpofe, obvioufly for the beneft of the infured, and comprehended within the fair meaning of the Policy

Convoy Pond v Nut, Cowp E 17 G III 601, 9   v alfo Str 1264   1 Atk 545   Delaney v Stoudar', T Rep M 26 G III

Warranty.

↲ But if a Factor of " a Public" Company, draw a Bill ✳ P 157.
on such Company, and any Member accept it, it shall not
bind the Company or any other Member of it because it
is only a private Act of such person, and not of the Company " directly, or by their Officer duly authorized for
" such purposes."

A servant, or " even" a Wife cannot accept a Bill without Moll B II.
an Authority from the master or from the Husband · unless c 10 § 27.
they usually made such Acceptances. Sty 307

Par.

Warranty.

† A Warranty to Sail on or before such a Day, makes the Sailing ac- † Hore v
cordingly an indispensable Condition without regard how it may have Whitmore, E.
been prevented 18 G III

§ A Warranty must be literally performed. nothing tantamount Cowp 784, 5.
will satisfy it excludes the consideration of an equivalent : other- § Pawson v
wise of a Representation, for in that it is sufficient if it be Sub- Watson, 785.
stantially performed And a Warranty may be written in the Mar- De Hahn v
gin of a Policy for thus it is still part of the instrument of Insu- Hartley, T R
rance Tr 26 G III,
343,

* The insured may recover on a partial though declaring on a total * Gardiner v.
Loss For this is not in the Nature of an Action of Debt it is an Croscale, Hil.
Action on the Case, a liberal and equitable Action in which the Plain- 33 G II
tiff may recover less, though not more, than the Sum for which he 2 Burr Manf
sues The Defendant, on this general Action, comes prepared to shew 904 908
that either no Loss happened, or none with which he is chargeable, or S C Bl
that he is chargeable but for part And if a partial Loss could not 198. 9
be recovered under such general Declaration, it would introduce great L N P 129
inconvenience, by making distinct Counts requisite for every Species of
Damage and every possible Quantum of Loss

Evidence of Acts done with an intention to deviate, but without
actual Deviation, shall not defeat the Policy ‡ ‡ Str 1249
Where the Defendants insured Goods to London, and until the Hil 19 G II
same should be safely landed there The Evidence was, that the Ship Foster v
arrived in the port of London, and the Owner of the Goods sent his Wilmer
Lighter and received the Goods out of the Ship but before they
reached Land, by an Accident they were damaged ‖ ‖ Sparrow v.
Held, that on this Evidence the Insurance was discharged but Caruthers,
that it would have been otherwise, had the Goods been sent off by the Tr 18 G II
Ship's Boat Str 1236

Where the Value saved comes short of the freight, the insured is
entitled to consider it as a total Loss ¶ ¶ Mic 10
Where a Ship goes out, and is not heard of within such time as G II Str
she, by the general course of Voyages should have been, this negative 1065
Evidence sufficiently infers the presumption she was lost at Sea, and ✳✳ Str 1199
though there be an Exception in such insurances, that it shall not ex- Green v
tend to captures and seizures, this shall not avail the underwriter Brown, Mic
because the presumption is that of such Accidents, notice would have 17 G II
arrived ✳✳ Robertson v
Lever, Hil
An Insurance on the Ship will not cover Seamens Wages. 26 G III

The T Rep 127
32

Par 5.

Collateral Acceptance.

12 Mod. 410.
Salk. 129
3 Bac. Abr 608
Com Rep. 76.
Lutw 891, 2
896, 9.
Carth. 129

A. draws a Bill upon *B* and *B* being in the Country, *C*, his Friend, accepts it: the Bill must be protested for the Non-acceptance of *B*; and then *C*'s Acceptance shall bind him to answer the Money

Moll. B II
c. 10. § 33

So if a Bill be not accepted, and a third Person accepts the Bill for the Honour of the Drawer, this shall bind him to answer the Money because he hath given Credit to the Bill and by consequence, he must answer the Money for which he hath given Credit

INDORSEMENT

Lockyer v
Offiley, E
26 G III
T. R. 252

The Voyage determined, which was the Object of the Insurance, the underwriter shall not be liable, though the Ship be lost in consequence of a cause which took place during her Voyage as if she be seized on account of an Act of Smuggling committed by the Master, for it is, at the strongest, only like the Case where a Ship was insured

Meretony and
Dunlope, E.
23 G III.

for six Months three days before the Expiration of that term, she received, what the Sailors emphatically express, her death's Wound, but by pumping, was kept afloat till three days after the time and, in that Case, the insurer was held not liable

Where every thing is done for the probable benefit of all parties concerned, and according to usage, the insured shall not suffer the loss and a transaction in the course of the Voyage, though not literally upon it, shall come within the Insurance

And therefore, in an Action brought against the Royal Exchange Insurance Company, upon a Policy on the Body, Tackle, Ordnance, and Apparel of the Ship Onslow, against Perils of the Seas, Men of War, Fire, and then, in general terms, from the Thames to all places beyond the Cape of Good Hope and back again, until moored

§ Kelly v R.
Exch Assur
Corp
E 30 G II

twenty-four hours in the River Thames ‖

*When the Ship got to Canton, the Captain laid up his Sails and Tackle on a Bank Saul, * according to the Custom in that Navigation A Swedish Ship took Fire, which burnt the Tackle of the On-*

Cun og C 72
p 282, &c.
S C 2 Burr
Manst 341

flow; adjudged that the Insurers were liable.

Abandonment

After Notice of Loss, the Insured may abandon which is making a Renunciation to the Insurers, and the Insured comes in for so much as shall appear his Interest in the Adventure beyond the Value insured

Cunningham,
Art 69
p 278, 9

Gols v
Witner,
2 Burr Manst.
683

This Doctrine of Abandonment, and of the Loss which shall authorize it, was largely discussed in the Case of an Insurance on the Ship David and Rebecca, and another on the Goods on board the said Ship.

M'c 32 G II

The Case was this —The Ship was bound from Newfoundland to her Port of Discharge in Portugal or Spain, without the Straights, or England, to commence from the time of her beginning to load at Newfoundland

* Or Sand Bank.

A Bill, once accepted, cannot be revoked " by the Party   Moll II c 10.
" who hath accepted, it," although the Acceptor has advice   § 28
that the Drawer is broke because, by Acceptance, he hath   Styl. 370.
given Credit to the Bill; and after Credit given, the Acceptor has made the Bill his own, and, by Custom, the Payment is to be made where the Credit was given and the
Custom must be particularly alleged, being the Foundation
of the Action

VOL I.   I   TIT.

Newfoundland *for either of the above Places. and the* Insurance
*on the first Policy was, on the Body, Tackle, Apparel, Ordnance,
&c &c of the Ship*

The Adventure to commence from Newfoundland, *and to continue
during her Abode there, and until she should have been moored at An-
chor twenty-four Hours in Safety*

*The Ship and Cargo were valued at the Sum subscribed without
farther Account*

*And it was agreed, that in case of Loss, it should be lawful for
the* Insurers *to pursue, labour, travel, &c for the Recovery of any
part, and that the Loss should be considered as an Average Loss.*

The Plaintiff declared on a total *Loss, by* Capture by the French.

*The other Policy was upon any kind of lawful Goods or Merchan-
dize, laden or to be laden on board the said Ship And the Declaration stated diverse Quantities of Fish, and other lawful Merchandize,
to the Value of the Money insured, were put on board to be carried
from* Newfoundland *to her port of Destination and so continued (except such as were thrown over board as after mentioned) till the Loss
of the Ship and Goods*

*The Declaration then farther stated, that one fourth of the said
Goods were necessarily thrown overboard, in a Storm, to preserve the
Ship and the rest of the Cargo after which, the Ship and the Remain-
der of the Goods were taken by the* French

*On the Special Case it appeared, that the Ship departed from her
proper port, and on the 23d of* December, 1756, *was taken by the
French And that the* Master, Mates, *and all the* Sailors, *(except an Apprentice and Landman) were* taken out and carried to
FRANCE, *That the Ship remained* IN THE HANDS OF THE
ENEMY, EIGHT DAYS, *and was then retaken by a* British Pri-
vateer, *and brought into* Milford Haven *on the 18th of* January,
and that immediate Notice *was given by the Assured to the Assurers, with an offer to* ABANDON *the Ship to their Care*

*It was also proved on the Trial, that previous to the Capture by
the Enemy, a violent Storm arose, and that then part of the Cargo
was thrown over-board as in the Declaration alledged, and the rest
SPOILED, while the Ship lay at* Milford Haven, *after the offer
to abandon But some of these points seem to have been introduced
from a doubt what might be the Decision of the Court on the effect
of the Capture, &c. and to have had no essential influence on the
Determination.*

The

Tit. VI.

2 Indorsement.

" An Indorsement is is a signing by one who passes a Bill,
" whereby he, implicitly, acknowledges himself to under-
" take, that the same shall be paid as Cash "

*P 159.   * It is usual when Bills of Exchange are drawn, especial-
ly when they are payable at two or three Usances, for the
Deliverer to endorse them over to others in the Traffic of
Goods and Commodities and the Receiver of such Bills,
has not only the Original Credit of the Drawer at stake,
and

The Lord Chief Justice, *after noticing the indistinctness and
discordancy of the Rules concerning what should be held to be a Capture so as to alter the* property *as a possession after the Battle ended,
a carrying* intra præsidiæ *; or, by later and clearer Authorities, a
Sentence of Condemnation, observed, that the difficulty which
might arise on the Question, whether by the Facts in Evidence, the
property were changed, was foreign to this Case that being a
Point which it might have been necessary to decide between other parties, as against a Vendee, or Recaptor, but not between the Assured
and the Assurers*

That here was a Loss, *on which the general Question depended,
whether on the circumstances it amounted to a* Total Loss, *intitling
them to abandon the Ship and Cargo to the Insurers, for them to
make what advantage of the Salvage they could —or, in other
Words, whether the Insured had, under all the circumstances, upon
the 18th of January, 1757, an Election to abandon ?*

*His Lordship continued, the Loss and Disability was in its Nature
total a the time it happened During Eight Days, the Plaintiff
was certainly intitled to be paid by the Insurer as for a total Loss
And in Case of a Recapture, the Insurer would have stood in his
place. The subsequent Recapture is, at best, a saving only of a
small part . half the Value must be paid for Salvage The Disability to pursue the Voyage still continued The Master and Mariners were Prisoners. The Charter-party was dissolved The Freight
(except in proportion to the Goods saved) was lost The Ship necessarily brought into an English Port What could be saved might not
be worth the expence attending it*

*The subsequent Title to Restitution, arising from the Recapture,
cannot take away a Right vested in the insured at the time of the
Capture. But because he cannot recover more than he has suffered,
he must abandon what may be saved*

*I cannot find in a single Book, antient or modern, which does not
say, that in Case of the Ship being taken, the Insured may demand
a for a total Loss and abandon*

*And what proves the Proposition most strongly is, that by the gene-
ral Law, he may abandon in the Case merely of an Arrest or an Em
bargo by a Prince, not an Enemy Positive Regulations in different
Countries have fixed a precise time, before the insured shall be at Liberty*

and of the Acceptor, if the Bill be accepted, but also of
the Indorsees of such Bills · because, such Indorsees have
passed such Credit in their payments instead of Money, and
the Persons receiving such Bills, have Actions in their own
Names against either . for all their several Credits are at
stake when they have passed their Subscriptions instead of
Money.

* Who may Indorse.   * P. 160.

A NOTE, payable to a *Femme Sole*, who marries before Str 516
Transfer of it, must be endorsed by her Husband

In like manner, an Executor or Administrator, " may L N P 273.
" indorse a Bill of their Testator.

" And where Bill is endorsed to *A* and *B* as *Executors*, King and
" they may declare, as such, against the Acceptor   others Executors of Steven-

I 2   *Par.* fon, against

Thom T R.
Mic 27 G III,
berty to abandon in that Case   The fixing a precise time proves the 487
general Principle

Every Argument holds stronger in the Case of the other POLICY,
with regard to the GOODS

*No Capture by the Enemy, though condemned, can be so total a
Loss as to leave* no possibility *of a Recovery   If the* Owner *himself should retake at any time, he will be entitled · and by the Act
of Parliament, if an* English *Ship retakes at any time before condemnation, the Owner is entitled to Restitution upon stated Salvage.
This Chance does not suspend the demand, for a total Loss, upon the
Insurer   but Justice is done, by putting him in the place of the* infured, *in Case of a Recapture*

In questions upon POLICIES, *the Nature of the Contract, as an* v infra.
Indemnity *and nothing else, is always* liberally *considered.—In* ALL
Cases the insured *may* chuse NOT *to abandon*

In the second Part of the Usage *and* Customs *of the Sea, (a*
French *Book translated into* English) *a Treatise is inserted, called*
GUIDON   *Where, after mentioning the Right to abandon upon
a Capture, he adds, or any other such disturbance as defeats the
Voyage, or makes it not worth while, or worth the Freight, to pur-
fue it*

I know, that of late times, the privilege of abandoning has been
restrained *for fear of letting in Frauds.   And the Merchant can
not elect to turn, what at the time when it happened, was in its
Nature, but an Average into a total Loss, by abandoning   But
there is no danger of Fraud in the present Case   The Loss was*
total *at the time it happened*

*The Chief Justice then recapitulated the other circumstances of the
Case   and concluded, after remarking on them*

We are of Opinion, that the Loss was TOTAL BY the CAP-
TURE *and the Right which the Owner had, after the Voyage defeated to obtain Restitution of the Ship and Cargo, paying great
Salvage to the Recaptor, might be abandoned to the Insurers after
she was brought into* Milford Haven.

POSTEA

* P. 161   * Par 2

Ord-r of Liability

" If the *Bill* be an *indorsed-* Bill, and the *Indorsee* cannot
" get the Drawee to discharge it, he may call upon the
" Drawer or the Indorser, or, if the Bill has gone through
" many hands, any one of the *Indorsers*. for each *Indorser*
" is a *Warranter* for the payment of the Bill, which is fre-
" quently taken in payment as much (or more) upon the
" Credit of the *Indorser* as of the *Drawer* And if such
" *Indorser*, so called upon, has the Names of one or more
" *Indorsers* prior to his own, to each of whom he is properly
" an *Indorsee*, he is also at Liberty to call upon any of
" them to make him satisfaction, and so upwards. But the
" *first* Indorser has nobody to resort to but the *Drawer*
" only

* P 162.   *What is to be proved against the Indorser*

1 Salk 127   " In an action against the *Indorser*, the Plaintiff is not
L. N P 27,   " obliged to prove the hand of the *Drawer*, for if the Note
               " be *forged*, the *Indorser* is liable.

                                              " On

* p 380 400   POSTEA to the PLAINTIFF in both Causes   See the same Case *
of Parker's   in a Collection which contains Statutes respecting Navigation and Com-
Laws of Ship merce, from 28 E III 1354, to 13 G. III 1773 and adjudged
ring and Insu Cases, from 1 W & M to 14 G III
rance 1775
              And afterwards another great Cause came before the Court, which
              was on a special Case referred at Guildhall from the Sittings there,
              before L rd MANSFIELD, after Michaelmas Term, 1760, on an
              Insurance of a Ship called the Selby, from Virginia or Maryland
              to London, and if Goods and Merchandize therein, until she shall
              have moored at Anch r twenty four Hours.

Hor tm v   This was a VALUED POLICY and on a Special Case it ap-
Vau- 2Purr   peared —
1155 Parke's
L S I 427   That the Ship, after quitting her Port of Departure, was taken
              by a French Privateer that at the time of the Capture, she had nine
              Men on board, of whom the Captain of the Enemy's Ship took out
              Six besides the Captain, leaving only the Mate and one Man, and
              put a Prize Master and several Men on board to carry her to France
               Then SEVENTEEN DAYS after, she was retaken by an English
              Man of War, who sent her into Plymouth, where she arrived four
              teen Days after her Recapture the Day of her arrival being the
              Sixth of June
               That the Plaintiff living at Hull, informed of what had happened
              to his Ship the Selby, wrote, on the 23d of June, to his Agent in
              London, to acquaint the Defendant, that the Plaintiff did, from
              thenceforth ABANDON to him his Interest in the said Ship   That
              the Defendant, on being so acquainted, said, he did not think him-
                                                                          self

" On a *Bill* payable to *A* or *Bearer*, it is not neceſſary to L N P *ibid*
" prove a Demand on the *Drawer*, for there the *Indorſer* is
" in the Nature of an original Drawer

" But on a Bill payable to *A* or *Order*, Demand on the Mic 32 G II.
" Drawer is to be proved, in general, if Bill not accepted ; Heylyn v,
" but if accepted, then on the *Drawee*, who is the 2 Bur Manſ
" Acceptor 674

" Yet if the *Indorſer* have paid part of the Money, this 2 Str 1087.
" Proof is no longer neceſſary

* " As to *foreign Bills* of *Exchange*, the point of *Demand* * P. 163
" was ſolemnly determined in the Caſe of *Bromley* v *Fra-*
" *zier* There on *Action*, on the *Caſe* by the *Indorſee* againſt
" the *Indorſer*, the Objection upon general Demurrer was,
" that they had not ſhewn a Demand on the Drawer, in
" whoſe default only it is, that the Indorſer warrants And
" becauſe this was a point unſettled, and becauſe there are
" contradictory opinions in *Salkeld* 133 and 134, the Court
" took time to conſider of it And on the ſecond Argu-
" ment they delivered their Opinion that the Declaration
" was good enough on the ground of inconvenience and
" circuity, contrary to the Nature of this Mode of Negoti-
" ation, if it ſhould be otherwiſe. For * that the favour * P. 164.
" allowed

ſelf bound to take to the SHIP *but was ready to pay the Salvage,
and all other Loſſes and Charges that the Plaintiff ſuſtained by the
Capture*

*It was admitted on the ſpecial Caſe, that the Ship and Cargo ſuſ-
tained no damage by the Capture*

*On this, the Queſtion ſubmitted to the Court was, whether the
Plaintiff, on the ſaid 26th Day of* June, *had a Right to* ABANDON,
and hath a Right to recover for a TOTAL Loſs ?

Lord MANSFIELD, *in delivering the Reſolution of the Court,
after ſtating the Caſe as ſettled, the general Queſtion, and the points
made by Counſel, firſt admitted this a total loſs by the Capture but
that on the Recapture it would depend on circumſtances, whether
that total ſhould not be converted into an Average Loſs That in
point of Fact, the Loſs, in this Caſe, was ſo converted by the Recapture and this the whole was brought to the laſt Point, whether
the Loſs having been once total, a Right veſted in the inſured to recover the whole by abandoning, ſo as it could never after be deveſted
or taken from him by any ſubſequent Event*

On this the Chief Juſtice thus expreſſed himſelf

*The Plaintiff's Demand is for an Indemnity His Action then
muſt be founded upon the Nature of his Damnification, as it really
is at the time of the Action brought It is repugnant, upon a Contract
of Indemnity, to recover as for a total Loſs, when the final Event
has decided, that the Damnification, in Truth, is an Average, or
perhaps no loſs at all.*

Whatever

" allowed to this species of Contract was for commercial se-
" curity and dispatch, by such Bills passing from hand to
" hand, as if they were Cash And that accordingly the
" more Indorsements the greater Credit to a Bill, but
" which could not be, if the resort were necessary to the
" Drawer, in whatever part of the Globe, or however to
" be traced. And that as to the Notion that the Indorser
" warrants only *in default* of the Drawer, there is no Colour
" for it . for that every Indorser was in the Nature of a *new*
" *Drawer* And that at *Nisi prius* the Indorsee never was
" put to prove the hand of ,the *first Drawer*, where the
" Action was against the Indorser

Conformity of foreign and inland Bills.

" That every inconvenience in that Case suggested holds
" to a great degree, and every other Argument equally, in
" the Case of INLAND BILLS of EXCHANGE

* P. 165.   * " The COURT, therefore, in the principal Case, thus
" declared, We are all of opinion that to entitle the In-
" dorsee of an INLAND Bill of Exchange to bring an Action
" against the Indorser, upon failure of payment by the
                                                    " Drawee,

Whatever undoes the Damnification, *in whole or in part, must ope-*
rate upon the Indemnity *in the same degree. It is a Contradiction*
in Terms to bring an Action for Indemnity, *when upon the whole*
Event, no Damage has been sustained.

This reason is so much founded in sense and the Nature of the
Thing, that the Common Law *of England adopts it (though inclined*
to strictness). The Tenant is obliged to indemnify his Landlord
from Waste . *but if the Tenant do or suffer waste to be done in*
Houses, yet if he repair before any Action brought, there lies no
Action of waste against him . But he can not plead non fecit vastum,
but the Special Matter The Special Matter shews, that the Injury
being repaired before *the Action brought, the Plaintiff had* no
Cause of Action : And whatever takes away the Cause takes away
the Action *

Suppose a Surety sued to Judgment and afterwards, before an
Action brought, the Principal pays the Debt and Costs, and procures
satisfaction to be acknowledged on Record the surety can have no
Action for Indemnity , because he is indemnified before any Action
brought If the Demand or Cause of Action does not subsist at the
time the Action is brought, the having existed at any former time will
be of no Avail

But in the present Case, the Notion of a vested Right in the Plain-
tiff to sue as for a total Loss before the Recapture, is fictitious only,
and no founded in Truth For the insured is not obliged to abandon
in any Case. He has an Election No Right can vest as for a

* Sublatâ Causâ tollitur effectus

total

" Drawee, it is *not* neceſſary to make any Demand of, or 2 Burr Manſ.
" Enquiry after, the firſt *Drawer*   * If the origınal Bill 676
" be made payable to *A B* or Order, it is in its Nature ne- * P. 166
" gotiable and aſſignable, and is transferred by Indorſement More v Man-
" as amply without the words, OR ORDER, added to all ning, 6 G I.
" or ANY of the ſucceſſive Indorſements as with them For Comyns 311.
" the Transfer follows the Nature of the Bill itſelf, and is Acheſon v
" GENERAL, like that   Fountain.
                                                           1 Sir 557
    " Very different is a mere Authority to receive as ſervant Tr 9 Geo. I.
" or Agent   Edw & al v.
                                                           E I Comp.
    " And converſely, (ſince what is payable to a perſon by Tr 1 G III
" Indorſement of ſuch a Bill is payable to his *Order*) what 2 Burr 1216.
" is payable to his *Order*, may be demanded by the party's Carth 403
" ſelf As, pay the Contents of this Bill unto the Order 9 W. III.
" of Mr *Fiſher*   Mr *Fiſher* brought an Action . the De-
" fendant demurred, becauſe it was not-to *Fiſher* himſelf,
" but to his Order . but the Court held that *Fiſher* might
" well bring the Action And he had Judgment accord-
" ingly.

Indorſement.

total *Loſs, till he has* made *that Election He can not elect before
Advice is received of the Loſs and if the Advice ſhews the Peril
to be* over, *and the Thing in ſafety, he can not elect at all, becauſe
he has a right to abandon when the Thing is ſafe*
    *Writers upon the Marine Law are apt to embarraſs General Prin-
ciples with the poſitive Regulations of their Country but they ſeem all
to agree, that if the Thing is recovered* before *the Money paid, the
Inſured can only be entitled according to the final Event.*
    After citing RICCIUS *for the Sentiments of the foreign Juriſts, his
Lordſhip thus proceeds*
    In the Caſe of Spencer v Franco, *though upon a Wager-Policy,
the Loſs was held* not *to be total, after the Return of the Ship,* Prince Before Lord
Frederic *in ſafety, though ſhe had been ſeized and long kept by the* Hardwicke at
King *of* Spain *in a time of actual War*   Guildhall in
    In the Caſe of Pole v. Fitzgerald, *though upon a Wager-Po-* 1735
licy, *the Majority of the Judges and the Houſe of Lords, held there* Caſes in Dem.
was no total Loſs, *the Ship having been* reſtored *before the End of* Proc Wedne.
Four Months   13 Feb 1754.
    *The preſent Attempt is the firſt that ever was made to charge the
Inſurer as for a total Loſs, upon an Intereſt Policy after the Thing was
recovered And it is ſaid, the Judgment in the Caſe of* Gols v.
Withers, *gave riſe to it*
    *It is admitted, that Caſe was no way ſimilar Before that Action
was brought, the whole Ship and Cargo was literally loſt At the
time of the offer to abandon, a fourth of the Cargo had been thrown
overboard, the Voyage was entirely loſt, the Remainder of the Cargo
was Fiſh periſhing, and of no Value at* Milford Haven, *where the
Ship was brought in, the Ship ſo ſhattered as to want great and ex-
penſive Repairs, the Salvage one Half, and the Inſurer did not en-*
gage

* P 167.   * *Indorfement*

1 Salk 65.   " An indorfement to pay *part* of a Bill, fo as to fplit the
Haw ins v   " Entirety of it into different payments, is not good, be-
Cardee, M
10 W III   " caufe it multiplieth Actions: and an Ufage of fuch a kind,
B R Cartn.   " contrary to the Analogy of Cafes to the Nature of the
456 S C
L N P 271   " Tranfaction and to its own Principles, the Law will not
S P   " fuffer to obtain the Authority of a Cuftom

M 19 G III   " The Holder of a Bill of Exchange, may fue a fubfe-
          P   " quent *Indorfer*, notwithftanding an ineffectual Execution
Having again²
Mulcall, BL   " and Difcharge of a precedent one.
1235

                                   TIT VII.

                                   PROTEST

                    " Having treated of the feveral *Parties* fucceffively con-
                 " cerned in a Bill of Exchange, the *Drawer* and original
                 " *Payee*, the *Acceptor*, and the *Indorfers*, it is now fit to
                 " obferve the feveral Confequences, dependant on *Non-Ac-*
                 " *ceptance* and *Proteft*

* P. 168.   " * It has been remarked already, that a partial and condi-
                 " tional Acceptance may be good   However, the Holder
Str 1153   " of the Bill may *prot-ft*, if the *Drawee* offer any thing
L N P 270   " fhort of an abfolute Acceptance for the whole.

                                                        " For

gage to be at any expence, it did not appear that it was worth while
to try to fave any th ng
     But it is fa'd, though the Cafe was entirely different, fome part of
the reafoning warranted the Propofition now inferred by the Plaintiff
from it
     The great Principle relied upon was, that, as between the In-
furer and the Infured, the Contract being an Indemnity, the Truth of
the Fact ought to be regarded and therefore, there might be a total
Lofs by a Capture which could not operate a change of property And
a Recapture fhould not relate by Fiction, (like the Roman Jus Poftliminii) as if the Capture had never happened, unlefs the Lofs was
in Truth recovered
     This reafor ng proved, è converfo, that f the Thing in Truth
was fate, no artificial reafoning fhall be allowed to fet up a total
Lofs.
     The Words quoted at the Bar were certainly ufed, that there is
no Book, antient or modern, which does not fay — hat in Cafe of a
Ship being taken, the Infured may demand as for a total Lofs,
and ABANDON But the propofition was applied to the Subject
Matter and is certainly true, provided the Capture, OR the total
Lofs occafiona thereby, CONTINUE to the time of abandoning ar t
bringing t   Action
     The Cafe in before the Court d d not make it neceffary to fpecify
all the rigor of it.

                                                        F on

" For payment of a Bill of Exchange, after the day
" which it has to run, the Acceptor," by the Cuſtom of
London, " which is general in this Caſe throughout Eng-
" land," has three Days, " which are called" Days of
Grace which ſeems to be like the *Quarto die poſt*, on return of Writs which might have ſprung from the *Saxons*,
" thinking" it unbecoming a Freeman to do any Act immediately

When the three Days of Grace are out, " in caſe of
" Non-Payment," the party " who has tendered it, ſhould
" note the Bill with the Date of the tender and refuſal, and
" then it is to be proteſted, according to that Date, for L N P 271,2.
" Non-Payment "

＊ The *Proteſt* for *Non-Acceptance* or *Non-Payment*, muſt be ＊ P. 169.
made and ſent over in due and convenient time " And it Moll B 2 c.
" ſeems that," if the three Days of Grace end on a *Satur-* 10. § 17
day, the holder muſt proteſt it on *Monday*, and ſend it away 2 Keb 584.
by the next Poſt and if the Proteſtation, within the time Venir 45
be neglected, the Drawer will not be anſwerable, becauſe Mic 21 Car.
the Bill of Credit was given inſtead of Money and if the 11 B R
Deliverer neglect to proteſt it in due time, it is " he" has Barnard
given Credit to the Correſpondent, and therefore ought not K B 305
to be anſwered by the Drawer of the Bill.

" And

From the way of Reaſoning, (then uſed as reſulting from the cir-
cumſtances of that Caſe), it did by no means follow, that if the
Ship and Cargo had, by the Recapture, been brought ſafe to the
Port of Delivery, without having ſuſtained any damage at all, that
the Inſured might abandon.

But without dwelling longer upon Principles or Authorities, the
Conſequences of the preſent Queſtion are deciſive It is impoſſible that
a man ſhould deſire to abandon in a caſe circumſtanced like the pre-
ſent, but for one of two Reaſons, either that he has overvalued, or
the Market has fallen below its original Price The only Reaſons
which can make it the Intereſt of the party to deſire, are concluſive
againſt allowing it

It is unjuſt to turn the Fall of the Market againſt the Inſurer,
who has no concern in it, and could never gain any thing by its riſe.
And an overvaluation is contrary to the general Policy of the Ma-
rine Law, contrary to the Spirit of the Act of 19 G II a temptá-
tion to Fraud, and a ſource of great Abuſe Therefore no man ſhould
be allowed to avail himſelf of having overvalued

The Inſurer, upon the Marine Law, ought never to pay leſs upon
a Contract of Indemnity than the Value of the Loſs and the In-
ſured ought never to gain more Therefore, if there was occaſion to
reſort to that Argument, the Conſequences of the Determination would
alſo be ſufficient upon the preſent occaſion.

But upon Principles, this Action could not be maintained as for a
total Loſs if the Queſtion was to be judged by the ſtricteſt Rules of
Common

* P. 170.

Hill v Lewis,
Salk. 133

Allen v
Dockwra,
ceram Treby
C J Mic.
10 W III.
Salk. 127.

" And the convenient time of protefting for Non-Accept-
" ance or Non-Payment, is not arbitrary and vague, for if
" it were, that Certainty of Contracts, which is effential to
" Trade, would have no exiftence fince.

" And *Notice* of fuch Proteft, as early as reafonably may
" be, is neceffary to charge the Drawer otherwife the Law
" will imply the Bill paid, becaufe of the *Truft* and Confi-
" dence between the Parties, and the extreme inconvenience
" to Commerce, if a Bill might rife up to charge the Drawer
" at any diftance of time, when, in the meanwhile, all
" reckonings and accounts may have been adjufted between
" the Drawee and Drawer.

* P. 171.

L. N P 273,5

" * And, in general, it may be taken, that Credit given
" to one of the parties, without Notice to him who other-
" wife was liable, difcharges the other · for this is a deter-
" mining of the Election

Windham v
Wither and v
Trull, Str 515
Cunningham,
§ 5. ar. 6.

" And it is evident, that actual payment from one of the
" parties, amounts to fuch a Satisfaction, as may be given
" in Evidence, in bar of an Action brought by the fame
" Plaintiff againft another And therefore, where the Plain-
" tiff brought two feveral Actions againft the *Drawer* and
" *Indorfer* of a *promiffory Note*, the Court faid, they would
" have laid the Plaintiff by the heels if he had taken out
" execution on both.

" But

*Common Law · much lefs can it be fupported for a total Lofs, as the
Queftion ought to be decided by the large Principles of the Marine
Law, according to the fubftantial Intent of the Contract, and the
real Truth of the Fact*

*The daily Negociations and Property of Merchants, ought not to de-
pend upon Subtilties and Niceties but upon Rules eafily learned and
eafly retained, becaufe they are the Dictates of common Senfe, drawn
from the Truth of the Cafe*

*If the Queftion is to depend upon the Fact, every Man can judge of
the Nature of the Lofs before the Money is paid but if it is to attend upon fpeculative Refinements, from the Law of Nations, and the
Roman Jus Poftliminii, concerning the Change and revefting of Property, no wonder Merchants are at a lofs, when Doctors have differed
upon the Subject from the Beginning, and are not yet agreed*

*To obviate too large an inference being drawn from this Determina-
tion, I defire it may be underftood, that the point here determined is
that the Plaintiff, upon a Policy, can only recover an Indemnity according to the Nature of his Cafe at the time of the Action brought
er, at moft, at the time of his offer to abandon*

*We give no opinion how it would be in Cafe the Ship or Goods be
reftored in fafety, BETWEEN the offer to abandon, and the Action
brought, or BETWEEN the Commencement of the Action and the
Verdict And, particularly, I defire that no inference may be drawn
that in cafe the Ship or Goods fhould be reftored after the Money paid*

"But where the Drawer has no Cash in the hands of the
"Drawee, Notice of the Bill being dishonoured, is not ne-
"cessary to charge the Drawer.

"And where a Bill is tendered by the Holder to the
"Drawee, for Acceptance *before* it becomes due, * and is * P. 172.
"accepted, Notice must be given to the *Indorser* of the Blisard v Hrst,
"Non-acceptance ; otherwise he shall not be charged, if 5 Burr Mansf
"the Drawer, when it becomes due, fail of payment, not $\begin{smallmatrix}\text{Mic 11 G III.}\\2670\ 2\end{smallmatrix}$
"even though he have promised after it became due, to S. P Goodall
"take it up the promise being founded on a mistake of v Dolley,
"Liability $\qquad$ T Rep 712.
                                                            E 27 G III.

SECTION VI

Of Promissory Notes.

"A *Promissory Note* is a written Engagement, not under
"Seal, to pay a certain Sum of Money to a Person or his
"Order

"* It differs from a *Bill of Exchange*, which is an Order to * P 173.
"pay, including an *implied* Promise   3 & 4 A.c. 9.
                                                              L N P 272.
"In other respects, there is now a general Analogy esta-
"blished between *promissory Notes*, payable to a person or
"his Order, or to a person generally without Name as
"*unto Bearer*, and Bills of Exchange. Such Notes being
                                                            " now

---

as for a total *Loss*, the *Insurer could compel the Insured to refund the
Money, and take the Ship or Goods That Case is totally different from the
present, and depends throughout upon different reasons and principles*
 Here the *Event had fixed the Loss to be an Average* ONLY *before the Action brought*, before the *offer to abandon*, and before the
*Plaintiff had notice of any Accident consequently, before he could make
an Election*
 *Therefore, under these circumstances, we are of opinion, that he cannot
recover for a total, but for an* AVERAGE *Loss* only, the *Quantity
of which is estimated and ascertained by the Jury*
 And in the *Case* of Lewis and another v Rucker, is a *perspi- 2 Burr
cuous and full elucidation of the Nature and effects of a* VALUED Manf 1167.
Policy   E 1G III
 The *Case was on a* POLICY *upon Goods aboard the* Vrow Mar-
tha, *at and from St* Thomas's Island *to* Hamburgh, *from the
Loading at the said* Island, *till the Ship should arrive and land the
Goods at* Hamburgh
 The *Goods (consisting of Sugars, Coffee, and Indigo) were valued,
the* clayed *Sugars at* 30 l *per Hogshead, and the Muscovado at* 20 l.
They were warranted free from Average under 5 per Cent
 In the *Course of the Voyage, the Sea Water got in and when the
Ship arrived at* Hamburgh, *it appeared that every Hogshead of
Sugar was damaged The Damage made it necessary to sell im-
mediately, they were accordingly sold the difference between the
                                                                  Price*

"now unqueſtionably aſſignable, and *indorſable*, with the
"ſame general conſequences and rules as Bills of Exchange

➤ P 174
L. 2 P. 277

"➤ And this Analogy between *promiſſory* Notes and *Bills*,
"ſeems to take effect from the *Indorſement* for then a
"Note is an Order to pay the Money to the Indorſee,
"which we have ſeen, is the very Definition of a Bill of
"Exchange.

Tit. II.

What Notes ſhall be good as abſolute.

Morris v Lee,
Tr 11 G L
2d Ld Ra,m
1396
S C 1 Str 629

"We have already ſeen a Bill or Note muſt be abſolute
"at all Events it may be proper to adduce ſome inſtances
"of diſputed Notes, held to have been good within this
"Rule

➤ P 175

"➤ The *Inborſee* brought an Action, againſt the *Drawer*,
"upon a Note which appears to have been thus '—I pro
"miſe to be *accountable* to *A* or order for 100*l* value receiv-
"ed Verdict for the Plaintiff In arreſt of Judgment,
"it was argued, that this Note was not negotiable or aſſign-
"able under the Statute for that it was not to pay at all
"Events, and that he might account for it as a Factor,

➤ P. 176

"by laying out ➤ the Value in the purchaſe of Goods for
"the Uſe of *A B*.

"But the Court held, that this was a good aſſignable
"Note within the Statute that under all circumſtances ap-
"parent on this Note, "to promiſe to be accountable,"
"was equivalent to a promiſe to pay. He could not be any
"otherwiſe

---

*Price when they brought, by reaſon of the Damage, and that which
they might then have brought at Hamburgh, if ſound, was as 20l.
5s 8d per Hogſhead, to 23l 7s 8d*

*The Defendant paid Money into Court on the like proportion of
the ſum at which the ſugars were valued in the Policy, as the Price
the damaged ſugars bore to the Sound at the Port of Delivery The
only Queſtion at the Trial was, by what meaſure or rule the Damage,
under all the circumſtances of this caſe, ought to be eſtimated*

*The Plaintiff proved, at the time of the Inſurance ſugars were
worth, at London and Hamburgh, 35l a Hogſhead That the Price
having ſunk, on the Expectation of a Peace, orders had been ſent
before the Arrival of the Goods at Hamburgh, and before notice of
the Damage, to loſe no time if ſugars till the Price ſhould riſe above
50l He thought That the ſugars did riſe 25l per Cent, and
it was contended that it was conſequential difference in the product
ariſing from the neceſſity of Sale, ought to be included in the Damage*

*The Jury found agreeable to the Defendant's Eſtimate, upon the pro-
portion of the actual difference between ſound ſugars and thoſe damaged*

" otherwife accountable to *Indorfees*, and it being exprefsly
" to *A B.* or ordei, it muft betaken, that its transferrabi-
" lity, in the way of payment was in contemplation *Powys,*
" Juftice, indeed, feemed to ground himfelf much upon the
" Verdict but the Plaintiff, in this Cafe, feems to have
" declared on the Note, as in the Nature of a Specialty, and
" thus to have brought it however, * unneceffarily on the   * P 177.
" Record, and as the Verdict was entire, without dif- v Cunningham
" tinguifhing the other Count, which was general on an *infi*- Sect 2 art 5.
" *mul computaffet* (on thofe reafons as it may be prefumed),
' the other Judges were clear that the Verdict could not aid
" the Note . but that, if bad on the Statute, it muft remain
" unremedied by the Verdict They thought it good, and
" Judgment was for the Plaintiff

" On Error from *C B* Note to pay *A* or order, fix Weeks 2 Str 1217
" after the Death of the Defendant's Father, foi value re- M 18 Geo. II
' ceived, was held a good Note · foi that there was no Colerun
" contingency whereby it might never become payable, but
" only the time of payment was uncertain, which is the
" Cafe of all Bills payable at fo many days after Sight In
" *Communi Banco*, it held three * Arguments, and was ad * P. 178.
" judged good, by a folem Refolution, delivered by Lord
" *Chief Juftice* WILLIS.

" So a Note payable to *A* when he fhall come of Age, Cunningham
" which will be 12 *June* 1750 for it is payable at all Events, 304
" on 12 *June* 1750, and the coming of Age, is not a con-
" dition, but a circumftance here the Reafon is clear and fa- Str 24
" tisfactory It may not be fo eafy to reconcile the Cafe Andrews r
" with the principle, where according to a very fhort and Franklin
                       " early Hil 3 G 1.

raged fugars, when fold, at the Port of Delivery, to the value in-
fured
  On this the Plaintiff moved for a new Trial
  To this there were two Objections taken
  Inft, that this was altering the Meafure of Damages, in the Cafe
of a partial Lofs, from what would have been the meafure in the Cafe
of a total Lofs For then the prime Coft, or Value in the Policy, muft
have been paid
  To this the anfwer, recognized by the Court, was, that the different
Meafure of Value in the two inftances arifes from the Nature of the
Thing
  Where there is a total Lofs, no meafure can be taken but the prime
Coft, to afcertain the Damages, and he thus fulfils his Contract of
Indemnity he pays the Value of the thing he infures, fuch as it was,
at the Outfet He has no concern in the fubfequent Value, and fo it
it if part be intirely loft, the prime Coft is the meafure for that part
  But if part of the Cargo, capable of a diftinct valuation, as being
a entire individual, be fpoiled, as one hogfhead out of ten, no mea-
                             fure

" early Note of an eminent Reporter, it appears to have
" been held, that a promiffory Note to be paid within two
" Months after a certain Ship fhould be paid off, was good
" The only caufe there affigned is, that the paying off a Ship
" is a thing of a public Nature, which indeed eftablifhes the
" Notoriety of it, when it fhall happen: but there is ftill the want
" of Affurance that it ever will happen ; for the Ship and
" Crew will perifh I know * not that any fubfequent Cafe
" has been decided on the fame Principles, except the following
" On an Action upon a Note, in the following Form
" *I promife to pay* Mr James Lewis, *Eleven Pounds at the Pay-*
" *ment of the Ship* Devonfhire, *for value received*
" In this Cafe, *Hardwicke,* Chief Juftice, is reprefented
" to have faid, as to the Contingency of the Payment, the
" fubfequent Act of the Payment of the Ship makes it certain
" and therefore, though not a * *Lien ab initio,* yet became fuf-
" ficiently fo, and within the Statute, by the Fact happen-
" ing after. It is not like the Cafe of *Jocelyn* and *Laferre,*
" where it was held, that a Bill of Exchange, payable out
" of the particular Fund for growing Subfiftence, was not
" within the Statute. I think, therefore, the Declaration is
" proper enough but you may make your objection in Ar-
" reft of Judgment , for this will appear on the Record
" It

* P 179

Lewis v Orde,
Sittings at
Middlefex
8 Geo II
B R T and
Comm 26
Cunningham
§ 2 8

* P. 180.

fure can be taken from the prime Coft to afcertain fuch damage If
you can fix whether it be a third, a fourth, or a fifth worfe, you afcertain the Damage by a rule of mathematical certainty And here the
port of Outlet can be no Guide, but on account of the fubfequent actual depreciation it muft be decided by the Price at the Port of Delivery,
where the Voyage is completed, and the whole Damage known And
whether the Price there be high or low, the Difference between that
price for the damaged, compared with found Goods, equally fixes the
proportionate deterioration, and as the infured would pay the whole
prime Coft, if the Thing be wholly loft, fo if it be only a third, fourth,
or fifth worfe, he pays a third, fourth, or fifth of the value of the
Goods fo damaged, taken proportionably on the Value infured, that is,
if they are one feventh lefs faleable than found Goods, he pays on 30l
for prime Coft infured, one feventh, or 3l 2s 10d ¼
The fecond objection was from its being a valued Policy and it
once a time ufed to be argued, that a valued was equivalent to a wager
Policy, and that therefore there could be no Average Lofs, the Value
being fictitious
To this the Anfwer eftablifhed by the Decifion of the Court a
that valued Policy is not a wager Policy, or like, " Intereft or no
" Intereft If it were, it would be void by the Statute But the
the only effect of the Valuation is fixing the Amount of the prime
Coft juft as if the Parties admitted it at the Trial but that in
every argument, and for every other purpofe, it muft be taken that
it

* " It does not appear, that any Motion afterwards was * P. 181.
" made to bring this point to a more folemn Determination.

" In this Cafe, there was another Point on which the
" Judge gave his Opinion The Note being without the
" Words " Order," or " Bearer," he faid, he remembered
" a Cafe where it was held on Demurrer, that a Note with-
" in the Statute need not be in terms fo payable

* " *I promife to pay to* W. 100l. *in three Months after Date,* * P 182.
" *value received of the Premiffes in* Rofemary Lane, *late in the* Mic 2 G III.
" *Poffeffion of* T R   Ld Raym

" On Demurrer, the Court clearly held this to be a pro- 1545
" miffory Note within 3 & 4 *Ann, c* 9   Borchell v.
                                                                      Slocock, Cun-
Error on Judgment in *C B* , in Cafe, upon a promiffory ningham § 2
Note, entered into by *A* to pay fo much to *B* * " for a 12
" Debt due from *C* to the faid *B* And it was objected, * P. 183.
" that this not being for *value received*, was not within the Str 264
" Statute and *primâ facie*, the Debt of another is no con- Popplewell v.
" fideration to raife a promife But the Court held it to be Willon, Hil
" within the Statute , being an abfolute promife, and every ningham, § 2.
" way as negotiable as if it had been for value received 11.

* " But, *I promife to pay to* T S 50l *if* T S *doth not pay* * P 184
" *it within fix Weeks*, was held bad, on Motion in Arreft of Cunningham,
" Judgment, becaufe the Drawer was not the original Debtor, § 11. 13
" but might be a Debtor on a Contingency

                                                              " But

*the value was fo fixed as that the infured meant only to have an In-
demnity*

If it be undervalued, *the Merchant himfelf ftands Infurer on the
furplus if much overvalued, it muft be done with a fraudulent
view , either to gain contrary to the Statute againft Intereft, or with
fome View to a fraudulent Lofs The Court, therefore, will never
fuffer the infured to plead, that he has greatly overvalued, or that
his intereft was a Trifle only*

That it is fettled, that upon valued *Policies the Merchant need only
prove fome Intereft, to take it out of the Statute , becaufe the adverfe
party has admitted the Value, and if more was required the agreed
Valuation would fignify nothing But if it fhould come out in Proof
that a Man had infured* 2000l *and had intereft on board' to the Value of
a Cable only, there never has been, and I believe there never will be,
a Determination that by fuch an Evafion the Act of Parliament may
be defeated*

*That there are many conveniences from allowing valued Policies .
but where they are ufed merely as a Cover to a Wager, they would be
confidered accordingly*

*That the effect of a Valuation is only fixing, concluſively, the prime
Coft which in an open Policy, muft be proved ; in a valued one, is
agreed.*

*That to argue there can be no Adjuftment of an agerage Lof. upon
a valued Policy, is in this inftance directly againft the Terms of the
Policy*

"But where the Note is jointly *and* severally, or even
"jointly *or* severally, this is well on a separate Action against
"either, no less than on a joint Action

* P. 185
R--- Abbot
Co p 832
Tr 18 G I.L

* "And accordingly, on ERROR from the COMMON
"PLEAS, on Action upon a PROMISSORY NOTE made by
"*two*, who *jointly* or *severally*, promised to pay And in
"that Form the Plaintiff had declared against the Defen-
"dant.

"Mr *Wood* argued for the Plaintiff in Error, that it was
"not sufficiently alledged that *he* had ever promised to pay the

1 S r 76
Hi 4 G

"Note in Question; and cited a Case where this very Point
"had been made, and had prevailed

"That was the Case of *Butler* and *Maliffey*, where upon
"a promissory Note the Plaintiff set forth that the Defen-
"dant and another, *conjunctim vel divisim*, promised to pay

* P 186

"On this there was a DEMURRER * and, *per Parker*,
"Chief Justice, the Plaintiff might have brought it against
"either or both, for he had his Election If the Action
"had been against both, he should have declared as he now
"does, but that it is not right in the Action against one only.
"For he should have declared *generally*, that this Defendant
"by his Note promised to pay, and a several Note by two
"would have been good Evidence As where there are se-
"veral Obligors, and one only is sued, no mention is made
"in the Declaration of the other Obligors He that speaks
"in

Policy itself that being expressly subject to Average, if the Loss of any sort of sugars exceed 5 per Cent

That the Difference between the Price of the damaged Goods actually produced and the prime Cost (or Valuation in the Policy) cannot be the Rule, as it was contended it ought to be for that this would in some cases make the Underwriter in the Rise or Fall of the Market, subject him in some cases to pay vastly more than the Loss, in others, deprive the insured of a full satisfaction though there was a Loss

Considered Circumstances of the Case and from the particular circumstances of the Case for value of the 30l valued in the Policy, because it appears the sugars were laid there for that, if the Damage from the sea water had not made a re-exportation necessary.—

He therefore delivered the opinion of the Court, that the Jury rightly directed on the general nature of the Contract And Correct that the Goods shall come safe in the due Exercise of the Contract or else to indemnify the Plaintiff to the amount of the prime Cost or Value in the Policy If they are to be lessened in Value through Damage at sea, the Nature of a Contract of Indemnity speaks necessarily that the Merchant is to be put in the same Condition (Reference being had to the prime Cost or Value in the Policy) in which he would have been, if the Goods had arrived free from Damage; that is by being paid such proportion of the aliquot part of the prime cost or value in the Policy as corresponds

" in the disjunctive says true, if either member of the *dif-*
" *junctive* be verified, whereas he that speaks in the con-
" junctive affirms both parts to be true

" The Plaintiff, in that Case, had leave to discontinue, on
" payment of Costs

VOL I.   K   " He

*with the proportionor aliquot part of the Diminution in Value occasioned
by the Damage. That the Duty accrued upon the* Ship's *arrival, and
landing her Cargo at the Port of Delivery. The insured had then a
right to demand satisfaction The adjustment could never depend upon
future Events or Speculations*

*That if these were to be regarded, it would be productive of the
greatest inconvenience and injustice, and that the Right and Measure
of satisfaction which accrued at the landing being incapable of variation from subsequent Contingencies, it appeared as plain as any proposition in* Euclid *that the Rule by which the Jury had gone was the
right measure*

* *A Merchant insures his Goods from* London *to* Sallee, *and there*   *Cunningham,
to be landed The Factor, on his Arrival, sells the Cargo on board   C III § 6
without unlading the ship and the Buyer agrees for the Freight to   art 14.
the Port of Venice *Before she breaks Ground, the Ship takes fire.
Held that the assured and Buyer are absolutely without Remedy . for
the property of the Goods becoming changed, and Freight being contracted* de novo, *was equivalent to a discharge of the Policy by landing of the Goods.*

|| *In an Action brought on a Policy of Insurance of a Ship, it appears* ||LdRaym 724
in Evidence that the Ship was condemned by the Process of Law,   Cunning 309.
ord seized by this sentence the Property *and ownership are destroyed,
and there is no remedy on this Policy of Insurance*

† *And it seems, by the Case of* Grant v. Innes, *that the Premium*   † Cunning.
may be insured as well as the Ship and Freight, under a general Insu-   317
rance on Ship and Freight

§ *If an Insurance is made on a Ship generally, and the name of the*   § Cunningh.
ship expressed, according to the said Policy, upon the Keel of the Ship   C III § 6
of such a Burthen} this Assurance does not extend to the Goods when   art 52
the Ship only is named   §Malyne s Lex
                                                                            Mercator, 116,
‡ *Goods insured, and a Ship disabled the Goods put into a Boat*
or Lighter, which afterwards is found to be an Enemy's Ship, and   ‡ Vi Cunning.
seized, the Insurers shall answer it being a Loss incurred bona fide   ut supra
under the necessity of the Moment   art 48

*Policy of Assurance to warrant a Ship for twelve Months The
ship did perish within the time of twelve Months, accounting twenty-
eight Days to the Months This Evidence held not sufficient to maintain the Action, and that the Policy was discharged*

This was cited in Sir Wollaston Dexie's *Case on (the computation
of time under the statute of Usury) in the* 29 Eliz *and so far as I
have yet observed, it is the oldest reference in our Books to an obligation in the Nature of a* Policy of Assurance *And the more remarkable, as the very term is used, so that the Custom of such undertakings
seems by that time to have been pretty well settled. Insurers in this
Country used to meet, before the building of the* Royal Exchange, *at
a House situate where* Lombard-street *now is, and called the* Pawn-
house,*

* P. 187.
2 Str 819.
M. 2 G II.

*" He also cited the Cafe of *Ovington v Neale*, which was
" much ftronger, to the fame purpofe: for that was upon
" *Error* from the *Common Pleas*, after Judgment for the
" Plaintiff, who had declared upon a promiffory Note, by
" which, as in the principal Cafe, the Defendant and *A B*
" *conjunctim aut feparatim* promifed

" And

er Lombard; *fo that it is probable both* Bills of Exchange *and thefe
Pol.. es were derived to us from thefe Refugees from* Lombardy.
About the year 1719, *the* Royal Exchange *Affurance Company, originally patronized by* Lord Onflow, *and that of the* London Affurance
by Iora Chetwynd, *were inftituted and an aid of* 600,000l *having been offered to Government, if they fhould obtain a full and permanent fanction, they were eftablifhed by Act of Parliament in th*

6 Geo I c. 18 *Year already mentioned and by the laft Claufe the Companies are
fubjected to fpecific Penalties, if they fhall lend Money to the Crow-
otherwife than on Credit of Parliament, the Prerogative thus wifely,*

1 Leon. 95
Guarrough
art. 71 *and with a becoming fpirit, giving its concurrence in fupport of an
effential principle of the Conftitution*

*In fuch a Country as this the Inftitution could not fail of advancing
rapid, and vigoroufly to its perfection, fo that it has not only been long
fince verified with refpect to its extent and Indemnity with us, that they
infure again ft Strefs of Weather, Pirates, Rovers, Rocks, Lightning,
almoft every detriment that can happen; (there being hardly any mif-
fortune for which provifion is not made, either particularly or by the
general fcope of a Policy of Infurance) but with regard to their confideration an affect, the good fenfe and experience of refpectable commercial men, with the equity, clearnefs, and confonancy of a feries of
judicial decifions, have concurred to found a fyftem clear, liberal, folid,
and comprehenfive, by which the event of Queftions, refpecting mercantile Interefts might generally be forefeen fo as to be previoufly adjufted or fatisfactory Grounds, or if brought into Litigation fuch Queftions are now terminated without difficulty, without delay, and an
Appeal for fome Years fcarcely in a fingle inftance has been made*

*Before we take leave of this branch of our fubject, it appears proper
to lay before the Reader fome Cafes which have been determined on the
teca ng principles mentioned in the cafe. That Fraud, either by mif-
reprefenta on pofitively, or negatively by fuppreffion of Truth in the
formation of the Contract or t, fubfequent mal-practice under it, abfolutely forfeits all claim to the ftipulated Indemnity*

*It is hard y r n fit to advert to the grofs fpecies of Impofition in-
ftances by the cafe hereto e this head, fuch as fending out of the
ocean d , e, fame fhip difguifed, to appear like a new and found
o e er n g to e t knowledge that the fubject of the infurance
is tt , t nt to a confiderable Value on Articles of little worth,
c t u g them to profit by the Policy*

" loft or not loft" *will be good,
e en the p y offering proceeds with good Faith, under a real want
of information as to the Event, it will not avail him to have inferted
thofe words, if it appear in Evidence that either directly or by advice he knew, at the t me the Ship to have been actually loft.*

A 4

" And there, by the Court, by the prefent Declaration,
" he only fays he has this *or* fome other Caufe of Action:
" and Judgment was *reverfed*, for want of the Plaintiff's
" fhewing a Title to bring a feparate Action againft one of
" the Makers of the Note.

  * " Lord MANSFIELD If *or* is to be underftood as a   * P. 188,
" *disjunctive*, who is to elect whether the Note fhall be joint
" or feveral? Certainly the Perfon to whom it is payable If
" fo, the Plaintiff has made his *Election* But *or* in this Cafe
" is fynonimous to *and*. They *both* promife that they or one
" of them fhall pay . then *both* and *each* is liable *in folidum*.
" The Nature of the tranfaction forces this conftruction. It
" is faid that the Judges fhould be *aftute* in furtherance of
K 2   " right,

And in another Cafe, Holt *Chief Juftice obferved, that if Goods
had been infured as the Goods of an* Hamburgher, *when in Fact
they were the Goods of a Frenchman, at that time an Enemy, this
infurance would have been void and the fame, it may be added,
would be the Cafe if the Infurance were on the Goods of a perfon ftated
in the Policy to be of one Country, when in Truth he was of another,
though neither at enmity with this · for upon many accounts it is not
the fame rifque*

  *So where a Ship was to go under Paffes not applicable to the Name
fhe bore at the time of making the Infurance, and the Goods on board
were of the fubjects of a Country not warranted by the Policy . it was
by the Chief Juftice admitted that on each of the reafons the Condition of the Policy was not performed*

  *And thus the Concealment of a Fact material to the Contract (and
indeed any fact is material which the Contracting party wifhes to learn,
as fuppofing it may concern him with refpect to the tranfaction depending,) the fuppreffion, therefore, of a Fact, which relates to the object of the Policy, either in its real or apprehended tendency, deftroys
the Infurance*

  *T o had a doubtful Account of his Ship that was at fea ; namely,
that a Ship, defcribed like his was taken He infured her without
giving any Information to the Infurers, either as to the hazard or circumftances which might induce him to believe that his ship war in great
danger, if not actually loft*

  *The Infurers bring a Bill for an Injunction, and to be relieved againft
the Infurance as fraudulent*

  Lord CHANCELLOR (Macclesfield) *the infured has not dealt fairly
with the Infurers in this cafe He ought to have difclofed to them what
intelligence he had of the ship's being in danger, and which might induce him at leaft to fear that it was loft, though he had no certain account of it . for if this had been difcovered, it is impoffible to think
they would have infured at fo fmall a Præmium but either not at
all, or on a longer . fo that the concealment of this Intelligence is a
Fraud*

  He decreed, therefore, the Policy to be delivered up with Cofts ,   2 P W 170.
but the Præmium to be paid back and allowed out of the Cofts.   Trin 1723

Cunningh § ut
And   fupra art 1.

" right, and the means of recovering it   And therefore one
" is afhamed to fee either hitch or hang upon pins or parti-
" cles, contrary to the true manifeft meaning of the Con-
" tract

" And

And though in that Cafe, no Action being at Iffue, the cautionary
Protection fought, could only be given in a Court of Equity , had the
Caufe with thefe circumfances come to Trial in the other fide of the
Hall, the infured would have there been precluded by the Evidence
of fuch Facts   For where a Queftion is equitable in its Nature, the
fame Principles of Decifion pervade all the Courts

Smith v Fon-tereau
H.! 16 G II
2 Str 1183
Cunningh
P 174

The next Cafe was an Action at Law, and fhews that a Concealment of a known or fuppofed hazard will be equally deftructive of the
benefit which the infured might otherwife have claimed under the
Policy, whether the fubfequent Lofs be of the fame Nature with the
precedent Danger or not.

On the 25to of Auguft, 1740, the Defendant underwrote a Policy
from Carolina to Holland   It appeared the Agent for the Plain
tiff had, on the 23d of Auguft, received a Letter from Cowes,
dated 21ft of Auguft, wherein it was faid—The 12th of this
Month I was in company with the fhip Davy (the fhip in Queftion) at twelve in the Night, loft fight of her all at once   The Captain fpoke to me the day before, that he was leaky, and the
next day we had a hard Gale   The Ship, however, continued her
Voyage till the 19th of Auguft, when fhe was taken by the Spa-
niards, there was no pretence of any knowledge of the actual Lofs
at the time of the Infurance, which was made in confequence of a
Letter received that day from the Plaintiff abroad, dated 27th of
June before

The Chief Juftice declared, that as thefe are Contracts, upon
Chance, each party ought to know all the circumftances.   And he
thought it not material that the Lofs was not fuch a one as the Letter
imported , for thofe things are to be confidered in the fituation of them
at the time of the Contract, and not to be judged by fubfequent
Events   he therefore thought it a ftrong Cafe for the Defendant, and
the Jury found accordingly

* 3 Burr Manf
1905

* The Cafe of CARTER v BOEHM, was an INSURANCE governed by the fame Principles as the common Marine Infurances, and
therefore proper to be adduced under this head   after remarking
thofe point, which were peculiar to it, and fhewing that they did not
affect the general Principles of the Decifion.

This was an Infurance for one year, from the 16th of October,
1759, to the 16th of October, 1760, for the Benefit of the Go
VER .OR of FORT MARLBOROUGH, in the Ifland of Sumatra,
in the EAST INDIES, indemnifying againft the Event of the Fort
being taken by, a foreign Enemy.   The FORT was taken by Count
d'Eftaign within the year

It was in Evidence, that the Governor had a real Intereft, by
the Value of his Property in the Fort, greatly above the Amount
infured

That he was guilty of no Fault in the Lofs of the Fort

That

* " And BULLER, *Juſtice*, ſaid, if the Note had been a * P. 189.
" Note only, not a joint and ſeparate Note, the Defendant
" could only have pleaded in *abatement* , it would not have 2 Sid 189
" been *error*

" The

That it *was not a Fort proper or deſigned to reſiſt* European Ene-
mie. , but only for Defence againſt the Natives • that the Office of the
Governor *was not military but mercantile and that it was only a*
ſubordinate Factory to Fort St George
    The *Caſe farther included two Letters , the firſt dated the* 16th *of*
September, 1759, *which was ſent to* England, *together with*
the Inſtructions for inſuring, and which repreſented that the French
had, the preceding year, a deſign on foo. to attempt taking that ſet-
tlement by ſurprize, and the probability of that deſign reviving; the
weakneſs of the Fort , its being badly ſupplied with Stores, Arms,
and Ammunition, and the impracticability of maintaining it in its
ſtate againſt an European Enemy
    The *letter, dated the* 22d *of* September, 1759, *and ſent to his*
Brother by the ſame conveyance, confeſſes his being then more afraid
than formerly, that the French *ſhould attack and take the ſettlement,*
and aſſigns farther inducements to that opinion from their inability of
muſtering a Force to relieve their friends on the Coaſt, *ſo that rather*
than remain idle they might pay the Fort a Viſit.
    It *was alſo objected the Governor had not diſcloſed the Condition of*
the Place Of every thing which could differ this Caſe from that of
a merchant ſhip lying in harbour, and inſured for the ſame time in a
diſtant port againſt an hoſtile attack, the Queſtion was ultimately
cleared, for the COURT *agreed (on ſome or all of the Reaſons ſpe-*
cified by the Chief Juſtice, *among which were its being no military*
Fort, and the Governor really in a mercantile capacity , and that even
the Captain of a Ship was allowed to inſure Goods he had on board,
or his part, if he be a part owner, and the Captain of a Ship, under
like circumſtances to inſure his ſhare, and that on principles of
public Convenience, little was to be apprehended from the Example)
that they were not warranted to ſay the POLICY *was void upon*
his Account
    It *went, therefore, ſolely on the Queſtion of Concealment; and in*
diſcuſſing that Queſtion, theſe Principles were ſtated by the Chief
Juſtice *in delivering the Judgment of the Court*
    INSURANCE *is a Contract on ſpeculation the ſpecial Facts upon*
which the Chance of the Contingency is to be eſtimated, lie moſt commonly
in the knowledge of the inſured only, to whoſe Repreſentation there-
fore the Underwriter truſts upon Confidence that he does not keep back
any circumſtance in his knowledge, to miſlead the Underwriter into a
belief that ſuch circumſtance does, not exiſt, and to induce him to eſti-
mate the Riſque as if it did not
    The *keeping back ſuch circumſtance is a Fraud, and therefore the*
Policy is void And although the Non-communication *ſhould happen*
through Miſtake, and not through any fraudulent Intention, ſtill the
Policy is void, for the Riſque really run is different from the Riſque
underſtood and intended to be run

The

* P 190.
Str 271
Cunningn
§ 2 10

* " The Court held in *Error* from *C B.* that a Note to
" deliver up *horses* and a *wharf*, and to pay money at a parti-
" cular day, could not be counted on as a good Note within
" the Statute and therefore reversed the Judgment

* P 191
Str 299
Plea 6 G 1
Taylor v
Dobbins
Cunningn 124.

* " A Note alledged to have been *written* by the Defen-
" dant needs not to be averred to have been *signed* by him
" for it might be—I, *A B* promise to pay,—which would
" be as valid as, *I promise to pay* signed *A B*

" It

The Policy *would be equally void against the Underwriter if he
concealed, and an Action would lie to recover the Premium as if
he insured a Ship on her Voyage which he privately knew to be arrived*

The governing Principle is applicable to all CONTRACTS *and
dealings*

GOOD FAITH FORBIDS EITHER PARTY, BY CONCEALING
WHAT HE PRIVATELY KNOWS, TO DRAW THE OTHER INTO A
BARGAIN FROM HIS IGNORANCE OF THAT FACT, AND HIS BE-
LIEVING THE CONTRARY.

*But either party may be innocently silent as to Grounds open to
both to exercise their Judgment.* Aliud est celare aliud tacere
Cic. de Offic.
L lii. 14. neque enim id celare quicquid reticeas, sed cum id quod tu scias
id ignorare, emolumenti tui causa, velis eos, quorum intersit id
scire.

*This Definition of Concealment, restrained to the efficient Motives
and precise Subject of any Contract, will generally hold to make it
void in Favour of the Party misled by his Ignorance of the Thing
concealed.*

*There are many Matters as to which the Insured may be innocent-
ly silent He need not mention what the Underwriter knows, what
way soever he came to the Knowledge* Scientia utrinque par PARES
contrahentes facit

*He need not mention what the Underwriter ought to know, what
he takes upon himself the knowledge of, or what he waives being
informed of*

The Underwriter needs not be told general Topics of speculation
He is bound to know the Causes which may occasion natural *Perils,
as the difficulty of the Voyage, Seasons, Probability of Lightning
Hurricanes, Earthquakes. He is bound to know Causes of* political
*Peril from the Ruptures of States, from War, and the various ope-
rations of it*

*If an Underwriter insures private ships of War, by sea and on
shore, from Ports to Ports, from Places to Places, any where, he
needs not be told the secret Enterprizes on which they are destined,
because he knows some expedition must be in view and from the
Nature of his Contract, he waives the Information If he insures for
three years, he needs not be told any circumstance which shews it may
be over in two: or if a Voyage with Liberty to deviate, he needs not
be told what tends to shew there will be no Deviation.*

Men

* " It very foon came to be fettled, what at this day when * P. 192.
" Notes have acquired fuch extenfive currency and confe- Salk 25
" quence we can hardly bring ourfelves to fuppofe ever Ld 1 Anne
" could have been doubted, that the Delivery of a promif- Meredith and
" fory Note was a good Confideration on which to found an Shute
" *Affumpfit,* the Note being *Evidence* of a Debt S C
2 Ld. Raym.
* " And where a Bill or Note is taken without a precedent 759
" Debt, Cafh being given for it or the like, this is confider- * P. 193.

Men argues differently from natural Phænomena, and political Appearances: they have different Capacities, different Degrees of Knowledge, and different Intelligence But the means of Information are open to both each profeffes to act from his own fkill and fagacity, and therefore neither needs to communicate to the other *

The Reafon of the Rule which obliges Parties to difclofe, is to prevent Fraud, and to encourage good Faith. It is adapted to fuch Facts as vary the Nature of the Contract, which one privately knows, and of which the other is ignorant

The Queftion, therefore, muft always be, as intimated in the Outfet, whether there was under all the circumftances at the time the Policy was underwritten, a fair REPRESENTATION or a CONCEALMENT, fraudulent if defigned, or, though not defigned, varying materially the Object of the Policy, and changing the Rifque underftood to be ran

The Court were of opinion, that in this Cafe there was no Concealment or Non-communication of any thing which ought to' have been difclofed by the infured that the fuppofed probabilities in the Letter were Matter of mere general fpeculation, upon which the Underwriters, from their local fituation, had even greater opportunity to have formed their Judgment That no Attack was in Evidence, or hoftile Attempt againft the Place, till long after the Infurance propofed and made. That by infuring againft a total Lofs in general Terms, the expectation of the infured of the danger of a total Lofs, fhould the Place be attacked by an European Force, was fuggefted in the Nature of the Propofal, fo that, in Fact, the Contingency infured was, whether the Place would be attacked by an European Force, its incapacity for Refiftance being prefumed in the Terms and Circumftances of the Contract, fo that the Fort, under this Policy and the circumftances of the Cafe, ftood as a fhip under the implied Condition of being fea-worthy, anfwerable, (for all that appeared,) V S C 1 Bl R 593. and adequate to the purpofe for which it was intended, of Defence againft the Natives, and it muft be taken to have been infured, under the certainty of a total Lofs, if a Ship of War, or a European Enemy fhould come up the River againft it And that a contrary Conftruction would render the Rule againft Concealment, affigned to prevent Fraud, an inftrument of Fraud, of which and every Rule it might be faid, as of the Statute of Frauds, it fhall not be turned againft itfelf.

* Ubi enim Judicium Emptoris eft, ibi Fraus Venditoris quæ Cic. ut fupra. poteft effe? may be fafely applied in the fenfe and with the limitations here intimated.

" ed

" ed as a fale of the Bill or Note , but where there is a pre-
" ceaent Debt the Bill in itfelf fhall not be payment, unlefs
" the particular Contract of the Parties, or their fubfequent
" Act make it fo.

*P. 194.

Jefferies v
Auft n.
Mic 12 G L
2 Str 674.
and v Guich-
ard & Roberts,
1 Bl 445
Mic 4 G III

*P. 195.

Lond 1781.
B IV C. 6.
P 427.

* " The *Confideration* of a Note may be enquired as be-
" tween the *Drawer* and *Payee*, but generally when the
" Note has been paffed in a courfe of payment, neither want
" of confideration, nor fraud in the commencement, nor
" fatisfaction, unlefs endorfed on the Note itfelf, can be
" given in Evidence to defeat the Claim of the Holder, to
" the Value which * it purports to convey   And this from
" Principles not only explained in the Books of the Profef-
" fion, but noticed and adopted by the very able Author
" of *Remarks on the influence of Climate, &c. on Manners,*
" *Laws, Government, &c*   It is indeed of the Effence of
" Commerce that no latent Bar fhould impeach the Validity
" of an apparently good transfer of negotiable Interefts;
" otherwife they would foon ceafe to be negotiable

*P. 196.

* " But to this there is one Exception founded on the too
" zealous Anxiety of the Legiflature to fupprefs an evil ex-
" clufively injurious to Individuals, and frequently a fource
" of unfufpected Ruin to their deareft and beft deferving
" connections , but which, after all the remedy or preven-
" tion, rather depends on the Manners, and not on Laws

EXCEPTION *of* GAMING SECURITIES.

9 Anne
Ch. 14. § 1

" The Statute, entitled, " *An Act for the better preventing*
" *of exceffive and deceitful Gaming,*" enacts that all NOTFS,
" BILLS, BONDS, Judgments, Mortgages, or *other fecu-*
" *rities and conveyances* whatfoever, by any perfon or per-
" fons, *where the whole or any part of the confideration* fhall be
" for Money or other valuable thing won by GAMING, or
" for repayment of Money lent or advanced for fuch pur-
" pofe, *fhall be utterly void, fruftrate, and of none effect, to* ALL
" INTENTS AND PURPOSES *whatfoever*

*P 197
Bowyer v
Barpton
Tr 14 G II
2 Str 1155

* " Upon a Cafe ftated at *Nifi prius*, upon an Action
" brought by the Plaintiff as *Indorfee* of feveral *promiffory*
" *Notes*, it appeared the Notes were given by the Defendant
" to one *John Church*, for money by him knowingly advanc-
" ed to the Defendant, to game with at dice   That *Church*
" indorfed them to the Plaintiff for a full valuable confide-
" ration , and that the Plaintiff had not notice, or was privy
" to the Notes being given for a gaming purpofe
" Upon this a Queftion arofe on the Claufe of the Sta-
" tute laft recited, whether the Plaintiff could maintain this
" Action againft the Defendant   And after two Arguments,
" the

" the Court were of opinion he could not for that it is
" making use of the security to some intent and purpose, if
" he can pay his debts with it besides the evasion which
" would take place even when an Indorsee might be privy to
" the transaction ; from the difficulty of proving notice.
" And * though it will be some inconvenience to an innocent * P. 198.
" man, yet that will not balance the considerations on the
" other side. And it is but the common hazard of taking
" notes of infants or *femmes couvertes* And the Plaintiff is
" not without his remedy, as he might sue *Church* on his
" Indorsement

" And in this Case, notice is taken of the opinion thrown Mic. 8 W III
" out, extrajudicially, by HOLT, in *Hussey's* Case, which B R
" was on the statute of *Charles* ; which provides, that if any 16 Car. II. c 7.
" person shall play otherwise than with and for ready Money, § 2
" and shall lose any sum thing or exceeding the sum of one
" hundred Pounds, at one time or meeting, upon Ticket or
" credit, or otherwise, and shall not pay down the same, *the*
" *party losing shall not be compellable to pay or make good the same*
" BUT the Contract and Contracts for the * same, and * P. 199.
" for every part thereof, and all and singular Judgments,
" Statutes, Recognizances, Mortgages, Conveyances, Assu-
" rances, Bonds, Bills, Specialties, Promises, Covenants,
" Agreements, and other Acts, Deeds, and Securities what-
" soever, which shall be obtained, made, given, acknowledg-
" ed, or entered into for security or satisfaction of or for the
" same, or any part thereof, shall be utterly void, and of
" none effect

" It was holden that by this Clause *Assumpsit* was no
" longer maintainable against an Acceptor of a Bill drawn
" for payment of a gaming Debt but HOLT, concurring in
" this, held it would have been otherwise if a Bill had been
" assigned on good Consideration, and the stranger so taking
" it, not being privy to the illegal Contract, had brought
" the Action   Salk 344
* " This *Dictum* of that great Man has been strongly ques- * P 200.
" tioned , even to the extent of saying, that all the learned
" part of the Bar wondered at it It may be proper to con-
" sider a little the intent and operation of this Statute.

" It has been observed, in a Case presently to be cited, Robinson v.
" for another reason, that the Statute of *Charles* makes void Bland
" the CONTRACT in the instances upon which it attaches ; 2 Burr Mansf
" the Statute of *Anne* the SECURITY alone And the Point 1080 1
" under Consideration seems to turn upon this, whether in
" the Statute of *Charles,* SECURITIES which are after men-
" tioned are made void, in so far as the inforcing of them
" would execute the illegal Contract , or void *to all intents*
                                                      " and

" and purpofes (which words are not in that Act) fo as ne-
" ceffarily to deprive *Strangers* taking without notice, and
" for valuable confideration, of all benefit, from a Note free
" from fufpicion on the face of it, and which in many ref-
" pects paffes, and is by Law confidered as Money in aid
" of the public convenience and freedom of commercial
" Contract

* P. 201. * " In the hand of a Stranger, it is not a fecurity for the
" performance of any Contract between the original parties
" If the Drawer, the Acceptor, or any of the Indorfees are
" of Credit and known refponfibly, it is in the contempla-
" tion of a Stranger, portable Cafh It is neither his Duty
" nor in his power to come at the Original Confideration
" and we have feen already, that where that Confideration
" is fraudulent, and the Security, as between the Parties,
" null at Common Law, as being for performance of a
" void Contract, this fhall not change the nature of a Bill
" of Exchange or promiffory Note affignable (which is now
" the fame thing), fo as in other inftances to affect a Stran-
" ger If it does on this, it muft be on the clear and ne-
" ceffary effect of the Statute Now in this Statute the
" Claufe which fays *Securities* fhall be void, immediately
" follows, and refers to that which fays, the party fhall not
" be compellable to pay, for it then fubjoins, without any
" intervening words, BUT all' bonds, &c and Securities
" whatfoever, which fhall be given, &c for payment or fa-
" tisfaction of, or for the fame, fhall be void and of no ef-
" fect If this provifion is fatisfied by their being void, as
" between parties and privies under the Contract, it will
" not be extended farther to an operation fo unfavourable,
" but by abfolute Neceffity of Law

" Now the Gamefter, the original Payee, when he in
" dorfes the Note to a Stranger, who becomes a purchafer
" of it for a valuable Confideration, has received the advan-
* P 202. " tage of the Contract and Security, he has Cafh or Va-
" lue for it and Strangers, into whofe hands it may fuc-
" ceffively pafs from an innocent Indorfee, may be thought
" to ftand on a footing wholly independent of the Contract

4 Bac Ac- " And this Sentiment appears to be adopted in *Bacon's*
6:: IV " Abridgement, and to be favoured by the different Mode of
171. " expreffion in the Commentaries, when treating of the ef-
" fect of the Statute of *Charles* and that of *Anne* And no
" Decifion occurs contrary to HOLT's Idea. It is perhaps
" as becoming in the Law as in Philofophy, not to wonder
" without adequate Caufe and poffibly the learned part of
" the Bar would have done no injuftice to that character by
" a lefs

" a lefs empaffioned reception of the Sentiments on this oc-
" cafion of that very learning and difcerning Judge

" And HOLT himfelf, in affirmance of this Opinion, puts 2 Mod 279.
" a Cafe much ftronger being on a Bond which is not re- Mic 29
" garded as Currency in the Place of Cafh, but as a fpecial Car II C B.
" Security that Cafe had actually been decided within little
" more than twelve Years of the Statute . *A* won 100*l* of
" *B* and being indebted in that Sum to *C* he takes *B* with
" him to *C*, and there *B* acknowledges the Debt, but fays
" nothing of the Confideration, (of which *C* remained
" wholly ignorant), and confents to give Bond to *C* for the
" Debt of 100*l* * which *A* owed to *C* *B*. is fued by *C*. * P. 203.
" on this Bond, who pleads the Statute of *Charles* in his De-
" fence, ramely, that it was for payment of a Gaming
" Debt. Now, a Contract, that *B* would make Security
" by Bond, Mortgage or Judgment to *A* for fuch Debt, is
" clearly pronounced Void under the Statute · and though
" *C*, if privy to the Confideration of giving the Bond, could
" never have recovered under it, yet *C* innocent, and a
" Stranger to the Tranfaction, and accepting only a Secu-
" rity for payment of a legal Debt, was held by the whole
" Court not to be within the Statute This appears to go
" the whole extent of the Dictum of the *Lord Chief Juf-*
" *tice* HOLT, and beyond it and to be a direct fatisfactory
" Decifion in point upon this Queftion on the Statute.

" In the Cafe of *Robinfon* and *Bland*, which will require 1 Bl R
" to be hereafter mentioned for another important Principle 237 and 256.
" contained in it, the Action was on the Cafe upon Promifes S C
" The Declaration confifted of three Counts· the *firft*, on a Bill 2 Burr Manf.
" of Exchange, drawn by 'Sir *John Bland* (whofe Sifter and 2 G III
" Adminiftratrix was the Defendant) at *Paris*, 31ft of *Au-*
" *guft*, 1755, payable in *England*, at ten days after Sight,
" for the fum of 672*l* payable to the order of the Plaintiff.
" The fecond Count was for Money *lent* and advanced, the
" third for Money *had* and *received*, by the Defendant to the
" Ufe of the Plaintiff

" There was a Verdict for the Plaintiff, fubject to the opi-
" nion of the Court on a Cafe referved which, * fo far as * P. 204
' material to the prefent occafion, comprifed the following
' Facts.

Notes Void on the Statute of ANNE, *for Money lent for*
GAMING

" That the Bill was given for Money on Account of Play
" at *Paris*, which was fairly loft, 300*l*. Money *lent* by the
" Plaintiff

" Plaintiff for the above purpofe ; 372*l.* Money *loft* to the
" Plaintiff at the fame time

" *The Court* was of Opinion, that the SECURITY for Mo-
" ney loft or lent for the purpofe of Gaming, was rendered
" void by the Statute of *Anne* fo that upon the *firft Count,*
" the Plaintiff could not recover

" But as to the CONTRACT, *the Court* was of Opinion,
" that the Money WON was not recoverable the *Contract*
" and *Security* being both defeated by the Statute of *Charles*

" But that, as to the Money LENT, the Plaintiff was en-
" titled to recover fuch LOAN, not being prohibited by the
" Statute of *Char'es,* and the SECURITY only being affected
" by that of *Anne,* the CONTRACT at large remaining open
" to be decided according to the Merits of the Confideration,
" which, in this Cafe, the Court, held fufficient to entitle
" the Plaintiff, and that he muft accordingly recover for fo
" *much* (with Intereft up to the time of Judgment), on his
" Counts of *general* ASSUMPSIT

" Judgment was accordingly entered up on the Verdict
" but under Rule to ftand as Security for 300*l* the Principal
" Money lent, and 75*l* Intereft

Gilb R 49
.39
⚹ P 205.

" The Plaintiff declared on a *promiffory* Note the De-
" fendant pleaded, that by the Statute of ANNE to make
" void Notes or other Securities given to induce a * Creditor
" to fign a Bankrupt's *Certificate, (a)* the Plaintiff ought
" not to maintain his Action, for that on fuch day, he,
" the Defendant *deceffor devenit* And that before that time
" and hereunto, he was and is indebted to *I S* in 100*l*
" and above that a Commiffion iffued, and Commiffioners
" proceeded and made a *Certificate* of his (the Defendant's),
" having conformed in all things to the Statute, &c and that
" the faid *I S* refufed to fubfcribe the *Certificate,* until he
" the Defendant, fhould give him a Security, namely, the
" Note in the Declaration mentioned, or a like Note,
" whereupon the Defendant gave the Note, in the Declara-
" tion fet forth, to the Plaintiff in Truft for *I S* to induce
" him to fubfcribe the faid Certificate

(a) Neither this Act nor the Title occurs in Ruffhead's *Edition
It is afterwards cited under the Title of* 4 *&* 5 Anne, *in this
Cafe A Statute of that Date (c 17) is expired But there is
at prefent by the Statue* 5 G II *a Claufe pronouncing void all
Bonds, Bills, Notes, Contracts and Agreements, as a Confideration
or to the intent to perfuade a Creditor to fign a Certificate, the party
fued to be at Liberty to plead the general Iffue, and give the Act and
the fpecial Matter in Evidence.*

" The

" The Plaintiff demurred, and on Argument, it was con-
" tended, that the Plea was general and bad: that it amount-
" ed to no more than the *general Issue*, which he might
" have pleaded, and given the Consideration in *Evidence*
" under the Statute

" The Court seemed to be of Opinion, that though he
" might well have pleaded the general Issue in this Case,
" yet that having introduced a special Plea, he ought to
" have shewn that he was such a Bankrupt as was entitled
" to his Discharge since otherwise, the Creditors for whose
" Benefit, equally and impartially, the Provision was framed,
" would not be prejudiced by the Note or Certificate, and
" the Mischief would only fall where the Fraud was in-
" tended

* " *Bills* of *Exchange* and promissory Notes are within the ✱ P 206.
" Statute of Limitations. '

Eq Ca Abr
602 Renew
v Axton, Hil
2 & 3 T ll
Carth 3
v. etiam 226.

SECTION VII

Of SECONDARY EVIDENCE.

" *Voluntary Affidavits* have already been considered. Little
" requires to be said of the Evidence of LETTERS.

Letters

" These, however, are sometimes the very Basis of the
" Charge as where the Contents of them constitute an *overt*
" Act of *Treason*. But in this Sense, they do not properly
" relate to this head

" They are *Secondary* Evidence, where they are adduced
" *Collaterally* to the Charge and thus *Letters* may be read
" in Evidence, from the Wife to the Defendant, on an
" Action, of which there are too many examples though
" he cannot read them in his favour

" *Letters* too are not unfrequently read in proof of a pro-
" mise of Marriage.

TIT. II.

Tradesmen's Books.

" The Statute of JAMES enacts, that a *Tradesman's* SHOP- L. N. P 282
" BOOK shall not be *Evidence* AFTER a Year This might
" infer a Surmise of Parliament, that of itself it was Evi-
" dence, generally Yet it is not so, unless under circum-
" stances *for defect of vetter*

" Thus,

Price v the
Earl of Tor-
rington, Cor
Holt. C T
Salk 285 Tr
2 Ann.

* P. 207

" Thus, where an Action was brought by the Plaintiff,
" being a Brewer, for Beer fold and delivered ; it was
" proved that the ufual way of the Plaintiff's dealing was,
" that the Drayman came every Night to the Clerk of the
" Brewhoufe, and gave him an Account * of the Beer they
" had delivered out, which he fet down in a Book for that
" purpofe, to which the Draymen fet their hands, and that
" the Drayman was dead   They proved his hand-writing
" to the Book. and this was held good Evidence of the
" Delivery, otherwife of the Shop-Book fingly, without
" more.

Salk 690
Hil 11 W III

" And in an earlier Cafe, on a Taylor's Bill, a Shop-Book
" was allowed Evidence, it being proved that the Servant
" accuftomed to make the Entries was dead, and that it was
" his hand to the Book.

Clerk & Bed-
ford, M.c.
5 G II
L N P 282.

" But where the Plaintiff to prove Delivery, produced a
" Book which belonged to his Cooper who was dead, and
" whofe Name was fet to feveral Articles, as Wine deliver-
" ed to the Defendant, and a Witnefs was ready to prove
" his hand, it is faid, that Lord Chief Juftice *Raymond*
" would not allow it, for that it differed from Lord
" *Torrington*'s Cafe, becaufe there the Witnefs faw the Dray-
" man fign the Book every Night

L N P 283
3 May 1738

" Upon an Iffue out of Chancery, to try whether eight
" Parcels of *Hudfon's Bay* Stock, bought in the Name of
" Mr *Lake*, were in Truft for Sir *Stephen Evans*, his Af-
" fignees, the Plaintiffs, fhewed firft, that there was no
" Entry in the Books of Mr *Lake* relating to this Tranf-
" action   Secondly, fix of the Receipts were in the hands
" of Sir *Stephen Evans* · and there was a Reference to the
" Back of them by *Jeremy Thomas* (Sir *Stephen's* Book-
" keeper), to Book B B of Sir *Stephen Evans*   Thirdly,
" *Jeremy Thomas* was proved to be dead   The Queftion
" was, whether the Book of Sir *Stephen Evans* referred to,
" in which was an Entry of the payment of the Money,
" fhould be permitted to be read   And the Court of *King's*
" *Bench*, on *Trial at Bar*, admitted it, not only as to the
" Six, but likewife as to the other two, in the hands of Sir
" *Berlby Lake*, the Son of Mr *Lake*

* P. 208.

L N P 283
fupr c ea by
Lc haraw
r Non gome-
ricard Turner

" And in *Smartle* and *Williams*, where the Queftion was,
" whether the Mortgage Money was really paid ; a Scri-
" vener's Book of Accounts, the Scrivener being dead, was
" holden to be good Evidence of payment

Tit.

Tit. III

Depositions, &c *poft Mortem*

" We come now to the laft Species of Written Evi-
" dence, and the moft proper to precede *parol* Teftimony,
" for it is indeed only parol in its Origin, and not admitted
" till the direct Verbal Proof ceafes to be attainable, I
" mean *Depofitions* and Examinations at Common Law, in-
" troduced as Evidence after the Death of the party by
" whom they were made and acknowledged

" And firft," *Exemplifications* of *Depofitions* in *Equity*. Barnard K B,
" thefe" fhall be delivered to the Jury if the party be dead, 348.
and the Exemplification are under the Great Seal: but if
the Exemplifications contains the Teftimony of fome that
are living and fome that are dead, it fhall not be delivered
to the Jury, becaufe, when the Parties are dead, their Depofitions are the greateft Evidence that the Nature of the
thing is capable of, and equal to Evidence *Viva Voce*, and
ought to be as carefully confidered and examined. which
cannot eafily be, unlefs they are carried away by the Jury,
for the bare reading of them in Court is not likely to make
the fame Impreffion, befides, this Evidence does not derive
Credibility from any Act of the *Nifi Prius* Court, but they
have it intrinfically in themfelves, from the Self-Evidence of
their own Seals, and therefore, wherever they are removed Styl Prac.
they remain the fame* but if fome of the Witneffes are Reg 294.
living, it is not the higheft Evidence

* " But it fhall not be prefumed that Witneffes are dead, * P 209.
" fo as to admit their Depofitions in a Court of Common
" Law, where it is apparently fuppofeable that they con-
" tinue living

Proof of the Death neceffary to introduce them

" And therefore, on Trial of an Iffue directed from the Benfon v Olive
" Equity fide of the Exchequer, in the year 1732, the De- cor Reynolds,
" pofition of a Witnefs examined fifty (h) years before, C B
Mic 5 G II.
" namely

(h) It is upon a Principle analogous to this, that the Rule is Beverley v
founded, that a period, which by any reafonable intendment a perfon Beverley, et al,
in being may furvive, fhall not be fuch a precedent Efate as fhall con- 2 Vern 131
ftitute a vefted remainder in the perfon, whofe intereft is to take effect
after the Death of him, to whom fuch a Term is devifed
Thus, where A devifed Lands to B his eldeft Son, for the Term
of fixty Years, if he fhould fo long live, and from and after his deceafe to his grandfon D. the fon of B, in Tail B and D fuffered
a Recovery.

V supra, 100,
103

" namely, in 1672, was offered to be read, without any
" Evidence of his being dead The *Chief Baron* would not
" admit it; diftinguifhing it from a Deed, which proves
" itfelf after thirty years. for that a Deed had fome Au-
" thenticity from the folemnity of hand and feal (probably
" he

*a Recovery an objection was taken to that Recovery, for that th-
Devife to B. being only for fixty Years, if he fhould fo long live,
and after his deceafe to D the freehold, during the Life of B was in
abeyance It was argued that the limitation of the Estate Tail,
expectant on the term of fixty years, was good And Lord Derby's
Cafe was cited as in point That the devife over, from and immediately after the deceafe of B ought to be intended of his dying
within the Term, which was highly prefumable, B being then upwards of forty years of Age But the Court held it would be
hard to make fuch construction on the Words of the Will, as to fay
where a Term is limited to a man for fixty years, if he fhall fo long
live, and from and after his deceafe, to another, that it must be
meant, from and after his deceafe within the term For fuppofe he
outlived the Term, fhould the remainder-man take in the life of the
first devifee? That would be a construction contrary to the words and
intention of the Teftator.*

Cited, Litt.
Rep 370
as of 34 Eliz.
C B.

*Lord Derby's Cafe was this. Covenant to ftand feized to the
Ufe of himfelf for Life, Remainder to another for eighty-nine years,
if Ferdinand his fon fhould fo long live, Remainder after the Death
of Ferdinand to a fecond fon in Tail The Queftion was if the
fecond Remainder in Tail were good. And it was adjudged fo to
be. for that it was for eighty nine years, which is longer than
by intendment of Law a man fhould live. but that if it had been for
ten years, if Ferdinand fhould live fo long, then it had been a
void Remainder*

In the Cafe of Napper and Sanders, *A made a Feoffment to
the Ufe of herfelf for life, and after, to the Ufe of the Feoffees, for
80 years, if B and C fhould fo long live and if C furvived B
then to the Ufe of her for Life, and after the Deceafe of C to the Ufe
of D in Tail, with remainders over The Queftion was, whether the
Remainders fubfequent to that for the Life of C were contingent or vefted*

*In this Queftion there were two points the first foreign to the pre
fent confideration, whether the contingency on which the Eftate for
Life to C was limited to depend, fhould extend to all the fubfequent
remainders, and it was determined that it fhould not.*

*There remained then the other point, neceffary to the decifion of
the queftion, namely, whether fuch remainders were not to be deemed
contingent in regard of the poffibility of the joint lives outftanding the
term of eighty years, in which event, fuppofing A the feoffor, to be
dead, there would be evidently no preceding eftate fubfifting, nor, confequently, the remainders capable of taking effect.*

*Lord Derby's Cafe was cited, and it was adjudged that the Re
mainders vefted immediately*

" he muſt have added to this effect, and became original
" proof, to which the atteſtation of Witneſſes was but a
" circumſtance ſubſervient, but in the inſtance under con-
" ſideration the *vivâ voce* Evidence is, in Courts of Com-

Vol I   L   " mon

In another Caſe it was ſaid by Hale, *Chief Juſtice, that a Feoff-*   Weale v Low-
ment for ninety-nine years, if A *ſhould ſo long live, and, after his*   er, Pollex 674
Death to the Uſe of B *in fee, ſhall not be contingent, but it ſhall*
be preſumed his life will not exceed ninety-nine years, otherwiſe if it
had been limited but for twenty-one

See for theſe Caſes a Work, which, for the importance (in a pro-   Fearne on
feſſional and public view) and intricacy of its ſubject, and the clear-   Conting
neſs and ſtrength of reaſoning, merits early to be ſtudied, and never   Rem & Ex
to be wholly laid aſide, by the Lawyer, who would unite the higher   Deviſes, 11, 15[?]
knowledge and principles of his profeſſion with practical experience   Hargrave's
ſince Caſes without order, and a firm regular connection of well-   Notes, 20 b.
eſtabliſhed inferences, which the Mind acquires an habit of deducing
from an exerciſe of its powers in the attentive ſtudy of a juſt ſyſtem,
impart a defective, fugitive and fallacious intelligence The Trea-
tiſe, to which reference is here made, may be expected to have that
direct influence in fortifying the Judgment of a Student which the
Mathematics more remotely (as to the object of legal Attainments)
are obſerved to exert After the admirable COMMENTARIES *on the*
Laws of England, and the nervous Copiouſneſs of PLOWDEN's
Reports, we might ſay of that Treatiſe of HALE's *Hiſtory of the*
Common Law, BACON's *Reading on the Statute of Uſes, and*
SHEPHERD's *Touchſtone, and* DODDERIDGE's *Engliſh Lawyer*
—nocturna verſate manu, verſate diurna After a year
or two thus ſtrenuouſly employed, if he ſhall peruſe the Law
of Evidence, FOSTER's *Treatiſe on the Crown Law, and with it*
HALE's *Pleas of the Crown, and inform himſelf, from the few Au-*
thors who have treated on the ſubject, concerning the courſe of Pro-
ceedings and general Principles of the Conſtitution of the COURT *of*
CHANCERY *(not neglecting* WOOD's *Inſtitutes of the Law of Eng-*
land for they are an excellent ſpecimen of diſtinct and cloſe Arrange-
ment, and by no means, even now, ſuperſeded in their Utility) will
it the young ſtudent be ſo grounded, that the year before his Call
to the Bar he may attend the Courts to great Improvement? And
having acquainted himſelf with leading Caſes in a few of our beſt
modern Reporters, among whom I know not that any can with more
advantage be read than SIR JAMES BURROW, *for the* COMMON
LAW, *and* PEERE WILLIAMS, *(ſtill a modern, from the Paucity*
of Chancery Reporters) for his admirable Caſes, chiefly in EQUITY,
would he not enter on the practice with a well-grounded hope, and a
ſenſe of the real magnitude and extent of the objects which the Pro-
feſſion comprehends? Would he not, if unſucceſsful, he ſuſtained by
a not unbecoming conſciouſneſs, and if ſucceſsful, enjoy his honourab e
acquiſitions with a ſentiment proportioned to the means by which he
attained them? This indeed may ſuppoſe a later Call to the Bar
than juvenile impatience or parental wiſhes may well admit as other-
wiſe it would interfere with academical exerciſe at the ſeaſon beſt
adapted for claſſical and ſcientific ſtudies But the dubious benefit of
a few

"mon Law, the primary Proof, and Depofitions are re-
"ceived in its room only from the neceffity of the Cafe)
"He faid if proper enquiry and fearch had been made, and
"no account could have been given of him, he would have
"admitted it at fuch a diftance of time."

* P 210   * EVIDENCE *of* VERDICT *and oath of* DECEASED *Witnefs*
on *Trial.*

12 Mod 318   Another way of perpetuating the Evidence of a party de-
Barnard. K. B.   ceafed is, by giving the Verdict in Evidence, and the *Oath*
243   of the party deceafed " upon that Trial "

V fupra, 65, et   " Now concerning this there are thefe Rules." Where
paffim   you give in Evidence any Matter fworn at a former trial, it
muft be between the fame parties becaufe otherwife you
difpoffefs your Adverfary of the Liberty to crofs examine
befides, otherwife you cannot regularly give the verdict in
evidence, and where you cannot give the verdict in evidence,
you cannot give the Oath on which it was founded, for if
you cannot fhew there was fuch a caufe, you cannot fhew
that any perfon was examined in that Caufe, and without fhewing that Caufe, no man's oath can be given in Evidence

* P. 211.   " And for this purpofe it hath been holden that, the *Poftea*
" is fuffic ent Evidence of a Verdict, that is, fo far as to
S.r 162   " entitle you to introduce an account of what a Witnefs,
" fince dead, fwore at that Trial

EXAMINATIONS *of deceafed Perfons.*

Pra't Ch J.   " Declarations of a *dying* perfon are frequently part of
Hil 5 G 1   " the Evidence given in fupport of an Indictment (after his
Str 162   " deceafe) of Murther   On this fource of Evidence fome
S r 199   " points arofe in the melancholy Cafe of Mr. *Luttrel*
S C Ha gr
St 1
Vol VI.
P 202—4.

*a few years fercer ty will not bear a competition with the advantages,
both profeffional and general, of being contented not to affume the
Garb and Name of the Profeffion till well grounded in its Theory,
and even fomewhat difciplined in its Practice   of which opportunities
are not wanting fince a very commendable and antient Inftitution
has been revived* * *Five years fpent in this manner, the latter
half perhaps in one of the Law Societies, might introduce him to
the Bar not too young to be refpected on the firft occafion which fhould
call him forth, nor too old for the full gratification (probably to be
continued for a number of years) of every juft and liberal view,
with full increafing j tiifaction to himfelf and the Community*

* *Alluding to voluntary Exercifes in which Law Queftions are
debated.*

" This

" This Gentleman being mortally wounded, his account
" of the Facts, together with his sentiments on the circum-
" stances leading to the event, was reduced to writing by a
" Clergyman, at the request, and in the presence, of two
" Justices The writing was not signed by the deceased, and
" one of the Justices took it with him into *Wales* The
" Clergyman took a Copy of it. There were also three
" several conferences on the same general purport which the
' declaration was meant to have proved, namely, charging
" the Defendants with having barbarously murdered him.

" The *Copy* was offered to be given in Evidence, but the
" Court would not admit it. the Counsel for the Prosecu-
" tion not having shewn that the Original was lost, but it
" appearing, on the contrary, that they might have pro-
" duced it if they had applied in due time

* " There then arose a Question whether any of the De- * P. 212.
" clarations of the deceased, touching the Cause of his
" Death, could be Evidence The Court was unanimous
" that the Declaration at the second conference could have
" no account given of it that would be Evidence, that being
" the conference in which the Declaration was reduced to
" writing But the first and third were held to be distinct
" Facts, of which Evidence was receivable, and the decla-
" ration of the deceased at these conferences was accordingly
" admitted, the CHIEF JUSTICE *dissentient,* as considering
" the first, second, and third, to be all to the same effect,
" like supplemental Answers in Chancery, so as to consti-
" tute but one fact, of which he best Evidence was not pro-
" duced, and therefore he *was* of opinion they could not be
" let to give an account of the first and third conference "

† In an information of *Perjury,* on a Trial in Ejectment * P 213
on *Not Guilty,* the Defendant " insisting" that what he T Raym 170.
swore was true, in Proof of the Perjury one was produced
to prove what a person deceased swore at the former Trial
in Ejectment. And this was allowed to be good Evidence ;
because it doth not go to the Proof of the charge itself that
the Defendant swore, but only to the falsity of the fact that
was sworn " And it was held" that the Charge itself,
which consists in the Proof of " the Truth of the Fact, and
the Contrariety of" what the Defendant swore might be directly proved by Evidence, " which might be" cross-exa-
mined by the Defendant, but " that" the falsity of the
fact to which the Defendant swore may be made out by any
other Proof because, in this Case, you must give the Verdict
in Evidence to prove the Perjury, in as much as the Cause
in which the Perjury * was committed must be set forth in your * P. 214.

L 2   information, V infra.

information ; and by confequence be proved on your Iffue. And when you have proved that the Defendant fwore in the Caufe, you may fhew the whole Matter *viz* how his Teftimony ftood oppofed by the Evidence of the party deceafed

WITNESS *examined before* CORONER—*dead, fick or kept back.*

t Hawk P C 429
Ch 46 § 6.
Keb 55
H. H P C.
306
Ch. 24
2 H H P C
284. 5
Chap 38
2 Keo 18, 9
1 Lev 180

Kel 55
2 H. Pl C
429
2 Keb 19
H P C.
Ch 45
St. Tr 265
3 St Tr 8, 9
2 H. H P C.
284. 5
* P. 215

A Witnefs " is" examined before the Coroner, but upon the Trial is either dead, or fo ill that he is not able to travel if oath be made of the Truth of this Faƈt, the *Examination* of fuch Witnefs, fo dead or unable to travel, may be read, but the Coroner muft firft make oath that fuch examinations are the fame that were taken before him upon oath, without any Addition or Alteration , becaufe the *Examinations* are, in thefe Cafes, the utmoft Evidence that can be procured, the Examinant himfelf being prevented in coming by the Aƈt of God

And much more fo are fuch Examinations Evidence, and to be read on the Trial when it can be proved on oath that the Witnefs is detained and kept back from appearing by the means and procurement of the * prifoner . for he fhall never be admitted to fhelter himfelf by fuch evil Praƈtices on the Witnefs, that being to give him Advantage of his own Wrong

EXCEPTIONS *in the admiffion of this Evidence.* CONFESSION.

In an Information againft *Paine* for compofing and publifhing a Libel againft the late Queen *Mary*, which was called her Epitaph The Cafe was that *Paine* wrote the Epitaph, but it was diƈtated to him by another, and that afterwards *Paine* put it into his ftudy, and by miftake delivered it to *B.* inftead of another Paper It came at length through feveral hands to the Magiftrates, who fent for *B* and examined him upon oath in the Abfence of *Paine* *B* died before the Trial of *Paine*, which was at Bar , and the Court would not allow the Examination of *B* to be given in Evidence, becaufe *Paine* was not prefent to crofs-examine . and though it is Evidence in *Indiƈtments* for Felony in fuch Cafes, by Force " of the Statute," yet it is not fo in *Information* for Mifdemeanours, or *Appeals* of Murder

1 & 2 P & M.
- 3
2 & 3 P & M.
c 10

- P 216

And upon this " Statute the Confeffion of the Prifoner " (though it is not to be exhibited to the Grand Jury) may " on the Trial be read in Evidence againft * the Prifoner " fuch" Examination and Confeffion " being taken" before a Juftice of Peace

" And

" And of this the following particulars are to be obferved: Burn, J P l. 537.
" The Examination of the *accufed* ought not to be upon
" oath the reafon of this refults from the moft obvious
" Principles of Juftice, Policy, and Humanity
It is proper that he fet his Name " or Mark to it "
" This Information being upon the Trial duly proved by
" the Juftice, who, if it may be, fhould be perfonally pre-
" fent, or his Clerk," is Evidence againft the Party himfelf
who made it ; but cannot be made ufe of againft any others.
This Confeffion " to be Evidence, muft be voluntary, H H P C Ch 38 p 284.
" for, as the excellent Sir MATTHEW HALE notices, it muft
" fatisfactorily appear that the Prifoner confeffed freely with-
" out menaces or any fpecies of undue influence impofed upon
" him, and that he has often known (he fubjoins) the Pri-
" foner acquitted againft his Confeffion upon the Examina-
" tion. for that the reafon of thefe Examinations being at
" all Evidence is, that they are taken before Judges of Re-
" cord, authorized and required by Act of Parliament, and
" who have jurifdiction concerning the Crimes upon which
" they are taken.
" If it appear, therefore, that any of the requifite circum-
" ftances are wanting, this fpecies of Proof will be rejected ;
" and the laft Circuit Sir *George Nares* ever went, he, though
" finking under his illnefs, exerted his accuftomed Vigilance
" and * Benevolence in the Cafe where the Admiffibility of * P. 217
" a Confeffion in Writing was rendered doubtful by circum-
" ftances at the time of making it If practicable, it may
" feem always beft where the confeffion of the Printer is
" taken, that it be in the prefence of one or more indiffe-
" rent perfons unconnected with the *Profecutor*, the *Magif-
" trate*, or the *Prifoner*, (or at leaft the two former), that it
" may be proveable to have been deliberately and freely
" made
" In the Cafe now to be ftated it was difallowed, as being
" before a Jurifdiction deemed not relevant to the *criminal*
" Iffue
" *Welfh* forcibly took away Mrs *Pickering*, and married H H P C. II Ch 38 P 285
" her, and thereupon a temporary Act of Parliament was
" obtained, enabling *Commiffioners* therein named to hear and
" determine that Marriage, and to diffolve it if there were
" caufe. In that Cafe Mrs *Pickering* herfelf was examined
" touching the Manner of the Marriage, as a fupplemental
" proof, and died pending the fuit *Welfh* was afterwards
" indicted upon the Statute 3 *H* VII for Felony in this Fact :
" and it was moved, that this Examination of Mrs *Picker-
" ing* might be read in Evidence againft the Prifoner, but
' it was denied. becaufe it was a proceeding according to
" the

"‧ the Civil Law, in a Civil Court; becaufe that fuit was
"originally at the inftance of Mrs *Pickering*, in her own
"Caufe, for her own Intereft, and therefore at Common
"Law not allowable, though the Commiffioners on that
"Examination, were Judges conftituted by that which was
"then allowed to be an Act of Parliament

"And this Examination of a perfon charged with Felony
' not amounting to a Conviction *ipfo Facto*, but only to
' a part of the Evidence againft the Prifoner, is not to be
"introduced as Evidence till after the Plea of *Not Guilty*,"
"becaufe the Trial ought * to be of Record, folemn, in
"open Court, that determines upon the Fate of Life and
"Death

"The Reader may obferve that under this head of Writ-
"ten Evidence is included here the Oath of a party
"deceafed, on a former Trial, which, feparately confidered,
"would belong to unwritten Proof: but fince it is ne-
"ceffarily connected with the proceedings on Record in the
"former Trial, not being receivable till at leaft the Postea
"be given in Evidence, and fince it could not be referred to
"the general character of unwritten verbal teftimony, which
"is by living Witneffes fpeaking to their own knowledge, and
"not (unlefs in fome rare inftances of exception) to that of
"other perfons, or the Declarations of others, on the whole
"it feems that the oath of the deceafed Witnefs, as attach-
"ed in a manner to the written Evidence by Record, has
"its proper place in this concluding divifion of written Evi-
"dence

"It has been a controverted point with refpect to a Wit-
"nefs examined before the Coroner, and who afterwards,"
on all endeavours ufed againft the Trial cannot be found

"On the Proof of this it hath been thought his Exami-
"nation may be read in a Cafe of Felony at Common Law "
becaufe it is to be prefumed that the Witnefs is dead, when
he cannot be found after the ftricteft Enquiry. "And in
"merely Civil Cafes," where a Witnefs is loft, and cannot
be found, you may, upon oath of the Matter, ufe his Depofition, "then" it is the beft Evidence that can poffibly be
had of the Matter "and" when a Witnefs is fought, and
cannot be found, he is in the fame circumftances as * to the
party, "and as to the expedience of fupplying for the pur-
"pofes of information to the Court upon the Queftion, the
"want of this verbal Teftimony," if he were dead "and
"public Juftice will not reject any Evidence, where better
' is not attainable, unlefs in the reception of it there would
"be given of inconvenience

"And

" And it was refolved by the Judges, on their previous K•l 55 v. Rt.
" confultations with each other, touching the Courfe of form Ld
" Law on points likely to arife on the Trial of Lord *Morley,* 2 Hawk. P. C.
" before the HOUSE of PEERS, for *Murder* 430

" That in Cafe oath fhould be made concerning any Wit-
" nefs, who had been examined by the Coroner, and was
" then abfent, that they had ufed all their endeavours to find
" him, and cannot find him, that is not fufficient to autho-
" rize the reading of fuch examination

" The extreme hazard of Abufe in this inftance is ma-
" n.feft.

" But there feemeth to be no doubt that even in capital Kel 55.
" Cafes," if it be proved that a Witnefs was fubpœnaed, and
fell fick by the way " fo as to be unable to travel," his Depofition may be allowed to be read, " the Coroner or other
" Magiftrate before whom it was taken, firft making oath
" that fuch Depofition is the fame which he took upon oath,
" without any Addition or Alteration whatfoever " for the
" Depofition is the beft Evidence that in this Cafe can pof-
" fibly be had, and that anfwers what the Law requires.
" And in general Terms this hath been already expreffed.

BOOK

※ P. 220.

*BOOK II.

PART I.

CHAPTER I.

Of Unwritten Evidence

We now come to confider the unwritten Evidence, or Proofs from the Mouth of Witnesses

SECTION II.

Witnesses

And where we muſt conſider

1. Who are totally excluded from Credit, " or, in other
" Words, what Exceptions go to the *Competency* or *Admiſ-*
" *ſibility*

2 By what rules we may diſtinguiſh the Truth of contradictory Evidence; " or, in other words, what circumſtances
" augment or impair the Credit reaſonably to be given
" to a Witneſs."

TIT II

Of Incompetency

Thoſe who are *totally excluded* from all *Teſtimony* are,

First, for Want of legal Integrity; " which is
" twofold

    1 *Preſumptive*; *from* Interest
    2 *Poſitive*, *from* Infamy.

Second, for Want of Discernment, which is alſo
twofold.

    First. *From* Non-attainment *of years of* Reason
    Second *From* Deprivation *or Defect of Reaſon*

Third, propter Jurisjurandi defectum *for want of a*
legal Oath

Fourth, propter Fidem publicam, *from* Professional Confidence.

⊁ P 221.

* Tit III.

1 *Witneſſes excluded by Intereſt*

Concerning *Perſons* intereſted in the Matter in Queſtion,
the general Rule is, that no Man can be a Witness for
himself.

" But

" But this Rule, though univerfal in civil Matters, does
" not exlude the party, who profecutes in the Name of
" ie CROWN, in *Right* and in *Behalf* of the PUBLIC.
or this, in ordinary Cafes of perfonal Wrong, there is
an obvious Reafon ; fince he doth not come for perfonal
" compenfation in the fhape of *Damages*, which are reco-
" verable only by a civil Action, nor is he by intendment
" of Law prefumed to come for private Revenge in the pu-
" nifhment of the Offender, but in pure Maintenance of the
" Laws and public Juftice
    " However, the Principle is yet more general , for, not
" to mention *Appeals* of *Murder*, which perhaps cannot
" with legal propriety be claffed under this head, fince the
" Law will not prefume an Intereft in the indulgence of an
" acrimonial and unfocial Paffion, fuch as Revenge is, a
" Party fhall profecute by Indictment where he hath a direct
" Intereft in the event, that is, where he hath been *robbed,*
" and the Goods are out of his Poffeffion, remaining in the
" hands of the Party charged And here, if he *profecute*
" to CONVICTION, he fhall have by the Statute a WRIT
" of RESTITUTION Nay, he fhall often be * without Re- * P 222.
" covery of his Goods, unlefs he profecute, for, on reafons
" eafily to be apprehended, he fhall not have *Trover*, or
" other *civil Action*, againft the *Felon*, for the TRESPASS
" mergeth in the FELONY.
    " The true and moft general PRINCIPLE, therefore, Gilb Rep 113
" which governeth this Diftinction, is, that *it concerneth the*
" *Community that* Crimes pafs not wholly unpunifhed And
" if the party fuffering might not profecute, few befide
" might have the certain knowledge of the Fact, or the Dif-
" pofition of bringing it to Trial, which muft combine to
" call forth the Exertions of PUBLIC JUSTICE
    " Yet fo far the Rule holds, being founded on a Principle
" not to be fuperfeded of neceffary Juftice That where a
" Perfon is to *difcharge* himfelf by fuch Evidence as would
" effect a Conviction, he fhall not be an Evidence in fup-
" port of a public Profecution Thus where a man is *in-*
" *dicted* for FORGERY, the party whofe hand is faid to be
" forged fhall not be admitted to prove the Fact charged, L N P 288,9.
" of Forgery ; for his hand, apparently, againft him is Evi-
" dence, till the contrary be proved, of an Obligation. and
" therefore he fhall not be permitted in the Indictment to
" make proof (while he hath intereft in the Queftion, the
" fuppofed Obligation ftanding in apparent Force againft
" him) that it was not his hand   •

† Intereft Reipublicæ ut ne fint Delicta impunita

                                                          " But

Where Interest excludes from Testimony in Support of criminal Prosecution.

"" But though in *criminal Cases*, the Exceptions are few "" indeed, in which a party interested in the Event * may not "" be a Witness, in CIVIL CASES, there is hardly at COM- "" MON LAW an instance where the Cause is so circum- "" stanced as that he may: and this upon clear reasons ope- "" rating such Exclusion ," for where a Man, who is inte- rested in the Matter in Question, would also prove it, it rather is a Ground for Distrust than any just Cause of Be- lief for men are generally so short-sighted as to look to their own private Benefit, which is near them, rather than to the Good of the World, "" which, though on the sum of "" Things really best for the Individual," is more remote, therefore, from the Nature of human Passions and Actions, there is more reason to distrust such a biassed Testimony than to believe it. It is also easy for persons who are prejudiced and prepossessed to put false and unequal Glosses upon what they give in Evidence; and therefore the Law removes them from Testimony, to prevent their sliding into Perjury and it can be no Injury to Truth to remove those from the Jury, whose Testimony may hurt themselves, and can never induce any rational Belief.

*P 223.

"" If it be objected, that Interest in the Matter in dispute "" might, from the Bias it creates, be an Exception to the "" *Credit*, but that it ought not to be absolutely so to the "" *Competency*, any more than the Friendship or Enmity of a "" party whose Evidence is offered, towards either of the "" Parties in the Cause, or many other considerations here "" after to be intimated · the general Answer may be this, "" that in point of Authority * no distinction is more ab- "" solutely settled, and in point of *Theory*, the existence of "" a direct Interest is capable of being precisely proved, but "" its influence on the Mind is of a Nature not to discover "" itself to the Jury, whence it hath been held expedient to "" adopt a general Exception, by which Witnesses so cir- "" cumstanced are free from Temptation, and the Cause not "" exposed to the hazard of the very doubtful Estimate, "" what quantity of Interest in the Question, in proportion "" to the Character of the Witness in any instance, leaves "" his Testimony entitled to Belief Some indeed are inca- "" pable of being biassed even latently by the greatest Inte- "" rest, many would betray the most solemn obligation and "" public Confidence for an Interest very inconsiderable An "" essential Exclusion, where no line short of this could "" have

* P 224

* V 4 Burr Mais -- 5.

" have been drawn, preferves Infirmity from a fnare, and
" Integrity from fufpicion, and keeps the Current of Evi-
" dence, thus far at leaft, clear and uninfected

" But Refentment or Partiality, when prevalent in a great
" degree, are apt to fhew themfelves in the Voice, Coun-
" tenance, and Air of the Witnefs, in the manner of his
" reprefenting facts, and often by the intermixture of his
" own fentiments and opinions, fometimes by an excefs of
" warmth, at other times by a folicitous referve, and in fome
" by an affectation of Candour.

‡ *Of* INTEREST *within the meaning of the* RULE *or* PRINCIPLE. ‡ P. 225.

To explain this Rule, " that *Intereft excludes Teftimony*," $^{a \text{ Atk Rep.}}$
ne muft confider what the Law looks upon as Intereft, $^{229 \text{ P W}}_{\text{Rep 432}}$
and it is, *where there is a certain Benefit or Difadvantage to the*
Witnefs attending the Confequence of the Caufe one way

And therefore, in the firft place, a naked *Truft* doth not
exclude a man from being a Witnefs. for fince there is no
falfe Bias on his Confcience, there is no reafon to exclude
him from Atteftation

Therefore a Guardian in Socage may be fworn for his
Ward.

An Infant bringing his Action by Guardian, the Guardian
on Record not allowed to be a Witnefs. becaufe if the Action be frivolous, the Expence of fuch Action will not be
allowed him in his Difcharge and therefore the Guardian $^{\text{Lent Aff 1714.}}$
that would be fworn to fupport this Action, fwears to the $^{\text{per Parker,}}_{\text{C J}}$
maintaining " of" his own Intereft, and confequently, is not
a competent Witnefs $^{\text{Str 506 548}}$

SECTION II

Of WITNESSES *interefted, and others not interefted, within the*
meaning of the Rule.

" It feemeth that" an Executor may be fworn in a Caufe $^{\text{Mod 107}}$
relating to the Will, where he is not refiduary Legatee;
becaufe he is no more than a Truftee, and has no Intereft

Where a Man has a Truft, coupled with an Intereft, he $^{3 \text{ P W Rep}}$
can not be fworn in the Proof of it, becaufe he is " re- $^{18r \text{ contra-}}_{\text{form Ed}}$
" garded" in Law as Mafter of the Eftate

" But when the Doctrine of Trufts was novel, much
" feverer hath been the Rule. and accordingly it hath been
" held, that" where *A* has the Freehold in Truft for *B*,
A cannot be fworn in Defence of it becaufe ✱ he is ✱ P 226.
looked upon in Law as Mafter of the Eftate for the *Ceftui* $^{\text{P W 220 is}}$
Cui Truft can not derive a legal Title in the Ejectment, and $^{\text{not contrary,}}_{\text{for that was in}}$
the *Chancery*.

the Truftee muft not be fworn to derive a legal Interest to himfelf

P. W 250.

" And although now, for a confiderable time, it is clearly " fettled, that in Equity, at leaft, a *Truftee*, MERELY as " fuch, is not precluded from being a Witnefs concerning " the Truft Eftate, yet in conformity to the antient Dif " tinction (too ftrongly it then feemed eftablifhed by Pre- " cedent), an highly refpected Authority declared his Idea,

By Hardw. Ch 2 Tr Atk Rep 229 Note to former Ed

" that" a Truftee, though merely nominal, cannot be examined at *Law*, though he clearly may in Equity. " This, if it were ftill held Law, would feem to merit " the Aid of the Legiflature, that Evidence might not be " excluded in this fingular inftance contrary to the general " Principles, and the other Rules of our Law concerning

v Lowe v Joliffe, Bl. 365, 6 E 2 G III Hale fuper Litt 6

" Admiffibility of Witneffes But recent and great Autho " rity appears for the admiffibility of an Executor in Truft, " and of a Common Truftee without Releafe "†

Tenant at *Will* has been allowed to prove Livery of feifin in the Leffor for a Man cannot be faid to get or lofe where he has only a precarious Intereft, and not fuch cer- tain Benefit or Charge out of the Eftate as he may recover in an Action. Now Tenant at Will can maintain no Action for the Poffeffion in his own Right, and therefore, by his Oath, he doth not defend any Eftate or Intereft of his own, he is but in Nature of a Bailiff or Servant to the Freeholder, and the Law does not exclude Servants to be fworn in behalf of their Mafters

" In thefe Terms the Doctrine on this head hath been " ftated but now, fince AGRICULTURE hath become an " Object of confideration, proportioned to its juft and great " importance, for this Caufe, and, in favour alfo of the

* P 227.

" free and certain poffeffion of property, * *Tenancy* at *Will* is " confidered as *Tenancy from Year to Year*, entitled to an " half Year's Notice, determining with the Commencement " of the Eftate or if it be thought more proper to ftate " the Propofition in thefe Terms, where on the Tenancy, " there is annual Rent referved, or where the Nature of " the Demife requires occupation for an Year certain, the " Courts of Juftice will conftrue fuch Demife, without any " fpecified Term, agreeably to the Nature of the Subject,

C mm 11 ch 5 s 147

" and the fair intent of the Tranfaction, fo as that it be " a Tenancy for a Year certain, renewed by Implication, " if timely Notice (of which the Limits have been fpe-

† Holt *and* Tyrrel, 1 Barnardift 12 E 13 G I 1727 *cited in the above Cafe, where, on a Trial at Bar, it was held that a Truf tee, without Releafe, might be a good Witnefs.*

" cified

" cified already), be not given of the Determination of the
" Contract

" And this Neceffity of an half Year's Notice, deter- Right on dem
" mining at the Period from which the Demife originally of Flower v
" commenced, is recognized not only with regard to *Lands*, T Rep E.
" but *Houfes*, in a Cafe very recently determined which 26 G III.
" was, a Demife by parol of a public Houfe at 10l per
" *Annum*, the Rent to commence from the Midfummer of
" 1781

" On the 26 *March*, 1785, a Notice was ferved to quit
" on the 29th *September* following

" A Verdict was taken for the Plaintiff at the *Salifbury* Af-
" fizes, fubject to the Opinion of the Court on the Special
" Cafe as above ftated

" It was much contended by Mr *Le Mefurier*, who argu-
" ed for the Plaintiff, that the reafons for protection and en-
" couragement of Hufbandry, had governed all the preced-
" ing Cafes that the Principle of the Rule failed with re-
" gard to Houfes , that in ftrictnefs fuch a Contract as that
" in Queftion, amounted to no * more than a Tenancy at   * P. 228.
" Will , and that the reafons of convenience would not
" warrant extending a conftruction as to the circumftance
" requifite to the efficacy of an half Year's Notice, to fuch
" inftances And that although ever fince the time of *H.*
" VIII half a Year's Notice to quit, had been held to be
" neceffary in the Cafe of a Tenant at Will, it was not then
" nor by any fubfequent Cafe required that fuch Notice
" fhould expire with the Year, and that at leaft there could
" be no Analogy from the motives for requiring this in the
" inftance of *Farms*, which, fhould make this correfpon-
" dence of the expiration of the Notice to any particular Pe-
" riod neceffary in the Cafe of *Houfes*

" But all the Judges then prefent (*abfente* WILLES) confi-
" dered the Diftinction as not affecting the Cafe which
" they held to be fufficiently ftrong on the general Principle,
" that Notice given to quit before the expiration of the
" Year, computed from the Term of Commencement, is
" contrary to the implied Agreement of a Tenancy from
" Year to Year, which a Tenancy on annual Rent is now
" underftood to be at leaft And therefore, Judgment for
" the *Defendants*

" It feemeth now therefore, that hardly any *Tenant* can Comm I c 9
" come in as a Witnefs, unlefs *Tenant* by *Sufferance*, which is, P 150, 1
" he who holdeth over without confent of the Landlord, Hargr Co Litt
" after the expiration of his legal Term an inconvenience, ch 8 § 68
" frequent when there was no better remedy than by *Eject-* n 3
" *ment* in fuch Cafes but of which little is now heard fince 4 G II c 28
" the § 18   11 G II c 19

" the Statute, early in the Reign of the late King, gave the
" Penalty of the double Yearly Value.

The equitable CESTUY QUE *Truſt clearly excluded by* INTEREST

* P 229

3 Cn. Rep 22

* " It is clear." the equitable *Ceſtuy que Truſt* can not be
ſworn to the Title : for Equity is a part of the Law of *England ·* and therefore, the Law ought ſo far to take Notice of
the equitable Intereſt, as to exclude the Owners of ſuch In
tereſt, who do really enjoy the Benefit of the Eſtate, from
any Atteſtation.

Mod 21
2 Keb 576

If a Man promiſe a Witneſs, that if he recover the Lands,
he ſhall have a Leaſe of them for ſo many Years, this excludes
the Evidence for here the Witneſs would have a fixed and
certain Advantage from the Verdict, and by conſequence,
his Atteſtation is to derive an Intereſt to himſelf

Mod 21

" The Caſe indeed thus put, bears a Complexion very like
" *Subornation* of *Perjury ·* at leaſt it amounts to that undue
" practiſing of Witneſſes which the Law abhorreth but ſo
" much is neceſſary to the Rule· for if the Intereſt be direct
" and dependant on the Event of the Cauſe, in favour of
" the party by whom the Teſtimony is tendered, it is imma
" terial in what manner or from what ſource ſuch Intereſt
" ariſes "

A *ſcire facias* was brought by the King to avoid a Patent,
and Exception was taken to the Witneſs, becauſe he was to
be Deputy to the Perſon that would avoid it · but the Exception was diſallowed : becauſe the *ſcire facias* is in the King's
Name , and therefore, " it" cannot be preſumed, that the
Intereſt was in another, which would deſtroy the very being
of the *ſcire facias ·* for no Judge ought to preſume contrary
to the Record " It ſeems the reaſon of this was, that
" there muſt have been preſumption on preſumption, and
" that of Fraud "

* P 230.

*TITLE III

If the Obligee deviſes the Debt to the Obligor, and the
Frecutor, in ſatisfaction of the Legacy, delivers up the
B d and the Bond is cancelled, and after the Validity of
t¹ Will is queſtioned, *viz* whether the Teſtator was *compos*
c not, the Obligor is ſaid to be a good Witneſs to the Will
I c uſe the Obligation being cancelled, he can never be charged at Law upon a cancelled Bond, for it is the Seal that
" carries " the Obligation "

" It may indeed be ſaid, that if the Will be a void one,
" the Executor may be liable to the perſon who ſhould have
" had

" had the Benefit of the Bond, whofe fecurity he hath rafhly
" deftroyed · but this doth not prevent the Competence of
" the Witnefs; nor even affect his Credit fo long as he is
" under no fufpicion of having fraudulently promoted the
" making of a falfe Will (as a forged one, or obtained by
" impofition), in order to procure a Difcharge of the Debt
" he owed to the Teftator "

But otherwife it is " held" in cafe of a *Mortgagee* for
though the Mortgage be cancelled, yet the Right being tranf-
ferred, doth not ceafe or go back again by the cancelling of
the Deed

Now the Mortgagee, at Law, hath an abfolute Eftate and
Equity " doth not allow" a Redemption, but by difcharging the Mortgage Money, " or by the Act of the Mortgagee,
" equivalent to fatisfaction by payment " fo, that in fuch
cafe, the fwearing the Teftator to be *compos* after cancelling the Deed of Mortgage, would ftill be in Defence
of his own Intereft. for the Eftate doth not come back to
the Mortgagor, but by Virtue of the Devife

* " And that the real intereft or equitable Lien on the   * P 231.
" Eftate is to be regarded, hath been confirmed by late   Goodtitle v.
" Cafes The Deeds ought to accompany the Title, and a   Morgan, E 1787, B R.
" prior Mortgage, if he hath fuffered the Deeds to be in   T R 755
" poffeffion of the Mortgagor, fhall not prevail againft a
" fecond Mortgagor without notice, who has all the title
" Deeds, and has taken the Affignment of the Truft Term
" for a valuable confideration

" Nor, on the other hand, fhall the poffeffion of a fatis-   T R 758, 9
" fied Truft Term and of the Title prejudice the true owner-   60
" fhip which will be confidered, not only in Equity, but
" at Common Law, in Trial of an Ejectment Now in   ⊦ Whence
" Evidence, the Court will ⊦ fee where the fubftantial Inte-   and Burgefs.
" reft is · and to this the Objection of Incompetency muft be   Bl 113
" allowed to apply, though the formal Intereft may be in   Willoughby v. Willoughby,
" another "   Canc l' R

If a Man makes a Feoffment to one, and afterwards makes   763
a Feoffment to another of the fame Lands, and the fecond   L R Aor 685
Feoffment, " reciting," that he was feifed in Fee at the
time of the Feoffment, makes diverfe Covenants, that the
Feoffee fhall quietly enjoy, &c after, upon an Iffue taken,
whether there were any former Feoffments, the Feoffor fhall
not be fworn to prove that there was not, becaufe the Feoffor,
in this Cafe, would be fworn to fave himfelf from the Breach
of Covenant in the fecond Feoffment, and therefore he is
concerned in Intereft in the Succefs of the Caufe, and ought
to be excluded from all Atteftation

Tit IV.

Interest, *where direct and absolute, applies as an* Exception *to* criminal *Cases*

" As hath before been noticed," in all public Profecutions, the Party injured may be a Witnefs, " with the Exceptions " already intimated, and now to be ftated more largely "

* P. 232 * " Thus the Party may be a Witnefs, where there is a Fine to the King, and no private Advantage arifing to him felf, " immediately or confequentially," from the Profecution but if there be any Advantage of private Benefit to accrue by the Profecution, the Party is equally excluded as in a private Action

Hardr 331. In an Information of Affault and Battery, the perfon injured may be a Witnefs becaufe here the Fine is to the King, and no private Benefit accrues to the party as the refult of the Profecution

But fuch Verdict in an Information, founded only on the party's own Oath, cannot (which we have already obferved) be given in Evidence in a Civil Action for that were indirectly to fuffer the party to atteft in his own behalf

But where, on any public Profecution, there arifes any private Advantage to the Profecutor, there he can not be a Witnefs becaufe that were plainly " and directly" to atteft in his own behalf ; which can never be admitted.

Hardr ubi fupr 2 Str 728. S.P. Therefore, on an Information of *Forgery*, the party whofe Right was prejudiced by the Forged Deed, can not be a Witnefs · becaufe (as was intimated above) there plainly refults a private Benefit to the party from the fuccefs of the Profecution

L N 289 " But this is one of the Objections to competency which " is removed by a *Releafe* Accordingly the principal Evi- " dence againft Dr Dodd, the party in whofe name the " Bond was forged, was admitted to give Evidence, this " proof being firft made I cite, for this the memory of the " tranfaction, recent on account of its particular circum- " ftances in the minds of many, and the account given in a " refpectable Publication We have before obferved, the

Ann Reg 1777 " point is fettled in Civil Cafes ; it is not lefs fo in criminal " ones '

* P 233 * So in an Information of *Perjury*, founded on the Statute, Hardr ubi fupr the Perfon injured by the Perjury, can not be a Witnefs 2 S 3 -37 becaufe " he" gains 'en Pounds on the Statute by Conviction 2 S - 1043 " But, of courfe, on an Indictment at Common Law, where 1124 " the Penalty does not go to the Informer, the party injured L N P 289 " may be a Witnefs "

So

So in an Information on the Statute of *Ufury*, the party to Co Litt the ufurious Contract can not be a Witnefs, (while he hath Ed 6 b Harg. an Interest in the Question), becaufe that were to avoid his 2 R Abr 689. own Securities, but after he hath paid the Money, he is a T R 191 good Witnefs, becaufe then the Party guilty is fined to the 7 Mod 118. King, and there is no Advantage to the Profecutor from the Information

" I fhall now mention a Determination, which throws " great Light on the general Theory and Diftinctions of this " Article, and fhall, for that reafon, quote it almoft *verbatim*.

TIT V

Diftinction between Intereft and indefinite Influence

" In the Cafe of *Abrahams* againft *Bunn*, which was an 4 Burr Manf " Action *qui tam*, on an ufurious Contract, on the Trial at 2251 " *Guidhall*, before Lord MANSFIELD, there was a Verdict " for the Plaintiff On a Motion for a *New Trial*, the " Ground taken, was the fuppofed *Incompetency* of the Plain- " tiff's Witnefs He was the *Borrower* of the Money, and " was called by the Plaintiff to prove the ufurious Contract.

" That this Witnefs *was* the *Borrower* of the Money fuf- " ficiently appeared, being directly fo charged in all the Counts " on the Record which were entirely on ufurioufly *taking*, there " being no Count which charged any *Bond, Affurance* or *Contract*

" " There was an Exception as to the *Form* and *Time* of * P 234. " taking the Objection, which belongs to another head, and " is prefently to be confidered but the COURT went on the " *Merits*, as if the Exception had been duly taken in point " of *time* and *form*

" The CHIEF JUSTICE, in delivering the Opinion of the " COURT, faid,

" There are two Reafons given for univerfally rejecting " the Teftimony of the *Borrower*

" 1ft, Becaufe 'tis to be prefumed really his own Caufe, " and that the nominal Plaintiff is fet up colourably by him

" 2dly Becaufe it would enable him to avoid his own " Securities, and difcharge himfelf of the Money borrowed

" The firft Reafon is *now* totally exploded for he is not " now prefumed to be a party in the Caufe

" As to the fecond, the Propofition laid down is too large ; " for there may be Ufury which can not affect the Debt or " avoid the Contract The Claufe which avoids the Con- " tract is, where the Ufury is for more than *five per Cent*. " But if a Contract be only for *five per Cent* and the Len- " der afterwards takes more, he is liable to be profecuted for " Ufury, and to pay the Penalty, though it does not avoid " the Contract And where it would affect the Debt, it + s Long's " may have been † paid. Cafe Sir T

VOL. I.   M   " All Raym 151.

" All the other Cases are loose Notes of *sayings*, or Opi-
" pinions at *Nisi pr us*, general Assertions, general Inferences,
" without particulars, without Argument, without Conside-
" ration, without any State of Pleadings or Facts

* P 235. * *Where the Proceedings can not be given in* EVIDENCE *to recover against the* WITNESS *in another Cause, the Objection,
generally, is to the Credit only.*

" This Question having now come before the Court, it is
" necessary to consider it with Accuracy and Precision
" The Objection to the *Competency* of the Witness can
" only be supported by arguing, either, that the Event of
" this penal Prosecution, in favour of the Plaintiff, will
" avoid the Bond, Assurance, or Contract of the Witness,
" and *discharge* him from the *Debt*, or that this Cause turns
" upon the *same* points and transactions, which, if proved
" in another Cause, would avoid the same
" The Foundation fails in both Propositions · and the
" Consequences would not follow in the last, if the Pre-
" mises were true

v supra.   " No *Contract* or Assurance appears here for Usury, or so
" much as to repay the Money   And if there was, the Re-
" covery of the Penalty, upon this Information, would not
" affect the Contract   The Judgment in this Action could
" not be g ven in Evidence in an Action for the Debt,
" though the Validity of the Contract depended upon the
" same Grounds as the Information.   That might indeed be
" a Prejudice, Influence, or Bias upon the Mind of the
" Witness ard go to his *Credit*, but not an actual Interest to
" go to his *Competence*
" This D st nction has not been sufficiently attended to at
" *N.f. Prius*   The Cases are contradictory, and it is im-
" possible to reconcile them

e. 285   " The great Deference to Lord *Chief Justice* HOLT's
\ c 10 \. III " Opinion made the Case of *The King* v *Whiting*, to be
2 5 r 1043 " followed for some time   Nay, *Lord* HARDWICKE im
P 9 G II   " plicitly fol'owed it in the Case of *The King* v *Nunez*

+ P 236   + " At that time there were many Cases both ways, a
" string of both Sorts · and among the rest, *Watts's* Case, in
" *Hardres*, that in Forgery, Perjury, or Usury, the party
" grieved shall not be admitted as a Witness, because he
" may receive a *consequential* Advantage from the Verdict,
" and *Parris's* Case, in 1 *Ventr* 49 where such a Witness
" was admitted   None of which Cases were considered or
" looked into

                                              " But

" But fince the Cafe of *Whiting*, and the Cafe of *Nunez*,
" there has been great light thrown upon the Diftinction
" between *Intereft* which affects the COMPETENCE of a † Firft Mod
" Witnefs, and *Influence*, which goes only to his *Credit* 26 Oct 1736:
" There have been the Arguments, and Judgment in the T 1736
" Cafe of *Rex* v *Bray*, Mayor of *Tintagel*, † where Lord and determin-
" Hardwicke fhook the Authority of *Rex* v *Whiting*, which ed on Friday,
" he there, in effect, contradicts, (though with guarded Burr
" Decency of Expreffion), notwithftanding his having before
" followed it in the Cafe of *Nunez* † † Lord Hard-
" Then came the Cafe of the *Eaft India Company* v *Goflen* wicke's Words
" There was alfo a Cafe of *Bailie* v *Wilfon*, (about the them in my
" proving of a Will) before the Delegates: who were Note), if that
" *equally divided*, whether the Objection fhould go to the frictly exa-
" *Competence* or *Credit* of the only Witnefs who proved a mined, I be-
" Codicil, fubfequent to a fecond Will, fetting up again the lieve it would
' firft Will, and therefore, no Sentence was given There- Objection went
" upon a Commiffion of Adjuncts iffued a Majority of rather to the
" whom (Mr ✝ Juftice *Dennifon* being one) held that it went the Competen-
' only to the *Credit* And fentence was given for the firft cy of the Wit-
" Will Upon a Petition for a Commiffion to review, it nefs. Burr
" was fully argued · and Lord *Hardwicke*, on the 15th of ✱ P. 237.
" *Jan* 1744, gave a folemn Opinion with the majority of
" the Adjuncts, that the Witnefs having adminiftered under
" the firft Will as Agent to the Executor, or as Executor *de*
" *fon Tort*, and being liable to Actions, the objection went
" only to the *Competency*, not to the *Competency*
" The folemn difcuffion in thefe three Cafes draw the
" Line between INTEREST, which goes to the COMPE-
' TENCE, and INFLUENCE which goes to the *Credit*, more
" clearly than had been before underftood
" It eftablifhed a Rule, that where the Matter was *doubt-*
' *ful*, the objection fhould go to the *Credit*
" It eftablifhed, that the Queftion in a criminal Profecu-
" tion being the fame with a Civil Caufe in which the Wit-
" nefs was interefted, went *generally* to the Credit, unlefs
" the Judgment in the Profecution where he was a Wit-
" nefs, could be given in Evidence in the Caufe where he
" was interefted I fay, generally, becaufe all Rules of
" Evidence admit of Exceptions
" After thefe Cafes, in that of *Rex* v *Broughton*, in
" 1745, Lord Chief Juftice *Lee*, over-ruled the three
' Cafes of *Rex* v *Whiting*, *Rex* v *Nunez*, and *Rex* v.
" *Lluis*, which opinion of his has been followed fince and
" approved

M 2 " There

There has been a remarkable Cafe in *Trinity* Term, 32 &
" 33 G II *Bartlet* v *Pickerfgill* The Defendant bought an
*P 238.   " Eftate for the Plaintiff   There was * no Writing, nor
" was any part of the Money paid by the Plaintiff. The
" Defendant articled in his own Name, and refufed to
" convey, and by his Anfwer denied any Truft   Parol
" Evidence was rejected, and the Bill was difmiffed   The
" Defendant was afterwards indicted for Perjury, tried at
" *York*, and convicted upon Evidence of the Plaintiff, con-
" firmed by circumftances, and the Defendant's Declara-
" tions   The Plaintiff then petitioned for a fupplemental
" Bill in the Nature of a Bill of Review, ftating this Con-
" viction   But the Petition was difmiffed, becaufe the Con-
" viction was not Evidence   22 *Nov* 1762
" This reafoning fhews too, that if it was neceffary, the
" Witnefs was competent to be heard as to the Debt being
" paid   What he fwore could not be Evidence in an Action
" for the Debt
" There is no Danger of Perjury from hearing him   The
" Defendant may produce the Security, and falfify him   If
" (as here) it is the Cafe of a Pawn, the Witnefs would
" fwear againft his own Intereft to fay untruly the Debt
" was paid and the Pledge returned   But either way the
" Debt is paid   For unlefs the Pledge be redeemed, it is a
" fatisfaction
" Suppofe a Witnefs produces a Bond or Mortgage can-
" celled—fuppofe he produces a Receipt,—there can be no
" Danger in hearing him   For the Jury are not bound to
" believe him   That depends on Circumftances, which may
" contradict or fupport his Teftimony
*P 239.   * " But if it be neceffary to prove Payment, and the
" Party is not to be heard as a Witnefs to prove fuch Pay-
" ment, the Statute would be as effectually repealed, as
" if the Borrower could never be a Witnefs at all   For
" they never would fuffer any Body elfe to be privy to
" the Payment, delivering up, or cancelling the Securities
" But to go further, all Objections to the Competence
" of the Witnefs muft either be *proved*, or drawn from him
" upon a *Voire dire*, or to take it in the utmoft Latitude,
" upon his *Examinatio*
" Here was no Proof of any Objection, or of any Debt
" remaining   The Witnefs fwore, that he fhould neither
" gain nor lofe by the Event of the Caufe, in every fhape
" in which the Queftion could be put   And he fhews it by
" giving an Account of the Debt being paid   He fwore,
" upon a *Voire dire*, that it was paid
                                              " Had

" Had the Defendant produced a Security, or proved the
" Pledge to be remaining in his Cuftody, it would have
" been a different Confideration, whether the Witnefs, who
" was the Borrower of the Money, could be examined to
" contradict this But *when the whole Ground of the Objecti-*
" *on comes from himfelf only, what he fays muft be taken together*
" *as he fays it* and then the Debt is paid

‘ In every Light, we are all of opinion, that, under all
" the circumftances of this Cafe, *Benjamin Abraham was a*
" COMPETENT *Witnefs*"

Tit VI

Different effect of General and particular Intereft

The Men of one County, City, Hundred, Town, Cor-
poration or Parifh, are Evidence in relation to the * " Rights, *** P. 240.**
" Privileges, Immunities, and affairs of fuch Town, City,
" &c" if they are not concerned in private Intereft in relation thereunto, nor advantaged by fuch Rights and Privileges as they affert by their Atteftation Men of the County
are Evidence on an Indictment for not repairing a Bridge
for, ‖ whether it be in repair or not, they are perfectly in- **‖ There feems**
different for every man for the convenience of his own **an evident**
tranfpofition in
Paffage is concerned to uphold the Bridge, and can not be **the former Ed**
thought to create an ufelefs Charge, fo that he is perfectly
indifferent, being equally concerned on both fides of the
Queftion

" And this which appears to have been before fettled at **1 A St 1**
" Common Law, is now expreſſly provided by Statute " **c 18 13**

But the Men of the County can not be fworn in a Caufe
relating to the Bounds of the County, in a fuit depending
between that and another County, carried on at a County
Charge becaufe every man is in fuch a Cafe concerned to
prevail in point of Intereft

" Formerly," if the Hundred " were" fued on the Statute of *Winton*, no Perfon of that Hundred, " it was held,
" could" be a Witnefs, becaufe every perfon's Intereft is
concerned in the Tax of the Hundred, and " he" therefore
fwears in his own Difcharge

" But now" Inhabitants of the Hundred " are" to be **Note to the**
admitted as Witneffes at Trials on the Statute of Hue and **former Ed St**
8 G II c 16
Cry
§ 15
The Inhabitants of a Parifh cannot be Witneffes in relation
to Common, or the *Modus Decimandi*, becaufe * this touches *** P 241**
Hob 91, 2
the private Intereft of thofe Perfons, and the Lofs or gain **Cafe of**
falls upon their private Fortunes **Pooly, Doug**
Controv Elec
" So **II 236, 7.**

There has been a remarkable Cafe in *Trinity* Term, 32 &
" 33 G II. *Bartlet* v *Pickerfgill* The Defendant bought an
" Eftate for the Plaintiff There was * no Writing, nor
" was any part of the Money paid by the Plaintiff The
" Defendant articled in his own Name, and refufed to
" convey, and by his Anfwer denied any Truft Parol
" Evidence was rejected, and the Bill was difmiffed The
" Defendant was afterwards indicted for Perjury, tried at
" *York*; and convicted upon Evidence of the Plaintiff, con-
" firmed by circumftances, and the Defendant's Declara-
" tions The Plaintiff then petitioned for a fupplemental
" Bill in the Nature of a Bill of Review, ftating this Con-
" viction · But the Petition was difmiffed, becaufe the Con-
" viction was not Evidence 22 *Nov* 1762.

" This reafoning fhews too, that if it was neceffary, the
" Witnefs was competent to be heard as to the Debt being
" paid · What he fwore could not be Evidence in an Action
" for the Debt

" There is no Danger of Perjury from hearing him The
" Defendant may produce the Security, and falfify him If
" (as here) it is the Cafe of a Pawn, the Witnefs would
" fwear againft his own Intereft to fay untruly the Debt
" was paid and the Pledge returned But either way the
" Debt is paid For unlefs the Pledge be redeemed, it is a
" fatisfaction

" Suppofe a Witnefs produces a Bond or Mortgage can-
" celled—fuppofe he produces a Receipt,—there can be no
" Danger in hearing him For the Jury are not bound to
" believe him That depends on Circumftances, which may
" contradict or fupport his Teftimony.

* " But if it be neceffary to prove Payment, and the
" Party is not to be heard as a Witnefs to prove fuch Pay
" ment, the Statute would be as effectually repealed, as
" if the Borrower could never be a Witnefs at all For
" they never would fuffer any Body elfe to be privy to
" the Payment, delivering up, or cancelling the Securities

' But to go further, all Objections to the Competence
" of the Witnefs muft either be *proved*, or drawn from him
" upon a *Voire dire*, or to take it in the utmoft Latitude,
" upon his *Examination*

" Here was no Proof of any Objection, or of any Debt
" remaining The Witnefs fwore, that he fhould neither
' gain nor lofe by the Event of the Caufe, in every fhape
" in which the Queftion could be put And he fhews it by
' giving an Account of the Debt being paid He fwore,
" upon a *Voire dire*, that it was paid.

" Had

P. 238

* P. 239

"Had the Defendant produced a Security, or proved the
"Pledge to be remaining in his Cuftody, it would have
"been a different Confideration, whether the Witnefs, who
"was the Borrower of the Money, could be examined to
"contradict this But *when the whole Ground of the Objecti-*
"*on comes from himfelf only, what he fays muft be taken together*
"*as he fays it* and then the Debt is paid

"In every Light, we are all of opinion, that, under all
"the circumftances of this Cafe, *Benjamin Abraham was a*
"COMPETENT *Witnefs.*"

Tit VI

Different effect of General and particular Intereft

The Men of one County, City, Hundred, Town, Cor-
poration or Parifh, are Evidence in relation to the * "Rights, * P 240.
"Privileges, Immunities, and affairs of fuch Town, City,
"&c" if they are not concerned in private Intereft in relation thereunto, nor advantaged by fuch Rights and Privileges as they affert by their Atteftation Men of the County
are Evidence on an Indictment for not repairing a Bridge
for, || whether it be in repair or not, they are perfectly in- || There feems
different for every man for the convenience of his own an evident
tranfpofition in
Paffage is concerned to uphold the Bridge, and can not be the former Ed.
thought to create an ufelefs Charge, fo that he is perfectly
indifferent, being equally concerned on both fides of the
Queftion

"And this which appears to have been before fettled at 1 A St 1
"Common Law, is now exprefsly provided by Statute " c 18 13
But the Men of the County can not be fworn in a Caufe
relating to the Bounds of the County, in a fuit depending
between that and another County, carried on at a County
Charge becaufe every man is in fuch a Cafe concerned to
prevail in point of Intereft

"Formerly," if the Hundred "were" fued on the Statute of *Winton,* no Perfon of that Hundred, "it was held,
"could" be a Witnefs, becaufe every perfon's Intereft is
concerned in the Tax of the Hundred, and "he" therefore
fwears in his own Difcharge

"But now" Inhabitants of the Hundred "are" to be v Note to the
admitted as Witneffes at Trials on the Statute of Hue and former Ld St
Cry 8 G II c 16
§ 15
The Inhabitants of a Parifh cannot be Witneffes in relation * P 241.
to Common, or the *Modus Decimandi,* becaufe * this touches Hob 91, 2
the private Intereft of thofe Perfons, and the Lofs or gain v Cafe of
falls upon their private Fortunes. Poole, Doug
Cont ov Elec.
"So II 236, 7

L. N. P. 283   " So in an Action on a Policy of Insurance, any who " have insured on the said Ship shall not be Witnesses "

v Str 414   So neither shall a Sailor who hath Wages due, be a Witness concerning the safety of a Ship supposed to be lost, " for he is interested in the Event of the Question since, if " the Ship be lost, the Crew lose their Wages "

v Parker 286   So in a Corporation, the Inhabitants and Freemen are Witnesses to any thing relating to the Public, where they are not concerned in Gain or Disadvantage in relation to their private Fortunes, but where any Loss or Disadvantage is consequent to the Witness upon his Trial, he must be excluded

1 Ventr 351t
2 Show 146
3 Keb. 295
   In an Action on the Case, brought by the Mayor and Commonalty, concerning the Water Bailage, a Freeman of London may be a Witness· because the Freemen are not concerned in the Privilege by immediate or private Interest, nor do they get or lose by Consequence of the Trial " Yet " at that Period (32 Car II) this did not pass unanimously " and on the Tender of a Bill of Exceptions, the Counsel " by whom these Witnesses were offered, appear to have " thought it safest to waive the Point "

Sid 109.   So in a Gift to a Corporation, any Member may be Witness if the Gift be public in relation to their Buildings, Schools, or the like, because no man gets or loses by the Event of the Trial

*P 242   * But as to the Custom of Foreign-bought or Foreign-sold in a Corporation, none of the Freemen are to be admitted as Evidence, because every Man's private Interest is concerned in the Consequence of the Trial, and where a Man is concerned in the consequence of the Trial, he can not support it by his Oath.

But in an Action brought by Parishioners for embezzling the Stores, now by St 3 & 4 W & M c 11 § 12 the Parishioners may be Witnesses (Alms-men excepted) for the Statute, in Behalf of the Poor, hath set aside the Rules of the Common Law in that instance and since the whole Riches and Improvement of the Nation arise out of the Labour of the poorer sort, it is but reasonable that the Materials of their Labour should be abundantly secured against
27 G III c 29   all mismanagement

" And now the Inhabitants of every Parish, Township, " or Place, shall be competent to prove an offence within " their Limits, notwithstanding the Penalty (provided " " exceed net twenty pounds,) &c given to the Poor of
L. N. P. 194   " such Parish, &c or otherwise, in Exoneration thereof

" And where part of the Penalty goes to the Corporation, " the Votes of Freemen have been rejected as Witnesses
‹ It

" It is no good Exception to a Witnefs that he hath Com- L N P 285
" mon *per Caufe de Vicinage* of the Lands in Queftion, for
" this is no Intereft, but only an Excufe for Trefpafs

" An inhabitant not rated to the Poor, nor receiving Alms, Say Rep 180.
" is a *competent* Witnefs for a Penalty, a Moiety of which is N to form. Ed.
" given to the Poor of the Parifh

" But the Intereft which excludes, muft be certain, and L N P, 284.
" not contingent For which reafon the Heir at Law is a Salk 283
" competent Witnefs . for his Eftate is precarious, at the
" Will of the Owner, and he therefore hath no abfolute
" Intereft , but he who hath a *vefted* Eftate in *Remainder*, is
" not competent, for he hath a certain Intereft And ac- Cor Treby,
" cordingly the Heir of a Bankrupt was admitted, to fwear Mic 10 W III
" a Debt due to the Bankrupt "

CONTINGENT INTEREST *does not exclude Intereft Contingent.*

* " Illegal Intereft is not to be prefumed The Law will * P. 243.
' not prefume an Intereft contrary to the legal or conftitu-
' tional quality of the fubject

" Thus where a Party, being an inhabitant, was offered
" to prove that *outfitters* had no *vote* in the choice of *repre-*
" *fentatives*, on the ground that he was *interefted*, fince by this
" proof he would enhance the Value of his own Vote, the
" Anfwer was, that a Vote for Members to ferve in Parlia-
" ment was not of the number of thofe Rights whofe value
" is diminifhed by increafing the number of thofe who have
" a concurrent title , that fuch Vote had, in the eye of the
" Law, no Analogy to *faleable* property , and that it had
" been the conftant practice to admit a Voter under an indif-
" puted Title to give Evidence concerning the Rights of Dougl contr
" Election , and his *Evidence* was accordingl, allowed by the El 360, 1 IV.
" Committee "   69, 9

Tit. VII

Party cannot be a Witnefs in his own Caufe

From " this" Rule " concerning Intereft," a Corollary
may be deduced,

That the Plaintiff or Defendant cannot be a Witnefs in his Norton and
own Caufe for thefe are the Perfons that have a moft imme- Moult Hil
diate Intereft · and it is not to be prefumed that a Man who 1701
complains without Caufe, or defends without Juftice, fhould
have honefty enough to confefs it

And therefore, an Anfwer in Equity is of little Weight in
" favour of the party," where there are no proofs in the Caufe

to back thefe Suggeftions: becaufe, though it is the Conftitution of the Court to the Parties upon Oath to difcover
the fecret Practices complained of, yet there is very little
Credit to be given to a Man's Oath " in his own behalf,"
where there is no probable circumftance to fupport it

" The Defendant B, had lent Money to C, on a Mort-
" gage of C's Eftate, and the Plaintiff A, being alfo about
" to lend Money to C, D, a Witnefs depofed that C, upon
" Enquiry, made from Inftructions by the Plaintiff, had de-
" nied an, prior incumbrance

* " The Defendant in his Anfwer, denies the Charge of
" Concealment   An Iffue directed to try the Fact, and
" the Plaintiff, to admit the Anfwer of the Defendant B,
" to be read on the Trial

" However, an exceeding ftrong Cafe is put, where the
" Plaintiff was allowed to benefit by his own Teftimony   It
" is this

" The Defendants had taken out an Execution contrary
" to an Injunction of the Court of Chancery   And it was
" alledged, that fome of the Bailiffs who ferved the Execu-
" tion, had found Money hid by the Plaintiff in a Wall of
" his Houfe, to the amount of 150l which they had pur-
" loined, and otherwife dore great damage to the Goods of
" the Plaintiff   The Lord Chancellor ordered the Defen-
" dants to make good the Money, and fatisfy the Plaintiff,
" all the Lofs which he would fwear he had fuftained

" This Cafe manifeftly went on the Ground of the juft
" odium, entertained both in Law and Equity againft Spo-
" liation, † particularly under Colour of Law   and the
" Neceffity of the Cafe, the Wrong-doers, having from
" the Nature of the Tranfaction, deprived the Plaintiff of
" the regular Proof by which the amount of the Injury
" fhould have been otherwife afcertained   I think it muft
" be prefumed, that there was ftill fome Evidence indepen-
" dent of the Plaintiff's Oath, to induce a Belief, that the
" fum of Money fo charged, as taken from him, had been
" laid by for Safety   and then in a Cafe fo peculiarly cir
" cumftanced, we may perceive fatisfactory Principles in
" fupport of the Decifion.'

* TIT. VIII

Exception 1, Common Law or by Statute

" And in general, there are Exceptions to the Rule not
" admitting an interefted Witnefs, partly at COMMON LAW,
" and partly by Statute

† In Casum Spoliator, et in Subfidium Spolicto præftandum omne
præfumitur

" Thus,

" Thus, where from the Nature of the subject proof can- 2 Roll's Abr.
" not otherwise be expected, a party shall be admitted as 685, 6ᵇ 3 Mod 115.
" Witness whose Interest otherwise is sufficient to exclude 10 Mod 103.
" him for, where the Law could receive no Execution, Fortes 246 Ventr 351
unless a party interested were a Witness, there he must be 12 Mod 340.
allowed, for the " Law" must not be rendered ineffectual
by impossibility of Proof. And where the " Law" can have
no force, but by the Proof of the Person in Interest, there the
Rules of the Common Law, " respecting Evidence in general,"
are presumed to be laid aside. " or rather the subordinate are
" silenced by the most transcendant and universal Rule, that
" in all Cases, that Evidence is good than which the Nature
" of the subject presumes no better to be attainable "

Therefore, " before the express provision of the Legisla- V supra, and Douglas Con-
" ture," the Party robbed might be Evidence on the Statute trov Elect
of *Winton,* to charge the Hundred for otherwise the Bene- Sudbury, vol
fit of the Statute would be excluded, as no other person can II p. 161, 2.
be supposed present in such a Transaction to give their Evidence

" So where the Question was, whether the Defendants Rex v Phipps
" had a Right to be Freemen, though it appeared there and Archer, at Cambr perLee
" were Commons belonging to the Freemen, yet an Alderman Ch J
" was admitted to prove them no Freemen, it appearing that L N P 289.
' none but Aldermen were privy to these Transactions

* " So in Actions by Informers for selling Coals without * P 246.
" measuring by the Bushel, the Servants were admitted as L N P 289.
" Witnesses for their Master notwithstanding 3 G II in-
" flicts a Penalty upon them for not doing it though *Eyre,*
" *Ch Jus* did, on that Account, in two or three instances
" refuse to receive them.

" So, where the Question was, whether the Master had ibid
' deserted the Ship *(Sussex)* without sufficient Necessity; E I Comp and Gosling,
" a Sailor who had given Bond to the Master (as a Trustee 16 G II
" to the Company) not to desert the Ship during the Voyage,
" was admitted Evidence for the Master, it appearing all the
" Sailors entered into such Bonds

" So, where a Son having a general Authority to receive
" Money for his Father, received a Sum, and gave it to the
" Defendant, the Son (though his Testimony might seem to
" fall under another Exception, as well as that of Interest,
' which will be explained hereafter) was admitted as a good L N P
" Witness in *Trover,* brought by the Father to recover the 289, 90. Salk 289
" Money, his Testimony being corroborated by other cir- Cor Holt
' cumstances

" So, in Trover against a Pawn Broker, the Servant em- L N P 290.
" bezzling his Master's Goods, and pawning them, admitted Mic 1752
" to prove the Fact C B.

" Thus

Willes and
Harris, Dou-
glas Controv.
El II 275. 4
and Note D.
" Thus in a Caufe which originated in the Exchequer on
" a Bill brought by the Plaintiff, as impropriator of *Tythes*,
" in the Parifh of St. *Keavine* in *Cornwall*, the Court di-
" rected an Iffue, which was tried at the Summer Affizes, in
" 1774, before Mr. Baron EYRE Several *Fifhermen* were
" called by the Defendant to prove the Manner of Tything
" Fifh · the Counfel for the Plaintiff objected to their *Evi-*
" *dence*, as they had an Intereft to *negative* his Claim But
" the Judge faid, the Objection proved too much, as it would

* P 247.
" deprive the Plaintiff of the only means he could have * of
" proving the *Cuftom* . and the Evidence was admitted But
" the Counfel for the Plaintiff, excepting to the admiffion
" of any Witneffes who had followed the Occupation of Fi-
" fhermen within *fix* Years, fuch being under a prefent liabi-
" lity, in cafe the Plaintiff fhould fucceed, the Judge ruled
" accordingly, that no Witnefs fo circumftanced fhould be
" admitted "

On Rejection or Admiffion of Informer as a Witnefs where enti-
tled to part of the Penalty

13 Car II.
3 Mod. 114
P. Str.
On the Statute concerning the hunting of Deer, which
gives a forfeiture on Conviction, before " a Juftice upon
" the Oath of one or more CREDIBLE Witneffes," the In-
" former " hath been allowed as a" good Evidence though
he hath part of the Penalty

Str 316 Rex v
Tilly, Tr
6 G I
Ret to former
Ed.
" However, by a later Authority, a Conviction for this
" very offence was quafhed on this very Ground, that the
" Informer was the Witnefs, and was intitled to a part of the
" Penalty.

Rex. - T Ser-
geson, Efq
- Str 1181
Hil 16 G II
" And where an Information was moved againft a Juftice,
" for not condemning a horfe taken out of a team, under
" the Statute which requires proof to be made before a Juf
" tice of the caufe of forfeiture,—the Cafe was this the
" party who feized, tendered his own Oath, the Defendant
" fcrupled to take it, or to determine the Affair in the Ab
" fence of the Owner or Driver

" *Per Curiam*, both were reafonable Objections Why is
" not the perfon who feized, and is to have the benefit
" of the forfeiture, within the reafon of excluding Informers
" where there is a Penalty ? Making *proof*, muft mean *legal*
" *proof* · the other alfo is but natural Juftice

" Here the Court appears to have recognized both Prin

* D 248.
10 Mod 156
Fort [246
Alt. 247, 1
" ciples, that of not condemning a perfon without giving
" him an opportunity of being heard, (which, if * the Juf-
" tice had done, he would defervedly have been brought to
" condign Cenfure), and this other of not condemning upon
" the

" the Teftimony of a Witnefs, who is to gain by the Con-
" viction, as alike grounded in immutable and natural Equity
" The Information was difcharged , and with Cofts "

On the Statute of *Conventicles,* " the Informer hath [16 Car II. ch 4 exp 22 Car II. ch 1.]
" been held a good Witnefs, though he hath not only part
" of the Penalty, but comes in the moft invidious character to
" criminate an Act of Worfhip at which he has been pre-
" fent and this hath been allowed on the Principle, that
" the Nature of the Cafe excludes the Prefumption of bet-
" ter Evidence

" And it muft be obferved, that the Prefumption of Im-
" poffibility to adduce better Evidence, muft be a Refult of
" the Nature of the Subject as conftituted by General Law
" or if depending on particular circumftances, thofe muft
" be fuch as entitle a Witnefs otherwife incompetent, to be
" heard by the fault of the contrary party . for an accidental
" want of fuch Proof as the Law allows, will amount to a
" legal Inability in the Plaintiff to recover in rare Cafes,
" and proceeding ufually from his own negligence, this may
" be inconvenient to the Individual , but it importeth no
" lefs than the Certainty of the Rules of Decifion and the
" confequent Security of the Public And the Law regard-
" ing the Welfare of the whole, which is that of Individuals
" too, as parts of the Syftem, muft prefer the fuffering of
" a particular inconvenience, rather than the admitting of a
" public mifchief "†

Some have extended this " Rule of admitting a Witnefs,
" who hath an Intereft in the Queftion, in default of a difin-
" terefted Witnefs (when the Nature of the Cafe fuppofes
" fuch an one not to be adducible), * fo far as" to the *Bye* [* P. 249.]
" *Laws* of a Corporation . and it is faid, that in an Action
" brought by the Corporation of Weavers, in *Norwich,* for
" the Penalty of a Bye Law, which ordains that no Weaver
fhould work at his Trade in Harveft , one of the Corpora-
ton " was" allowed " as" Evidence, though the Penalty
was due to the Corporation, left the Bye Law fhould be eluded, which was made for a Common Benefit

But *quære* for no Body of Men feem to be authorized to
make a Law and atteft the Breach of it, where it turns to
their own Benefit

On an Information *qui tam pro Domino Rege,* on the Act
of Navigation, the Informer was, on folemn Debate, allowed to [See 10 Mod · 194, 2nd Str 316 Contra N. to form Ld.]
be a Witnefs, though he was to have half the Forfeiture .
and this *ex Neceffitate Rei,* otherwife the Statute would be
eluded

---

† *Lex potius vult pati privatum incommodum quam publicum malum*

" And

Glo Rep 111.
Regina v Cob-
bold.

" And in general, the Rule prevails which was recognized
" by the Decision of the Court, in the Cafe of an Infor-
" mation on the Statute of 5 *Anne*, *c* 14 for the preferva-
" tion of the Game There the *Informer* was the *Witness* ·
" Mr *Salkeld* forcibly argued that the Common Law of *Eng-*

See al.o Rex v.
S one, Lord
Raym 1545.
and 2 Burr
270

" *land*, the Laws in general of civilized Nations, and of uni-
" verfal Juftice, would no more permit a Man to be his own
" Witnefs than his own Judge And upon this Exception,
" fingly, the Conviction was quafhed.

" But Statutes have infringed on this Rule, and Evafion,
" efpeciall v in Cafes where the Revenue is concerned, ha.e
" made their way in practice, which reduce the Obfervance
" of it almoft to an ineffective form An apparently difin-
" terefted Witnefs is fet up · who, if a conviction takes
" place, has a regularly allotted portion with the Informer

2 Sid 51
Feb 13. T
Raim 32
See StyL 482

" A Perfon" who has part of the Land, fells *bona fide*,
and for good confideration ·* if it be after he is fummoned
as a Witnefs, or after he has had Notice of Trial, the
Court will not admit his Evidence

* P. 250.

Par 2

Nominal Defendants not excluded

* If any perfon be arbitrarily made a Defendant to prevent
his Teftimony in the Caufe, the " Plaintiff" fhall not pre
vail by that Artifice, but the Defendant, againft whom nothing
is proved, fhall be fworn notwithftanding for here the De
fendant does not fwear in his o wn Juftification, but in the Juf
tification of another, with whom he is " unduly" joined
in the Action : and were not this allowed, it were but for
the Plaintiff to turn all the feveral Witneffes into Defendant ,
and he might be able to prove what he pleafed without Con
teft. therefore, if there be an Action of Trefpafs againft
one of them, he may be Evidence againft the other

But this Rule muft be underftood where there is no manner
of Evidence againft the Defendant for if there be Evidence
againft one, though in the Judge's opinion, not enough to
convict him, yet fuch perfon can be no Witnefs for the other,
becaufe his Guilt or Innocence muft wait the Event of the
Verdict ; for the Jury are Judges of the Fact, and not the
" Bench "

L N P 285,6

" In Trefpafs. if one of whom the Plaintiff defigned to
" make ufe as a Witnefs, be by Miftake made a Defendant,
" the Court on Motion will give leave to omit him, and
" have his name out of the Record, even after Iffue joined
" for the Plaintiff can in no Cafe examine a Defendant, whil
" la

" he continues such on the Record, though nothing be proved
" against him   And therefore, in an Information for a
" Misdemeanour, the Attorney General *(Trevor)* offering
" to examine a Defendant for the King, which the Court
" would not permit, he entered a *Nolle profequi*, and then
" examined him

⁜ " And if a material Witnefs for the Defendant in Eject- ⁜ P. 251.
" ment, be made a Co-Defendant, the right way for him is
" to let Judgment go by Default but if, by pleading, he
" admit himfelf to be Tenant in Poffeffion, the Court will
" not afterwards, on Motion, ftrike out his Name   But in
" fuch Cafe, if he confent to let a Verdict be given againft
" him, for fo much as he is in poffeffion of, it feems he may
" be a Witnefs for another Defendant

" In Trefpafs, the Defendant pleaded *Quod Actio non:*
" for that *Richard Mawfon*, named in the *fimul cum*, paid
" the Plaintiff a Guinea in Satisfaction · and Iffue thereon;
" the Defendant produced *Mawfon* and *per* Eyre, Ch' J.
" he may be examined for what he has now to prove can
" not be given in Evidence in another Action ; and in effect,
" he makes himfelf liable by fwearing he was concerned in
" the Trefpafs

" But if the Plaintiff can prove the Perfons named in the
" *fimul cum* in Trefpafs, were, *bonâ fide*, made Parties to the
" fuit, which muft be by producing the Original and Procefs
" againft them, and proving an ineffectual endeavour to ar-
" reft them, the Defendant fhall not have the Benefit of
" their Teftimony "

Trefpafs againft *A* and *B* for two Horfes. Evidence Hale fuper,
againft *A* as to one, and the Queftion is, if he may be a Litt 6 b Str.
Witnefs for *B* in relation to the other and it feems, that if [633]
1 were the fame Fact, and the Trefpafs committed at the
fame time and place, he may not be a Witnefs, becaufe he
fwears to difcharge himfelf , but ⁜ if they were not a fingle ⁜ P 252.
Fact, but two diftinct Trefpaffes at different times and
places, arbitrarily joined in the fame Declaration, then they
may be Witneffes one for the other, becaufe the Oath of
one of them, has no influence on the Crime laid to his
Charge, but merely goes in Difcharge of the other.

Tit IX

Husband *and* Wife *not* Evidence *for or againft each other*

" There is one peculiar Species of Intereft, and com-
" bined too with the principle of confidential obligation,
" which

"which is feparately to be diftinguifhed And this founds"
the fecond Corollary on the General Rule, which is,

Co. Litt. 66
4 St Tr 608
2 H. P. C.
279

That Hufband and Wife cannot be admitted to be Witneffes for or againft each other

For if they fwear for the Benefit of each other, they are not to be believed, becaufe their Interefts are abfolutely the fame; and therefore, they can gain no more Credit when they atteft for each other, than when any Man attefts for himfelf

And it would be very hard that a Wife fhould be allowed as Evidence againft her own Hufband, when fhe cannot atteft for him. fuch a Law would occafion implacable Divifions and Quarrels, and deftroy the very legal Policy of Marriage that has fo contrived it, that their Intereft fhould be but one · which it could never be if Hufbands were permitted to deftroy the Interefts of the Wife, nor could the Peace of Families be well maintained, if the Law admitted any Atteftation againft the Hufband

Brownl. 47

The Wife, in Cafe of High Treafon, is not bound to difcover her Hufband's Treafon, although the Son is " compellable" to reveal it

T Raym 1

Yet in Cafe of High Treafon, the Wife is admitted as Evidence againft her Hufband, becaufe this " has been " fuppofed to be," for the public fafety, which is to be preferred before the Intereft or Peace of private Families, and the Ties of Allegiance are more obligatory than any Relation whatever †

* P 253
Hott 116.
St. Tr. 2659
H. H P C
301
H P C 431
—2
Rufh. Coll
P 2 Vol. I
fo 04—9
Str 633
Comm 1 Ch.
15 P 443
T Raym
1 Ventr
2 Kc8 403
pl 8

* In the Cafe of the Lord *Audley*, where the Hufband was charged to have affifted to the Rape of his Wife, the Wife was allowed a Witnefs, becaufe it was a perfonal Force done to her, and of fuch fecret violence there could be no other Proof but by the Oath of his Wife

But, " on the whole," this piece of Law hath fince been exploded, that in a perfonal Wrong done to the Wife, the Wife may be Evidence againft the Hufband, becaufe it may be improved to dreadful purpofes, and muft be a Caufe of implacable Quarrels, if the Hufband chance to be acquitted

" And in a very recent Cafe, fingular indeed, and I be-
" lieve without Example in this Country, where a Wife
" was the Profecutrix and fole direct Witnefs in proof of
" an execrable Charge againft her Hufband, which came
" before the Grand Jury for the County at large, at the
" Summer Affizes at *Bury*, in 1784, the Judge recom-

De Offic. Ed.
Dab I 17

† *Cari funt Parentes, cari liberi, propinqui, familiares, omnes omnium caritates Patria una complexa eft pro quá quis bonus dubitet mortem oppetere fi ei fit profuturus ?*

" mended

" mended in his Charge, that the Bill fhould not be found,
" if unfupported by any other Evidence fince otherwife a
" Caufe very peculiarly unfuitable to be brought without ef-
" fect before the public Ear, would come to Trial with a
" legal Neceffity of the Prifoner being difcharged from the
" Indictment, for Want of Evidence *competent* to go to the
" Jury "

There is a great Difference between a Wife *de Facto* and
a Wife *de Jure* for a Wife *de Jure* cannot be an Evidence
for or againft her Hufband, but a Wife *de Facto* may as
if a Woman be taken away by Force and married, fhe may
be an Evidence againft her Hufband, indicted on the Statute againft the Stealing of Women for a Contract obtained by Force hath no Obligation in Law .† and therefore
fhe is a Witnefs in this Cafe as well as in any other Cafe 3 Hen VII.
c 2 Anno
1486
1 Ventr 243 4.
whatfoever

A marries with *B* and after with *C*, and by *C* has Iffue
D *C.* is an Heirefs to certain Lands, and leaves them to
defcend to *D*   And between *D* and a collateral * Heir to * P. 254.
C the Queftion of Title arofe . and the Queftion was, whether *B* could give Evidence of her Marriage with *A* It
was objected that by the very Teftimony of *B* fhe fuppofes
herfelf the Wife of *A* and confequently can depofe nothing
againft his Intereft, and he by this fecond marriage, " fup-
" pofing it were good, which fhe impeaches," is intitled to
be Tenant by the Courtefy. But to this it was anfwered,
that the Trial in this Cafe could be no Evidence in the Queftion between *A* and the collateral Heir , and therefore the By *Gould*, Juft.
Wife of *A* might be a Witnefs

But it was objected before HOLT on another Trial be- 2 Lord Raym.
tween the fame Parties, that the other Wife was no Wit- 752
nefs in this Cafe , becaufe fhe by her Oath gains an Intereft,
" namely, the ftrengthening of the Reputation of her Mar-
" riage with *A* " and fo doth not ftand as a fair and un-
prejudiced Witnefs, and he refufed to admit her to be a
Witnefs

" But perhaps the Matter was lefs debated as her Tefti-
" mony was not neceffary to the Caufe. for they proved
' the Marriage of *A* with *B* by other Witneffes, to the
" fatisfaction of the fpecial Jury "

† Ex vi injuftâ non oritur Contractus

Par 2

No other Relation held incompetent to be a Witness

But no other Relation is excluded · becaufe no other Relation is abfolutely the fame in Interest · but by the Civil Law † *Servants* and Children were excluded becaufe the Parents and Mafters had an abfolute Power over them, and therefore under that Law they fwore with manifeft Intereft to themfelves. " or if you will rather fay that nothing is in " a legal fenfe an Intereft which depends on the Fraud, or " Force, or arbitrary will of another, it may be more ge- " nerally expreffed * that they are excluded as not pof- " feffing that civil *free Agency* which is neceffary to the " character of a Witnefs, and are confidered as politically " included in the perfon of him whofe Dominion over " them is unlimited We find, however, in the DIGEST, " an Exception to the Incompetence of fervile Teftimony " when the Truth was not attainable by any other Proof

" Yet is not the Idea dreadful of a Child Evidence " againft a Parent, or a Parent againft a Child, in capi- " tal Cafes, or Children of the fame Parents againft each " other ?

" And where the Evidence tends merely to fettle the " Truth of the Fact as between other Parties, the Wife's " Teftimony fhall be admitted, though it go to a Fact which " fhe could not be allowed to prove or difprove, if the " Action were directly againft her Hufband Thus where " an Action was brought againft the Defendant for the " Wedding Cloaths of his Wife, the Wife's Mother " was allowed an Evidence to prove the Cloaths were " purchafed on the Credit of the Father, and not of the " Defendant

" And the Declaration of a Wife may be admitted though " relative to a Fact which charges the Hufband, in the fame " manner as his own Declaration, when it is not offered as " direct Evidence, but only as corroborating the Credit of " what has been before offered in proof by a *competent Wit-*

Margin notes:

Anon T L C. in the paffage cited in the foot Note, where the Author ex- empts the fra- ternal, parent- al, and conja- gal Relation See to the fame effect the *C de o the D o Tafcary* A t XXVIII

* P. 255.

Str 504. Note to former Edi- tion.

S r.

---

† D 22 5

‡ *Idonei non videntur effe Teftes quibus imperari poteft ut Teftes fiant.*

h C 4 20, 8

‖ *Servos pro Domino, quemadmodum adverfus eum, interrogari non poffe non ambigitur*

Quelque grand que foit le droit focial il cede, & doit toujours ceder au lieu de la Nature

Jura fanguinis nullo Jure civili dirimi poffunt

D 22, 5

† *Servi refponfo tunc credendum, cum alia Probatio adeurendam veritatem non eft*

" loes

" nefs And this feems to have been the Principle of the
" Cafe of the Nurfe Child but the Reafon of the Dif- Str. 527.
" tinction comes more properly to be confidered under the
" Article, HEARSAY

" And fo lately, in an Action for Damages againft the
" Driver of a Stage-coach, tried at *Bury* Affizes in the
" fpring of this year 1787. The Carriage in which * the * P. 256.
" Hufband and Wife were was overfet, and the Wife much
" hurt The Declaration of the Wife that the Accident
" was owing to the inattention of the Hufband was given
" in Evidence, to corroborate the Proofs of the Defendant's
" Witneffes "

SECTION IV.

Of Incompetency from INFAMY.

The " next" fort of Perfons excluded from Teftimony,
" for want of Integrity, are *fuch as are ftigmatized*

Now there are feveral Crimes that fo blemifh, that the Co Litt 6 b.
Party is ever after unfit to be a Witnefs· as Treafon, Fe- Salk 461
lony, and every *Crimen falfi*, as Perjury, Forgery, and the 5 Mod 74 S C.
like

And the Reafon is very " clear," becaufe every plain 2 Str 1148
and honeft Man, affirming the Truth of any Matter under where Affida-
the fanction of an Oath, is entitled to Faith and Credit, this Caufe, on
fo that under fuch Atteftation the Fact is underftood to be which the De-
fully proved
But where a Man is convicted of Falfity and other Crimes v ould have
againft the common Principles of Honefty and Humanity, aided himfelf.
his Oath is of no Weight, becaufe he hath not the Credit 2 Balftr 154.
of a Witnefs, and there is greater Prefumption againft him Br L. IV
than can be on his behalf   c 19 § 2
                                                               Fl L IV
For the Prefumption is benign and humane to every Man c 8 y -
produced as a Witnefs, that he will not falfify or prevaricate Bro Ch 15
in Matters of fuch Importance as all Affairs of Juftice are· 2 Hawk P C.
but where a Man is a notorious and public Criminal, this 432 § 19,433
Prefumption fails him and from thenceforth he is rather to § 21, 2, 3
be intended as a Man profligate and abandoned than one
under the Sentiments and Conviction of thofe Principles
that teach Probity and Veracity, and confequently the producing " of" fuch a Man is ineffectual, becaufe the Credit of his Oath is overbalanced by the Stain of his Iniquity.
† The common Punifhment that " indicates" the *Crimen* * P 257.
falfi is being fet in the Pillory and therefore they anciently
held the Law to be, that no Man legally fet in the Pillory Co Litt 6 b.
could be a Witnefs. for they thought it a ridiculous Thing, 5 Mod 15
                                                               Skinn 578, 9
VOL. I.   N   and Ld Raym 39
                                                               S C

5 Mod 74.
Holt, 753
12 Mod. 72
12 Vin. Abr
28 pl 9
Will Rep
B R. 18
Ventr 349
2 Sid 51, 2

and boding ill to a Caufe, when a Perfon thus ftigmatized appeared in Court to atteft any thing; but the Rigour of this is reduced to Réafon for now it is held that unlefs a Man be put in the Pillory, for *Crimen falfi*, as for Perjury, Forgery, or the like, it is no Blemifh to a Man's Atteftation for a Man may be pilloried for fpeaking fcandalous Words of the Government, which yet in doubtful and factious Times ought not to be taken as a Prefumption againft his common Credibility †

    " Otherwife if the Crime be recognized by the Law as " infamous in its Nature, though not attended with what is " termed infamous Punifhment "

SECTION V

Of REHABILITATION *of Teftimony.*

    " We are now led to confider how far Teftimony may be " reftored which has been fufpended by Crime : or how far " a Witnefs infamized may be rehabilitated by *Pardon*

    " Of Pardons there are two Species in Reference to this " Point · the one which is called a *Statute Pardon*, the other " a Pardon at COMMON LAW.

Owen, 150.
Moor, 872
Browne, 10
Hob 617
Cuddington v
Williams.
Roll's Abr
87, pl 6
Tr 13 T
T Raym 370,
380
Goab 288
S il 328
Kevl 38
Ventr 349

*⸸ P 258

4 H VII
c 13

    " A general Statute Pardon is fuch as paffes on an Ac" ceffion, or other memorable occafion "

One attainted of Felony or of cheating, after a general Statute Pardon, was allowed to be a good Witnefs.

    " A Pardon by *Common Law* is either by *Prerogative*, or " by *Privilege* that by *Privilege* was anciently by * Com" PURGATION, and is now called benefit of Clergy and " this relates to all Felonies, whether at Common Law " or newly created, if not expiefsly taken away by Act of " Parliament By Clergymen it is held claimable on the " repetition of a clergyable offence indefinitely, but to lay" men only once: fo that if fuch be again guilty of the " fame or any other clergyable offence, they are liable, on " conviction, to fuffer death and they can no longer inter" pofe this privilege either as a *declinatory* Plea, or after fen" tence to avoid Execution. And very lately a perfon fuf " fered death for a clergyable Felony refpecting the copper " Coin, having once before been allowed the benefit of " Clergy on Conviction for the fame offence

    " The Statute which eftablifhed this limitation, in the " inftance of laymen, directs them to be alfo branded in

---

† *Ex Delicto, non ex fupolicio, emergit Infamia.*
C'eft le Crime qui fait l'infame, et non pas le fupplice

                                           " the

" the hand; both as a punifhment and as a mark to give
" notice .they have no farther claim to'this indulgence

" Formerly they were required to read, as the Teft of
" their Title to this Privilege: but the Legiflature of an en-
" lightened Reign, more beneficially for the individuals and 5 A c. 6.
" the Public, threw down this Barrier which denied Accefs
" to Clemency in favour of abfolutely unlettered Igno-
" rance, by mak'ng it alike to all whofe offences were
" within the benefit, and requiring them to work as the
" Condition of their Pardon   The Statutes of the early
" part of the following Reign fubftituted for *clergyable Lar-* 4 G I c 11
" *cenies,* Tranfportation to *America* for *feven years,* in lieu 6 G I c. 23.
" of branding or whipping, if in the difcretion of the
" Court fuch punifhment fhall be expedient, on penalty of
" Felony without benefit of Clergy on their return within
" the time

* " The burning in the hand has been by fome legal * P. 259.
" writers faid to be in the Nature of a Statute Pardon
" being a Condition on-performance of which the dif-
" charge from punifhment, and the reftitution to credit,
" took effect

" A Pardon by Prerogative is the Refult of the high
" Truft repofed in the Crown, and the power of difpenfing
" it is indulged to the King in the conftitutional character of
" *Pater Patriæ*   This is not the time for difcuffing the ex-
" pediency of fo reforming the penal fyftem, as that rarely
" an occafion fhould be prefumeable to call forth the ex-
" ertion ot this Power.   At prefent, rarely from a fevere
" Verdict founded on unfatisfactory Evidence, but often
" from the Inequality and Rigour of our criminal Code, this
" power hath interpofed.

" In every fuch inftance, if the Pardon be abfolute, then
" immediately when recorded, if conditional, then in like
" manner after performance 'of the condition, the *competency*
" of the party to be heard as a *Witnefs* is reftored or legally
" *created*

" It hath been faid that by a Statute Pardon" every
" one" within that Pardon is reftored " to Competency,
" and is to be confidered as" received into fociety as a Perfon of Credit, " for that" no man can be punifhed in his
Reputation when the public Voice hath difcharged him

But whether the King's pardon " has generally reftored   2 Brownl 47
" his Competency," hath been a Queftion   for fome hold   2 Bulftr 154
that the King's Pardon takes away the Punifhment indeed,   2 Sid 221, 2
but doth not remove the Crime. and that the Turpitude of   Abr 163 pl 6
the Crime remaining is ever a Prefumption againft his Evi-   Cro. Jac 622
dence   2 Str Tr
521—4 269.

Others

*P. 260 ⸰Others hold the King's Pardon reſtores the Reputation, and
2 Sta.e Tr 269 the Loſs of Reputation being part of the Puniſhment, the
3 St Tr 585, King's Pardon, that can take off the whole Puniſhment, muſt,
6 c, 552. 3
andrar icularly by neceſſary conſequence, reſtore the Reputation and "that"
4 S. T 610 the King, as conſtitutional Guardian of the Life, Liberty,
T R. 23, 369, and Eſtate of his ſubject, is the beſt Judge of the Conſe-
379.
quence of his Pardon

2 Haw P C. So that if any Perſon guilty of thoſe Crimes by which
433 § 22 the Credit is loſt, be afterwards pardoned, it muſt be ſuppoſed he hath repented of his Fault, and hath returned to a
better mind · and therefore that his Evidence is not dangerous
to the Life, Liberty or Eſtate of the ſubject "that is, in
"ſo far as to be excluded as incompetent . though the Jury
"doubtleſs will exerciſe their Diſcretion as to the Credit
"due to a Witneſs under theſe circumſtances, according to
"the Nature of his Offence

"But a diſtinction hath been taken where the Incompetence
"is the general conſtructive Reſult by Preſumption of Law,
"on conviction upon an infamizing charge, and where it is
T V 2 Salk "expreſsly included in the legiſlative ſanction as a conſequence
5 4. 689 "annexed to the particular offence, and that inſeparably, until
5 P 690 "the Judgment be reverſed."

Therefore the Law is now held to be, that on Perjury at
Common Law the Party pardoned may be a Witneſs becauſe
the King has a power to take off every part of the Penalty,
"and this effectively, comprizes a power to" diſcern whether it is fit the Offender ſhould be reſtored to Credibility
but if a Man be indicted for Perjury on the Statute, the King
cannot pardon "ſo as to diſcharge this Incompetency" for
5 E 27 c 9 the King is excluded and diveſted of that Prerogative by the
Aero 1 C2 expreſs words in the Statute ⸰ the Oath of ſuch perſon ſo of-
§ 6 § 7
V 2 Stk u' "fending to be received in any Court of Record, or, as the
L 2 "Statute elſewhere expreſſes it, "the Offender from thence-
"forthſhall be reputed and diſabled for ever to be ſworn in any
"of the Courts of Record"

⸰ P 261   *SECTION   VI.

2 Rarm 3 . An Indictment of Perjury, and Verdict thereon, and no
P 122 Judgment entered, cannot be admitted to weaken the Credit
L 2 Gariel, of any Witneſs for if there be no Judgment entered, the
P 1 4 G 'li Allegata muſt be ſuppoſed defective, and a man cannot be
Co×p 2 intended to make competent Proof upon inſufficient Allega-
tions

SECTION

SECTION VII

Perfons EXCUMMUNICATED *not* WITNESSES

Perfons excommunicated cannot be Witneffes · becaufe by
the Laws of the Church fuch Perfons are excluded from human converfation   Nay her laws go fo far as to excommu-
nicate fuch who converfe with them   and confequently they
cannot be admitted to receive any Queftions from a Court of
Juftice , befides, they thought that 'thofe who were excluded
out of the Church were not under the influence of any Religion

   " When one confiders the feveral Caufes of *Excommunica-*
" *tion* exclufively recited by the Statute, it is impoffible not
" to be furprized that they remain as unrepealed exceptions
" to the *Competence* of *Teftimony*

   " The firft is HERESY, which, whatever it may mean, im-
" plies a fenfe of religious obligation, and of confcientious
" Acceptance of *Chriftianity* itfelf as divinely revealed   How
" then does it prefume a Man to have no regard to the ut-
" tering of an injurious falfehood in the prefence of the
" Deity, and in repugnance to that Religion the Truth and
" Authority of whofe general Doctrine he admits!   Another
" Caufe is Error in Opinion in Matters of Religion and Doc-
" trine received and allowed in the Church of *England*   Now
" if the Church of *England* were really infallible, it would be a
" misfortune to differ from her in any point , but certainly no
" ground of civil incapacity, efpecially fo as to preclude a Court
" of Juftice from * being informed by a Perfon labouring under
" that misfortune   Another Caufe is *Simony* which as a cor-
" rupt trafficking may indeed affect the Credit of a Witnefs
' though the offence is conftitued fo ftrangely, that eccle-
' fiaftical Right and Wrong upon this fubject enter com-
' monly in a manner very perplexing to a lay imagination,
" fhould it attempt to define the principles of morality or
" fenfe by which the Boundaries have been fettled   A re-
" mark not very diffimilar may be applied to *Ufury*

   " *Incontinence,* under which Cenfure antenuptial Com-
" merce was till very lately included, & though the Parties
" fhould have made the *Amende honorable* by intermarrying,
" is another of the recited Grounds of *Excommunication* , as it
" being unguardedly awake to the Impreffion of Nature de-
" monftrated an Infenfibility to the Voice of Truth

   " PERJURY, in an ecclefiaftical Court, ftands in the Clofe
" of the Catalogue   And this, under due Conviction in
" the Courts of Common Law, forms, as we have feen, and
                                    " juftly,

Margin notes:
Carr Comm.
B C VI Ed.
Elzev 1635
P 135

5 Eliz c 23
v Morgan's
Brit Lib
p 215, &c
Lond 1766

* P. 262.

† 27 G III.
c 44

" juftly, a decifive Exception to the Competency But if
" Excommunication take place on this as an ecclefiaftical
" Charge, this extenfive civil Confequence is thus anticipated
" by the fentence of a *Forum* whofe Rules of *Evidence* are
" far different from thofe of the common Law   .

" Even in Popifh Countries, the civil Terrors annexed by
" this fulmination of the Church, are made to yield to a
" fteady and ferene Ray of Juftice † In *England*, if the

+ V T L. C. " Cognizance of teftamentary, matrimonial, and fome other
II 112—14 " Caufes be judged expedient to remain under the ecclefiaf-
" tical Jurifdiction, it will be expedient that they have Pro-
" cefs to affift them, like other Courts, in the Inveftigation

* P. 263. " of fuch * Caufes But Excommunication is clearly as
" unfuitably applied to the Contumacy of a Witnefs in a-
" Caufe depending at Doctors' Commons, as in a Caufe
" depending in Chancery or the King's Bench "

SECTION VII

Of POPISH RECUSANTS.

2 Bulftr 155,6   The fame Law has been faid to hold place in relation to
2 St. Tr 425 *Popifh Recufants* " for that by the Statute of " *James*" they
bn. Crawley,
216 contra, are in the fame Condition with perfons excommunicated
and *Hawkins,* " But the learned and judicious Serjeant *Hawkins* thinks the
ut infra.   ' Difqualification does not extend to this The Words of the
" Act are,—*Every Popifh Recufant convicted* fhall ftand and be
" reputed to all Intents and Purpofes difabled, as a Perfon
" lawfully excommunicated

" That fuch Perfon fhould not be *competent* as a *Witnefs* in
" any Caufe hath been the *Inference* from thefe Terms but
' the Author already cited obferves, that this Conftruction

Hawk P C " feems over fevere for that this, like all other penal ftatutes,
23, 4   " ought to be conftrued ftrictly, in limitation of the Penalty,
" and that the Purport of the Words may be fully fatisfied
" by the Difability to bring any Action

" Indeed a Difability introduced againft a party ought not,
" by the force given to any general Terms, to operate a
" failure in the Courfe of public Juftice The perfon may
" be underftood difabled as to any Intereft of his own but
" the Competence of Teftimony is an Intereft of public
" Juftice "

Co Litt 6 b Perfons outlawed may be Witneffes they are punifhed in
their Properties, but the Outlawry " doth not affect their
" Competence if it have any Influence, it, at moft, termi-
" nates in their *Credit* as *Witneffes*'

" In

THE LAW OF EVIDENCE.

"In *civil* or *criminal* Caufes, no perfon at **Common** * P. 264.
"Law could be admitted to give Evidence otherwife than
"upon Oath excepting Witneffes for the Prifoner who
"were not fuffered to be fworn againft the Crown, that is,
"on criminal Profecutions, as if the Crown had an Intereft
"in the Death, Forfeitures, Imprifonment, or Difhonour of
"the Subject. and as if, in favour of fuch Intereft, the fcale
"were to be rendered unequal between Government and the
"accufed In the Dawn of a female Reign this ignominious ¹ A S ² c. ₉.
"and cruel partiality was effectually renounced Anno 1701.

SECTION IX

Exception in favour of the Teftimony of Quakers

"But it being apparently juft and expedient that perfons
"who believe a folemn Affirmation made under the confci-
"oufnefs of an omniprefent Deity to be the only allowed
"Mode of attefting to a Truth in Controverfy, fhould be
"admitted as *Witneffes*, under a fanction fubftantially the
"fame, and the fame civil Confequences, the Statute of ⁷ & ⁸ W III.
"*William* III introduced an intended Remedy. which how- c 34.
"ever was found unfatisfactory, being indeed an *Oath*, al-
"though not an imprecatory one. and therefore an Affirma-
"tion in the fimple and proper Senfe was fubftituted, but
"this right of being heard on Affirmation is expreſsly limited
"to *civil* Cafes †

Tit. II

A Suit profecuted by Action, *though given with a penal Intent,
is a civil Cafe within the Statute in favour of the Teftimony of
Quakers*

"On this it has been contended that an Action to recover
"a Penalty given by Statute on an offence which was a *crime*
"at Common Law, was not a *civil* but a criminal fuit within
"the meaning of the ftatute The Cafe is a recent one, and
"opened a very liberal Inveftigation not only of the import
"and effect of the Statute but of the Nature of Atteftation.
* "This was an Action of *Debt* upon the Statute againft * P 265
"*Bribery* Atchefon v
"On behalf of the Defendant on a Motion for a New Everett, Cowp.
"Trial, it was contended, that *Evidence* not legally admif- 381 Hil
"fible had been received, by allowing the teftimony of a B. R v St
"*Quaker* which it was argued, fhould not, in this Inftance, ² G II c, c 14

† *In Teftimonio injuratus recipitur Nemo.*

"have

"have been permitted, the Caufe being fubftantially, and
"within the meaning of the Statute, a *criminal* one. For
"that the Mode of Recovery, and the confiderable Sum
"allotted to the Informer, went not as a perfonal fuit for a
"private Benefit, but as a Reftriction on a *Crime* at *Common*
"*Law* —that the fignal Penalties and Difabilities, confe-
"quent on the Judgment, proved it both in principle and of
"fect a criminal fuit

"For the Plaintiff, it was argued that the Evidence was
"rightly received That whatever the Object of the Ac-
"tion, as countenanced by the Legiflature in a Public View
"might be, the Form was *Civil*,—the legal Characters of
"the fuit, ranked it with complete Certainty in the Clafs of

r - & 5W III
c 34 §1, 2, 3
6 Anno 1696

"*Civil Caufes*,—that the Intent of the Statute correfpond-
"ed with the Terms of it, in thus fixing the Line, and pro-
"tecting this Body of Citizens from private coercion or re-
"venge, to which they would remain liable, if where the
"fuit was commenced by an *individual*, and could not there-
"fore be difcontinued by the *Crown*, a *Quaker* fhould be
"driven to the Alternative of violating his confcience by
"taking an Oath, or incurring a contempt, by refufing to

* P. 266

"comply with the *fubpœna*, of the party for that * purpofe
"Here the Action, the Declaration, the Plea, the Judgment,
"the Operation of the Infolvent Act, which confeffedly
"would difcharge this like any other *Debt*; all demonftrate,
"that this is truly a Civil Caufe, within the Letter and the
"Spirit of the Act

"That a Point of which the Analogy would govern this,
"had been already decided. where an Action had been

7 & 8 W III
c. 12

"brought againft the Sheriff, for a *falfe* Return The Judg-
"ment concluded with a *fit deferders in mifericordia*, inftead of
"a *captiatur* The Plaintiff had a Verdict and Judgment
"the Defendant brought Error on which one of the Caufes
"affigned, was the irregularity in the conclufion of the Judg-
"ment as already ftated and urged, that it was not amen-
"dable within the Statutes of *jeofails*, as being not on a *civil*
"but a *criminal* Suit

"The *Judges* in the *Exchequer Chamber*, though differing
"in opinion as to the regularity of the Judgment, were una-
"nimous, that if wrong, it was aided by the Statutes of
"*Jeofails* For that aiding in the fta ute 4 G II c 26 ex-
"cepts criminal Cafes from thofe S atutes, whether the Sta-
"tute giving double damages on a *falfe return*, be *penal* or
"*not but*, as this is *not* a *criminal profecut on*, the defect is
"aided by the Statute

"Lord Mansfield, in delivering the opinion of the
"Court, after adverting to the Cafes in which this Queftion
"had

‹ had been touched, rather than decided, and noticing the
‟ fituation of the *Quakers*, before the time of paffing the
‟ Act, expreffed himfelf to this effect .—

* ‟ A more liberal way of thinking prevailed after the * P 267.
‟ Revolution The principles of *Toleration* were explain-
‟ ed and juftified by confequence of the Writings of
‟ *Locke*, *Somers*, and other great men of thofe times And
‟ a Statute paffed, which, though not general, was very ex-
‟ tenfive in the relief it afforded to fcrupulous confciences.
‹ That Statute was 1 *William* and *Mary*, *c* 18. commonly
‟ called the † *Toleration* Act

‟ In the *thirteenth* Section of that Statute, the Legiflature
‟ takes Notice, that there was a Sect called *Quakers*, who
‟ had religious Principles in which they differed from the

† The Form in the Toleration Act, is this —
I do fincerely promife, and folemnly declare before God and
the World
In the Statute of 7 & 8 *W* III the Affirmation is,—
I do declare, in the Prefence of Almighty God, the Witnefs
of the Truth of what I fay
In the Statute of *G* I. it is rendered unexceptionable , being
only as quoted in the next Page Thus a fingle Law, founded
in due Attention to the Rights of Humanity, is the fource of fucceffive Improvement.
A very refpectable Perfon, not a Quaker, was greatly offended
with the Multiplicity and imprecatory Claufe of the civil oath of
his Country He remonftrated in a grave and becoming manner .
but hardly, in any inftance has the Dignity of a wife and virtu-
ous Republic more fuffered than by the Treatment, which, on
that occafion, he experienced
Vogliamo che in qualunque cafo e circoftanza in cui fia permeffo
deferirfi il Giuramento a qualunque Perfona per qualunque caufa,
debba il Giudice, o Miniftro proceffante, primade ferire il Giuramento cerziorare le perfone fopra l'obligo che porta feco il Giuramento , fpegiandogliene, l'effenza, e l'importanza—e fi fe trat-
terà di perfone di Religione diverfa della noftra, a tali perfone fi
f i preftare il Giuramento, (previa la detta cerziorazione fecondo
l'ufato, ma,) con il piu refpettato e temuto loro rito PENAL
CODE of the GRAND DUKE of TUSCANY , Art XII Dated
Pifa, 30th *Nov* 1786 I owe the Perufal of this Code to him,
who for a Courfe of Years, with a Conftancy of felf Denial,
and an intrepid Perfeverance of Exertion not to be defcribed,
fcrutinizes the Globe to diminifh the Crimes and alleviate the Mi-
feries of its inhabitants, purfuing Horror and Peril in their moft
horrid Receffes, under the influence and protection of divine
Philanthropy
The Cafe in *Siderfin*, was a Queftion of extremely great importance in point of Property and one of the lateft in which
the Ufe of a perfon's particular Seal was confidered as requifite
to prove the Authenticity of a Deed v. p 269.

‟ eftablifhed

" eftablifhed Doctrine of tne *Church* of *England*. and that
" one of their religious Scruples was the taking an Oath ac-
" cording to the Form prefcribed by the Law of *England* to
" Chriftians · and therefore, the Act enables them to give
" affurance of their fidelity and allegiance to the State by
" what I may call *another* form of Oath · becaufe it is ap
" pealing to the Deity for the veracity of what they fhall
" fay.

· & 6 W III
c. 34

" This Statute was followed about fix Years after by ano
" ther, which allows a *Quaker* to *affirm* in Cafes where other
" perfons are required to take an Oath but ftill this affirma-
" tion retains the fubftantial characteriftic of an Oath

* P. 268
8 G I c 6

* " But in the Year 1721, the Statute paffed, which,
" after reciting that the Forms prefcribed, in Lieu of the
" common Abjuration Oath, the Declaration, and the At-
" teftation, in Courts of Juftice, were not found fufficient
" to avoid the inconveniences which they were meant to obvi
" ate, by reafon of difficulties remaining among the faid *Qua*
" *kers* concerning them, reduces the whole to a more fimpl-,
" but folemn Affirmation, by omitting the Appeal to the
" Divine Prefence, the Affirmation being thus .—I do fo-
" lemnly, fincerely, and truly declare and affirm

" And the fecond Section, after giving to this Affirmation
" the fame force and effect in all Courts of Juftice, as if
" fuch *Quaker* had made it in the Form prefcribed by the
" Act of *William*, annexes all the civil confequences of Per-
" jury, to the wilfully, falfely, and corruptly fo affirming,
" in the fame manner as that Statute had done

" And on this liberal and fecure footing, the Evidence of
" *Quakers* in *Civil* Caufes ftands at the prefent Day

" It has been truly faid, that fince the Cafe of *Omichund*
v *Barker*, and another Cafe of great Authority determined
" fince, the Nature of an Appeal to Heaven, which ought
" to be received as a full Sanction to Evidence, has been more
" fully underftood I there argued, and the Judges, in deli-

* P. 269.
" vering their Opinions * agreed, that upon the principles
" of the Common L v, there is no particular Form effen-
" tial to an Oath to be taken by a Witnefs But as the pur
" pofe of it is to bind his Confcience, every Man of every
" Religion, fhould be bound by that Form which he himfelf
" thinks will bind his own Confcience moft

" Therefore though the Chriftian Oath was fettled in very
" early times, yet *Jews* before the 18th of *Edward* tne
" *Firft*, when they were expelled the Kingdom, were per
" mitted to give Evidence at *Common Law*, and were fworn,
' not on the Evangelifts, but on the Old Teftament No
" diftinction

" diftinction was taken between their fwearing in a *civil* and
" in a *criminal* Cafe.

" It is objected, that the *Quakers* are the only people in
" the world who ever refufed to *fwear* but, in *fubftance,*
" their affirmation is the fame thing the *form* only is diffe-
" rent, for an Affirmation is a moft folem Appeal and At-
" teftation to the God of Truth

" There is a remarkable Cafe reported in *Siderfin,* where
" Dr *Owen,* Vice-chancellor of *Oxford,* in the Year 1657,
" being called as a Witnefs, refufed to kifs the Book ; but
" defired it might be opened before him, and he lifted up his
" right hand The Jury prayed the Opinion of the Court,
" if they ought to give the fame Credit to him as to a Wit-
" nefs fworn in the ufual manner ; and GLYN, *Chief Juftice,*
" told them, that in his opinion, he had taken as ftrong an
" Oath as any other Witnefs : but, faid he, if I were to be
" fworn, I would kifs the Book.

" * There is a Sect in *Scotland,* at this Day, who hold it   * P. 270.
" to be Idolatry to kifs the Book. But their own form of
" fwearing is much more folemn At *Carlifle,* in the Year
" 1745, upon a Profecution of fome of the Rebels, there
" was no Evidence but of this Sect , and a Cafe was fent
" up for Advice, whether they could be received as Wit-
" nefles It was the opinion of thofe who were confulted
" here, that the Evidence might be received , but it was
" not an object, and the Profecution went no further

" The Chief Juftice then adverts to the Hiftory of the
" progrefs of the Bill for admitting the Teftimony of *Qua-*
" kers on Affirmation in the Reign of *William* III He at-
" tributes the exception with regard to *criminal profecutions,*
" to a ftrong prejudice in the minds of great men at that
" period He fhews that the Act, a *temporary* one, being 13 W. III c 4.
" carried with difficulty, was afterwards continued for eleven
" Years , and in the Reign of *Q. Anne,* two unfuccefsful
" efforts were made to render it perpetual, which was not
" effected until the Year of the Acceffion of the prefent Fa-
" mily to the Throne But that neither then, nor in the fub-
" fequent enlarging and amending Statute, any alteration
" was made to the Exception of criminal Caufes , which,
" in fome inftances, bears harder upon the *Quakers,* and
" leaves them in a worfe condition than when their fect firft
" arofe The Statute of *Anne,* having afterwards interven-
" ed, and putting the examination of Witnefles for the Pri-
" foner on the fame * footing of Teftimony upon *oath,* with * P 271.
" thofe for the *Crown.* So that if a *Quaker* be indicted of a
" capital Offence, he can not now call *Quakers* as Witnefles in
" his behalf.

                              " That

" That it is not possible to say, why the Exception was
" made, yet since made, it must be followed.

" That however it is not of a Nature to admit any ex-
" tension by Equity For that in *remedial* Cases, the con-
" struction of Statutes is indeed extended to cases within
" the reason or within the Rule of them But where it is
" an hard positive Law, and the reason not very plainly to
" be seen, it ought not to be extended by Construction

" That we come then to this Question, Is the present
" a criminal Cause? A *Quaker* appears, and offers himself
" as a Witness, can he give *Evidence* without being sworn?
" If it be a criminal Cause, he can not

" Now there is no distinction better known than between
" *civil* and *criminal* Law, or between *criminal Prosecutions*
" and *civil Actions*.

" Mr Justice *Blackstone*, (and all other antient and mo-
" dern Writers on the subject) distinguishes them *Penal*
" *Actions*, in our system of Jurisprudence, were never yet
" put under the head of *criminal* Law The construction
" of the Statute must be extended by Equity to make this
" a *criminal* Cause It is as much a *civil* Action, as an
" Action for *Money had* and *received* The Legislature,
" when they excepted to the Evidence of *Quakers* in *criminal*
" Causes, must be understood to mean Causes *technically*
" criminal, * and a different construction would not only
" be injurious to *Quakers*, but prejudicial to the rest of the
" King's Subjects who may want their Testimony The
" Case of Sir *Watkyn Williams Wynne* v *Middleton*, is a very
" full Authority, and alone sufficient to warrant the Dis-
" tinction between civil and criminal Proceedings In that
" Case, the Question was, whether the Statute 7 & 8 W
" III was *penal* or *remedial* The Court held it was not a
" p nal Statute But supposing it was to be considered as a
" *penal* Statute, yet it was also a *remedial* Law, and there
" fore, the Objection taken was cured by 16 & 17 *Car* II.
" c 8 Now the Exceptions in that Statute, and also in
" St 32 H VIII c 30 and in St 18 *Eliz* c 14 are of
" *penal* Actions and *criminal Proceedings* But Lord *Chief*
" *Justice* WILLES, in delivering the solemn Judgment of
" the Court, says, there is another Act which would de-
" cide of itself, if considered in the light of a new Law,
" or as an Interpretation of what was meant by *penal*
" Actions in the St 16 & 17 *Car* II This is the Statute
" of 4 G II c 26 for turning all Law proceedings into
" *English* and it has this remarkable Conclusion, that every
" Statute or *Jeofails* shall extend to all forms and proceed-
" ings in *English*; (except in *criminal* Cases) and that this
" Clause

* P 272.

1 Wils 125
2 Str 1227

C- 22

v § 1, 2.

" Claufe fhall be conftrued in the moft beneficial manner.
" This is very decifive

" No Authority whatever has been mentioned on the
" other fide, nor any cafe cited where it has been mention-
" ed, that a *penal* Action was a *criminal* Cafe The fingle
" Authority mentioned againft receiving the Evidence of a
" *Quaker* in this Cafe is, an *Appeal* of *Murder* But that
" is only a different Mode of profecuting an Offender to
" Death Inftead of proceeding by Indictment in the ufual
" way, it allows * the relation to carry on the Profecution * P. 273.
" for the purpofe of attaining the fame end which the
" King's Profecution would have had, if the Offender had
" been convicted, namely, execution and therefore, the
" Writers on the Law of *England* clafs an Appeal of Murder
" in the Books under the Head of *Criminal* Cafes (†)

" With refpect to a *Quaker's* giving Evidence in *criminal*
" Cafes, his Lordfhip obferved, that the Quaker was liable
" to an *Attachment* on refufal but intimated that by the
" Act of Toleration he would be exempted from any penal
" confequences, his diffent touching the *lawfulnefs* of an
" oath being no longer liable to be treated as a *crime,* nor
" he to be fubjected to *punifhment* for a refufal founded
" on it

" And to evince that where the end was *civil,* though
' the *form* was that of a *criminal* fuit, the teftimony of a
" Quaker was receivable by the Statute, he inftanced *Rex*
" *v Turner,* where on a motion to quafh an appointment 2 Str 1219
" of *Overfeers,* though in the King's Name, the end being Hil 18 G II.
" a *civil remedy,* the *Affirmation* of a *Quaker* was allowed Lee, Ch J
" to be read

" The Refult is, that where the Form is *civil,* though the
" fubject may be *penal,* or where the Form is *criminal,* but
" the object a *civil* remedy, the Evidence of a Quaker fhall
" be admitted being excluded in proper *criminal* Caufes,
' where the Form and the Object both denominate the fuit
" a Profecution for a public Offence

(†) Thus GLANVILLE, who held that great office of *Capitalis
Jufticiar us Angliæ* (an office apparently fuperior to that of either
Chancellor or Chief Juftice in the prefent day,) under HENRY
the SECOND, commences his Book § by this divifion *Placitorum* § L I c 1.
aliud eft CRIMINALE, *aliud* CIVILE *Item placitorum crimina-
lium aliud pertinet ad Coronam domini Regis, aliud ad viccomitem
pro inciatum*

‖ And afterwards he ranks the *Appeal* of the *Wife* for the *death* ‖ l XIV c 3
of her *Hufband* amongft the criminal Caufes Co.Litt. 284,7

Incapacity

Incapacity from Want of Difcernment

The CHIEF JUSTICE concluded thus: " We are not " under the leaft embarraffment in the prefent cafe. for there " is not a fingle Authority to prove that upon a penal Action " a *Quaker's Evidence* may not be received upon his *Affir* " *mation.* Therefore I am of opinion that Mr Juftice *Nares* " did perfectly right in admitting this *Quaker* to be a Wit " nefs upon his Affirmation, and confequently that the Rule " for a New Trial fhould be difcharged

SECTION X

Peer to be examined on Oath

V Foft, 140 —53

" But although on Trial before the Lord *High Steward* " and *Peers,* out of Parliament, (in which Cafe the Peers " are in the Nature of a *Jury)* or before the *King* in *Par* " *liament,* which is by the *Houfe* of *Peers* in its judicial Ca " pacity when Parliament is fitting, (the High Steward, if " any be appointed, being only as Speaker *pro Tempore,)* " the Peers give their Verdict or Sentence upon their *Honour,* " perhaps meaning not merely their perfonal dignity and " eftimaticn, but their *Barony,* which as *Pares maximæ Cur æ* " they hold as a folemn Truft by the Tenure of the due " performance of the Duties of their Office; yet if a *Peer*

Cotm I c. 12 p 402

" be examined as a *Witnefs,* he fhall give his Evidence on " Oath · and accordingly, on the laft Trial on an Indict- " ment of High Treafon, in levying War againft the King, " the Lord Vifcount *Stormont* was fo examined, he being at " that time one of the *fixteen*

SECTION XI.

Of INCAPACITY *for want of* DISCERNMENT

Co Litt 6 b L N P 293 H P C B 1I c 6 § 27 Poun1 47 Mofeler, 72

" We are now to confider Perfons under" thofe who are excluded from Teftimony by want of Difcernment · " and " this either,

" 1 Propter Ætatem " 2 Propter defectum Rationis

TIT II.

" 1 *Of incapacity by reafon of years*

CHILDREN under the Age of *fourteen,* are not, " as of " courfe," admitted as Witneffes. and yet at * twelve they are

are obliged to fwear Allegiance in the Leet. There is no time fixed wherein they are to be excluded from Evidence; but the reafon and fenfe of their Evidence is to appear from the Queftions propounded and their Anfwers to them "And as Children of very ténder years are capable of being "legally confidered as being capital offenders, much more "are they capable of being *Witneffes*

"And *Hale* thinks that even in a capital Cafe where the "Information from the party injured is peculiarly effential, "it may be expedient to hear an Infant, though the Court "fhould think it unfit to fwear her"

The Evidence of a Child of 6 years was refufed by the Lord Chief Baron himfelf on an Indict-ment of a Rape, and afterwards on an Indict-ment for an Affault with in-tent to commit that offence Str 700 E 12 G H H P C, 634, 5

Tit. III

2 *Of Incapacity by reafon of Want of Underftanding, by Idiocy or Infanity*

Ideots and *infane* Perfons are obvioufly incapable of being "*Witneffes* but this muft be underftood of fuch as mani-"feftly are within the defcription of this deplorable Cala-"mity · otherwife a *defect* or *inconftancy* of underftanding not "clearly to this extent will affect their credit but not their "Competency to be examined, but where they appear" perfectly incapable of any fenfe of Truth, "they are" plainly and neceffarily excluded

"Yet of an *infane* Perfon it might, for Defect of other "Evidence, merit to be confidered, whether, in *civil* Cafes "at leaft, the Teftimony of fuch might not be *admiffible* "upon points where his underftanding did not appear to be "fubject to difturbance it being well known that in many "of thefe melancholy inftances, efpecially where the refult "of fome violent paffion, the party affected is entirely "cool, clear, and recollected in his Ideas, and as free as "other perfons from the delufions of a perverted imagin-"ation, in every thing not connected with the Caufe of his "Infanity

* "With regard to perfons who have only temporary * P. 276. "fits of *Madnefs*, (then ufually termed *Lunacy*), and at other "times are in all refpects of found reafon, thefe are then "confequently as capable of teftimony as of any other legal "Act.

SECTION XI

EXEMPTION propter FIDEM PUBLICAM or Incapacity *on account* of profeffional *Confidence.*

"We are laft, on the head of *Competency*, to confider "the Cafe of thofe who being *profeffionally* engaged as of "Counf l

"*Counfel* for a party, or as Solicitor, Attorney, or oth-r
"Law Agen*, are poffeffed by virtue of fuch confidential
"chara&er, of fa&s which are under the Inveftigation of a
"Court of Juftice.

† Rayner 111
—12
and L. N P.
284, 5

"This point hath been largely and well treated by the
"Author † of *Readings* on Statutes in the Reign of *George*
"the *Second* · and from him chiefly will be cited what ap
"pears of moft importance under this head

"The general Principle is derived from hence That
"formerly, in the fimpler ftate of Society and Laws, Per-
"fons appeared for themfelves, and condu&ed their own
"Claims or Defences, without needing the Affiftance of
"men educated to the formal pra&ice of the Law When
"the extenfion of property, the encreafe of Laws, the
"magnitude, number, and fubtilty of legal Queftions ren-
"dered this no longer fafe or pra&icable, the Attorney, as
"the Name indicates, became the legal Reprefentative of
"his Client in the Caufe The Anfwer of the Agent was
"the Anfwer of the Principal, and whatever the party
"could have done perfonally, was conclufive when tranfa&-
"ed in his place by his legal Proxy It was therefore con-
"verfely juft that the Attorney fhould neither be compelled
"nor permitted to anfwer Queftions pointed at the Dif-

+ P 277

"clofure of Fa&s, which to divulge would be inconfiftent
"with the Nature of fuch Reprefentation, being * of tha*

III Com 3-o
Theo- of Ev
95
L N, P 284

"kind to which the party could not perfonally have been
"obliged to anfwer

"But there are Limitations refulting from the principle
"of this Rule

Cutts and
Pickering, E
24 Car II
1 Ventr 197

"Thus, an Attorney or Solicitor may difclofe a Fa&
"communicated *prior* to his being *profeffionally* confulted by
"the party who afterwards became his Client

11 St. Tr 253

"So alfo of a fubfequent Fa& during his Retainer, if in
"its Nature unconne&ed with the profeffional Truft, as
"neither being, nor prefumably taken to be, relative to

Obf of Sir J S
2 Str 1122

"the legal Bufinefs on which he is employed, or as being
"fuch as equally was open to his knowledge had he not
"ftood in that relation

"Farther, if the Fa& to which an Attorney or Solicitor
"is examined be fuch, as that on the proved or admitted
"circumftances of the Cafe, or on the ftate of the Quef-
"tion upon which either Party relies, the Truth cannot
"be inveftigated but by examining a perfon under this pro-
"feffional Confidence, he fhall be confidered as free from
"the generally implied obligation to fecrefy, at leaft where

V 12 V n
Ab- 38 pl 1

"the point to be afcertained by his Evidence cannot cri-
"minate his Client.

"And

" And where an Attorney is Witnefs to a Deed, the Rayn 117, 8.
" Confent of his Client that he fhall atteft the Inftrument Ld Say and
" carries with it an abfolute implied Confent that he fhall Mich 10 A.
" be examined concerning the Execution of the Deed   10 Mod 41
" Where the original Ground of Communication is Sir O Brdg-
" *Malum in fe.* as if he be confulted on an *Intention* to com- Advice of all
" mit a *Forgery*, or *Perjury*, this can never be included the Judges,
" within the Compafs of profeffional Confiderce being 58
" equally contrary to his Duty in his Profeffion, his Duty
" as a Citizen, and as a Man but if fuch offence, as For-
" gery, for Example, *committed* without his being *privy*,
" comes to his knowledge in the courfe of confidential
" tranfactions with his Client, in * the way of bufinefs, he * P 278.
" fhall not be compelled to affift in proving it
" But this Privilege, or rather this incapacitation, (it Rex v Dixon.
" being more for the protection of the Client, and of the 3 Burr Manf.
" Faith of a Truft effential to civil Society than for the fake 1687, 8
" of the Agent) is underftood of *Law Agents*, not of Agents
" in a popular and general fenfe, otherwife it might be
" moft inconveniently extended to *Stewards*, and even com-
" mon fervants
" In Ejectment on a Trial at Bar, the Evidences, which Sir Samuel
" as the Plaintiff infifted, would have eftablifhed his Title, Jones v Coun-
" and avoided the fettlement of the Defendant, were locked chefter, ut fu-
" in a Box, which had been in the Cuftody of a ftranger, pra.
" who before the Trial delivered it to the *Earl* of *Bedford*,
" a Truftee for the Defendant.
" The Earl, prefent in Court, was requefted to deliver
" the Key, that the Box, which was brought into Court,
" might be opened He faid, that being a *Truftee*, he con-
" ceived he was not obliged to fhew forth any Writings
" that might impeach her eftate, and if he fhould, it would
" be a breach of the Truft repofed in him, which was fa-
" cred and inviolable
" The court faid, that they could not compel him to de-
" liver the Key but *Hales* faid it was advifable for him to
" do it For he held, though it is againft the Duty of a
" *Counfellor* or *Solicitor*, &c to difcover the Evidence with
" which he who retains acquaints him, yet a *Truftee* may
" and ought to produce Writings, but that *there* they could
" not rule him to do it

* SECTION XII   * P. 279.

EVIDENCE on HEARSAY.

" We now come to the loweft fpecies of *parol* Evidence.
" The *Light* which Evidence hitherto confidered throws on
VOL I   O   " a Caufe

" a Caufe was *primary* and *direct* , but of this *secondary* and re-
" flected for where better can be adduced the Rule is, that
" *Hearfay* is full Evidence

III Comm.
368
L. N. P 233,
294, 5.

" Yet of certain Queftions *Hearfay* is full Evidence, when
" from the Nature of the fubject no other can be expected
" as in common Opinion to general Character which refts
" upon general Eftimation , but otherwife of particular Facts

" So of a Prefcription, which excluding direct Proof from
" written Evidence, and running beyond the reach of pre-

Skinner v Ld
Bellamont,
Worcefter 1744

" fent knowledge, is well proved by referring to the Account
" given by difinterefted parties long fince deceafed

Bifhop of Meath
v Ld Belfield,
1747

" So even of an antient Prefentation to a Benefice, under
" circumftances, this being good by parol, the general Re-
" putation of the Country that B was in by the Prefentation
" of *A.* was allowed as Evidence, the Parifh Regifter being
" filent.

Grimwade and
Stevens, Kent,
1697

" So of a Defcent, or Family Relationfhip, Teftimony
" concerning the common Reputation and Belief in the Fa-
" mily is frequently given in Evidence for Defect of better

Davies v Pierce
Tr 27 G III.
T R. II. 53

So Declaration of *deceafed* Tenants, that a certain piece of
Land is parcel of the Eftate which they occupied, is admiffible Evidence

1 Mod. 283
Tr 29 Car II.
B. R.

" So where it comes in corroboration of Teftimony of a
" Witnefs, by fhewing him on the former occafion to have
" declared agreeably to his prefent Evidence

V fupra.

" So in Iffue, on the Legitimacy of Plaintiff or Defen-
" dant, Evidence of what the Parents have been heard to
" fay is admiffible , not as a detached fource of direct Evi-
" dence, but as an Inducement to the Belief of the Witnefs
" one way or the other

≠ P ^80
Pendrel and
Pendrel
2 Str 925

" Where a party is living and producible as a Witnefs,
" the Declarations of that party fhall not be given in Evi-
" dence on the one hand, till the party hath been produced
" and examined to the point to which fuch fuppofed Decla-
" clarations refer, on the other

" What a Witnefs hath heard from a Criminal volun-
" tarily , without force or undue influence of any kind, con-
" feffirg the charge, is Evidence againft the criminal on the
" Trial, but not againft a third Perfon

" It has been already feen, that fince beft Evidence,
" which the Cafe, circumftanced as it ftands, will allow, is
" always required, † *parol* proof cannot be given of what
" a deceafed

---

† On the Cafe of a Man convicted of Murder on the Declaration
of the Deceafed, fupported by ftrong circumftantial Evidence, Sir
George Nares, in converfing on the fubject, quoted this Paffage
Have

" a deceafed perfon faid, on his death-bed touching the
" Caufe of his Death, when thofe Declarations were re-
" duced to writing, and might have been fo given in Evi-
" dence , but where they were not fo reduced, this Evi-
" dence is admiffible . though the *Credit* of it much depends
" on the Memory and Temper of the Witnefs by whom it is
" related

V fupra, 211.

Trial of Bam-
bridge
Harg St Tr.
IX 261

" Such Declarations, well authenticated and fupported by
" circumftances, have undoubtedly their Weight, from the
" fituation in which they are uttered

* " On the other hand, an extremely able Writer fhews
" the various fources of Error and Mifreprefentation arifing
" from this fpecies of Proof, by what an affaffinated Perfon
" may have been heard to fay relative to the Caufe of his
" Death At prefent this is but hinted ; its proper place
" will occur hereafter, in treating on the *probability* refulting
" from Teftimony And this Difcuffion it will foon be fea-
" fonable to commence. It remains, however, a general
" Rule fubject only to neceffary Limitations, that no Evidence
" fhall be admitted upon oath of what a man faid when he
" was not upon oath

* P. 281.

Dougl II 397.
8, and 308, 9.

CHAP. II.

GENERAL OBSERVATIONS

" There remain a few general Obfervations on this Article
" of *Competency*

Par 2.

Effect of the Objection where doubtful.

" Firft, wherever it is *doubtful* whether the Objection
" fhould go to the *Competency* or to the *Credit*, the Witneffes
" ought to be heard · for no Evidence fhould be rejected that
" is not clearly and decidedly inadmiffible

V fupra, 237.

Have I not hideous death before my view,
Retaining but a quantity of life,
Which bleeds away, even as a form of wax
Refolveth from his figure 'gainft the fire ?
What in the world fhould make me now deceive,
Since I muft lofe the ufe of all deceit ?
Why then fhould I be falfe, fince it is true
That I muft die here, and live hence by truth.

Jonv. A V
Sc IV
Capell's Shak-
fpeare, 5

O 2

Par.

Par. 3

Time of excepting.

" Then, as to the time of taking the Exception

" Evidence muſt be opened before it is offered, that the
" Court may judge of its Nature and Circumſtances, ſo
" as to be able to diſcern whether it ought to be offered to
" the Jury

" And then, after a Man hath been examined *in chief,*
" hath gone through his whole Evidence, and been croſs ex-
" amined, the *Exception* to his *Competency* comes, in ſtrict-
" neſs of Law, too late . † and, in this reſpect, the ſtrict-
" neſs of Law is very wiſe it always ſaves time, and it pre-
" cludes Abuſes which might otherwiſe take place

* " In the ſtrict antient Method, if a Witneſs was ſuſ-
" pected to be intereſted, he was examined by the party lia-
" ble to be prejudiced by his Teſtimony, on a *voire dire,* to
" diſcloſe the Truth concerning ſuch circumſtances But as
" the Queſtions put with this view, were generally in a
" great degree the ſame which would be afterward repeated
" on the examination *in chief,* it has been permitted, for the
" diſpatch of Juſtice and the mutual convenience of the
" parties, to examine *conditionally,* (as it were in the nature
" of a *de bene eſſe*), ſubject to *exceptions* of *Competency* reſerv-
" ed, to be argued if judged material, at the Cloſe of the
" Evidence.

" But where a Verdict is clearly ſatisfactory on the Me-
" rits, this Exception to the Competence of ſome of the Wit-
" neſſes, will be of no Weight to induce the granting of a
" new Trial; though it might have had ſome in a doubtful
" Queſtion.

Tit. II

Inconvenience in the Effect of Exceptions to Competency.

" A remark has been made by a Gentleman, to whom
" the Public is obliged for valuable information on a great
" branch of *conſtitutional* Law, that there is a conſiderable
" inconvenience attendant on the Mode of taking Exceptions
" to *Evidence* for that the Counſel, who offers Evidence,
" againſt the Competency of which the other ſide has to ex-
" cept, has already the advantage of whatever prejudice or
" improper impreſſion, ſuch Evidence may be likely to con-

Marginal notes (left column):

1 St. Tr 129
old Edition.

4 Burr Manſf.
2152 v ſupra.
T R. 718, 9
E 27 G III.

* P. 282.
3 Comm 370
Turner & al v
Peart, T R.
701 ſupra.

T R. ut ſupra.
717—20

Douglas contr
Ei. III -31, 2

† *Vigilantibus, non dormientibus, ſubveniunt Jura.*

" vey

" vey with it, by stating its purport and tendency to the
" Jury, who may too probably infer, when objection is
" to its Admissibility, that it is therefore, of course, both
" true and fatal to the party objecting. Yet the * Re- * P. 283.
" medy intimated, that perhaps it might be an improvement,
" when Questions of Admissibility are raised, that the
" Jury, as well as the Witnesses, should withdraw till the
" point be argued and decided, may feem neither ef-
" fectually to meet the inconvenience at present fub-
" fisting, nor to be free from disadvantages of its own,
" and those of a kind yet more to be avoided · possibly this
" may be one of the instances in which some disadvantageous
" circumstance is attached inseparably to a great and peculiar
" benefit, not as a corruption or deviation, but as admitted
" into the original frame of a sublime Institution; which,
" if more guarded in this point, must have been so by the fa-
" crifice of something more essential "

CHAP III

We come now to consider the Scale of *Probability*, and to v fupra, p. 2.
compare the several Degrees of Evidence. All Certainty,
as we have shewn, arises from the Knowledge of a Man's
own proper Senfes " and is either direct" by Intuition,
" or reflective," by comparing his Ideas and thoughts one
with another

SECTION II

On Degrees of Probability in Testimony

Probability " arifeth from the Teftimony of others,
" concerning a Subject proveable to their Senfes, when fuch
" Teftimony is in" Agreement with a Man's own Thoughts
" and Obfervations.

Tit. II

Order of Proof

And here it is to be first confidered, that in all Courts of
Justice, the Affirmative * ought to be proved · for it is fufficient barely to deny what is affirmed, until the contrary be
proved · for Words are but the Expreffion of Facts, and
therefore, when nothing is faid to be done, nothing can be
proved · and this is a Rule, both in *Common* and *Civil* Law;
the

† Actori incumbit Probatio.

* P 284. " the Civil Law fays, * the Proof lies on him who makes
" the Allegation, for it is againft the Nature of Things to
" prove a Negative "

But in a Cafe where the Affirmative is *primâ facie* proved,
the other fide may conteft with oppofite Proofs . and this
is' not properly the Proof of a Negative, but the Proof
of a Propofition, totally inconfiftent with what is affirmed

And therefore, when the General Iffue is in the Negative, the Plaintiff muft always begin with his Proof becaufe the Defendant cannot prove the Negative, 'and the
Charge beginning by the Plaintiff, he muft take it out of his
Evidence . as if the Defendant be charged with a *Trefpafs*,
he need only make a general Denial of the Fact, and if
" Evidence be given, which uncontradicted, will" prove
the Fact, he can only prove a Propofition inconfiftent with
the Charge · " as" that he was at another Place at the
time when the Fact was fuppofed to be done, " or that
" the Ground was his own where he had a right to be ,"\ or
the like

But where Law " implies an Affirmative," contained in
the Iffue, there the oppofite Party " may" be put into the
Proof of it by a Negative · as in the Iffue *ne unques accouple
en loyal Matrimonie*, the Law will fuppofe the Affirmative,
that the " Marriage was lawful, at the fame time, the
" Plaintiff having averred a general Illegality, the Defen-
" dant, from the Neceffity of the Cafe, is put to fhew on
" what Marriage, under what circumftances and qualifica-
" tions he relies It is therefore, in Truth," the Defendant
* P 285 " muft * begin, " by offering Evidence to fupport the Le
" gality of the Marriage.

18 G II c 20 " So on a Suit againft a *Juftice* of Peace, for exercifing
3 Burn 21, 2 " that Office, *not* being qualified according to the Statute, it
" lies on the Defendant to prove his *Qualification* "

L N P 298 In an Information againft Lord *Halifax*, for refufing" to
" deliver up the Rolls of the Auditor of the Exchequer, the
\ Co Litt " Court put the Plaintiff to prove that he did not deliver
L III § 534 " them for a perfon fhall be prefumed duly to execute
" his office till the contrary appears And this might be
" prved by pofitive Facts, fuch as Refufal, their remain-
' ing in his Poffeffion, and the like.

- Co f s λ t " The truth is, that in legal Queftions, the general nega-
‹ I . t ve ferm is convertible, (often by various diftinct Subfti-
I ν ι ι ∧ ‹ n ns of litigated Fact), into a pofitive one In fuch
‹ il ces, therefore, where it fuffices for the Plaintiff ge-
" i ll to deny the exiftence of any legal Qualification,

D \ al t 2   , Ci ncumbit Probatio, qui dicit, non qui negat.

" under

" under which the Defendant might juftify, it is incumbent
" on the Defendant to prove the particular circumſtances
" which contradict the Negative And this is not proving
" a Negative, which in a direct Senfe is impoſſible, but
" it is proving an Affirmative repugnant to the general Ne-
" gation †

" As in the cafe juſt intimated, the plaintiff charges, that
" the Defendant hath acted as a Juſtice of the Peace, not
" having qualified purfuant to the Statute. The Defendant
" proves his Property, and proves his Compliance with the
" Requiſitions of the Statute. The Nature of the Quef- ,
" tion puts the Proof on the Defendant. If he fail in that
" Proof, then the general Negative of Qualification, com-
" prized in * the Plaintiff's Charge is converted into an ∗ P. 286.
" Affirmative, that the Defendant, having an Eſtate
" amounting in the whole to lefs Value than the Qualifi-
" cation by Law required, did exercife the office of a Juf-
" tice of the Peace ; or that the Defendant having neglect-
" ed to take and fubfcribe the oath of Qualification, hath
" acted as a Juſtice , or that his Qualification, if any, con-
" fifteth in Lands which he hath omitted to fpecify in the
" Oath prefcribed , or in the Notice directed in default
" thereof, to be given in Writing before the Trial Now
" thefe pofitive requifites, being Acts to be performed by
" the Defendant, it is for him to prove that he hath per-
" formed them."

In a Writ of Right, the Evidence muſt begin from the
Tenant, if the Mife § is thus joined —And the Defendant
putteth himfelf upon the great Aſſize of our Lord the King,
" and prayeth that Recognition be made, whether he hath
" the better Right of holding the Tenements with the
" Appurtenances to him and his Heirs as Tenant thereof
" as he holdeth, or whether the faid Plaintiff, of holding
" the faid Tenements with the Appurtenances as he above
" demandeth." fo that in this Cafe, the Defendant's Iſſue
" is in the Affirmative, and therefore, the Proof muſt begin
from him

† Actor quod adfeverat probare fe non poſſe profitendo, reum C IV 19 23
neceſſitate monſtrandi contrarium non adſtringit cum per rerum
naturam factum negantis probatio nulla fit

§ Et Def fe pon in magn Aſſiz Dom Reg. et petit Recog-
nitionem fieri utrum ipfe majus Jus habeat tenendi tenementa cum pertinentiis fibi et hæredibus fuis ut tenens inde, ficut
illa tenet, an præd. querens habendi eadem Tenementa cum per-
tinen' ut illa fuperius pet.

SECTION

SECTION III.

Loweſt Proof in a general Senſe, cæteris paribus

The fiſt and loweſt Proof, is the Oath of one Witneſs
only and there is that Sanction and Reverence due to an
P. 287. Oath, that the Teſtimony of one Witneſs * naturally obtain-
eth Credit, unleſs there be " ſtronger" appearance of probability to the contrary

Now that which ſets aſide his Credit, and overthrows his
Teſtimony, is the Incredibility of the Fact, and this Repugnance of his Evidence for if the Fact be contrary to all
manner of experience and obſervation, it is too much to receive it upon the Oath of one Witneſs; or if, what he ſays,
be contradictory, *that* † removes him from all Credit, for
Things totally oppoſite, cannot receive Belief from the Atteſtation of any Man " And of theſe Objections, the for-
" mer is *extrinſic* to the Teſtimony, the latter is *internal*
" Any ſuppoſed Fact, not plainly impoſſible, may be proved
" by ſuch force of teſtimony in the Number, Character,
" and Situation of the Witneſſes, as ſhall induce a manifeſt
" Improbability of their ſpeaking falſely · for difficulties
" external to the teſtimony are ſubdued and comparatively
" loſt, when the Teſtimony under all its circumſtances, is
Prıce's IV " entitled to Credit it then communicates its general Cre-
Diss 422—3. " dibility to whatever Queſtions of Fact it is offered, it
" being evidently inconſiſtent, that the antecedent improba-
" bability of the Event ſhould affect the Credit of actual
" Proof, that it has taken place It has no ſuch effect on
" the moſt improbable incidents, if a man's own Senſes and
" immediate Obſervation, aſſure him of the certainty of
" their having taken place; it has proportionably no effect
" on matter of Evidence, where the general Credibility of
" the Witneſſes is fully eſtabliſhed, and no intereſt or undue
" motive is reaſonably imputable to render them ſuſpected
" on the particular point

" The moſt unlikely and the moſt familiar occurrences
" are, as to their exiſtence or non-exiſtence, determinable
" by the ſame natural means of Obſervation, according to
" the Quality of the Fact to be aſcertained Either is
" therefore proveable, not according to the previous
" Grounds for expecting it, but to the reaſons for acqui-
" eſcing with juſt Cauſe in the Truth and Knowledge of
" the Witneſſes

ſ *Allegans contraria non eſt audiendus.*

" An

* P. 288.

* " An *essential* Repugnance, is an intrinsic Discredit to " Testimony, which destroys the credence which might " otherwise be given to any Witness on any Question, as " already hath been noticed "

SECTION IV

Two Witnesses.

The *Second* † Degree of Credibility, is from the Oaths of *two* several Witnesses· and is " considerably higher" than the " general" Credibility which arises from the Oath of one Witness only. For here, if they agree in every circumstance, there must be two perjured, or it must be true what these Witnesses allege " and" depose, but if, upon their Examinations, they " materially" disagree in circumstances, then they fail in their Credit, because their Contradictions cannot be true

T I T. II.

There are some Cases in the Law, where the full Evidence of *two* Witnesses is absolutely necessary

Par. 2.

Where necessary.

First, where the Trial is by Witnesses *only*· as in the Case of a Summons in a real Action· for a Man's affirming, is but equal to another Man's denying, and where there is no Jury to discern of the Credibility of Witnesses, there can be no Distinction made as to the Credit of their Evidence. for the Court doth not determine of the Credibility of one Man in preference to another, for that must be left to the Determination of the Neighbourhood. ‡ therefore, where a Summons is not proved by two Witnesses, " in the " instance stated," the Defendant may wage his Law of non Summons

* P 289.

* The *second* Case (" which before was mentioned") is in Chancery, and that is where there is but *one* Witness, contradicting the Answer, for there the Credibility is equal unless it appears from the Nature and Face of the Fact that the Answer is not to be believed· and the Course of the Court in such case is to direct a Trial at Law to ascertain the Credibility of that Witness by a Jury, which is the common

---

† *Proximus huic, longo sed fortior intervallo.*
‡ *Vicinus Facta Vicini præsumitur scire.*

standard

ftandard on which the Credit of an *Englifhman* is to ftand and fall on all Events

The *third* Cafe in which the Law requires *two* Witneffes, is *High Treafon*, and this not fo much from the natural Equity of the Rule, that every Man's Allegiance is fuppofed till the contrary is proved, and the Negative of the Prifoner is equal to the Affirmative of the Witnefs, and therefore the Treafon ought to be proved upon him by two Witneffes, for then the fame would be good in Cafes of Felony, where every Man's Honefty is prefumed till the contrary is proved, and yet there it is fufficient to prove the contrary by one Witnefs, but the Law hath appointed two Witneffes in this Cafe, becaufe a Court Faction might, in many Cafes, cut off their enemies without a fufficient Proof and now by the late Statute two Witneffes are required to every *overt* Act of Treafon

"The Words of the Act (one of the noblest Exertions "of humane Policy and legiflative Wifdom that our Code "can boaft,) are thefe That no Perfon fhall be INDICTED "(fo that Evidence before the Grand Jury is comprized "within the provifion of the Claufe) tried or attainted of "High Treafon whereby any Corruption of Blood fhall "be made, or of Mifprifion of fuch Treafon, but by and "upon the Oath and Teftimony of *two* lawful Witneff's, "either both of them to the fame *overt* Act, or one * of "them to one, and the other to another overt Act of the "fame Treafon unlefs the party indicted or arraigned fhall "willingly without Violence, in OPEN COURT, confefs the "fame, or fhall ftand mute, or refufe to plead, or in Cafes of "High Treafon, fhall peremptorily challenge above the "Number of thirty five of the Jury, any Law, Statute, or "Ufage to the contrary notwithftanding

"And that if two or more diftinct Treafons of diverfe "heads or *kinds* fhall be alledged in one Bill of Indictment, "one Witnefs produced to prove one, and another to prove "another of the faid Treafons, fhall not be deemed or taken "to be two Witneffes to the fame Treafon within the mean- "ing of this Act

"On the Conftruction of this Claufe it hath been held, "that to *collateral* Points *one* Witnefs fufficeth

"That a *Confeffion* before *Magiftrates* out of Court, "freely made and duly taken, may be given in *Evidence* "and if it goes to the *overt Act* directly, it muft be proved "by *two* Witneffes, and is then proper to be left to the "*Jury* as corroborative of other Evidence, though not as "conclufive, like a *Confeffion* in open Court, and a declara- "tion of the party concerning his fhare in a Fact *collateral* "to

Margin notes:

2 Hawk P C 256, 7, 8, 428 1 Raym 407 Kel 9

7 W III c 3 Anno 1695 § 2

Comm IV 357

⁑ P 290

Tef on H T ch III p 10, 242 Foft 241, 2

" to the Charge, it feemeth remains proveable by a *fingle*
" Witnefs

" *Petit* Treafon is alfo entitled to the Benefit of the fta- 1 E 8 c 12.
" tutes of *E* VI requiring two Witneffes And this was 5 E VI c II
" lately exemplified in the Cafe of a Woman indicted for
" this Crime committed againft an aged Lady to whom fhe
" was fervant There being but one Witnefs, fhe was ac- V Fofter, 107,
" quitted of the *Treafon*, and found guilty of Murder, and on P T
" though not otherwife laid in the Indictment than as in- Difc II Ch IX
" cluded in the charge of Petit Treafon   P 323—7, 8, 9.

* Two WITNESSES *required in* PERJURY, *and the Reafon.* * P 291.

" In Cafe of an Indictment of PERJURY, our Law re- Comm IV.
" quireth it to be proved by *two* Witneffes, as otherwife 358
" deeming it in equal balance, that one Witnefs fhould
" falfely affert this Charge as that another Man fhould have
" been guilty of this Crime, or, in other Words, that the
" Perjury of an Individual is as prefumeable to have been
" committed by the *Accufer*, on the depending Trial, as by
" the *accufed* on a former one. †

" As an univerfal Rule, the principle of the two ad-
" mirable Writers, to whom Philofophy and Humanity are
" fo much indebted, feems to fall juftly under the obferva-
" tion of the Author of the *Commentaries* on the Laws of
" *England* Doubtlefs one affirming and one denying is not IV Comm.
" a judicial Equilibrium in the univerfal Nature of fuch 357
" Cafes, ‡ the *negative* of the accufed amounting to little
" more than a demand that the Guilt charged againft him
" may not fubject him to Sentence and Punifhment till duly
" proved by fair Evidence When the Accufer has fup-
" ported his Charge, though but by one Witnefs, the fcale
" in general cafes certainly preponderates againft the accufed,
" though in STATE CRIMES, (from the peculiar hazard
" which would refult if the legal Circumfpection, and even
" Jealoufy, as to Evidence were not very ftrong) and on a
" Profecution for PERJURY, from the Nature of the Quef-
" tion, two Witneffes are required

                                                    Two

(†) Thofe Laws which condemn to Death on the depofition † Sp of L. 13
of a fingle Witnefs are fatal to Liberty In right reafon there c 3
fhould be two, becaufe a Witne s who affirms, and the accufed
who denies, make an equal balance, and a third muft incline
the Scale.

‡ *Più d'un teftimonio neceffario perche fin tanto che un afferifce,* ‡ Becc. ‡ 13
e l'altro nega, niente v'è di certo, e prevale il diritto che ciafcuno ha P 56.
d'effere creduto innocente.

                                                    On

*P. 292.

* " Thus the Cafe of *Petit Treafon* depends on pofitive
" Provifion, founded probably on the Heinoufnefs of the
" Offence, which was deemed to require more full Evi-
" dence the Wifdom and Benevolence of our ancient Law
" proceeding on a contrary principle to that fanguinary
" Maxim of the *Roman* Code, that the greateft Crimes de-
" mand only a flighter proof + In *Perjury* the Requifition
" of two Witneffes is founded in the peculiar Name of the
' Crime charged, and in *High Treafon* it is eftablifhed," no,
fo much on the natural Juftice of the Rule, that every

§ Theorie de
L ... ...
n. ... ...
17... Ch. III
S 8 pr 3 T
II. p 120, 1

On this point an eminent French Author expreffes himfelf
very ftrongly. He calls the reafon given by *Montefquieu* the Reafon of *Nature* he adds, that the Jurifconfults have affigned a
farther one derived from the knowledge of the human heart, its
paffion, its corruption, its fallibility, and the Guard againft thefe
by requiring the Evidence of two at leaft He fays, *Le Nombre
des temoins fuffifans pour faire condamner un homme eft fixé à deux
dans tous les gouvernemens C'eft la feule preuve qui ait un caractere
legale et qui porte l'empreinte de la certitude*

*Car me les crimes demeureroient impunis fi l'on introdurfoit dans le
tribunaux ce pyrrhonifme où jettent les erreurs de vos fens et les vices de
cœur humain, il faut s'en rapporter au temoignage defintereffe conftant,
et uniforme de deux temoins non fufpects depofant du même fait fur
tout lorfque le corps du delit eft conftate*

+ In atrociorious leviores conjecturas fufficere

+ Py 29 Car
II c. 9

*Though the Writ for burning an Heretic be abolifhed, ‡ yet the ob-
noxioufnefs to Perfecution for religious Opinions is very far from
being yet entirely removed. Some of the moft perplexed Points of
Theology, and on which contrary Judgments have been formed by
men of ackrowledged Talents, Learning, and general Piety, and even
the formulary of devotion of a particular Church, and the fenfe of
certain Propofitions, than which nothing of more fingular fabric ever
iffued from the human brain, all thefe have been eftablifhed by pains
and penalties as if Parliaments were either the infallible Judges
of myfterious Truth, or had the power by their mandate of creating
Truth. The Church, indeed in the height of its Afcendance in this
Country, punifhed Herefy as Treafon of an infinitely higher atro-
city, than any Offence againft the freedom and being of the Community, to which that denomination could politically be annexed Gra-
vius peccat qui divinam quam qui temporalem lædit Majeftatem,
was a Principle that never fhould have induced Men to arrogate the
Defence of the Honour of the Deity, by arms the moft unfuitable
DEORUM INJURIÆ DIIS CURÆ is a fafer and a jufter Principle.
It is for Omnifcience to judge, for Omnipotence to defend, and for infinite Goodnefs to promote the Reception of thofe Truths in which Human Society has an Intereft of a Nature wholly diftinct from its civil
Obligations The Eftablifhment which fprung from corrupt and fe-
rocer Chriftianity, when they made Herefy worfe than High Treafon, made Affent to their arbitrary Impofitions, a Duty paramount to
all others, and Fidelity to the Common Rights of Society, and to the
entire Obligations of Confcience, the worft of Crimes*

v 9 & 10 W
III c 32
1 Eliz c 1 & 2
13 & 14 Car
II c 4

1 Car II c 2
22 Car II c 1
1 W & M ft
1 c. 18
Com IV,
c 4

Man s

Man's Allegiance is suppofed till the contrary is proved, and the Negative of the Prifoner is equal to the Affirmative of one Witnefs, and therefore the Treafon ought to be proved upon him by two Witneffes, for then the fame would be good in Cafes of Felony, where every Man's Honefty is prefumed till the contrary is proved, and yet there it is fufficient to prove the contrary by one Witnefs, but the Law has appointed two Witneffes in this Cafe, becaufe, " as already intimated," a Court Faction might, in many Cafes, cut off their Enemies on fuch Articles without fufficient Proof

" When the ecclefiaftical Ufurpation on the Confciences
" and Lives of Individuals, and on the protective So- T Raym 408.
" vereignty of the State, affumed the Trial of *Herefy*, this H H P C
" one Barrier, feeble as it was, ftood againft their Cruelty," 410 N b
that two Witneffes were required; becaufe this was to be 17 Deut, c
ined by the Canon, and they followed the Rule of the *Mofaic*
Law, that required two Witneffes in every capital " Cafe "

Single Evidence of an ACCOMPLICE *infufficient to convict.* * P 293

" Sometimes the Evidence of a fingle Witnefs, though
" *admiffible*, fhall not be left to the Jury as *competent* to con-
" vict, if not fupported by other Teftimony.
" Thus there are Cafes of *Felony* in which an accomplice
" fhall, under pofitive Law, be received as *Evidence* The
" *Common Law*, indeed, (except in the Cafe, and under the
" particular circumftances of thofe whom it termed *Appro-*
" *vrs*), rejected fuch Teftimony and pronounced that, in
" fuch Cafes, that no Man fhould be heard againft the fafety
" and legal Eftimation of another, who, by the very Terms
" of his Evidence, *infamized* his own But the Statute Law v Rex
" admits Accomplices in certain inftances to bear Witnefs in v Bate Nifi
" fupport of the Charge yet fo admits them, that in mat- Pr 22 June
" ter of Felony, the Evidence of an Accomplice alone fhall 1780
" not go to the Jury for Deliberation on the Guilt or Inno- v 4 & 5 W &
" cence of the Prifoner but they will be regularly inform- 6 & 7 W III.
" ed by the Judge, that there is no Evidence againft the c 17
" Prifoner on which he can legally be convicted † c 23
" In profecution for *Mifdemeanour*, it is otherwife held 5 A c 31
" and it feems to be now received for Law, that in Cafes v ut fupra
" fhort of Felony, fuch Evidence muft be received, and may
" fingly be fufficient to Conviction 2 R Rep 81
" There is indeed one cafe, where a perfon who is both an Styl 207 283.
" Accomplice, and otherwife a party interefted, is admitted Cro Cir 341
" from Neceffity and for want of other proof and her Evi- 350 470
2 Bulft 341
348 350 355

† *Allegans turpitudinem fuam non eft audiendus*

" dence,

" dence, if confiftent, is not only *admiffible* but *conclufive.*
" And that is on the Statute of *Eliz* " where the Mother of a
Baftard Child is allowed Evidence to prove the reputed
Father · and this is for Neceffity, becaufe otherwife, fuch
fecret Lewdnefs would go totally unpunifhed : but then, if a
Woman charges two Perfons, fhe lofes her Credibility, but
if fhe keeps conftantly to the charge of one only, it is a fufficient proof, the Statute having fet afide the Common Law
in that particular.

* P. 294
2 Hawk P C
258 § 142.
Sir T' Jones
233 3 Keb 68
H. P C 261.
Bro Coro. 220.

* In Treafon for counterfeiting the Coin, one Witnefs only
is fufficient · becaufe this does not relate to State Criminals,
and there is no danger of oppreffion from a Court Faction

On the WEIGHING of EVIDENCE

We come now, " though generally and imperfectly," to
fet the feveral bounds of Credibility where there are con
trary Proof " but this Subject is fo unlimited, and branches
" into fuch an infinity of undefcribable particulars, that it
" feems to admit of little more than a mere Outline, and
" even this, it will be difficult to mark throughout with the
" due force and precifion the reft muft be left to Integrity,
" found Difcretion and Humanity, exerted on particular
" Cafes as they arife "

In contrary Proofs if Mens fwearing can be " reafonably
" and probably" reconciled, fuch Interpretation fhall be put
upon it as may make them agree becaufe every one fhould
be fuppofed, " fo far as a fair conftruction without prejudice
" to others will extend," to fwear the Truth, and no Man
fhall be intended to fwear a manifeft Perjury ; therefore
that Conftruction fhall be taken that would make them agree
rather than fuch whereby they muft neceffarily oppofe each
other

One affirmative Witnefs countervails the Proof of feveral
Negative becaufe the Affirmative may fwear true, and the
negative alfo : for the Negatives may commonly be, that they
know nothing of the matter ; the Affirmative fwears that it is
and fo the Affirmative may be true, and the Negative alfo
for the thing that the one fwears muft be true, though the
other know nothing of the Matter " and this is the true
" Idea of negative Evidence."

÷ P 295   * But where the Affirmative and Negative oppofe each other
in contradictory Propofitions, the Evidence is to be weighed
according to the Rules hereafter mentioned.
" Thus if a perfon be charged with a *Robbery* committed
" in *London,* to affert that he was at *Bath* the whole Day of
" which the Robbery is charged to have been committed

" and to the proof of which time the whole Evidence in fup-
" port of the Profecution is precifely applied, this is not fo
" properly negative Evidence, as an *affirmative* contradictory
" Propofition; but if two Witneffes, on the part of the Pro-
" fecution, fwear to the Stature, Voice, Complexion, Co-
" lour of the Horfe, and another fwears that he did not
" obferve fome of thefe particulars, this is negative Evidence,
" which may well confift with the affirmative, as of feveral
" perfons prefent, one might not hear or fee what was heard
" or feen by others.

" Yet in fome inftances, as the difcharge of a Piftol and
" feveral Cafes of no infrequent occurrence, the negative
" of a credible Witnefs, prefent on the fpot, and at the ve-
" ry time when the fact, if real, muft have happened,
" weighs much againft the Credit of affirmative Teftimony:
" fince thefe are Facts to which every Eye and Ear within the
" fame diftance muft be prefumed fenfible

" But affirmative contradictory Propofitions, according to
" their refpective force of Proof, deftroy each other · fo that
" even in the Cafe inftanced, though no Evidence, in gene-
" ral, is weaker or more fufpicious than that of which the
" tendency is to prove the *alibi,* it may, from the number,
" the character, the confirmatory circumftances of proof
" from the feveral Witneffes, in points that exclude the idea
" of preconcerted Agreement, be fo ftrong as to overbalance
" very clear, probable, full and refpected Teftimony on the
" contrary fide "

* If there be " feveral" Witneffes " *on each fide,*" and
 preponderating as to Number, they are to be weighed as
to their Credit

If a Witnefs be produced, and another be " called in Evi-
dence on the contrary fide, to impeach" his Credit, his
Credit is leffened in proportion to that of the oppofite
Witnefs

If a Witnefs be produced, and another be " offered" in
Deftruction of his Credit, and a third be produced to fupport
his Credit, the Credit of the firft Witnefs is to be fupported
in proportion to the Credit of the firft and third Witnefs to
the fecond

" The party who has called a Witnefs, fhall not call other
" Evidence merely to fupport his Credibility, till the other
" fide have gone into Evidence to impeach it "

The Credit of a Witnefs is to be judged from his State and
Dignity in the World for Men of eafy circumftances,
" and educated in principles of Honour," are fuppofed more
hardly induced to commit a manifeft Perjury. " but this is a
" Prefumption extrinfic and limited."

* P 296.

Dougl Contr
El III
163,—4

Theorie der
L. C 124.

Then

Their Credit is to be taken from their "religious and " moral" Principles : for Men atheiftical and loofe, are not of the fame Credit as Men of good Manners and clear Con verfation, " and hence, formerly, a very unwarrantable " turn was given to a circumftance in the Mode of giving " Teftimony in capital Profecutions"?

* P 297   * In Cafes of Treafon and Felony, no Witneffes were" fworn againft the King. " Of this Notice has been taken al- " ready," and the Reafon not " improbably was,", becaufe Men think it an Act of Piety to fave the Life of a Man, and tnerefore, may ftretch a little beyond their knowledge, and for that Reafon, " were" not admitted to hurt their Confci ences by fwearing Hard, therefore, " it was indeed," to make any ufe of this Rule of Law to depreciate the Affirma tion, as if of lefs Value than an Oath: for the party affirming, declares he was willing to take his Oath, and cannot be admit ted · fo tnat " if" Advantage, " under thefe circumftances," were taken of the Authority of an Oath, above that of a na Led Affirmation, " this" were to turn the Rules of Law into oppreffion and Injury Where there is only Judgment " in- " ferior to capital," there Witneffes " were" admitted againft th. King ' and if the preceding Solution be allowed of the " original Ground of the Rule, the Diftinction is exactly " fuch as would refult from it . it being obvious that" the Reafon of the Rule, " fo underftood," does not extend to fuch Cafes

Their Credit is to be taken from their perfect indifference to the point in Queftion · for we rather fuppofe that the fa vour and regard to a Relation, may draw a Man into Perjury, than that it fhould lie upon a Man wholly indifferent and unconcerned

If Witneffes are equal in Number and Credit " of Integri " ty, the" Difcernment, " whofe Teftimony fhall be pre- " ferred," arifes from their " general means of Information " their apparent sincerity, or their particular skill

* P. 298.   * " By general means of Information may be underftood " fuch powers of perceiving and diftinguifhing, as to com- " mon Facts, as the Generality of Mankind, without the " Aid of any particular Science, ufually poffefs by means of " their fenfes and ordinary underftanding

" And this, under equal circumftances of local fituation, " with refpect to the object to be afcertained, may be, for " the moft part, nearly equal in refpect of the Eftimation it " may deferve in judicial Inquiries

" In criminal Queftions efpecially, what is too obfcure " for common Difcernment does not prefs with fufficient " Certainty in almoft any inftance to authorize Conviction,
" and

" and can rarely even be fubfervient to the more favourable
" fide, that of Acquittal.

" And in civil Matters the Facts moft frequently to be
" proved by Witneffes are fimple and obvious to the fenfes,
" as Deeds, Bills, &c though the inference on the whole
" Matter may be very complex.

" By *apparent Sincerity* we mean, when nothing in the
" Courfe of his Evidence renders fufpected the Depofition
" of the Witnefs and Fidelity of his Teftimony.

" By *particular Skill* we mean fuch as profeffional men of
" character and experience are prefumed to exercife when
" they give a folemn Opinion and Atteftation of their
" Judgment on Facts properly within their efpecial Study
" and Practice. Of this the moft ufual is the Teftimony
" of Phyficians or Surgeons, concerning the health of a
" Party, the Caufe of a fufpected Death, the Nature of a
" Wound or other Injury, and the means and manner in
" which it may be juftly believed or decifively concluded to
" have been effected, or, on the contrary, the *negative*, on
" Caufes of fufpicion, from circumftances apparently ftrong.
" The ftate of mind, as to fanity, is fometimes neceffary to
" be afcertained by men of medical knowledge ; * as where * P 299.
" a Will is difputed on the Ground of fuppofed Want of
" fuch Soundnefs of Mind and Memory as the Law requires,
" or where a Crime is charged.

" On the fame Principles, Merchants, with regard to
" their particular Cuftoms, not contrary to the general
" Law, Tradefmen concerning the Quality of particular
" Goods, Ship-builders, and other Artifans, concerning the
" State and Conftruction of Veffels, and other their refpec-
" tive fubjects of mechanical fkill, are entitled to Attention
" by Virtue of the Rule,—any one, not under particular
" bias, or apparent incapacity. may juftly challenge belief in
" the Art which he profeffes †

" In refpect of *general means of Information*, this may be
" noticed, that he who has obferved accurately an incident
" of any apparent confequence, remembers ftrongly, and
" for the moft part can relate circumftantially, the moft
" particulars affociated in his mind with the occurrence,
" and which partake in degree of the force of the general
" Impreffion, and thus the Reality of the Knowledge of a
" Witnefs, as to a particular Fact, will appear" from the
Reafons and Accounts " he" gives of " his" Knowledge.
For if one gives more clear and evident figns of " unaf-
" fected recollection" than the other, he is rather to find

† Cuilibet in Arte fuâ fidem (in quantum liceat) adhiberi oportet.

credit, for the Memory of the other side seems more faded, and therefore they appear rash in taking upon them, at least they do not appear so distinguishing in their Observations as those who give the Marks and Signs of their Memory.

V Finiication
of Mary Q. of
Scotland p 134.
—7 3c Ed
Ecinb 17-2

* P. 300

"Yet a Detail excessively circumstantiated is highly suspicious, and most so when either the Event was of no apparent importance to the Witness, at the time of its happening, so as to interest attention in a degree * so extraordinary, or the Suddenness or Alarm which would naturally accompany it, precludes the probability of such exact attention or remembrance ‖

‖ On this Article it seems right to quote at large a striking and instructive passage

Un particulier attaqué a minuit dans un grand chemin, frappé d'un coup de fusil déclare en mourant qu'il croit que son assassin etoit un homme qu'il désigna, parce qu'il avoit cru reconnoitre la voix de cet homme qui lui avoit demandé qu'il etoit, pour mieux ajuster son coup sur cette declaration, le particulier est arreté une fille entendue comme temoin declare avoir reconnu la même voix sur cette deposition on condamne l'accusé a mort, & preliminairement a la question Il s'y presente avec fermeté Son juge, en le tutoyant, lui demande le nom a ses complices Il repond, qu'il n'en ait point, puisqu'il est innocent On le traine au supplice, sur l'echaffaud il proteste de nouveau de son innocence, & meurt avec tranquillité Croiroit on bien que ce rapporteur recencit en triom he de cette expedition se felicitoit d'avoir condamné ce malheureux a mort? Il intituloit preuve complete la re union de deux faits que n'avoient pas même la fausse apparence des In dices Car d'abord peut on regarder comme une preuve la declaration a un mourant Christianisé, au mil eu des ombres de la nuit, au sein de l'effroi qu devoit lui causer la question terrible qu'un inconnu lui faisoit avoit il assez maitre de ses organes pour reconnoître surement la voix de son serviteur? Son esprit n'etoit pas preoccupé contre celui qu'il soupçonnoit? Enfin l' assassin pour se mettre en sureté lui même, ne pourroit il contrefaire sa voix? En supposant que ces presomptions dussent être comptées pour quelque chose, ne devoient elles pas dans la balance ère emportées par la preuve morale qui presentoit la conduite ferme au l'accusé? Conduite qui avoit tous les caracteres de l'innocence Si cette preuve morale n'etoit pas suffisante pour le faire declarer innocent, au moins elle l'etoit pour faire ordonner un plus ample reinformé La plus part des juges qui avoient souscrit a cet arrêt se jugerent etoien de cet avis, après lui avoir vu soutenir la question sans effet Mais une fausse honte les empecha de revenir sur leur pas comme si l'on se deshonoroit en retractant une injustice causée par un erreur Ceux d'entre eux qui existent encore & qui me lisent, fremiront peut-être Mais si le mot glaçant du farouche Ma

To C
2 II 1-7, 8

homet, il est donc des remords, ne fait aucune impression sur eux, l'azile de la sureté, n'est plus qu'au sein des forêts & le juste baigné de l'Assassin doit moins effrayer que l'air riant d'un magistrat ignorant & presumptueux

" Upon

" Upon the fame principle, efpecially" where the Matter
they atteft was tranfacted long before " the Trial, a Variance
" in fmall immaterial circumftances, attefted by different
" Witneffes, will ftrengthen inftead of impairing the fub-
" ftantial Credit of their Teftimony ," for it may be fuppofed that the little circumftances of things might be forgot-
ten · and it feems more like a ftory laid and concerted before-
hand, if in every particular and minute circumftance they
had both agreed in Evidence

Indications of Infincerity

" " It has been remarked, that a Witnefs may reafonably v fupra, 224↓
" become difcredited by evident indications of fubtlety or
" of rancour   It will be the fame if the party inftituting
" a capital Profecution for an atrocious perfonal Injury,
" fhould give Evidence with Indifference or Levity, or
" fhould appear to have been late in making any com-
" plaint

* Of Proof by Experts * P. 301.

" The Proof from the Atteftation of Perfons on their
" profeffional Knowledge, we may properly, with the *French*
" Lawyers, call Proof by Experts
" In proportion as *Experience* and *Science* advances, the
" uncertainty and danger from this kind of proof diminifhes.
" Formerly, when the Mother of an *illegitimate* Child
" was indicted for the Murder of it, if the *Lungs,* being
" immerfed in Water, would float, it was held a proof on
" which *Surgeons* might juftify an opinion that the Child was
" born alive, the inflated lungs, in confequence of the Air
" which had been drawn into them having been rendered
" fpecifically lighter than the Water   But this prefumption
" is now held infufficient, for that the Air included in the
" *Veficles* of the Lungs from other caufes may be adequate
" to the production of this effect in the lungs of a ftill-born
' Child.
* " In general it may be taken that when Teftimonies of * P. 302.
" profeffional Men of juft Eftimation are *affirmative,* they
" may be fafely credited ; but when *negative,* they do not
" amount to a difproof of a charge otherwife eftablifhed by
" various, and independent circumftances.
" Thus, on the view of a body after death on fufpicion
" of *Poifon,* a Phyfician may fee caufe for not pofitively pro-
" nouncing that the party died by *Poifon*, yet if the party
" charged be interefted in the Death, if he appears to have
" made preparation of poifons without any probable juft

P 2 " motive,

" motive, and this fecretly; if it be in Evidence that he
" has in other inftances brought the life of the deceafed
" into hazard, if he has difcovered an expectation of the
" fatal Event; if that Event has taken place fuddenly, and
" without previous circumftances of ill health, if he has
" endeavoured to ftifle Enquiry, by precipitately burying
" the Body, and afterwards, on infpection, Signs agreeing
" with Poifon are obferved, though fuch as medical men
" will not pofitively affirm could not have been owing to
" any other Caufe the accumulative ftrength of circum-
" ftantial Evidence may be fuch as to warrant a Convic-
" tion; fince more cannot be required than that the charge
" fhould be rendered highly credible from a variety of de-
" tacred points of proof, and that fuppofing poifon to have
" been emplo.ed, ftronger demonftration could not reafon-
" ably have been expected to have been, under all the cir-
" cumftances, producible.

* P 303

*CHAPTER II

On PRESUMPTIONS.

Having fpoken of *living* and " of" *written* EVIDENCE
" of *d rect* Facts," we now come to PRESUMPTIONS
" A Prefumption," as it is defined by the *Civilians*, is an
" Inference refulting from a certain fign of a Fact which
" is taken to be proved on account of its connection with a
" Fact directly proved †

" For,"

† Conjectura ex certo figno proveniens quæ alio adducto pro ve-
ritate habetur.

We here make the promifed Extracts from the Roman Law
concerning TESTIMONY.

In TESTIMONIIS *dignitas, fides, mores, gravitas examinanda
eft, et ideo Teftes qui adverfus fidem fuam teftationis vacillant, audi-
end non funt*

*Teftium fides diligenter examinanda eft ideoque in perfona eorum
exploranda erunt in primis conditio cujufque, et an honeftæ et in
civitate vitæ, an vero notatus quis et reprehenfibilis an locuples
vel egens fit, an inimicus et adverfus quem teftimonium fert, vel
amicus e pro quo teftimonium dat, fi careat fufpicione teftimonium*

Ideoque Divus Hadrianus, Vivio Varo legato provinciæ Ci-
liciæ refcripfit . *Tu magis fcire potes quanta Fides habenda fit
Teftibu. . qu et cujus dignitatis et cujus æftimationis fint et qui fim-
pliciter vifi fint dicere utrum unam eundemque medi atum fermonem
ettuler.t, an ad ea quæ interrogaveras, ex tempore, veri fimilia
refponder nt.*

Ejufdem quoque Principis extat Refcriptum *de excutienda fide
Teftium in hæc verba, Quæ argumenta ad quem modum probandæ
cuique*

" For," when the Fact itself cannot be proved, that which comes nearest to the proof of the Fact is, the Proof of the circumstances that necessarily or usually attend such Facts; and these are called Presumptions, and not Proofs, for they stand instead of the Proofs of the Facts till the contrary be proved

These Presumptions are twofold

1 Of Law, " which are necessary, and absolutely con-" clusive·

" 2. Of Fact, which are,"

1 Violent;
2. " merely" probable.

" There is a third sort of *weak* and inconclusive Pre-" sumptions, which are only noticed in a cautionary * view by * P. 304.
" reason of their frequent occurrence," for these light and rash presumptions weigh nothing, and therefore cannot come under " judicial" Consideration.

Presumption *of* Law.

" Presumptions in Law arise either from general
" Principles, or from *positive* Institution.
" Thus that the Averments of a Record are true is an
" irrefragable Presumption, against which every other spe-
" cies of Evidence, being inferior and subordinate from this,
" must contend in vain : of this and of its reasons sufficient
" has been said already.

tuique rei sufficiant, nullo certo modo satis definiri potest. Sicut non semper, ita sæpe, sine publicis monumentis cujusque rei veritas deprehenditur alias, numerus Testium, alias dignitas et auctoritas, alias veluti consentiens fama confirmat rei de qua quæretur fidem. Hoc ergo solum tibi rescribere possum summatim, non utique ad unam probationis speciem cognitionem statim alligari debere sed ex sententia animi tui æstimare oportere quid aut credas aut parum probatum tibi opineris.

Alia est Auctoritas præsentium Testium; aliud Testimoniorum quæ recitari solebant

Lege Julia de vi cavetur ne in reum testimonium dicere liceat ei, qui se ab eo, parenteve ejus liberaverit quive impuberes erunt: quique judicio publico damnatus, qui eorum in integrum restitutus non erit. quive in vinculis custodiáve publicá erit quive ad bestias ut depugnaret se locaverit quæve palam quæstum faciat feceritve qui- Ibid 3. *ve, ob testimonium dicendum vel non dicendum pecuniam accepisse judicatus, vel convictus erit. Nam quidam propter reverentiam personarum, quidam propter lubricum consilii sui, quidam vero propter notam et infamiam vitæ suæ admittendi non sunt ad testimoniorum fidem*

" And

" And again, if a party have acknowledged fatisfaction"
under hand and feal, the Prefumption is fo " abfolute," that
the Law admits not Proof of " the Money not having been
" paid , becaufe that were to let a Man invalidate his deed,
" which our own Law doth not permit ," for here, though
the payment of the Money is not proved, yet the Acquittance is proved, " which the Law intendeth could not be
" thus acknowledged with the higheft private Act of legal

*P. 305

" folemnity, the Deed of * the party" could not be without
fuch payment, " or other juft equivalent.

Comm L. Ch
18 p 472,3

' Thus where a Franchife has been held and exercifed
" beyond time of *legal Memory*, a Charter or Grant from
" the Crown fhall be *prefumed*," and this Prefumption is
a neceffary inference from the immemorial exercife of the
Franchife.

Comm II
Ch. 3 p 29.
Ibid p. 28

" Thus a difcharge of Tythes may be by immemorial
" Ufage, which *prefumes a fatisfaction*
" And, on the other hand, on the fame Prefumption of a
" lawful Origin, the parfon of one parifh may *prefcribe* for
" Tythes in another And innumerable inftances of conclu-
" five Prefumption might be cited, refulting from *general*
" Principles of the *Common Law*.

Winchelfea
Cafes 4 Bur
Manf 1962

" Thus upon Analogy with other Limitations, and for
" public Peace and Security, TWENTY YEARS of undifturb-
" ed Poffeffion of *corporate* Franchifes has been eftablifhed
" as a *Bar* to applications for the aid of the *difcretionary*

9 An c. 20
Cowp 75 7

" power of the Court of *King's Bench*, under the *Statute*
" empowering that Court to grant Informations in the Na-
" ture of *Quo Warranto*

*P. 306.

* " *Fraud* is not prefumable where the Facts do not
" neceffarily infer it, but *Prefumptions* of this fort too
" there are.

" Thus vifible poffeffion and apparent ownerfhip, cover-
" ing a fecret Transfer to another, is a Badge of Fraud,
" againft which *Creditors* were protected even by the *Com-
" mon* Law
" The Statute of *Elizabeth* applies by pofitive Provifion
" a Remedy of which the Law had not been unmindful, by
" virtue of its general Principles And therefore," if a

Hamberton v
Howgill
Hob 72.

Man, enfeoffed by Covin, to avoid the " Claims" of Creditors, pleads that he was feifed at the time of the Judgment by
Virtue of a Feoffment, and the Creditor, that he was not
feifed at the time of the Judgment, nor at any time after,
on this Iffue the *Covin* may be given in *Evidence* ; for this is
indeed no feifin, by the plain Words of the Statute, to avoid
the Extent of Creditors; " otherwife, it might have been,
" if the Iffue had been taken, not on the *Seifin*, but on the
" Feoffment ;

" Feoffment, for then, it feemeth, the Covin muft have
" been efpecially pleaded "

If the Heir pleads *Riens per Defcent*, and, to fhew that
there was nothing defcended to him, gives in Evidence a
Feoffment, the Plaintiff may, in oppofition, " as in the pre-
" ceding inftance," give *Covin* in *Evidence*, for this is to
deftroy the effect of the Feoffment, which indeed hath no
effect to defend and cover the Heir from the Actions of his
Anceftor's Creditors by the Defign of the Statute, and the
Creditor in this cannot be put to plead it, becaufe he could
not forefee any fuch fecret Feoffment, or know whether the
Heir would infift on it, till it is offered in Evidence, and therefore that is the proper time to encounter it with the proof of
the *Covin*

* A voluntary Conveyance hath no Badge of Fraud, unlefs * P 307.
the Party were then in Debt, or in Treaty for a Sale of the
Lands, for a Man may have reafon to fettle for the Good
of his Wife and Children, and if he hath a clear Eftate,
and no intention to fell, the fettlement muft be taken to be
a good one, for that cannot lie under a fufpicion where there
is no Difcovery made of an intent to ufe that fettlement to
fraudulent purpofes at the time of making it.

" And by *Prefumption* of Law, founded on ufage, even
" Copyholds are held *entailable* And therefore," if Copies
of *Court Rolls* be fhewn to prove a *cuftomary* Eftate, the En- Styl 450.
joyment of fuch Eftate, " by general Ufage of the Manor,"
muft be proved, otherwife it is not good As if the Cuftom
was to be proved of *entailing* Copyholds, you muft not only
prove from the Rolls that there were fuch Entails, but alfo
an Enjoyment under them accordingly, for the Rolls only
fhew, that fuch an Eftate was limited, and that the *Entailing*
of *Copyholds* was endeavoured, but this does not prove an
Ufage, unlefs the parties continued in poffeffion unlimitabed
under it for the Words of Limitation to a Man and the
Heirs of his Body make a *Fee fimple conditional* at Common
Law, and therefore, from the Words of the Roll, without Proof of the Ufage, you cannot collect that there was
a *Cuftom* of *entailing*

" Thus far of *Prefumptions* of *Law*, which are uncontrou-
" able, next of Prefumptions of Fact

* Presumptions *of* Fact   * P 308.

" And, firft, of fuch as relate to *Civil* Cafes
" Thus an undifturbed Enjoyment of *corporate Franchifes*, 4 Burr Manif
" though under twenty years, *may*, according to circumftan- 1963.—5
       " ces,

" ces, weigh with the Difcretion of the Court not to grant
" an Information under the Statute of *Anne*

" Thus a Poffeffion of Duties for 350 years, though a
" fpace fhort of the time of *legal* Memory, was held a *Pre-*
" *fumption* to be left to the Jury of a Grant of fuch Duties
" originally by Record

" Thus though the Poffeffion of one *Tenant* in *common* is,
" *primâ facie*, in Law the Poffeffion of the other, yet *thir-*
" *ty-fix* years holding, without Evidence of payment or
" demand of Rent, was held to have been *rightly* left to the
" Jury, as Evidence on which they were at liberty to pre-
" fume an actual oufter; or, in other Words, that the
" Tenant had difclaimed to hold as in common, and had
" held, during that Period, by an adverfe Title, in which
" cafe the Perfon claiming under the other Tenant in com-
" mon would be barred by the *Statute of Limitations* "

" If there be an old " Feoffment," and Poffeffion has
" long continued" with the " Feoffment," it is a violent
Prefumption of a Right, though *Livery* be not actually
proved· for though the fact of livery be not proved, yet
the circumftances ufually attending fuch Facts are really
" proved;" that is, the " Feoffment" and the long confequent Poffeffion

* The Mayor
of Kingfton
upon Hull v
Horner, Tr
14G III.B R
1774.
Cowp 102, 11.
and v 12Co.5
there cit-d
Doe ex Dem
F & T v.
Proffer
Cowp 217-20.

❊ P. 309.   *❊ Prefumptions of Fact, civil and criminal, and their Degrees*

If a Man gives a *Receipt* for the laft Rent, the former
is prefumed to be paid, becaufe a Man is *prefumed* firft to
receive and take in the Debts of the longeft ftanding efpecially if the Receipt b in full of all Demands, then it is plain
there were no Debts ftanding out

" And if fuch Acquittance be under *feal*, then it becomes
" a Matter of *fp.cialty*, from which refulteth the full *Pre-*
' *fumption* of *Law*, in the manner before ftated "

23G III c 49
24G III c 7.
Scf 1 " But now by a Statute, neither very popular nor appa-
" rently very productive, a Receipt (except on fpecialty or
" upon commercial or public payment) fhall not be given in
' Evidence as an Acquittance for the fum therein expreffed,
" unlefs on *ftamp* of 2d if the fum be above 2l and 4d if
" above 20l A lefs unfavourable Act led the way, by im-
25 G III.
c 28 " pofing a Duty ❊ on Legacies or diftributive fhares of in-

* 2s 6d for Legacy or fhare under 20l.
    5s above 20 l and under 100l.
    Additional 20s at 100l
    Additional 20s at 300l
    Additional 20s at 600l
    Additional 20s at 1000l

" teftate

" *teftate* Property (which was foon after doubled by another
" Statute)   Legacies or Shares of Wife, Children, or
" Grandchildren, are excepted from the additional Duties." c 5**8**. 20 G III.

Every Prefumption is more or lefs violent according as
the circumftances fworn are more or lefs " ftrongly connect-
" ed" with the Fact to be proved

" A *violent* Prefumption is required in *capital* Cafes. and in
" *civil* ones, where it goes in deftruction of a Right; a lefs
" Prefumption is fufficient to *fupport* a Right *prima facie*
" apparent

" In an action of *Trefpafs*, for breaking open the Houfe   Eldridge v
" of the Plaintiff, and deftroying his Goods, the Defendants   Mic 15 G III.
" juftified as Bailiffs of the Lord of the Manor, and that   Cowp 214-16
" by virtue of fuch their Authority, * they diftrained for *Quit-*   * P. 310.
" *Rents*   The Evidence was of *Payment* regularly, till the
" year 1736; a *refufal* in 1738, fince which time there had
" been no farther demand (nor had any payment been made)
" till within thefe few years, from the year 1736 to time
" of the Action

" That in 1736 an Action was tried between the Lord
" and the Owner of the Tenement in Queftion, for cutting
" down two Timber Trees growing thereon   a Verdict was
" given for the Tenant, fince which Payments had been
" difcontinued

" The Statute hath limited fifty years as the Term of Pre-   32 Hen VIII.
" fcription for *cuftomary* Rents and Services   fo that this   c 2,
" being but thirty-fix years from the demand could not be a   Anno 1530.
" Bar   But it was contended that it amounted to a *Prefump-*   Eldridge v.
" *tion* to be left to the Jury, the learned Judge † had ac-   Knott
" cordingly fo left it. but, on a Motion for a new Trial,   Cowp 214.
" the Court was of opinion, that there were no circumftan-   Anno 1774.
" ces on which the Prefumption could be fo raifed as to leave   * Mr Baron
" it to the Jury, for that the precife time of the refufal   Eyre
" commencing was in Evidence, and the probable caufe of it,
" not by *releafe*, but by the fuccefs of the Tenant in the
" Action concerning the Timber againft the Lord whom the
" fmallnefs of the payment might well induce not to bring
" an Action, and for thefe reafons a new Trial was granted.

CRIMINAL

If a man be found fuddenly dead in a Room, and   Co Litt 6 b
another be found running out in hafte with a bloody fword,   S P C 179 a
this is a violent Prefumption that he is the Murderer   for the   Hawk 11 P C.
Blood, the Weapon, the hafty Flight, are all neceffary con-   Ch 12 § 12.
comitants to fuch horrid Facts, and the next Proof to the   45 §7 46 2.
fight of the Fact itfelf is the Proof of thofe circumftances   1 S Tr 181
that do " thus indicate" the Fact.   3 St Tr 930.

CHAP-

* P. 311.

*CHAPTER VI

Of PAROL EVIDENCE *to explain a* DEED.

" We have hitherto treated of *parol* EVIDENCE, and
" *written* feparately   There is a Cafe, however, not very
" frequent, but exceedingly important, which concerns the
" *Admiffion* of *parol* Evidence to explain a DEED.

2 R. Abr 676
, 11.

" Thus" where a Man has *two Manors* called *Da'e,* and
levies a *Fine* of the Manor of *Da'e,* Circumftances may be
given in Evidence to prove *which* Manor he intended . for
fince the Fine is uncertain by the Identity of the Name, it is
fit that it fhould be reduced to a Certainty by Proof, that
the Fine   may not lofe the Operation which the Parties
intended

Meafe, Execu-
tor, v Meafe.
Cowp 47 S C.
C L. 457~60

" But   where Action of DEBT was   brought upon a
" BOND payable at a certain Day, the Defendant pleaded,
" that by *Agreement* between Defendant and Teftator of
" the Plaintiff the Bond only ftood as an *Indemnity* To
" this Plea the Plaintiff demurred, and the Queftion was,
" whether the Agreement pleaded could be given in Evi-
" dence, contrary to the exprefs Tenor of the Bond, pur-
" porting to be abfolute, for payment on the Day

" The Plaintiff contended, that the Office of *parol* Evi-
" dence extended no farther than to explain a Deed confift-
" ently with its general purport, and by no means to vary

Y 1P W 113
and 2 P W 127

" and change the Nature of the *fpecial Obligation* ; and that
" even on a Will the *uncertainty* to be removed by
" Evidence muft arife from fomething extrinfic to the
" inftrument

Max. of Law
L. T p 99

" And that excellent Obfervation of LORD BACON was
" cited, where he thus exprefles the Rule —There be two
" forts of *Ambiguities* of Words   The one is * *Ambigui-*

* P 312.

" *patens,* and the other *latens* † PATENS is that which
" appears to be ambiguous on the Deed or Inftrument , *latens*
" is that which feemeth certain, and *without Ambiguity,* for
" any thing that appeareth on the Deed or Inftrument , but
" there is fome *collateral* matter out of the Deed that breed-
" eth the Ambiguity

" AMBIGUITAS PATENS is never holpen by Averment
" and the reafon is, becaufe the Law will not couple and

Reg 23 L. T
Ll u j 2

† *Ambiguitas Verborum latens verificatione fuppletur , nam quod
ex facto oritur ambiguum, verificatione facti tollitur*

Ambiguitas Verborum patens nullâ   unquam verificatione
ambit. &c

" m.03

" mingle Matter of *Specialty*, which is of higher Account,
" in Law: for that were to make all Deeds hollow, and
" subject to Averments, and so in effect that to pass with-
" out Deed, which the Law hath appointed shall not pass
" but by Deed.

" THE COURT were agreed that the Plea was bad, and
" the objection decisive against admitting collateral Evidence
" to change the Nature of the Deed. That if there had
" been Merits, and it had sufficiently appeared this was a
" proceeding contrary to Agreement, the Court would have
" done Justice between the Parties in another Way."

BOOK

＊ BOOK III.

On the SUBJECT MATTER *of* EVIDENCE, *and the* ISSUES *or* MODES *of* SUIT.

CHAPTER I.

" WE have hitherto confidered EVIDENCE in its Form
" as *written* or *unwritten*, and in its DEGREE as *certain* or
" *probable* It is now time to regard it with relation to its
" OBJECTS or SUBJECT MATTER, and thefe will natu-
" rally conduct us to the *Iffues* or *Modes* of *Suit* appropri-
" ated to each "

CHAPTER II

" And in contemplating this extenfive Subject, we have
" adopted the Divifion of the † ROMAN LAW, acording to
" which we fhall confider all CAUSES to which EVIDENCE
" can be applied as divided into CLASSES, as founded either
" in CONTRACT or in TORT; and thefe may again be di-
" vided into ORDERS, by which they will be diftributed into
" Queftions of

" 1. Exprefs } CONTRACT { 1 *Private* } WRONG.
" 2 Implied }　　　　　　 { 2 PUBLIC }

" And thefe *Orders* fall refpectively into a farther Subdi-
" vifion of SPECIES,

Exprefs Contract,　1　By *Specialty*,
　　　　　　　　　　2. Without *Specialty*.

Implied,　　　1　*General*,
　　　　　　　2　*Particular*

" Thus we are poffeffed of the two well-known and great
" Branches of JURISPRUDENCE
　　　　CAUSES　　1. Civil,
　　　　　　　　　2　Criminal

" Queftions of *Contract* and of *private Tort* belonging to
" the *Civil*; Queftions of PUBLIC WRONG, to the *Criminal*
" JURISDICTION "

Po er I 123 † Sunt Jura, funt Formulæ de omnibus rebus conftitutæ ne quis
aut in *Genere Injuriæ* aut in *Remedii Ratione* errare poffit
Or, *as the* Attic *Jurifts*,
　　　Δίκαι ἰδιωτικαί
　　KATHΓOPIAI ΔHMOTIKAI

CHAPTER

CHAPTER III.

" And as every Caufe, according as it is referred, either by its Nature, or the Option frequently of the party, to one or the other of thefe Divifions, hath * its correfpon- *P. 314. dent ISSUE or MODE of Suit, our next point of Attention is to the feveral FORMS of *proceeding*, and the EVIDENCE adapted to each. And here it is proper to premife what is meant by an ISSUE, which is, *a Point material to the Queftion in difpute, and alleged conformably to the Nature of the Caufe affirmed on one fide, and competently denied on the other* If it be a Point of *Fact*, it is fimply called an *Iffue*, if it be a Point of *Law*, the Facts are then admit- Comm III ted, and it becomes an *Iffue of Law*, or *Demurrer*." 313, & Ch 21, p 314, &c.

CHAPTER IV.

" Having already obferved, that *Caufes Civil* are founded either in *Contract* or in *Tort*, it remains to confider them arranged, firft, under the head of CONTRACT.

TIT I

" And this muft be either *exprefs* or *implied*
" To the firft belong chiefly .
   " 1. *Debt*,
   " 2 *Sale or Exchange*,
   " 3 *Bailment, fpecial*,
   " 4 *Hiring, fpecial*.

TIT II

Of DEBT.

' A *Debt* is any Contract whereby a certain fum of Mo- Bl A. of L. E. ney becomes due. And it may be either, 77.
   " 1. *Of Record*,
   " 2 *Of fpecial Contract, by Bond or other*
   " *Specialty*;
   " 3 *By fimple Contract, as Note or other*
   " *Writing not under Seal.*

Par 2

For what Debt will lie.

" Firft, it is to be confidered for what debt will lie. In L. N P P II general it will lie where Damages can be afcertained by Ch IV p 167 the Averment.

" Thus

" Thus for *Amercement* in a Court Leet *Debt* will lie;
" and in the *Evidence* requisite to support this Action, it
" will be to be proved that he was an *Inhabitant*, at the
" time of the Amercement, as well as at the time of the
" Offence.

* P. 315.

* " So if a Statute prohibit the doing of any thing under
" a certain Penalty, and do not limit the Remedy by di-

L. N. P P II
Ch. IV p 168

" recting to sue in another Form, Debt will lie; but if it
" prescribe a different Method of Recovery, that Method
" must be pursued

" If a Man enter into a single obligation for payment of
" Money by *Installments*, Debt will not lie till the last Day
" of Payment is completed; for this is a Remedy founded
" on *Entirety* of Contract; the Contract being one, the
" Debt is also one, and not several for the several sums pay-
" able by Installment. but otherwise where there is a Bond
" with a penal sum conditioned to pay Money at several

Cotes&Howel.
M.c. 18 G II.

" days: for there the *Condition is broken*, and the Bond be-
" come *absolute* on failure of payment on any of the Days
" and *Debt* therefore will lie before the last day of payment
" is past "

T I T III.

Of DEBT *by* RECORD.

" Of Debt by Record sufficient has been in general im-
" plied in the precedent Observations on the high Nature
" and uncontroulable Validity of Records   It may here
" however, be observed that if Debt be due by Lessee under
" Indenture, and the Landlord accept a Bond for the Rent
" this doth not deprive him of his Election to sue by Action
" of Debt for the Rent as due by the Indenture, for his
" taking a security of an equal Nature is no Extinguish-

L. N P. 182

" ment of his precedent Right. but a JUDGMENT obtain-
" ed on such Bond is an Extinguishment, for this is para-
" mount, and his Remedy is now determined to the Judg-
" ment "

T I T IV

Of DEBT *by* SPECIAL CONTRACT

" In *Debt* upon *Bond* the Defendant is not to plead
" *debet*, but *non est factum*

" And this leads us to what may be given in *Evidence*
" the Plea of *non est factum*."

T i

Tit V.

Non est Factum

What may be given in Evidence on this Plea

If a Man seals an *Obligation*, and commands another to keep it till certain Conditions are performed, and * the Bond is delivered to the Obligee before they are performed, this * could never be his Bond till those Conditions were performed, and therefore this special Matter may be given in Evidence to prove *Non est Factum*

If an Obligation is delivered to the Use of another, and he disagrees to it, by this the Obligation has no force, and therefore it is no Deed, and this may be given in Evidence upon *Non est Factum*

Upon Debt against two, and *Non est Factum* pleaded, it is proved the Deed of one, and not of the other the Issue is maintained for a joint Action charges each with the whole Deed, and when the Issue is found that it is the Deed of one, it amounts to the total Cause of Complaint alledged in the Declaration against that Person, and consequently the Plaintiff ought to recover against him, since he is proved to be his Debtor.

" But where there is a *joint* Bond, and this appears on the
" Face of the Declaration, and one only is sued, he may
" shew this Variance on *Non est Factum*, otherwise it is only
" to be pleaded in *Abatement* "

A Man was bound to *Randolph*, and the Plaintiff declares of an Obligation to *Ralph* upon *Non est Factum* pleaded, it cannot be found the Deed to *Randolph*, for *Randolph* and *Ralph* are different Christian Names, and cannot denote the same Persons, so it is of *Edward* and *Edmond*

" Otherwise if it be a mere Misspelling, as *Jacob*, where
" the Party spelt his Name *Jacaob*, for now it is not a
" different Name, but a different Mode of spelling the
" Name "

If a Man confesses the Obligation, and pleads an Acquittance, he cannot conclude *Non est Factum*, (" either generally or with an *Issint*, of which hereafter") but must alledge " the special Matter, and conclude to the Court with" Judgment, *si Actio*, for it is really his Deed, though it be avoided by a contrary Agreement, which must be exhibited in the Court to judge of, so that the Validity and Essence of a lawful " *Defeazance*" of the Contract may be seen by the Court, before the Truth of the Fact be called in question before the Jury.

The

*[margin notes: a R Abr 683. * P. 316. Sav 71 Salk 174 c Co 119 b. Cro Eliz 54 Dy 163, 167. 2 Leon 111 And 4. Bendl 75. Danv Abr. 514 pl 1 5 Co 119. Dy 110. 5 Burr Mansf 2611—15]*

* P. 317.   * The Plaintiff brings an Action againſt *W. S.* on *Non*
eſt Factum, the Jury find a ſpecial Verdict, that *W. S* entered into an Obligation with the Plaintiff, by the Name of
T S. This is found for the Defendant· becauſe the Jury
do not find it the Obligation of *W S.* for the Jury cannot
find any Fact contrary to the ſpecialty put in Iſſue, and by
the ſpecialty it appeareth to be the Deed of *T S*

Dy 279 pl. 9
Cro Ja 558,
640.
Ow 48
Moor 897.
Rolls Abr 872.

Perk. 15. pl.
38, 9

" Yet the Reaſon given by *Perkins* is very ſtrong, that
" if properly pleaded, the Plaintiff ſhall recover on theſe
" Facts ; for *W. S* ſhall be concluded by his own Act from
" ſaying that it is not his Deed."

16 H. VIII. 7.
Sid. 450

A Man declares of an Obligation made to himſelf, and
on *Non eſt Factum* pleaded, the Jury find an Obligation
made to another of the ſame Name , this warrants the Iſſue
for the only Queſtion in this Action is, whether the Deed
profered in the Declaration be the Deed of the Defendant,
for if it were his Deed, ſealed and delivered to another than
the Plaintiff in the Action, he ought to *confeſs* the Truth of
the Deed, and *avoid* it, by pleading the ſpecial Matter

Styl. 78.

The ſame Law, if they find the Obligation to the Plaintiff and another, and that he brought the Action " ſole,
" which he ought not but" as ſurvivor Here the defendant might " have" demanded *Oyer*, and demurred to it,
" by way of Plea in *Abatement* ; but" ſhall not " take ad-
" vantage of it on the Plea of *Non eſt Factum* "

But where a wrong party is ſued, that bears the Name of
the Obligor, he may plead *Non eſt Factum* ; for then it is not
any Deed of his.

Styl. 414.
2 Co 4.
Cro J 136

The Plaintiff declares of a Bond dated 4 *Apr.* 24 *Eliz*
upon *Non eſt Factum*, the Jury find a Bond dated 4 *Apr* 24
Eliz. and delivered 30 *Feb* 23 *Eliz* this is a finding of the
Deed declared , " for if a Deed be without Date, or with
" a falſe or impoſſible Date, ſo as without Fraud, the Deed
" is good "

* P 318.

* If a Man pleads that the Obligation was made to another, and not to the Plaintiff, this is ill , " becauſe while
it affects the Form of a ſpecial Plea," it amounts " in ſub-
" ſtance merely" to the general Iſſue of *Non eſt Factum*,
" and ought therefore to have been ſo pleaded "

Sid 450
2 Keb 333
Ventr

Par 2.

What Diſabilities *are pleadable upon* Non eſt Factum

5 H VII 58
2 Co 9
Plow. 66

Upon *Non eſt Factum*, you may give, *not lettered*, in Evidence ; for when the Perſon who delivered the Deed is un-
learned, and the Deed is read and expounded to him in another

other fenfe than that which the Deed really contains, then did not the party agree to the written deed, it is not the expreffion of his Mind, nor to be accounted his Deed.

If a Man was blind, and the Deed mifread to him, he may plead *Non eft Factum*, and fuch Evidence will maintain the Iffue, for then indeed it is none of his Contract **Styl 78.** **2 Co 9**

" But it has been held, that" a Man cannnot give *Dureffe* in Evidence upon *Non eft Factum*, for the only Point in Iffue, and the Controverfy on *Non eft Factum*, is whether the Deed be the Act of the Party, fo that when the Act is proved to be done, the whole Matter denied by the Defendant is proved to the Jury, but if there be any circumftances to deftroy that Act, and avoid its binding Force, that muft be fhewn to the Court, that the Court may judge, and not the Jury, whether they are fufficient to avoid that Deed **5 Co 119.** **Plow 66**

 INFANCY *to be pleaded fpecially*, COVERTURE *may be given* * P 319. *in Evidence*

" And" upon *Non eft Factum*, a Man fhall not give *Infancy* in Evidence but he muft plead it and conclude to the Court with an *Hoc paratus eft verificare*. for the Infant is in Law reputed to have a contracting Power for his own Benefit, and to bind all the perfonal Eftate which is his own and therefore, has power to avoid his Agreements or not, " as ' they are for his Benefit or Detriment, when he fhall come ' of Age, and be of legal Difcretion to elect " and therefore, this cannot be faid to be a void Agreement, and fo the Iffue is not proved by this Evidence, fince the Iffue denies any agreement at all And accordingly, " leave was given ' to withdraw a Plea of *Non eft Factum*, and plead *Infancy* " **5 Co 119** **Plow 668.** **Moor 43** **3 Keb 228.** *** Ld Raym.** **315**

But *Coverture* may be given in Evidence on *Non eft Factum* for the Wife has no Will of her own, but is fubject entirely to the power of the Hufband, and he is to make all Agreements which are to bind the perfonal Eftate of the Hufband; and therefore, at the time of the making, it is no Deed at all **Olding v Arundel, Bl 357, Hil 2 C**

" But where the Wife has a feparate Provifion, fhe may, " under circumftances, charge herfelf by Deed **Corbett v. Poelnitz M 26 G III**

" And where a perfon, apparently of Age, has repre- " fented himfelf as being *really* of Age, he fhall not after " avoid his own deliberate and reafonable Obligation (though " it be not ftrictly for Neceffaries), by pleading of his own " Fraud, and giving Evidence to prove himfelf an *Infant*. **T. R 5.**

* T ɪ ᴛ. VI

5 Co 11c.
Hob 166 ac-
cordingly re-
commends the
fp ffin N E F
3 Co 59.
A¹ 58

"For the moſt part," where an Act of Parliament declares a Bond to be void, as Sheriff's Bonds againſt the
Statute of 23 *H.* 6. and uſurious Bonds againſt the Statute
of 13 *Eliz* yet this matter cannot be given in *Evidence*
on *Non eſt Factum*, but muſt be ſpecially pleaded and
ſhewn to the Court to judge of, for where a Statute declares a ſolemn Act to be void, it is not to be conſtrued
ipſo Facto void, but to be voided upon Appearance to the
Court, to be within the circumſtances mentioned in the
Statute, for " where there is a ſpecialty before the Court,"
it were prepoſterous, that the Statute ſhould be referred to
the *Jury* who are not Judges of the Law, as affecting
" ſuch Specialty

1 H. VII 15
Moor 43

"Therefore," if the Deed be only *voidable* at " Com-
" mon Law," the general Rule is, that you muſt conclude
to the Court with Judgment *ſi Actio*, becauſe the Court
may judge, whether you have offered ſuch matter as will
amount to the avoiding of the Deed: " and generally,"
the Law is the ſame " reſpecting theſe ſpecialties," whether voidable at Common Law, or void by Act of Parliament

ı *Par* 2.

Iſſint Non eſt Factum

1 H VII. 15
5 Co 119

* P 321

Where the Controverſy relates to the ſigning, ſealing,
or Delivery, of the Deed by the Defendant, he pleads *Non
eſt Factum*, generally: but antiently where the Deed was
ſigned, ſealed, and delivered, yet was originally void by
matter *dehors*, as by reaſon of *Coverture*, * or becauſe the
party had no Right in the Thing transferred by the Deed,
or it became void afterwards by Raſure, Interlineation, or
Addition, there the Defendant muſt have pleaded the Matter ſpecially, and concluded *iſſint non eſt Factum*, and this
was, that the Plaintiff might be apprized " of" the Point
of Defence for ſince there are ſo many various Modes to
make the Deed null and void, if all of them might be given
in Evidence upon *Non eſt Factum* generally pleaded, they
thought the Plaintiff could never come prepared to falſify
the Evidence of the Defendant, and therefore that Notice
muſt be given of ſuch foreign Matters as theſe, if you would
have them given in *Evidence.*

Another,

Another Reafon why this fpecial Conclufion with an *Iffint non eft Factum* was anciently referred to the Court was this, becaufe it generally contains Matter of Law, which, if it had arifen on proof of the Fact, " would have been" to be referred back to the Court by *Demurrer* to Evidence or fpecial Verdict, and therefore it is very reafonable that the Doubt of Law fhould be offered to the Court originally

But at this day the Law is otherwife " and" if a Man pleads, *delivered as an Efcrow*, and concludes fpecially *iffint non eft Factum*, the general way is to put it to the Jury, becaufe it is in effect to fay there was no Deed at all, but they may put it to the Court by an *hoc paratus eft verificare*, becaufe the Court will judge whether he exhibited fuch Matter as will make the Deed of no effect at all; and therefore fuch pleading is not apprehended to be vitious

* But if you plead a Breaking of the Seal, rafing, or addition after Delivery, you may conclude *Iffint non eft Factum*, but the better pleading has been reckoned to conclude to the Court with Judgment *fi Actio*, becaufe the Deed is not fo apparently void, but that it " may be expedient" to put it to the Court, whether thofe are circumftances that would avoid it * P. 322. Noy, 112 Moor, 30 Dall 105.

" Yet" you may give it in Evidence on *Non eft Factum*, for it difproves the Deed " The *Iffint non eft Factum* " upon Rafures, &c is much difcountenanced, fo far " back as the time of HOLT, as being unneceffary and in- " convenient " 6 Mod 271, 8

If a Man pleads *Quod Factum prædictum* was made and delivered without Date, and that the Plaintiff added a Date, and *iffint Non eft Factum*, " this has been held" not good, for at the beginning of the Plea he confeffes it to be his Deed, and to be made and delivered by him, which at the latter end he denies, and fo it is repugnant " But he might " have pleaded *Non eft Factum* generally, and given this " in *Evidence*" Cro Eliz. 800

Debt againft G B Executor of T B on a Bond made by T B The Defendant pleads *Quod fcriptum prædictum non eft Factum fuum*, whereas he ought to have faid, *Non eft Factum T B* After a Verdict this was held to be good, becaufe (*his*) fhall be intended his that the Plaintiff declares on, and that was the Bond of the Teftator, fince the Jury by their Verdict have confirmed the Relation to that Bond in the Declaration Latch 125

÷ " The Principle is obvious upon which," on *Non eft Factum* pleaded, a Man may give the fpecial Matter in Evidence, as Rafure, Interlineation, or Addition: being no * P. 323. 11 Co. 16, 7. V fupra, 104.

Q 2 more

more than this, " that" it is not neceffary to plead any Matter or Thing fpecially but what is exhibited to the Court to
judge of, and fuch Plea concludes with an Averment *that you
are prepared to verify*, and it feems incongruous to make
that abfolutely neceffary to be fhewn to the Court which is
fhewn to them in vain, and that doth not come under their
Judgment now when " you" fhew that the Deed is void,
you fhew that it is none at all, which amounts to the *general
Iffue* of *Non eft Factum*, and therefore you conclude not to
the Court, but to the Country, and thus" it " appears"
that it cannot be neceffary to fet it out to the Court, fince
it is not offered for their Judgment and Determination ‡

" And fuch Alterations will fupport the Iffue of *Non eft
Factum, though made fubfequent to the Delivery of the
Deed, for by them it is not now the Deed of the Party,
" and the Iffue is in the prefent Tenfe. "

In Debt upon Obligation the Defendant pleads, that there
was a *Schedule* annexed to the Obligation, the which Schedule is difannexed, and *Iffint 'on eft Factum* this is not good,
for here he confeffes the Deed, and avoids it, by faying that
the *Appendices* to the Deed are altered; " but he might have
" made a good plea, and" concluded to the Court with Judgment *fi Actio*, + allowing the Deed, but declining the
Plaintiff's Action, by faying that the " Plaintiff" himfelf
altered the Appendices thereunto relating

But on *Non eft Factur*, if the Seal were broken off after
Plea pleaded, it is the Deed of the Party

If the Deed be enrolled, you fhall not plead *Non eft Factum*, for by the acknowledgment of the Party it appears to
be the Party's Deed for there is that Credit given to the
Tranfactions in a Court of Juftice that the Party fhall never
fay he did not acknowledge it, + fo that though this Deed
be no Record (that is, no Act of the Court in the Decifion of Right and Wrong) yet it is in Court, and fo far to
be credited, that the Party fhall never deny the *being*
of fuch a Deed, " though he may its" operation " by

Marginal notes:
LNP 171
V Cowp 590

*P 324

9 H VI 60

Moor, 4

---

(1) Of Remedy after Verdict againft Defects and Irregularities
of Pleading &c (Comm III c 25 and the Statutes there cited
—14 L III c 6 anno 1340 9 H V c 4 4 H VI c 3
8 H VI c 12 and 15 32 H VIII c 30 18 Eliz c 14 21
J I c 13 and 17 Car III c 8 (ftiled in 1 Ventr 100 an
omnipotent Act, perhaps the firft inftance of the Abufe of that facred Term by applying it to Parliaments) 4 and 5 A c 16 9 I
c 20 5 G I c 13 anno 1718

+ *Probatio eiu ia fepti m allegantis eft fortiffima
Contra Praefumptione s Legis non receptun Probatio*

" a Plea

" a Plea properly adapted, which will hereafter be no-
" ticed "

If the Defendant pleads *Non eſt Factum*, and further de- 35 H VI 9 b
murs to the Obligation, the Demurrer is void, becauſe no
Man is allowed a Plea, " which is thus at once douole and
" repugnant," to alledge the Fact to be falſe, and the
Charge contrary to Law, but he muſt take one Plea that
he thinks moſt advantageous. for if he ſhould be allowed
ſeveral ways of Defence, it would multiply Contention
infinitely, as we find by the Practice of the *Chancery*,
where they judge upon innumerable Circumſtances, and
never reduce the Weight of the whole Cauſe to one Iſſue

" And though now by Statute *double* Pleading is to a 4 A c 16 § 4.
" certain extent allowed, yet it ſhall not be ſuch Pleading as
" militates againſt all Form and Reaſon and the Leave of
" the Court (which is of courſe, if the Pleas are regulat)
" is made neceſſary, in order to reſtrain this indulgence
" within due Limits

* " On this Iſſue reſpecting an Obligation by Specialty, * P 325.
" there are Pleas hereafter to be mentioned, which ſhall not
" be joined with that of *Non eſt Factum*

' Thus *ſolvit poſt Diem*, for it admits the Deed, and is 2 Bl 905, 6.
" therefore contradictory. the ſame of *Non eſt Factum* with Ibid 993
" *ſolvit ad Diem* "

Par 3

Riens paſſa par le Fait.

" This is naturally the next Plea to be conſidered and 5 H VII 8
" it has been a Queſtion whether " ſuch Matter as would B 3
" ſupport the Iſſue of" *riens paſſa par le Fait* can be given in 2 R Abr 677.
Evidence upon *Non eſt Factum* for, on the ' one" ſide, it I 25
may be ſaid, that on *Non eſt Factum* the operation of the
Deed is not in Debate, but whether the party ſigned, ſealed,
and delivered the Contract alledged in the Declaration ſo
that if the eſſential part of that ſort of Contract, " which
' the Law preſumes, when an Inſtrument, verified by legal
" ſolemnit, is brought in Queſtion as to its Exiſtence," be
proved,—the Execution of the Inſtrument with the required Forms,—they take it to be a proof of the Iſſue,
" as otherwiſe the Defendant ſhould not have reſted the
" Iſſue on a point which conteſts the Exiſtence of the Deed,
" when his real Defence ſuppoſes its *Evidence*, and impeach-
" es its *Validity* "

Others have ſaid, that where a Deed is of no effect to paſs
any Right, it is utterly void, " and therefore properly *no*
" *Deed*," as if a Man accept a Leaſe of his own Land by
Deed

Deed Poll, and where a Contract is void, and of no effect, it is reputed no Contract

" But its being no Contract in point of legal availment
" does not prove that it is no Deed the force and operation
" of the instrument is one Question its mere existence ano-
" ther, and it may seem strange, if a Man should, on the
" Trial, find himself compelled to defend his Right of con-
" veying when the Nature of the Issue calls on him to prove
" the Deed

* P. 326.

* Solvit ad Diem

" In one instance, however, *riens passa par le fait* must
" be pleaded, and Evidence that would prove *Non est Factum*
" between parties is proper to be given in support of it and
" that is where the effect of the Deed comes in Question
" with regard to the interest of a stranger, for" a stranger
shall not plead a *general* or special *Non est Factum*, as that the
seal is severed from the Deed, and *issint non est Factum*, but
he ought to plead *riens passa par le Fait* " since" a man ought
to try the Validity of a Stranger's Deeds no farther than
they regard his own Interest, and therefore he cannot deny
the Being of such a Deed, but only the operation of it as to
himself

**P Fl 197.
Part 3**

"In general, *Non est Factum* is the Plea where there
" is an original Defect of necessary requisites to the Consti-
" tution of the Deed, *riens passa par le fait*, where there
" is an incapacity to convey or to receive, either generally,
" extrinsic to the Deed, or particularly, in relation to that
" Mode of Conveyance"

Tit. VII.

2 Solvit ad Diem.

The *second Issue* is that of *solvit ad Diem* " for *riens passa*
" *par le Fait* generally terminates in a *Demurrer* but this
" now to be considered puts a Fact in Issue, in like manner
" as the precedent *Non est Factum* does for the *Jury*" And
to explain this Issue, it is to be considered that when any
Contract is founded on a *specialty*, it cannot be dissolved but
by specialty · for every Contract must be dissolved by the
same solemnity and notoriety with which it was made, otherwise there is more Evidence to suppose the Continuance of
the Contract than the Dissolution Therefore on a single
Bill, you cannot plead a naked Payment, without a Discharge
in Writing, because there is a solemn Contract by which
you are charged, + and there cannot be any Discharge but

* P. 327.

by

by Matter of equal folemnity; but you may plead *Payment at the Day*, becaufe the Condition is contained in the very Contract itfelf, and upon that Matter of Fact the force of the Contract depends, and when you difcharge yourfelf by pleading the Act required in the Condition, then is the Contract diffolved by fomething arifing out of the Contract itfelf, which is the fame Thing as if it were diffolved by a Contract of equal folemnity

Where I am bound to pay a " fingle" fum of Money to Sid 41. two, " generally," a Payment to any of them is fufficient, becaufe a Man cannot pay the fame " fum" to two feveral Perfons

" But a fpecial Payment may be required, which will not " be fatisfied by paying to a fingle Perfon "

Par 2

Payment to an Agent

Condition to pay Ten Pounds to *A* Payment to his Deputy " may be given in Evidence "†

The Payment to the *Scrivener* who has the Bond is *prima* Lit Rep 54. *Facie* a good Payment; becaufe he appears entrufted to re- Hetl 46 ceive it, and therefore on fuch Evidence it is prefumed to ² Keb 249: have come to the Party's hands but if it be proved, on the other fide, that the *Scrivener* broke, fo that the Money was never paid to the Plaintiff, this is no Payment to the Plaintiff but where a Man gets Judgment, Payment to his Attorney is well enough, for he is not only entrufted, and put in the Place of the Creditor, to get Judgment, but to take the Effect of that Judgment, and fince the Attorney might take out Execution, he may take the Payment of the Money inftead of Execution, therefore the Debtor ought to be indemnified by the Law

* Debt on Bond to a Bifhop, the Defendant pleads he * P 328 paid the Money at the Day to *T S* Bailiff of the Plaintiff, and by his Command, and " farther tenders an " Averment," that this came to the ufe of the Bifhop: " this Averment makes the Plea *double* (' though it might " have been fo combined with the entire Plea as to be " only Surplufage)," for if the Bailiff receives this by Command from the Bifhop, (though it does not come to the Bifhop's Ufe, yet it is a fufficient Difcharge to the Defendant " and when he fays farther that he is ready to " aver that the Money came to the Ufe of the Bifhop, this " makes two *Iffues* for one Iffue arifes on the Command- " ment, and the other, whether it came to his Ufe. And

† *Nam qui agit per alium agit per fe.*

" the

" the *Defendant* was ordered to *amend* his Plea which he did
" by leaving out the Averment that the Money came to the
" Bishop's Use †

" If Money be paid to an Agent for the Use of his Prin-
" cipal, the Consequence of this, under particular circum-
" stances, belongs more properly, to the Title AsۍۍMPSIT "

Mor 27
Cro Eliz 122
Dr 222 contra
S. 612
Caſ Temp
La Hardw 154

The Condition was to pay Money at a certain Day and
Place, and Payment was made *before* the Day, and an Acquittance given in Evidence, this was adjudged not to maintain the Issue, because the precise Day is parcel of the
Issue · but it is there said, they ought to plead the Payment
" specially, and the Acceptance of the Plaintiff   " But
" the Authorities on the Margin consider this Plea as good
" without the special Matter being more particularly aver-
" red, for that payment *before* the Day is payment *at the*
" *Day* "‡

* P 329   * SOLVIT AD DIEM, *where good, without shewing an Acquit-*
tance

Cro Eliz 884
9 H VII 41.
Deõ & S'uo
D 1 c 12
V supra, 16—
7

Debt on an obligation of *two hundred* Pounds Defendant
pleaded, that after the Day of the Writ purchased, *viz*
such a Day, *and, &c* he paid to the Plaintiff *sixty Pounds*
Parcel thereof, which he received —Judgment *de Brevi, &c*

† *Probably, the Plea on which he tendered the Averment was,*
que les deus bener a les maines de mesme l'Evesque; though the
Book has al œps   The former Edition has a Q ery (I imagine
added by the Editor) whether this were worse than surplusage
‡ But now by statute 4 *A c* 16 § 12 where an Action of
Debt s brought upon ary Bond which hath a Condition or Defeazance to make void the same upon Payment of a less sum at
a Day and Place certain, if the Obligor, his Heirs, Executors,
or Administrators have, before the Action brought, paid to the
Obligee, his Executors or Administrators, the principal and In
terest due by the Defeazance or Condition of such Bond, though
such payment was not made strictly according to the Con
dition or Defeazance, it shall and may nevertheless be pleaded in
Bar of such Actions, and shall be as effectual a Bar thereof as if
the Money had been paid at the Day and Place, according to the
Condition or Defeazance, and had been so pleaded

Note to the
former Edition

To this we may add, that where Payment is not made on the Day,
whereby the Bond is become absolute, and the Penalty incurred gene
rally, the Penalty is regarded in Law and Equity as the Form of
the security, yet in some Cases the Penalty is substance; as in bene-

C L 255, 6

ficial Leases for charitable purposes, where forfeitures go in aid of the
Poor, as in Mr Wilson's Donation to lend Money to young Trades-
men at one per Cent for the first Year, and two for the second, with
special Condition·

Upon

Upon fpecial Demurrer, adjudged for the Plaintiff: becaufe the Defendant did not fhew any Acquittance or Releafe proving this Payment, which if he had done, the Writ
would have abated for the whole but fince he did not produce any Deed of Acquittance, his Plea fhall be no more
than a naked Averment, which can never overthrow any
Obligation which is of an higher Nature, and confequently
cannot abate the Writ which is founded on it

" But this is to be underftood with the Qualification now Dy 52.
" fubjoined," in Debt on a fingle Bond, Payment without Moor, 12.
Acquittance is no Plea · for the Bond being a Contract with
folemnity cannot be avoided by a bare Averment, which is
inferior in its Nature to it otherwife in Debt on an Obligation *with Condition* for there, by the Nature of the Contract, and the *exprefs* Agreement of the Parties, Performance of the Condition is to be a full Difcharge of the Bond;
fo that if the Performance be pleaded and proved, it is a
full Bar

* In Debt on an Obligation of Ten Pounds, the Defen- * P. 330.
dant pleads that one *H* was jointly bound with him, to 5 Co. 117 b.
whom the Plaintiff had made an Acquittance, bearing Date
before the Bond, but delivered after it, in which he acknowledged the Payment of Twenty Shillings in full fatisfaction of the Ten Pounds, and adjudged a good Bar, for
if a Man acknowledges himfelf fatisfied by Deed, it is good
againft him, though he have received nothing, fince he fhall
not be allowed to contradict what appears under his Hand
and Seal

Condition to pay Seventy Pounds, viz Thirty-five Pounds Cro Eliz
at one Day, and Thirty five Pounds at another Day, at the 2 Danv.
Temple Church The Defendant pleads Payment of the Se- Abr 250
venty Pounds at *Ludlow*, and held good, *fecundum formam et* pl 14.
effectum reddendo fingula fingulis, as if he had pleaded Payment of the feveral Sums at the feveral Days

Debt upon a Bond · the Cafe was, that the Defendant did 22 E IV 25 2.
owe to the Plaintiff a certain Sum of Money by Bord, and Bro. Condition
certain Money for Wares fold , and *at the Day of Payment of* pl 181
the Bond he tendered the Money according to the Bond,
which the Plaintiff accepted, and faid it fhould be for the
Book Debt, and not for the Bond Debt , but the Defendant
faid he paid it on his bond, and no otherwife the Plaintiff
croffed his Book, and brought Debt on the Bond · and adjudged againft him, for the Defendant is to appoint the
Manner of Payment

* In Debt on a Bond of *two hundred* Pounds, conditioned * P 331.
to pay one hundred and *five* Pounds, the Defendant pleads Cro Ja 585.
Payment of the aforefaid fum of *one hundred* Pounds at the Danv Abr
                                                              Day 353 pl. 2.

Day: the Plaintiff replies, that he did not pay the said one hundred and five Pounds, and this he prayeth " may be en-" quired by the Country, and it was found for the Plain-tiff, and Judgment given for him, which was afterwards reversed, because the Plaintiff and Defendant do not join in a Point, and therefore there is no Issue or Verdict upon it

Cro Ja 549
3 Roll. R 135
Palm 74.

But where the Defendant pleads to Debt on Bond, Pay-ment of fifty Pounds on the 14th of *June*, &c and the Plaintiff replies, that he did not pay the fifty Pounds the SAID 14th of *August*, which at the Day aforesaid he ought to have paid him, and *Verdict* found that he did not pay it the 14th of *June*, yet it is no Error, for the Defendant's Plea was according to the Condition; and the Plaintiff's Replication, that he did not pay the said 14th, was good, for the Word *August* was superfluous, and the said 14th Day, without more, had been sufficient: but in the former Case there was another sum in the Plea of the Defendant than was in the Condition, and another sum in the Replication than was in the Bar; so that there could be no Issue

On Debt on an Obligation the Defendant pleads, that he paid at the Day, and *on this he puts himself " on the Country "* and the Plaintiff in like manner · and in *Error* it was insisted, that the Defendant ought to have concluded his Bar with, *and this he is ready to verify*, and then the Plaintiff ought to have replied, that he did not pay, and this he prays may be enquired by the " Country," so there had been an Affir

∗ P 332
Cro Car 316
Danv nb 354
p¹ 1
2 S·d 215
Keb 759, 76ζ
T Raym 58

mative ∗ and a Negative. but rejected. for there is an Issue, " for both parties join in putting the Question of " Payment to the Jury," and the Error is only the For-mality of joining it, so that it is aided by the Statute of *Jeofails.*

TIT. VIII

Where the Specialty, if any, is not the Ground of the Action,—

NIL DEBET

Cro Ja 227
253
b en·l 105
p ²lr 1
3 ır 16·
2 L o··al 220

If a Man makes a Lease for years, either by *Parol* or by *Indenture*, NIL DEBET is the GENERAL ISSUE· but in Debt upon an Obligation NON EST FACTUM, as is shewn, is the general Issue and the Reason of the Difference is this in case of a *Bond*, the Debt arises *on the Specialty* and therefore the consequence is, that you cannot disown " the " Debt' in the Issue, for then you would fall into this Ab furdty, that you would deny the Debt, and yet not deny the

the Deed which owns the Debt: now you cannot deny the Deed, which confesses the Debt under your Hand and Seal, without denying it to be your own Deed, which Issue is *Non est Factum*, and without disowning the Deed, you cannot disown the Debt, which arises on the Deed only.

But in Case of a Lease by Deed for Years, the Demand arises, not only on the Deed, but on the *taking of the Profits* in pursuance of that Contract, for there is no Debt until the Day of Payment, and this does not depend upon the Act of the Lessee only, as in the former Case the Debt depended upon the mere Act and Acknowledgment of the Obligor, but also on the Act of the Lessor in quitting the Premises: so that the denying " of" the Contract, by plead-ing *Non* * *est Factum*, could not be the general Issue, because not commensurate with the Declaration; for it might be the Deed of the Lessee, and yet no Debt might arise to the Lessor, because it is not the Deed alone that is required to make a Debt in this Case · now since an Act *en Pais*, as well as the Deed, goes to the creating " of" this Debt, by taking away the Act *en Pais* you destroy the Debt, and therefore shewing any Act that infers Impossibility of the Lessee's taking the Profits is good Discharge of the Debt.   * P 333.

But though this Obligation is not merely founded on the Contract, but on the taking of the Profits also, yet, in some Cases, I may charge my Lessee, though he never take the Profits, and this is where I charge the Lessee on his Con-tract, and as a " legally presumed" Taker of the Profits of my Estate and Freehold · and he cannot discharge himself from such a demand but by shewing his own Act or Laches in Excuse, which the Rules of Law will never allow as a good Excuse, and then in such a Case he is Pernor of the Profits *de Jure*, though not *de Facto*, so the Law looks upon him as my Tenant, and as taking the Profits of my Estate, because he cannot sufficiently excuse himself when I charge him with it.

Therefore, if I make a Lease, and quit the Possession, though the Lessee never enters, I may charge him in Debt for Rent. so if he enters and assigns the premises to another " And the modern Authorities are, since the privity of " Contract continues, that *Executor* or *Administrator* shall " answer for Rent, if *they* assign "   Rol Abr 605, pl 5
2 Sid 240
2 Ventr 209
3 Mod 325
Co Litt 54
5 Co 77, a, b

* But if my Lessee enters and assigns the Premises, I can * P 334 never charge him with *Waste* committed after Assignment · for though the Law Books own him as my Tenant *de Jure* in his own Contract, which by his own Act cannot be dis-solved, yet this is only to answer my Rent, which by his Contract he had undertaken to levy and pay me out of the
Profits;

Profits; but this suppofition of Law fhall not make him anfwer for the *wrongful* Acts of another, to whom he had a
legal power to affign it, and when the Penalty of the words
of the Statute is laid upon the very Tenant, for the fuppofition of the Law is framed to do every Body Right, but
not to do any Body an Injury

The Leffee for Years was anciently reckoned in the Nature of a Receiver or Bailiff of the Freehold, and therefore
upon any fuch Contracts he was chargeable as a Debtor to
the Freeholder, upon taking the Profits of the Eftate, that
in the eye of the Law do belong to the Perfon whom the
Law makes Tenant of the Freehold   Now nobody can be
fuppofed to continue another in the Poffeffion of the Eftate,
and to difcharge him on the Receipt of the laft Rent, if he
had not received what was formerly due, no more than a
Man would ftate accounts with his fteward, and difcharge
him on the Accounts of the Year before he had received

Co. Litt. 373
Dr 71 b
3 Co 55
2 Sid 44

what was precedent: the very continuing in the fame ftate,
and a Man's behaving fo well as to account for the Money
due this Year, is a Prefumption that he had done the fame
Thing formerly, or elfe a Man would not now have fuffered
it " and the Tenant being thus confidered in a view analo-
' gous to that of a Bailiff, a *prima facie* Prefumption at-
" taches, and" the laft Receipt is good " and ftrong" Evidence, " ftronger than would refult but for that Relation,

* P. 335

" * and conclufive until rebutted by contrary Proof." but if
this Acquittance be under Hand and Seal, then, " as hath
" been fhewn," it may be pleaded, and it is fuch *Evidence*
as nothing can be proved to the contrary · for this is Evi
dence by *Specialty*, and any Deceit or Miftake in former
Payments is but Matter *en Pais*, and therefore not of as high
a Nature as the Deed, and in giving *Evidence*, every thing

Mod. 118

muft be contradicted by a Matter of the fame Notoriety as
that whereby it is proved.

Eviction

Mod. 36, 118
Vin 358
2 Sid
Lev 97

Eviction, Expulfion, and any fufpenfion of Rent, is good
Evidence upon *Nil Debet*, for that amounts to difcharge and
fatisfy the " Caufe" of Complaint for then, " by the
' Fault of the Leffor," there was no Pernancy of the
Profits whereby I could become Debtor to him in the Reverfion and fo the Act *en Pais* is difcharged, which goes
of Neceffity to the creating of this Debt, " and this being
' a Matter *en Pais* may be given in Evidence to the Jury,"
yet others have held it ought to be pleaded.

If a ſtranger eviƈt the *Leſſee* of part of the I and, the whole Rent muſt be apportioned for though part be taken away, ſtill alſo ſome part remains, " and therefore" there is Part of the Conſideration Money remaining due to the Leſſor, for otherwiſe the Aƈt of the Law in the ſtranger's Recovery would do wrong to the Leſſor

" But" if the Leſſor enter into part, the whole Rent is ſuſpended, for the Leſſor cannot apportion it by a wrong-ful Aƈt of his own, for if the Party himſelf by his own Wrong doth hinder himſelf from the Benefit of his own en-t.e Contraƈt, the Jury ought not to divide it in his favour; " and" poſſibly the Leſſee would not have contraƈted for one part without the other

† " But where the Nature of the Diſturbance does not ✱ P 336 " conſiſt in an abſolute and total diſpoſſeſſion, as if the Hunt v Cope. " Party plead that the Leſſor pulled down a Summer Houſe, Hil 15 G III " whereby he was deprived of the Uſe of it, this may Cowp. 242 " amount to a *Treſpaſs* merely, which will not operate a " ſuſpenſion of Rent, and therefore on ſuch Plea the party " ſhall not recover on a *replevin* for Goods diſtrained for " *Rent* for *non conſtat* by the Plea that the Leſſor had done " any thing which would diſcharge the Rent but the *Leſſee* " might have pleaded that by this pulling down he was ex-" pelled and eviƈted from the Premiſes, and then the Faƈts " might have juſtified Verdiƈt in his favour on the Iſſue of " EVICTION

" And upon this Reaſon the Judgment in IRELAND for " the *Leſſee* was REVERSED "

— Ne unques ſeizi

In *Debt* for Rent upon a Leaſe, and NIL DEBET pleaded, 2 R Aor 677 *unques ſeiſi de la Terre* may be given in Evidence for if Pl 21 the *Leſſor* doth keep poſſeſſion againſt the *Leſſee* that he cannot enter, in as much as this Aƈtion ariſes not on the Contraƈt only, but on the *Pernancy* of the Profits, in pur-ſuance of the Contraƈt, there is no Rent due, and conſe-quently this is an Evidence that there is no Debt at all, and therefore proves the Iſſue

But if the *Leſſor* waives the Poſſeſſion, though the Leſſee R Abr 605 never " actually" enters, yet an Aƈtion of Debt lies for Rent, for the *Leſſee* did not enter and take the Profits, but ſince he might have entered and have taken them, he cannot make his own Fault and Laches any Part of the De-fence

But on the Plea of *Riens arrere*, or, *levie* " par" Di-ſtreſs, *ne unques ſeiſi de la Terre* is no good Evidence, for when

* P 337. * when a Man infifts that there is nothing behind of the Rent, or that it is already levied by Diftrefs, it fuppofes that he has already the Poffeffion of that for which he has already paid the Rent, or for which the Rent is already levied

Hil Aff. 1700. Debt for Rent on a Leafe. the Evidence to prove the Leafe was that the Plaintiff leafed the Houfe to the Defendant at a Rent, but no time mentioned, and it was agreed at the fame time that the Leffee was not to leave it without half a year's warning· for when the Rent is payable half early. and the Leffor permits him to continue any part of the half year, it is an Indication of his Will that he fhould continue the whole half year; and the like Law as to a Quarter's Notice, "1^{ſt}" the Rent payable quarterly. " But of *prefumed* Leafes from Year to Year, the Princi- " ples upon which they reft, and the Extent in which they " are applicable, mention has been made already, where " it appears that at this day the Notice to a Tenant who has " no certain fpecified Leafe muft be half a year, terminating " in fuch manner as to *complete* the annual period from the " *Commencement* of his Leafe There is only to be added, " as a point of Decifion, though indeed a neceffary and " obvious Corollary from the preceding Doctrine, that the

Butcher Wright " Tenant before a Mortgage or Grant of a Reverfion is **M c. 27 G III** " entitled to the fame Notice from the Mortgagee or **379—81** " Grantee "

Cro Eliz 222 Upon NIL DEBET pleaded, it was doubtful whether a **12 H VIII 6** Defendant might give in Evidence that his Leffor was bound by Covenant to *repair* the Houfes, and that he expended the Rent in *neceffary* Reparations: two Judges againft one held that this was a good Difcharge of the Tenant, becaufe it is very convenient that the Law fhould look upon this as a Payment, and not put the Leffee to fue his Covenant, for the Houfes might tumble down before the Tenant could have the effect of his fuit but the Judges differed in this, whether the Reparation ought to be pleaded or might be

* P 358 given in Evidence though the latter feems plainly to be the beft Opinion, becaufe, as it is a Difcharge, it amounts to Payment, and then it is very good Evidence on *Nil debet* for if the Rent be paid, it is no Debt, alfo, if it muft be plea led, it is the Plea of a collateral Agreement in fatisfaction of the Debt, and then no fuch Agreement can be proved for, though there was an Agreement that the Leffor fhould *repair*, yet there was no Agreement that the Leffee fhould expend his Rent on fuch *Reparations*

" And thus" on *Nil debet* the *Retainer* of the fame fum by *verbal* Agreement " for Reparations" was given in Evi- dence

dence, and allowed to be good; for this amounts to a Payment and when the Leafe is by Deed, it cannot be *pleaded* without Deed "and" fince fuch Expence in Reparation, "if pleaded," muft be pleaded as a Counter Agreement "in fatisfaction of the Debt, if the Leafe be by Deed, they muft plead this Counter-Agreement by Deed. otherwife, *ri folvitur eo Ligamine quo ligatur* laftly, the Plea amounts to the *general Iſſue* "and therefore by the Rule already "expreſſed, can be neither neceſſary nor regular." ^{Gouldſ 8o R Abr 6o5}

But it may be objected, that fince two Debts of equal Value in two feveral Perfons are no fatisfaction to each other, "on the general Principles of the Common Law," without Agreement, which muft be pleaded, why fhould there be any *Recouper* or Balance of Demands in this Cafe ?

It is true that two Debts of equal Value, "unconnected with the fame Tranfaction," are no fatisfaction to each other and the Reafon is, becaufe nothing can come in Proof but the Truth of the Matter alleged. "And the Common "Law held," that when one Debt is alleged in the Declaration, you "fhould" not encounter it with the Proof of another, to which no Man can come prepared for if one Debt were to balance another, in this Manner, all the Tranfactions during the * Parties whole Lives "might" k run over in every fingle Action, which would make fuits perfectly infinite but it is not unreafonable to balance Demands arifing on the fame Contract and in the fame Action. for the Law, to avoid Circuity of Action, confiders the whole Matter of the fame Demand, and doth not take it a part to break it into feveral Actions, for that is contrary to the Office of a Judge, which is to determine, and not to multiply Controverfies and therefore, if a Diffeizor difburfes Money in Repairs to have a Rent Charge iffuing out of the Land, it fhall be recovered in Damage. for the Law balances the Damage in View of the whole Matter, and not on a partial Confideration of the Damage merely belonging to the Diffeizin · for that would create another Action and fo in this Cafe the Law confiders the Money expended in Repairs as paid to the Leſſor * P. 339.

Upon NIL DEBET, Payment, "as hath been before no-"ticed," is good Evidence to difcharge the Debt. for the Iffue is in the prefent Tenfe, whether there be a Debt or not at the inftant when the Iffue was taken, and there is no Debt where it is paid.

Releafe

Releafe under Hand and Seal muſt be pleaded

But on *Nil debet* a *Releafe* cannot be given in *Evidence* for though a Debt, when it is releaſed is no more than when it is paid, yet when it is diſcharged by Releaſe under Hand and Seal, it muſt be pleaded and ſhewn to the Court, that it may appear to the Court to be diſcharged with thoſe apt Words and Solemnities which the Law requires to make a legal Contract; for *verbal* Contracts in ſuch Caſes are not ſufficient " in the Way of Plea," becauſe they are *nuda Pacta,* which create no Obligation

*P 340

Shetelworth v Neville, T R. Mic 27 G III 454—7

" And analogous to this, on *Debt* upon *Bond* againſt the " *Heir* of the *Obligor,* the *Heir* pleaded that he expended " Money in repair of the Premiſes liable, *over and beyond* " the Amount of the Rents and Profits: and on *Demurrer* " this was ruled a *bad* Plea.

Set off

Par 2.

V Rayn.Read 24—36

" By Statute 2 G II c 22 § 13 made perpetual by 8 " G II c 24 § 4 mutual Debts may be ſet off one againſt " the other, and pleaded or given in Evidence, upon No- " tice

" And by the latter Statute (which indeed ſeems to have " been the true intent and operation of the preceding one, " only that Doubts and Diverſity of Sentiment on this head " were deemed to require the legiſlative Interpoſition) Debts " of different Degree, as by *ſimple Contract* and by *Specialty,* " may be *ſet off* one againſt the other

" But not ſo Debts in *different* Rights, for theſe are not " *mutual* Debts

V Rayn. ut ſupra, and Collins and Collins 32 & 33 G II 2 Burr Manſ &c, 6

" This excellent Bill was introduced by Lord Chancellor " TALBOT and by it the Circuity and Expence of reſort- " ing to a Court of Equity in ſuch inſtances is ſaved, and " ſet off, where duly pleaded within the Statute, made equi- " valent to Payment

Corp 56

" But in Coverant *unliquidated* Damages cannot be pleaded " by way of ſet off

Trouۥes v Wihr, T R 457 It 27 G III

" And where the Plaintiff had been diſcharged out of " Execution on Judgment at Suit of the Defendant, on " giving ſecurity which was afterwards ſet aſide for Infor- " mality, and the Defendant pleaded the Value originally " ſecured by this Judgment as a *ſet off* the Court held that " this Plea could not be ſupported for the Judgment was " gone by the ſecurity taken, though the Defendant, who " accepted

" accepted that fecurity as fatisfaction, had neglected to
" make it effectually fo, by omitting an effential requifite
" in the Form "

* Where a Matter may be intended different ways on the * P. 341.
Allegation, fo as to make or not make a Right in the Plaintiff, fuch Allegation is not good, but if it is " open to"
Evidence to fettle the Doubt, there the Matter fhall be intended for the Plaintiff, if found for him` as if in *Debt*
for *Rent*, the Plaintiff fets forth that *A* was poffeffed of
Lands for ninety-nine Years, who demifed the premifes to
the Plaintiff for 2½ years; and then *A* granted the Reverfion to the Plaintiff, and fo for Rent Arrear he brought his
Action Now, if upon the Allegation " the Plaintiff hath
not fet forth fo much as to fhew an" efficacious Grant, yet
if the Defendant pleads *Nil debet*, and it be found for the
Plaintiff, there what was before doubtful on the Words of
the Declaration, " is now" afcertained for if there was
no effectual Grant proved, there could be no Debt to the
Plaintiff, an effectual Grant muft be fuppofed to be proved,
otherwife there could be no Debt and fo the " Grant"
muft be fuppofed " an" effectual Grant, for the Jury muft
not be intended to give a falfe Verdict, and fuch Conftruction can never be made of the Allegation, as cannot be made
without falfifying the Verdict

Tit IX

Of Debt *merely on* simple Contract

" Hitherto we have treated of Debt as arifing either
" from public Matter of Specialty, as by *Record*; or
" expreffly grounded on *private Specialty*, as by *Bond*, or
" connected with Matter *en Pais* originating in Specialty, as
" for Rent accruing from the actual or legal *Pernancy* of
" *Profits*, under a Demife by Indenture We are now to
" confider briefly of Debt as merely refting in simple Con-
" tract And here the Action is nearly difufed firft, be- Comm III
' caufe the Plaintiff muft recover the entire fum laid in his ch 9 P 154
" Declaration, or nothing, and, *fecondly*, becaufe when
" this Action is founded on fimple Contract, the Defendant
" * may *wage* his Law and clear himfelf of the Demand * P. 342.
" upon Oath, of which more remains to be faid in advert-
" ing to extraordinary Modes of Trial

" If brought againft an *Executor* for the Debt of the Tef-
" tator, it fhall be brought in the *Detinet* only

" It can properly be brought for Money only: for the
" suit of or Recovery of Goods and Chattels belongs to
" the kindred Action of DETINUE

Comm II
c 3' p 511

" And here it may be proper to notice, that among Debts
" by *simple Contract* the priority in the marshalling o *Assets*
" has been allowed to *servants wages* by respectable autho-
" rity.

SECTION V.

Of SALE or EXCHANGE.

" Of Sale, with respect to *personal* property, in which
" view alone we are now led to consider it, there are these
" chief particulars to be observed.

Par 2

Definition

Comm II. 30
5 446

" SALE is a transmutation of property from one man to
" another, in consideration of some price or recompence in
" Value If it be a commutation of goods for goods, it
" is more properly an *exchange* but if it be a transfer-
" ring of *goods* for *money*, it is called a *sale*

Par. 3.

Observations

" The Progress from the simple and natural to this
" latter artificial Mode of Traffic has been already con-
" sidered

" But with regard to the *Law* of *Sales* and of *Exchange*,
" there is no difference: they are to be treated therefore
" under the single denomination of *Sale* And it is to be
" observed what *Evidence* will in general establish or affect a
" Sale: *first*, where the VENDER *hath*, and secondly, where
" he *hath not* the property in him: referring farther parti-
" culars to the Action of *Trover*.

TIT. II.

1 *Where the Vender* hath *the Property.*

* P 543

* " Where the Vender hath in himself the property of
" the Goods sold, he hath the liberty of disposing them to
" whomsoever he pleases, at any time and in any manner,
" unless *Judgment* has been obtained against him for a *Debt*
" or

" or *Damages*, and the Writ of *Execution* actually delivered
" to the Sheriff for then by the Statute of *Frauds*, the Sale 29 Car II c 3.
" shall be regarded fraudulent, and the property of the
" Goods shall be bound to answer the Debt from the time of
" delivering the Writ

 " Indeed at *Common Law* it was bound from the *teste*, or 8 Rep 171.
" issuing of the Writ, and any subsequent Sale was fraudu- 1 Mod 188
" lent but now in favour of *Purchasers*, the Law is thus
" far altered, though it still remains between the *parties* ·
" and therefore, if a Defendant dies after the awarding,
" and before the delivery of the Writ, his goods are bound
" in the hands of the Executor

 " Nor is a Bill of *Sale* valid against Creditors, if the 3 Co 81 *
" ostensible property continue untransferred Twyne's Case.
                Comb 33
 " It is no sale without *payment*, unless the contrary is 7 Mod 95
" agreed of which *delivery*, on the part of the *seller*, is 13 Mod 5
" *conclusive* Evidence against the *Buyer*, and so is *Tender* of Mace v Cadell
" payment at the price agreed, against the *Seller* Cowp. 232, 3.

 " EARNEST accepted, if but a *Penny*, and delivery, if
" but a Part of the Goods, is payment or delivery to *bind*,
" the bargain

 " And by the Statute already cited, no contract for the
" sale of Goods to the Value of 10*l* or more, shall be
" * valid, unless the buyer actually *receives* part of the * P 344.
" Goods sold by way of *earnest* on his part, or unless he
" gives part of the Price to the Vender, by way of *Earnest*
' to bind the bargain, or unless some Note in Writing be V supra, 146
" made and signed by the party or his Agent

 " And with regard to goods under the Value of 10*l* no
" Contract or Agreement for the sale of them shall be valid,
" unless the goods are to be delivered within one year, or
" unless the Contract be in writing.

 " By sale the property is so vested, that if the Thing sold Noy 42
" perish, the Loss is the Buyer's after Earnest paid and
" he must make good the full price, though it never come
" to his hands

 " But though the Contract is complete by payment of
" *Earnest*, the *Vendee* cannot take away the Goods without Hob 41
" paying the full Price,. otherwise than by permission of the
" Owner

T I T   III.

Of Property transferred where not in the Vender

 " In general, *Sales* in MARKET *overt* bind the Right on Comm II 449
" account of the Notoriety of the Contract

         " In

Wood, B II
Ca. 2. p 211. " In LONDON every Day, except *Sunday*, is a Marke⸗
" *overt*, and the sales in *shops* there for valuable considera-
" tion are good

" But this Rule is held not to bind the King so as to di-
" vest property from him · and reciprocally, if goods are
" stolen and seized by the Officer of the Crown, and by
L T 158 " him sold in Market *overt*, the Owner, using due Dili-
" gence, shall recover them, for if he sue the Felon to
" conviction upon the same Felony, he shall have a Writ of
" Restitution

* P 345   ** Par 2.*

Pawnbrokers.

" And in a particular *Trade,* from the peculiar Danger of
" *Fraud,* and the oppressions it would produce, the proper-
" ty is not immediately changed by sale
1 J I c. 21 " By the Statute of *James,* the sale of goods wrongfully
" taken to a *Pawnbroker* in *London,* or within two Miles, is
" not to alter the Property
30G II c 24.
§ 5—13
24C III c 42
27 G III § 8 " This Trade was regulated in the Reign of the late
" King; and in the *present* two Statutes have passed con-
" cerning it

" Power is given, by the last of these Statutes, to a *Jus-*
§ 12 " *tice* of the *Peace,* on the Oath or Affirmation of one Wit-
" ness, to restore to the *Owner* goods unlawfully pledged,
" and pawned Goods are deemed forfeited at the expiration
§ 13 " of the year, which Term is extended to three Months be-
" yond the year, on *Notice* from the Owner in writing

Par 3

HORSES

-P & M c 7
31 Eliz c 12 " Another Exception is deduced from the Nature of the
" Property, for, with regard to *Horses,* no property is
" gained, although sold in Market *overt,* unless exposed to
" sale in an open place for such sales, between ten in the
" forenoon and sunset, and unless brought by the Vender
" and Vendee to the toll-gatherer or book-keeper, the toll
" paid, (if any) and the Horse, with price, colour, marks,
7 P 3-6 " and name, addition and abode of the Vender and
" Vendee entered in a Book for that purpose, nor even
" then is the property lost, if within six Months, the
" Owner puts in his Claim before some Mayor or Justice
" of the District, and within forty days after proves it by
                                                              " the

" the oath of two Witneffes before fuch Mayor or Juftice,
" and tenders the Price *bona fide* paid in fuch Market

Of BAILMENT *fpecial*, fee hereafter under the general
Title, BAILMENT

HIRING *fpecial*, which is a fpecies of Bailment, fee under
the fame Head

CHAPTER II

" We now come to Actions founded on Contract, exprefs
' or implied, with uncertain Damages and here every
" Thing of chief Importance will naturally fall under the
" comprehenfive Title of *Affumpfit*

ASSUMPSIT

" The Action of ASSUMPSIT is founded on *Contract*,
" either *exprefs* or implied, and it is either *general* or *fpecial*
" The general *Indebitatus affumpfit* bears a near Affinity to L N P B II,
" the Action of Debt It differs, however, in being de- Ch 2 p 128.
" tached from *fpecial*, and limited to *fimple Contracts*, and in —56
" the eftimability of the Value of the Demand, which is
" liable to be apportioned according to the Proof which the
" Plaintiff eftablifhes
" It will lie for thefe general Caufes.
      " 1 Money lent,
      " 2 Money laid out and expended to the Ufe of
      " the Defendant,
      " * 3 Money had and received to the Plaintiff's * P. 347.
      " Ufe,
      " 4 Goods fold and delivered,
      " 5 A fum certain on Work and Labour,
      " 6 On Account ftated,
      " 7 A *Quantum meruit* for Labour,
      " 8. A *Quantum valebant* for Goods

TIT II.

1 ASSUMPSIT *for Money lent*

" An *indebitatus affumpfit* will lie for Fines on Admiffion Douglas, 695.]
' to *Copyholds, Tolls*, and Profits of an Office 3 Burr 1717.
" Upon an *Affumpfit* againft in Executor or Adminiftrator, T R 619
" the Plaintiff muft prove his Debt, though the Defendant
' have pleaded *plene adminiftravit*, for by that Plea, though
' a Debt be admitted, yet the *Quantum* is not, and it differs
" therefore from an Action of Debt, in which the Plea of
" *plene adminiftravit* is an Admiffion of the Debt

                                          " *Affumpfit*

" *Affumpfit* will not lie on a promife by Defendant to pay
" Debt and Cofts on a Judgment, for this would be con-
" verting a *fpecialty* into a *fimple Contract* Debt

" *Affumpfit* will lie for Money lent to play with, as al-
" ready fhewn at large, for this action goes on the Con-
" TRACT.

Stevenfon v. Hardie.
2 BL 872—4.
H 13 G III.
C B I T

" *Affumpfit* will lie for *Loan* to the Wife at the *requeft*
" of the Hufband; for it is in *reality* a Loan to the Huf-
" band

* P 348.

*1 Burr Manff.
376*

* " *Affumpfit*, as we have feen before, will *not* lie on a *pro-*
" *miffory Note* or *Bill of Exchange* · but it will lie for the
" *Debt*, and the Note may be given in Evidence · but now
" the *Revenue* Laws have varioufly interpofed refpecting this
" fpecies of commercial tranfaction

15 G III c.51

" And, firft, under the Idea of preventing troublefome
" and prejudicial circulation of Bills for fmall Value, no
" *promiffory* Notes, or *Inland* Bills of Exchange, were to
" be negotiated or transferred for a fum under *twenty* fhil-
" lings

23 G III c.49.

§ 2

§ 4

§ 5

§ 6.

" And Bills of Exchange and promiffory Notes for lefs
" than 50*l* are fubjected to a Stamp Duty of *Sixp-nce*, if
" more than 50*l* to a Stamp Duty of *one* fhilling with an
" Exemption in favour of Bills drawn payable on Demand,
" on a Banker living within ten Miles of the Perfon draw
" ing, and of Bills in *Scotland* not exceeding *twenty-one* fhil-
" lings. Bills under 10*l* payable on Demand to pay only
" *three pence*

*Moulfdale v. Brennll
2 Bl.R.820—1*

" In the *Exchequer Chamber*, on Error from the *King's*
" Bench, it was held that *Affumpfit* will lie for not paying
" the Confideration of the Affignment of an uncertain
" Debt; and the Judgment of *B R* was accordingly af-
" firmed

*1 Cowp 437
43—5
Mart s a v
Hind*

" The Rector of a Parifh gives the Plaintiff a *Title* to
" the Bifhop by appointing him Curate with *Salary*, and
" promifing to continue him till he fhall be provided of fome
" ecclefiaftical preferment

* P 349

* " The Plaintiff brought *affumpfit* for the Salary on this
" Title, The defendant objected that the title is not to the
" Curate, but as an *Indemnity* to the Bifhop and that the
" Plaintiff was appointed Reader of *extra* prayers in the faid
" Church with Salary

" The Court was of opinion, that it was a *contract to the*
" *Plaintiff* from which, as a Matter of Fact, made known
" to the Bifhop, he derives, indeed, an affurance of Indem-
" nity but this refufing merely from the undertaking in
" favor of the Plaintiff, cannot be ftated as an objection to
" his action upon this Title.

" The

" The Court farther held, the *Readerſhip* was not an *ec-*
" *cleſiaſtical preferment*

" On *Aſſumpſit*, the Plaintiff declared that his Wiſe's
" Father, being ſeized of certain Lands, ſince deſcended
" to the Defendant, and about to cut 1000*l* worth of Tim-
" ber from the ſaid Lands, the Defendant promiſed to the
" Father that in conſideration, that he would forbear to fell
" the Timber, he would pay the ſaid Daughter 1000*l*

" After Verdict, it was moved in Arreſt of Judgment,
" that the Father ought to have brought this Action, (and
" it may be obſerved, this ſeems to be impoſſible, for till
" after the Father's Death, without felling the Timber,
" the Conſideration could not * accrue); for the Huſband
" was not party to the *meritorious* Conſideration   The Court
" was of opinion, the Conſideration was ſuch as well to
" maintain the Action brought by the Huſband. and Judg-
" ment was accordingly for the Plaintiff

Dutton v Poole, Mic 29. & Mic 30 Car II 1 Ventr 318 & 332 L.N.P. 133, 4

* P 350.

Tit. III

2 *Money laid out and expended*

" We now come to that ſpecies of *implied* ASSUMPSIT,
" which ariſes from *Money laid out and expended to the Uſe of*
" *the Defendant*

" There is little occaſion to inſtance in the ordinary Caſes
" of frequent occurrence, and which will eaſily be per-
" ceived to fall under this Action   it will be more adviſable
" to advert to a few leſs obvious, or illuſtrative of Prin-
" ciples

" On an Action for Money *paid, laid out, and expended to*
' *the Uſe of the Defendants*, the Caſe was this

" The Pariſh of *St Vedaſt* and *St Michael le Quern*, be-
" came united Pariſhes by Act of Parliament after the Fire
" of *London*, and ſince that time one ſet of Officers had
" ſerved in the two Pariſhes, the Election of whom had
" been always made in a joint Veſtry   In the year 1759,
" the ſexton's *ſalary* was ſettled at 20*l per Annum*, which
" was paid *jointly* by both Pariſhes

" The overſeers of *St Vedaſt*, had paid the Sexton laſt
" choſen the entire ſum   and brought this Action to recover
' a Moiety

* " The Defence of the Pariſh of St *Michael le Quern*
" was, that the laſt Election was not a joint one   that they
" claimed a Right of chooſing a ſeparate Sexton   and had
' given Notice to St *Vedaſt*.

Comm III. 162

Mouldſale, v. Birchall

T P 21, M. 26 G III.

* P 351.

" The

" The Court determined, that be the Merits of the Elec-
" tion as they might, *this* Action would not lie For that
" Money laid out and expended, could not be thus charged
" on a party against express Notice to the contrary

L N P. 147 " But it will lie on Money laid out and expended in per-
" formance of an Act which I was under *moral Obligation*
" to perform ; if another person does it without my re-
" quest, and I *after* promise to pay But of this more here-
" after, when we speak of the *Assumpsit* for work and la-
" bour done

Harris v.
Hunchback " On Action of *Assumpsit*, the second count was for Mo-
1 Burr. Manf " ney *laid out and expended* A note was given in *Evidence*
373 " in these Words :—This is to certify, that it is my request
" that you pay to Mr. *D* on account of Master *H* (an *In-*
" *fant*, Grandson of the Defendant), for the Workmens
" use, the Sum of 15*l* as Witness my hand *S H*—Held
" that the Note supports the Declaration

Tit IV

3 Money had *and* received

" We now come to the most *equitable* and extensive of
" this Species of Action every one of which is founded
" in *Equity*, and directed by the Rules of *substantial Jus-*
" *tice*

* P 552.   * " Let us, first, therefore, see against *whom* an Action
" for *money had and received* will not lie

Par 2

Against whom it will not lie

L N P 155. " It will *not* lie against a *Receiver* or *Collector* to recover
Sapl. field v
Ewa. " an *over-payment* , for where a Man receives Money for
Tr 27 G II " another, under Pretence of Right, and *pays it over*, the
Sadler v Evans
Tr 6 G III " Law will not suffer the Right of the Principal, while he
Whit cad v. " retains any Colour of Right, to be tried in this Action
Bro banks. " against the *Receiver* ; whether such Receiver be a public
Cowp 6?
Cam, neil v " or a private Agent . otherwise if the Receiver have had
Hall " *Notice* not to pay over, and yet pays it over, notwith-
Cowp 205
L N P 153 " standing
Co p 566, " But it will lie for Money paid in pursuance of an evi-
568 " dently void Authority
L N P tt un
1 R m 42 " *A* took cu Administration to *B* and appointed *J S*
L N P 153 " his Attorney, who received Money, and *paid* it to the *Ad-*
Sib " *mul frater* afterwards a Will appearing the Executor
M c 2 A.
Jacob v Allen " brought an *indebitatus assumpsit* against the Attorney , and
" it

" it was holden by *Trevor*, Chief Juſtice, at *Guildhall*, that
" the Authority being void it was a Receipt of ſo much
" Money for the Uſe of the Plaintiff on an implied Con-
" tract, for which *indebitatus aſſumpſit* well lies

" Yet perhaps it may be thought, that if the Attorney I am happy to
" was not privy to the exiſtence of the Will afterwards diſ- find that there
" covered, and had no notice from the Plaintiff touching is great Autho rity for this
" the payment over, that the Party who ought to have Doubt
" been ſued was he who took out Adminiſtration ; the Prin- See 4 Burr Manif 1986
" cipal, not the Agent

* " It will not lie for Money paid for the releaſe of * P 353.
" Cattle diſtrained, as *damage feaſant* becauſe it gives no * Lindon and
" notice to the Defendant, whether the *Merits* or the *Form* Hooper
" will be brought in queſtion, and if the merits, it is un- Hil 16 G III Cowp. 414—9.
" certain what juſtification the Plaintiff will ſet up • whereas
" in *Treſpaſs* or *Replevin*, the Right claimed for the Cattle
" to be on the ſpot where taken muſt ſpecially appear on
" the Record

" Nor (for like Reaſons) is it a proper Action to try a Power v Wells.
" Warranty Cowp 818, 9

' It will not lie where a Contract is *open* for there the Towers v
" Right is not to the *whole* Money, but to the *Damages* Barrat
" and then he muſt ſtate the *ſpecial* Contract Hil 26 G III T R 133—6

" It will not lie where a Perſon has paid Money, which Tarmer v
" in *Conſcience* he *ought* to pay, though, by availing himſelf Arundel C B.
" of an advantage from a general proviſion of Law, he Tr 12 G III.
" might have *avoided* payment, as in the Caſe of a *bonâ* Bl R 824, 5,
" *fide* Debt, which is barred by the Statute of Limitations, Bize v Dicka-
" or a Debt contracted during Infancy, which in *Juſtice* he ſon T R 286
" ſhould diſcharge

" Still leſs does it lie for Money which a Man has paid Smith v.
" for an illegal and unjuſtifiable Conſideration as Money Stotesbury.
" to bribe a Sheriff's Officer to accept Bail, or where 2 Bl 204.
" the Keeper of a *Lottery Office* has paid Money to the in- Browning v.
" ſured, in conſequence of Tickets inſured, contrary to the Morris
' Statute L 18 G III. 790—3

" But it will lie to recover the Premium on ſuch Inſu- Jiques and
" rances Golightly

➤ " Nor where the demand, though in ſtrictneſs legal, 2 Bl 1073—5
" is hard and unconſcionable, and the Plaintiff might have * P 354.
" had a remedy more ſuited to the ſtrictneſs of his Caſe ; Cowp 116
" for this Action is analogous to a *Bill* in *Equity* Teſſons v

" It will not lie for the *Nominee* of a perpetual Curacy Brooke, 793
" till he is in poſſeſſion and he is not in poſſeſſion without —7
" *licence* from the Biſhop T R 399

" Otherwiſe of a *Donative*. 3 Wilſon, 335

Par.

Par. 3.

Cafes of a particular Nature where it is the proper Remedy

" It is now time to confider Cafes of a fpecial Nature,
" in which it will lie.

" It will lie for *Notes* or *Money* againft a third perfon
" into whofe hands they are come *mala fide*, provided their
" identity can be afcertained

" The Facts upon the Cafe referved were the following

Chefter State
and Johnfon
Cowp 197–
200.

" *David Wood*, Clerk to the Plaintiff, a Brewer, and re-
" ceiving Money from the Plaintiff's Cuftomers, and alfo
" negotiable Notes for the Plaintiff's Ufe, in the ordinary
" courfe of bufinefs, paid feveral fums *with the* SAID
" *Money and Notes*, at different times, to the Defendants,
" upon the chances of coming up of Tickets, in the State
" Lottery of 1772, contrary to the Act of the faid year

" The Plaintiff and the fureties of *Wood* gave him a re-
" leafe

" The Queftion was, whether *Wood* was an admiffible
" Witnefs?

* P. 355.

* " 2 If admiffible, whether on this Cafe the Plaintiff
" is entitled to recover in this Action?

" It was decided, that *Wood* was an *admiffible* Evidence

" That this being a liberal Action, if the Defendant can-
" not in Confcience retain what is the fubject of it, the
" Action will lie.

" That it is not a Cafe of *equal criminality*, where the rule
" † would prevail in favour of the Defendant The Plain

So 1 Burr 442
and Golghty
s Revenue.
C L. 88

" tiff does not ftand in the Place of his Clerk the money
" was all along the Mafter's, and the property continuing
" unchanged, the Plaintiff is well entitled to recover

Felham v
Te—
E. 13 G III
C L 207, &c
and Cowp 416
419 S C cited

" On a *Conviction* of a Churchwarden for Neglect of
" Duty, the *Overfeers* levied the Penalty, but had *not paid it*
" over, or applied it to the Ufe of the Parifh

" The Conviction being quafhed, an Action for *Money*
" *had and received* was brought againft the Overfeers to re-
" cover the Penalty. It was objected that the taking was
" tortious, and therefore *Trover* or *Trefpafs* fhould have
" been brought

" The Court was of opinion, that the Plaintiff might
" well waive the *Tort*, and that this Mode of Action was
" in favour of the Defendant The Plaintiff could recover
" nothing

† In pari delicto potior eft conditio defendentis.

" nothing but what was confcientioufly due; the Defendant
" loft no defence which he could make *bona fide*.

* " In *Affumpfit* for Money *had and received* to the Ufe of
" the Plaintiff, *proof* that the Defendant was a married
" Man, and that pretending to be fingle, he had married
" the Plaintiff, and made a Leafe of her Land, and received
" the Rent, would be fufficient to maintain the Action,
" for, though the Defendant not having a Right to receive,
" the Tenants were not difcharged by his Receipt, yet the
" Recovery in this Action would difcharge them

* **P. 356.**
L N P 133.
Salk 28
Haffer v
Wallis
Hil. 6 A B R.

" It will lie where Money has been *extorted*

L N P 132.

" Thus, on Action for Money *had* and *received*, the Facts
" on the referved Cafe were, that about three years before
' the Action the Plaintiff pawned plate to the Defendant
" for 20*l* and at the three years end came to redeem it,
" and the Defendant infifted to have 10*l* for the *intereft* of
" it, and the Plaintiff tendered him 4*l* knowing 4*l* to be
" more than legal Intereft † the Plaintiff, however, at length,
" not being able otherwife to obtain his Goods, paid the
" 10*l* and brought this Action to recover the Excefs be-
" yond legal Intereft

Aftley v
Reynolds.
Mic 5 G II.
2 Str 915.

" The Court thought this a payment by compulfion ·
" for that the Plaintiff might have fuch neceffity for his
" Goods that *Trover* would not anfwer and the Plain-
" tiff accordingly had Judgment, which was ordered to be
" entered *nunc pro tunc*, the defendant dying during the Ar-
' gument

* " So where the Nurfe of the Plaintiff's inteftate went
" off with the Money he had about him, a Cafe within a
" nice fhade of difference from *ftealing*

* **P. 357.**
Thomas and
Whip

" B owes Money to *A* and pays it to *C* as Attorney of
" *A* whereas in reality *C* had no Authority from *A B* is
" liable ftill to *A* for the Money, and his Remedy is againft
" *C* by this Action

Tr 1 G I.
L. N P 130.
Robfon v
Eaton T R 62
M 26 G III

" But the whole Doctrine of this fpecies of *Affumpfit* has
" no where been more clearly elucidated than in the Cafe
" of MOSES and MACFERLAN· with which, therefore I
" fhall clofe this Title on the Action for Money *had and re-*
" *ceived* The Cafe was this

E 33 G II
2 Burr Manuf.
1006—12
S C 1 Bl 219
—21

Par

---

† The implied Limts of the principle in the *Roman* Law—*Quod
quis fciens indebitum dedit, hac mente ut poftea repeteret, repetere non
poffit* D XII 6, 50 are therefore, *ultro*, ex malâ fide.

Par. 4.

The leading Cafe, Mofes *and* Macferlan.

" The Plaintiff in *this* Action, *Mofes*, had indorfed to
" the Defendant in the faid Action, *Macferlan*, four feveral
" *promiffory Notes* made to *Mofes* himfelf by one *Chapman*
" *Jacob*, for 30 fhillings each, for value received, bearing
" date 7th *Nov* 1751, and this was done in order to en-
" able the Defendant, *Macferlan*, to recover the Money in
" his own Name againft *Chapman Jacob*, but previous to the
" indorfing of thefe Notes by *Mofes*, he was affured by
" *Macferlan* they fhould be of no prejudice to him, and
" there was an AGREEMENT figned by *Macferlan*, whereby
" he engaged *exprefsly, that* MOSES *fhould not be liable to the*
" *payment of the Money, or any part of it, and that he fhould*
" *not be prejudiced, or put to any Cofts, or any way fuffer by*
" *reafon of fuch his Indorfement*
" Notwithftanding this exprefs CONDITION and AGREE-
" MENT, the Deferdant in this Action fued *Mofes* in the
" *Court of Confcierce* upon each of the four Notes, as In
" dorfer

* P. 358 * " *Mofes*, by his folicitor, tendered the before-mention-
" ed *Indemnity* to the Court upon the firft of the faid Caufes,
" and offered to give *Evidence* of it, *and of the Agreement*, by
" way of Defence this the Court of Confcience *rejected*,
" and refufed to receive Evidence in proof of the Agree-
" ment, thinking they had no power to judge of it and
" gave Judgment againft *Mofes*, on the Footing merely of
" his *Indorfement*
" This Decree was actually pronounced in only *one* of
" the *four* Caufes but the Agent of *Mofes* paid the Money
" into Court upon *all the four Notes*, and it was taken out
" of Court by *Macferlan*, by order of the Commiffioners
" The whole Matter, as ftated, thus appearing in Evi-
" dence before Lord MANSFIELD, at *Guildhall*, there was
" no Doubt but that on the *Merits* the Plaintiff was en-
" titled to the Money, and accordingly a Verdict was
" there found for *Mofes*, for 6l (the whole fum paid into
" the Court of Confcience) fubject to the opinion of the
" COURT of KING's BENCH on the following Queftion
" Whether the Money could be recovered in THIS FORM
" of *Action*, or whether it muft be recovered by an *Action*
" brought upon the SPECIAL AGREEMENT only ?
" In delivering the Opinion of the Court, Lord MANS-
" FIELD ftated thefe Refolutions.

" He

* " He laid afide the Objection intimated at the Bar, * P 359.
" though not included in the Grounds on which the Cafe
" was referved, as if the Decifion of the Court of Con-
" fcience had bound this Queftion

" That this was not a Cafe of again agitating a Queftion
' once decided by a competent Jurifdiction this Queftion
" had never been decided by the Court of Confcience ; the
" Ground of this Action is confiftent with their JUDG-
" MENT it difputes not the Decifion of the Commiffioners
" on the Indorfement it proceeds upon a point not included
" in their fentence

" If the Commiffioners had been wrong in waiving Cog-
" nizance of this collateral Matter, it is fufficient that they
" did waive it but they appear to have done right in fo
" refufing as otherwife, on Defence againft a promiffory
' Note for thirty fhillings, they might go into Agree-
" ments and Tranfactions of a great Value, and thus by
" their Judgment indirectly conclude a Balance of a large
" Account

" The Plaintiff comes therefore before the Court on a
" Queftion entirely open, the Ground of this Action being,
" not that the Judgment is wrong (which never could be
" brought over again in any fhape) but that for a Reafon of
" which the Plaintiff in this Action could not avail himfelf
" againft that Judgment, the Defendant ought not in Juf-
" tice to KEEP the Money

" Money may be recovered by a right and legal Judg-
" ment and yet the Iniquity of keeping the * Money may be * P 360
" manifeft upon Grounds which could not be a Defence to
" that Judgment

" As fuppofe the Indorfee of a promiffory Note, having
" received the Money from the Drawer, recovers the fame
" Money from the Indorfer who knew nothing of the pay-
" ment

" Suppofe a Man recovers upon a Policy for a Ship pre-
" fumed to be loft, which afterwards comes home, or upon
" the Life of a Man prefumed to be dead, who afterwards
" appears, or upon a Reprefentation deemed to be fair,
" which comes out afterwards to be grofsly fraudulent

" The very Mode of ftating the Queftion for the Opi-
" nion of the Court, admits that the Judgment is no Ob-
" ftacle to the Application of the Plaintiff, Mofes, for that,
" were it indeed affected, would be fo alike by an Action
" UPON the Agreement itfelf, or upon the prefent one de-
" rived from the Equity of the Plaintiff's Cafe, arifing out
" of the Agreement

" That

" That it remained therefore only, within the Terms of
" the Queſtion ſaved at *Niſi prius*, whether the Plaintiff
" might elect to ſue by this Form of Action for the *Money*
" only, or muſt be turned round to bring an Action upon
" the Agreement

" That the Action, as brought for Money had and re-
" ceived, was equally beneficial to the *Plaintiff*, whom it
" allowed to *declare generally*, and prove the ſpecial circum-
*P. 361   " ſtances of his Caſe on the Trial, and * to the Defen-
" dant, who can be liable no farther than for the Money
" he has received, and to that has every equitable Defence
" on the general Iſſue ſecure at the ſame time againſt
" farther litigation, as Judgment upon this favourable
" Action would be a *Bar* to the Plaintiff's proceeding on
" the Agreement, though upon that he might have reco-
" vered more

" That it is not only thus on Principles of *Reaſon* and of
" *public Utility*, but thus by many Precedents by one par-
" ticularly, which was very ſolemnly conſidered, when Sir
" PETER KING was *Chief Juſtice* of the COMMON PLEAS,
" that was an Agreement in Writing to transfer five ſhares
" in the *Welch* Copper Mines, when the Books ſhould be
" opened the Books were opened the party who made
" the Agreement refuſed to transfer, whereupon the Ac-
" tion was brought for the Conſideration Money paid
" The objection then was, that this Action, for Money
" *had and received*, to the Plaintiff's Uſe, would not lie
" but that an Action ſhould have been brought for *Non-*
" *performance of the Contract*   This was over-ruled by the
" *Chief Juſtice*, who notwithſtanding left it to the Jury
" whether they would not make the Price of the ſaid Stock
" as it ſtood when it ſhould have been delivered, the Meaſure
" ſure of the *Damages* which they accordingly did

" And a Caſe being made for the Opinion of the Court
" of *Common Pleas*, the Action was reſolved to have been
^ P. 362   " well brought, and that the Recovery was * right, being
" not for the *whole* Money paid, but for the Damages of
" not transferring the ſtock at *that* time, which was a Loſs
" to the *Plaintiff*, and an advantage to the *Defendant*, who
" was a Receiver of the *Difference* to the Plaintiff's Uſe

" That the Damages recovered in that Caſe ſhew the
" *Liberality* of this Action for though the Defendant re-
" ceived conſiderably more, yet the DIFFERENCE MONEY
" only was returned *againſt Conſcience*, and the Plaintiff
" therefore, *ex æquo et bono*, ought to recover no more
" agreeably to the Rule of the *Roman* Law—*Quod Ca-*
" *di*

" *dictio indebiti non datur ultra quam locupletior eft factus qui*
" *accepit* †

" And the Court there faid, that the *extending* of thefe
" Actions depends upon the Notion of *Fraud·* whence it is
" at the *Election* of the fufferer either to difaffirm the
" Contract *ab initio*, by reafon of the Fraud, and bring
" an Action for Money *had and received*, to recover a pay-
" ment for which he has no *Confideration*, or to *affirm* the
" Contract, and bring an Action for the *Non-performance*
" of it

" That this equitable Action being *very beneficial* ought
" much *to be encouraged*, as it lies for nothing which *in Ho-*
" *nour* and *Honefty* has been rightly paid fo that even on
" an *ufurious* Contract the Principal and *legal* Intereft fhall So of *Trover*,
" not be refunded in this Action, and as it will lie for for the like
Reafon
" Money paid by *Miftake*, by *Impofition*, under Oppreffion, T R 153
" Extortion, or other under Advantage

" Our next is Goods fold and delivered at a Price cer-
" tain

---

† Is qui non debitum accepit, ab eo qui per errorem folvit re I 111, 15
obligatur, daturque agenti contra eum propter repetitionem *con-* I IV 13
dictitia Actio nam perinde ei *condici* poteft, *fi apparet eum dare
oportere*, *ac fi mutuum accepiffit*

Si *metu* coactus aut *dolo* inductus, aut *errore* lapfus *Titio* pro-
miſiſti, iniquum eft te condemnari, ideoque tibi datur exceptio
rei cauſâ, aut doli mali, aut *in factum compofita*, ad impug-
nandum actionem

Si quis *indebitum* ignorans folvit per hanc Actionem condicere
poteft   nam hoc natura æquum eft, *neminem alterius dam-
no fier locupletiorem*

Si procurator tuus *indebitum* folverit, et tu ratum non habeas
poffe repeti *Labeo* fcripfit quod fi *debitum* fuiſſet non poffe repeti,
Celfus, quoniam cum quis procura²orem rerum fuarum conftituit,
id quoque mandare videtur ut folvat creditori, neque poftea ex-
pectandum fit ut ratum habeat

Judex fi male abfolvit et abfolutus fua fponte folverit, repetere D XII 6 1
non poteft   14

Hæc Condictio ex bono et æquo introducta, quod alterius apud al- § 6
terum SINE CAUSA *deprehenditur, revocare confuevit*   Ibid 28

Actione Condictionis EA SOLA *quantitas repetitur quæ* indebita 66
foluta eft

Multo facilius quantitatis indebitæ interpofitâ fcripturâ con- C IV 5
dictio competit   Ibid § 3

* T I T. III.

4. *Goods fold and delivered at a certain Sum.*

" This is not greatly different from the Action of *Debt,*
" except in that circumftance of its being clear of the
" *Wager* of Law

" We will firft on this fubject confider Contracts, which
" may be the fource of this Action, when made by a Wife,
" an Infant, a *Factor*, or other Agent

Par 2

CONTRACT *by the* WIFE

" Generally," the Wife cannot by Contract bind the
Hufband for the Hufband is the fuperior and governing
power, and the Law hath entrufted him with the Conduct
of the whole Family and therefore the Wife's Acts in lar
gaining are wholly void and if found by fpecial Verdict
are not fufficient to bind the Hufband

But the Act of the Wife contracting is *prefumptive* Evi
dence to perfuade the Jury of the Contract of the Hufband
for if the Hufband permits another to contract for him, it
is his own Contract and this, " as will be feen, furnishes
" a Ground of Action on the implied Agency even in the
" Cafe of a ftranger much more in this neareft of Rela
" tions therefore" where the Wife, cohabiting with the
Hufband, takes up Goods in his Name,' this *primâ facie* is

the * Contract of the Hufband for it is to be prefum
that the Hufband will truft fo near a Relation to act for
him.

But if at the time of the Contract the Wife were abfent
ed from the Hufband, this is fo far from being the Contract
of the Hufband, that it is rather the contrary for it canno
be prefumed that an Hufband fhould truft a Wife elop d as
his Agent to Act for him fo that her contracting in his
Name is no Evidence to charge him

The ufual Employment of the Wife cohabiting with the
Hufband is good Evidence · but this is no conclufive Evi
dence for poffibl, fhe might have been always employed
with ready Money fo that it is ftill a ftronger Evidence,
the Hufband has paid the Debts of the Wife where fhe has
been entrufted

Again, that the Things were neceffary for the Hufband
and Wife and the Family is good Evidence of a Contr
to bind the Hufband · for though the Things are of ne
ceffi

ceffity, yet poffibly that Neceffity might be otherwife provided for. and they muft be neceffary not only for his Degree but to his Eftate alfo, to make the Evidence nearer to conclufive.

* Again, it is good Evidence to prove the Contract of the * P 365. Hufband, that the Things bought by the Wife came to the Ufe of the Hufband and his family. and yet this is not abfolutely conclufive; " for though *prima facie* it prefumes " Notice," he poffibly, " may be able to prove" that he had no Notice that they were bought " on Credit, otherwife " he would not have ufed them;" " and he may fhew this " by fhewing a fpecial warning not to give credit: for" if the Hufband forbid any perfon to truft his Wife, and he do truft her, this is " conclufive" Evidence that the Hufband never defigned, " or could by him, after fuch Notice, be " underftood, to affent," to contract with him by means of his Wife, and therefore he cannot charge the Hufband on any fuch Contract.

If the Hufband be abfent from the Family, and Goods are bought by the Wife, this is good Evidence to prove to the Jury, that the Wife did contract in the place of her Hufband, but this is not abfolutely conclufive, for poffibly

---

† *Of this factitious Neceffity— de la bienfeance * —as fome of the* * D'Alembert
beft French Writers term it (adopting the popular Language, but re- and Rouffeau.
ftraining the Application within philofophic Limits) SHAKESPEARE,
*with the Energy of his ftyle, fentiment, and expreffion of Cha-
racter—*

> *O! reafon not the need! our bafeft beggars*   LEAR.
> *Are in the pooreft thing fuperfluous.*
> *Allow not Nature more than Nature needs,*
> *Man's Life is cheap as beafts thou art a lady,*
> *If only to go warm were gorgeous,*
> *Why, Nature needs not what thou gorgeous wear'ft;*
> *Which fcarcely keeps thee warm*

In his fufferings he acquires an exacter fenfe of mere real Neceffity, and of the inattention which Wealth and Power create to the abfolute Wants of others, in minds occupied with their own imaginary ones.

> *Poor naked Wretches, wherefoe'er you are,*
> *That bide the pelting of this pitilefs ftorm,*
> *How fhall your houfelefs heads and unfed fides,*
> *Your loop'd and window'd raggednefs defend you*
> *From feafons fuch as thefe Oh, I have ta'en*
> *Too little care of this! Take Phyfic, Pomp,*
> *Expofe thyfelf to feel what Wretches feel,*
> *That thou may'ft fhake the fuperflux to them,*
> *And fhew the Heavens more juft.*

Actus neceffarii pro legitimis habentur, modo jufta fit Neceffitas.

he left ready Money, or made fome other Provifion for his Family

"But in this, and every fimilar inftance," there is a great Difference between Evidence offered to the Jury, and Evidence offered to the Court on a fpecial Verdict, "and "the Contract in this Cafe is a Fact to be found by the "Jury from the Evidence before them· for it is a Matter "en Pais, of which they are the proper and fole Judges "Thus" if they find that the Wife contracted * for Ne- ceffaries in the Abfence of her Hufband, this is good Evi- dence to perfuade the Jury that the Hufband did contract, and that his Will was concurring and went along with her in this Tranfaction but if this be found and offered to the Court, the Court cannot judge it is the Contract of the Hufband.

* P. 366.

For the Jury are the only Judges of the Fact, and they are to make the Deductions and *Conclufions* as to the *Truth of the Fact* from the Evidence before them But the Court cannot make any Deductions or Conclufions as to the Truth of the Fact, ("or, in other Words, the Conclufion of "Fact, as between the parties involved in the Evidence") unlefs they flow neceffarily and demonftratively from the Evidence which the Jury have ftated: for they are not Judges of *probable* or *improbable*, but of *lawful* and *not lawful* If therefore the Jury do only lay before the Court fuch "Evidence" as would induce a Man to believe that the Contract of the Wife was confirmed of the Hufband they cannot adjudge it to be fo: "for the Jury, by not finding "this, have impliedly negatived it;" and "the Court" not being Judge of the Probability of Fact, but of the Law only, if the Jury do not lay before them the *infallible* figns of a Contract, the Judges, who are to intend nothing, cannot adjudge it to be a Contract

"And this leading Principle fhould be kept in Mind ' wherever a fpecial Finding on an Iffue before the *Jury*, "is to take place: it applies, upon Analogy of Reafon, to "Orders of Seffion

* P 367
Comm I 442,
Le W 66, 7
S·k 118, 119
L N P 134
Tongwo ta and H icamore.
Ex 10 W III

* "If, during the *Cohabitation*, a *Wife* contracts Debts for "*Neceffaries* which the hufband hath neglected to provide, "he is obliged to pay for them

"If a Man put his Wife out of Doors, this amounts to "a general Credit for Neceffaries; and a perfon who has "fupplied her with thefe, notwithftanding a Warring not "to truft her while fhe lived with the Hufband, fhall reco ' ver againft the Hufband

"If

" If a married Woman lives oftensibly as a *Femme sole,*
" she shall not be permitted to take credit in that charac-
" ter, and defeat the remedy by pleading herself a married
" Woman

" Where the Husband had *abjured* the Realm, under the ^{Comm.IV 392.}
" privilege of sanctuary, to avoid suffering death as a
" Felon, the Wife was liable to be sued as a *Femme sole.*
" TRANSPORTATION hath been held to render her suable
" in like manner

" And where there was a separate maintenance, and the
" Husband resident in *Ireland,* the Wife was held suable as
" if sole

" When there is a separate maintenance, and the Huf- ⎫Sparrow v.
" band lives in *England,* a Case in the *Common Pleas* was ⎬Caruthers
" determined on the Ground of its being taken to be ne- 2 Bl R 1197,8.
" cessary that the Name to the Husband should be joined Ringstead v
" for conformity   A later Case, however, seems to disal- Lanesborough
" low this Necessity Hil 23 G Ill.
Lean v Schutz.
" And in a preceding Case it was ruled that merely to Bl R 1195.
" aver *Elopement* would not warrant a suit against the Wife Barwell v
" singly · for that Elopement had not the * same legal sense Brooks
' which modern Conversation seems to annex to it, and Hil 14 G Ill.
B R
" implied no more than that she had absented herself with- Hatchet v
" out his concurrence. S Baddely
Bl R 1079.

Par 3.   * P. 368.

Goods sold and delivered to an Infant

" Though an Infant may bind himself for *Necessaries,*
' yet a Contract for things otherwise allowable under that
" Description is not suable against an Infant living with V Bambridge
" the Parent, who is presumed to provide his Child with and Pickering
" sufficient Necessaries, and if he does not, it is the Parents Mic 10
" should be sued " G III Bl R.
1315

Upon *Non Assumpsit* the Defendant may give Infancy in
Evidence in Discharge of the Promise ; but if a Man were
at Issue upon *Non est Factum,* Infancy cannot be given in
Evidence but must (" as already has been declared") be
pleaded   For where the Issue relates to a solemn Contract,
which Contract had a " presumptive" Obligation at the
time of making, that is a full Proof of the Issue ; for " the"
solemn Contract " carrying its own" Force, the Court
ought to see that it is legally dissolved · but where there is a
Contract in Issue that " hath not " such presumption in
its favour, being not executed with " legal" solemnity,
there a Man may give in Evidence, on the general Issue,

S 2   that

that it had no Obligation by reafon of Infancy. For where there are not Solemnities of Contract exhibited to the Court, it is not neceffary that the Court fhould fee the Difcharge of that Contract: and therefore if the Plaintiff, on the Iffue, proves himfelf an Infant, it amounts to the Proof that he could not *affume*, and therefore no *Affumpfit*

* P 369

* " And generally under this head it is proper to obferve, " that the" Contracts of " an" Infant are not void, but voidable, " at his Election, when to his Prejudice · and on " this Principle, where" an Infant brought an Action for fix Pounds, for which the Defendant became indebted by a Contract to cut his Grafs, and carry it away, paying him fix Pounds, it " was held" no Objection to fay that the Plaintiff is an Infant, and fo could give no fuch permiffion, " for the Infant" was entitled to an Action for cutting of his Grafs, " as it fhall not lie in the Mouth of the contract- " ing Party to fay that the Act of the Infant was good to " entitle him to the Grafs, and yet not of Force to fub- " ject him to payment for it " and therefore here is a good Confideration, if the Infant will abide by his Bar- gain

" And on the like Principle that Contracts by an Infant " are good when clearly for the effential Benefit of the In- " fant, and that it is expedient parties fhould be encou- " raged thus to contract with one by the Certainty of fuch " Contracts being legally eftablifhed as are fairly within this " Defcription, the Validity of his Engagement for Necef- " faries under the Limitation already ftated depends, fucn " are meat, cloathing, and requifite inftruction, and the " Contract for thefe fhall bind the *Infant*

" Some Acts alfo he is impowered to do for the benefit " of the Community and this is not improper to be here ' noticed, as it illuftrates the reafons of the Law concern- " ing the Contracts and other Tranfactions of an Infant

* P 370

" Therefore it has been held that an Infant * fhall prefent " to an Advowfon, left an Avoidance fhould be incurred, " and this one fhould have prefumed to mean the Guardian " *jure Infantis* . but a ftrange Method has been preferred of " executing this Truft in behalf of the public; for *in the* " *excellent Notes* on the Firft *Inflitute* of *Coke*, it is re- " marked, that in another Work he extends this Doctrine " fo far as to fay that the infant fhall prefent, whatever his

3 Inft 156

" Age may be But that fome fuppofe the Guardian to " have the Right of prefenting in the Name of the Infant, " while others, again, admit the Right of the Infant in ge- " neral, but add, that if the Infant be of fuch tender years " as not to have any difcretion, then the Guardian fhould " prefent

" prefent for him · but that however the Law now feems Vin Abr.
" fully fettled in the Extent of Lord *Coke*'s opinion by a Guardian.
" determination of Lord *Chancellor* KING, in a Caufe be- Q pl 2.
" fore whom an Advowfon had been conveyed to *Truftees*,
" on Truft, to prefent fuch perfon as the Grantor, his
" heirs or affigns fhould by Deed appoint and on the prin-
" ciple that an Infant *of any Age* may appoint, his Lordfhip
' confirmed an appointment by an infant heir, though it
" appeared that the Child was *not a year o'd*, and that the
" Guardian guided the Child's pen in making his mark and
" putting his feal: yet the learned Annotator well obferves, 2 Eq C Abr.
" that although this Decifion may remove all doubts about Infant B pl 3.
" the legal Right of an Infant of the moft tender years to Vin Abr Col-
" prefent, it remains to be feen whether circumftances would Watfon's Cler-
" not induce a *Court of Equity* to controul the exercife, gyman's Law.
" where a prefentation is obtained from an Infant with- 140
" out the concurrence of the Guardian * This, one 3 Atk 710
" may add, would be an Interpofition which could hardly * P. 371.
" fail of taking place and indeed, can it be fuppofed that
" the fignature but now ftated was regaided other than as
" an aukward and burlefque Mode, by which the Guardian
" did, in the Name of the Infant, an Act neceffary to be
" done, and which the Infant, was fubftantially incompe-
" tent to perform?

" *Affumpfit* for Goods fold: the Defendant pleaded *Non-*
" *age* the Plaintiff replied, they were for his, the Infant's, L. N P 154.5.
" neceffary livelihood, and Provifion for the Maintenance Cro Ja 494
" of his Family. the Defendant rejoined, that he kept a
" Mercer's fhop at *Shrewfbury*, and bought thofe Wares to
" fell again, and traverfed that he bought them for Necef-
" faries and *Demurrer* thereupon.

" And by the *Court* · This buying for the Maintenance
" of his Trade, though he gain thereby his living, fhall
" not bind him · for an Infant fhall not be bound by his
" Bargain for any thing but for his Neceffity, *viz* Diet
" and Apparel, and neceffary Learning †

" But Mr Baron *Clarke*, where the Defendant in fuch an
" Action before him gave his *Non age* in Evidence, directed

† *With regard to the moral and religious Inftruction of Infants,
and others of the poorer Clafs, the Example of Mr.* RAIKES, *of*
GLOUCESTER, *has extended far. two Objects, however, effential
to the Perfection of the Plan, have not every where been equally regarded that the Inftruction be perfectly fimple, free, uncircum-
fcribed to any Sect or Eftablifhmen. · that manual Induftry be encouraged to go,* pari paffu, *with intellectual Improvement.*

" the

"the Jury to give a Verdict for the Plaintiff; it appearing
"he had been set up in the Farm, and bought the sheep of
"the Plaintiff in the way of farming, and said, he thought
"the Law ought not to put it in the Power of Infants to
"impose upon the rest of the World And the *Scotch* Law
"* is agreeable to this Determination However, in the
"Case of *Wyvall* and *Champion*, at Guildhall, LEE, Chief
"Justice, would not suffer the Plaintiff to recover for To-
"bacco sent to the Defendant, who set up a shop in the
"Country, he appearing to be an Infant, for the Law will
"not suffer him to trade, which may be to his undoing

"A *Copyhold* Estate devolved upon the Defendant when
"he was an Infant of six Years of Age a Fine was af-
"sessed, and on his coming of Age, he was admitted to
"the Estate † *Assumpsit* was brought for this fine and,
"upon a Case reserved, the Question was, whether *Assump-*
"*sit* would lie for the Fine, which the Jury found to be a
"reasonable one The Court held clearly the Action lay
"And *per* YATES, Justice, if *Assumpsit* had been brought
"against the Infant *during his Minority*, it would have lain
"Debt, in this Case, may not lie against an Infant, because
"he cannot wage his Law, but if an Infant take a Lease
"for Years, and hold, he may be charged in Debt for that
"Rent. If an Infant be bound for Necessaries, he is for
"an old Fine, which is necessary to entitle him to receive
"the Rents and Profits of his Estate, thereout to provide
"Necessaries. But in this Case it is clear beyond all Doubt
"as he has confirmed the Contract by his Enjoyment since
"he came of Age.

"Lord

Margin notes:
Erskine's Prin-
ciples, L. I.
T 7 § 21.
Str 1085

* P 372

Evelyn, Bart.
v Chichester
B R Trin.
5 G III
3 Burr. Manif.
1717

† *The Nature of an Exemption on account of Infancy, or from the*
Lapse of Time, is justly and vigorously represented by a celebrated
Author. and it is pleasing to observe, that the statement of a truth
so frequently requisite to be observed in common Life has not failed of
that Attention which may contribute to diffuse the knowledge, or
awaken the remembrance, of it in the Mass of the Community. It
deserves to be here repeated, and with pleasure I transcribe it

Paley's Moral
P- 1 of B III
Ca 4.

As the Right of Property depends upon the Law of the Land, it
seems to follow that a man has a right to keep and take every thing
which the Law will allow him to keep and take, which in many
Cases will authorize the most flagitious chicanery If a Creditor
upon a simple Contract neglects to demand his Debt for six Years, the
Debtor may refuse to pay it. Would it be right therefore to do so,
where he is conscious of the Justice of the Debt? If a person who is
under twenty-one Years of Age, contract a Bargain (other than
for necessaries) he may avoid it by pleading his minority. but would
this be a fair plea where the bargain was originally just? The
question

* " Lord BACON, in his Maxim to illustrate his eighteenth * P 373.
" Rule, that *Proximity of Relation is equivalent to a perfonal*
" *Intereft*, fays, that if one under Age contract for the
" nurfing of his *lawful* Child, the Contract is good, and fhall
" not be avoided by Infancy

* " We may add the Contract of an Infant to maintain * P. 374.
" his illegitimate Child is alike good and would have been
" fo even prior to the ftatutes for taking order concerning
" the maintenance of baftard Children

" So Neceffaries for an Infant's Wife are Neceffaries for
" him · but if provided only in order for the Marriage, he
" is not chargeable though fhe ufe them after

" But though Goods not neceffaries be delivered to an
" Infant, if after full Age he ratify the Contract by a Pro-
" mife to pay, he is bound

" Yet where an Infant has given fecurity, which by Law Capper and
" is null, it has been held that his Ratification, when of Davenant
Tr 29 Car II.
B. R

diftinction to be taken in fuch Cafes is this with the Law, we ac-
knowledge, refides the difpofal of property, fo long, therefore, as we
keep within the defign and intention of a Law, that Law will jus-
tify us, as well in foro confcientiæ as in foro humano But when
we convert to one purpofe a rule or expreffion of Law, which is in-
tended for another purpofe, then we plead in our juftification not the in-
tention of the Law but the words, that is, we plead a dead Letter,
which can fignify nothing . for words without meaning or intention
have no force or effect in Juftice, much lefs words taken contrary
to the meaning and intention To apply this diftinction to the example
juft now propofed, in order to protect men againft demands from which
it is not probable they fhould have preferved the Evidence of their
difcharge, the Law prefcribes a limited time to certain fpecies of
private fecurities, beyond which it will not enforce them, or lend its
affiftance to the recovery of the Debt If a man be ignorant or
dubious of the juftice of the demand made upon him, he may confcien-
tioufly plead this limitation · becaufe he applies the rule of Law
to the purpofe for which it was intended. But when he refufes
to pay a debt, of the reality of which he is confcious, he cannot, as
before, plead the intention of the ftatute and the fupreme Authority
of Law

Again, to preferve Youth from the practices and impofitions to which
their inexperience expofes them, the Law compels the payment of no
Debts incurred within a certain Age, nor the performance of any
engagements, except for fuch neceffaries as are fuited to their condi-
tion and fortunes If a young perfon, therefore, perceive that he has
been practifed or impofed upon, he may honeftly avail himfelf of the
privilege of his non-age to defeat the circumvention, but if he
fre'ter himfelf under this privilege, to avoid a fair obligation, or an
equitable Contract, he extends the privilege to a Cafe in which it is
not allowed by intention of Law, and in which confequently it does not
in natural Juftice exift.

Age,

" Age, could not have any effect: for that the Contract,
" otherwife voidable only, was fo extinguifhed by giving
" the Bond, that nothing remained to raife a confideration
" for the Promife

Borthwick v.
Carruthers.
T R E
27 G III.
648, 9

" To an Action for Goods fold and delivered the Defen-
" dant pleads *Infancy* · now the Plaintiff may allege, *that*
" *after the Defendant attained his Age of twenty-one, he rati-*
" *fied and confirmed the feveral Promifes and undertakings in the*
" *Declaration fet forth* · and then if the Defendant rejoin that
" *he did not,* the Plaintiff has only to prove a Promife, and
" the Defendant muft prove he was under age at the time of
" making fuch Promife.

Zouch ex Dim.
Abbot v Par-
fons. 1 Bl. 575

" On the Principles concerning legal incapacity, with
" relation to the Acts of Infants, much curious Learning
" is to be feen in the Cafe cited in the Margin

* P. 375   * Par 4.

FACTOR

L N P 130
Confalez v
Sladen.Tr 1 A
Guich
Salk M. S

" Where a Factor beyond fea buys or fells Goods for
" the Perfon to whom he is Factor, an Action will lie
" againft him in his own Name, for the Credit will be
" prefumed to be given to him in the firft Cafe, and in
" the laft the Promife will be prefumed to be made to
" him, and the rather, as it is fo much for the Benefit of
" Trade.

" However, a Factor's fale does, by the general Rule of
" Law, create a Contract between the Owner and the
" Buyer: and therefore if a Factor fell for payment at a
" future Day, if the Owner give Notice to the Buyer to
" pay him, and not the Factor, the Buyer would not be
" juftified in afterwards paying to the Factor.

" Yet under fome particular circumftances this Rule
" would not take place As where the Factor fells the
" Goods at his own Rifque, being to anfwer to the Owner
" for the Price, though it be never paid for in fuch Cafe
" *he is* the Debtor to the Owner, and not the Buyer

" Where a Factor is authorized to fell in his own
" Name, though he is not anfwerable for the Money, if
" not paid, yet he has a Right to receive the Money, and
" to hold it in difcharge of Money due from his *principal*
" to him

Drinkwater v
Goodwin E.
15 G III
Cowp 256

" He who buys goods of a Factor has not a right, under
" fuch circumftances, to with-hold payment to the Factor,
" on the ground that the *principal* is indebted to the Buyer
" in the fame or a larger fum.

Par

SERVANT, *or other Agent.*

" A fervant may be confidered as an *Agent* or *Factor* for
" his Mafter, and circumftances will prove with greater or
" lefs ftrength that he is fo.

" If the fervant has been ufually employed in making
" fimilar Contracts, the Credit given to him is juftly deem-
" ed to be given to the Mafter

" The Nature of the Employment in which the Ser-
" vant is retained, compared with that of the Article for
" which he is reprefented to have treated as by Commif-
" fion from his Mafter, is to be regarded as inducing a pro-
" bability, or otherwife material to guide the Difcretion of
" the Jury

" It is" good Evidence againft a Father that Phyfic was Keb, 439.
delivered to his Daughter on his Requeft.

TIT. IV.

5 *A Sum certain for Work and Labour.*

" This has much Affinity to the *Indebitatus affumpfit* firft
' mentioned. It will lie for *Wages* afcertained.

TIT V.

6 *On Account ftated*

" The *Affumpfit* on *Account ftated* will not lie againft an
" *Infant*.

" This Action comes in the place of the ancient and L N P 127,8.
" more fpecial Action of Account, in which the Judgment
" was that the Defendant *account*, and then the Court affign-
" ed *Auditors*

" Though thefe Actions of general *Affumpfit* are emi- May and King,
" nently liberal in their Form and in their Effect, yet they Ca. K B 537.
" have this in common with other Modes of Suit, that the
" Plaintiff's Proof muft tally with fome * of the Counts
" of his Declaration And therefore if, in an Action for * **P.** 377.
" Work and Labour, and Money lent, the Evidence were
" that there had been mutual Dealings between the parties,
" and that they had come to an *Account*, and that the De-
" fendant upon the Balance, was indebted to the Plaintiff
" (*ex gr* 5*l*) and had promifed to pay, the Plaintiff ought
" to

" to be nonfuited, unlefs there were likewife a Count upon
" an *infimul computâffet*

Thompfon v
Spencer B R.
E 8 G III.
V fupra

" Till lately it was a received Notion, that in a Count
" upon *infimul computâffet*, the Plaintiff was obliged to prove
" the exact fum laid But this idea is now exploded, and
" the Plaintiff may recover part of the fum laid on this
" Count, as on a *Policy of Infurance*, or any other

1 Snow 215

" In *Affumpfit* upon an *Account ftated*, Proof that the De-
" fendant and the Plaintiff's Wife reckoned that the De-
" fendant had borrowed at one time 40*s* at another time
" 40*s*. and another time 4*l* and that this came to 8*l* is
" good Evidence.

Tit VI.

7 *Goods fold on a* quantum valebant

Comm. III.
c 9 p 161.

" When Goods are fold at a *certain* agreed Price, the
" Remedy is by Action of *Debt*, or by the more ufual and
" fafer Action *indebitatus affumpfit* But Goods may be fold,
" and many are daily, without any Agreement, for a cer-
" tain Price and then the Law, from the Nature of the
" Tranfaction, implies a Promife to pay what they are
" reafonably worth: of which the ordinary Price of Goods
" of like Quality is Evidence

" And as to the fale which founds the *Affumpfit*," Delivery of the Goods is Evidence of the fale on the *Quantum
meruit* · becaufe they fhall be fuppofed to be delivered on
the Bargain, and with Expectation of the Price of them.

₮ P 378.

Tit. VII

8. Affumpfit *for Work and Labour done on a* Quantum meruit

" Of much affinity to the preceding is this *Affumpfit,*
" which, for Induftry and Skill employed on my Account,
" affigns an adequate Confideration, and prefumes me to
" have engaged to pay it

" And even a *tortious* fervice may acquire a Right to
" this Confideration, as otherwife the injurious Party would
" profit by his own *Wrong* On this Principle a curious
" and important Decifion took place before Sir GEORGE
' HAY.

The Court of
Admiralty,
29 June, 1775
Parke's Cafe
P 13 23-27
Jeets

" The Cafe was this:—*George Rogers* alias *Rigges*, a
" Negro, aged about nineteen, had been a fervant to feve
" ral Gentlemen in *England*, and in the fummer of 1760,
" being then out of place, became acquainted with *John*
" *Latter*, and *John Seffins*, who contracted with *Arthur*
" *Jonn*

Jones for the fale of him · an Affignment was accordingly Shark or SLAVERY Append. 79. drawn and figned by *John Latter*, by which *Rogers* was transferred to Meffrs *Mafon* and *Jones*, as a flave, for the fum of twelve Guineas

" In *Auguft*, 1776, fome time after the fale, *Rogers*, under fome falfe Pretences, was carried on board the *Britannia*, then lying at *Deptford*, of which *Mafon* and *Jones* were Owners, and was there againft his Will forcibly detained.

" When the fhip fet fail, he was fo far enlarged as to be fuffered to go on deck, and not being entered on the fhip's Books as Mariner, nor having any particular office or wages affigned, he was fet to work about the fhip's Duty in general, till he was appointed as Affiftant to the Cook: in this employment he ferved fometimes as Affiftant, and fometimes as principal Cook, during the whole Voyage.

" The * fhip failed to the Coaft of *Africa* in the SLAVE * P. 379. TRADE, and from thence to *Porto Rico*, where he was offered to fale by the Captain of the *Britannia* as a prime flave: but having found an opportunity of making known his ftory to the *Spanifh* Merchants, they refufed to purchafe him He returned therefore with the fhip, in which he ftill acted in his former capacity of Affiftant Cook, and upon their Arrival in the Port of *London*, in *May*, 1768, when the other Mariners were paid and difcharged, he was ftill detained on board againft his Will

" At length he made his efcape, and by the affiftance and advice of Friends, applied to Mr *Faulkner*, a Proctor of Doctors Commons, to be enabled to recover a recompence for his lofs of time and labour Mr. *Faulkner* accordingly wrote to *Arthur Jones* for that purpofe · a Meeting was appointed, in confequence of which *Jones*, *Seffins*, and another, feized *Rogers*, forced him into a Coach and carried him away, removing him to another fhip, and there chaining him to the main-maft till he was releafed by the Authority of the Court of *Admiralty*

' In the beginning of 1774, Mr. *Torriano* was retained to commence an Action againft *Arthur Jones*, as one of the Owners, for the purpofe of recovering the ufual Wages, or other recompence

" The Caufe was brought to a hearing on the day fpecified in the Margin, when the Facts being proved as ftated, 29 June, 1774. the principal Queftion was, *How far the Plea of* SLAVERY, *fet up by the Defendant, could be admitted in bar of the demand of Wages?*

* " In behalf of the Negro, it was urged that this kind * P. 380. of flavery never, by the Law of *England*, had exiftence

" in

"in this Country. They cited the Cafe of *Knowles* and
"*Somerfet* before Lord MANSFIELD, in which the Negro
"was *difcharged*, who had been brought up in Obedience
"to the Writ of *Habeas Corpus*, the Caufe of his Deten-
"tion on the return being ftated, which was a delivery of

Harg S Tr
XI 339

"the faid Negro by order of his Mafter, *Charles Stewart*,
"to the faid Captain, on board the veffel called the *Anne*
"*and Mary*, then lying in the river *Thames*, at *London*, in
"the parifh of St. *Mary le Bow*, in the Ward of *Cheap*, to
"be fafely kept, carried and conveyed to *Jamaica*, there
"to be fold as the flave and property of the faid *Charles*
"*Stewart*

Pre-ogative
Court, 11 May,
1773
Sharp, utfupra
Append 77

"They alfo cited the Cafe of *Cay* and *Crichton*, in which
"an exception to an Inventory was taken on account of a
"Negro being omitted; where the Judge, Dr *Hay*, dif
"allowed this exception, for that a *Negro* had been adjudg-
"ed by the competent Jurifdiction not to be the fubject of
"Property in *England* and therefore ordered the Article,
"charging defectivenefs for the omiffion of the Negro, to
"be ftruck out of the exceptive Allegation

"In the principal Cafe the Decree was fubftantially as
"follows

"There are, faid the Judge, two principal points in this
"Cafe.

"1ft. Whether fuch a fervice is proved, as ftated in the
"fummary Petition, as to intitle the Plaintiff to the Wages
"demanded.

* P 381.

* "He obferved that the fervice was proved by the ful
"left Evidence but that no Wages having been ftipulated,
"he could not be allowed a fpecific fum as for WAGF,
"afcertained by Agreement but that if the Plea of *Sla-*
"*very* would not interdict a Compenfation, he would be
"intitled to a recompence *in quantum meruit* And that,
"with refpect to the *fecond* point, whether the Plaintiff,
"being a SLAVE, could be legally intitled to any reward for
"his fervice, he thus expreffed himfelf.

"That the practice of buying and felling SLAVES wat
"certainly very common in ENGLAND before the Cafe of
"SOMERSET in the Court of KING's BENCH, 1772 but,
"however it might have been the Law of the *Royal Ex-*
"*change*, he hoped it never was *the Law of the Land*

"That the Opinions of Lord HARDWICKE and of Lord
"TALBOT, when Attorney and Solicitor General, had been
"quoted in fupport of this practice, and had been formerly
"confidered as giving too much countenance to it, though
"feeming

" feeming originally to have only applied to the Queſtion,
" whether any difference was created by Baptiſm

" But that by a late Determination of one of the ableſt
" Judges who ever preſided in this Kingdom, theſe Opi-
" nions have been held to be miſtaken and unſound , and
" there can be no farther doubt that the claim of ſlavery is
" not maintainable by the Laws of ENGLAND.

* " That the Law, of Courſe, was the ſame before that   * P. 382.
" opinion as ſince , and conſequently refers to all ſales of
' this Nature, which are every one illegal , and that there-
" fore the pretended Sale, in the preſent Caſe, in 1776,
" was an abſolute Nullity, and when the Allegation, ſtating
" the Sale, was admitted, on behalf of the Owners, had
" *Rogers* appeared under proteſt, upon this point of Law,
" his Exception would have been received in bar of the
" Plea

" That the Owners ſeemed to have acted under a miſ-
" taken Notion of Right: but the Claim of SLAVERY
" being clearly againſt the Law of this Country, and it ap-
" pearing that *Rogers* had always acted in ſome uſeful Ca-
" pacity during the whole time of his having been on
" board, he was entitled to a QUANTUM MERUIT for
" his ſervice, and this, on the circumſtances, he fixed at
" 15 *ſhillings per Month*, and condemned the Owners in
" Coſts †

Par 2.

No Action for a Counſellor to recover his Fees.

" But a *Counſellor* cannot have this, or any other Action,   Comm III 38
" to obtain a pecuniary Conſideration for his Advice, the   Davis Pref
" Law of *England* concurring in this point with the De-   O A S. 415.
" licacy of the *Roman Law*, in not permitting a Price to
" be affixed to the performance of this honourable Duty,
" in which ſo many and arduous Queſtions muſt ariſe,

† *By the Exertions of the* Pennſylvanian *Society, and of other
public Bodies in the* AMERICAN STATES *by the Progreſs of the*
London *and* Mancheſter *Societies ; by the view in which this ſubject appears to be now contemplated in* FRANCE *, and by the viſible
general Tendency towards humanized Manners , there is reaſon to hope
that the* Non *importation of* NEGRO SLAVES *from* AFRICA *will
be accompliſhed ſoon, and the Negroes at preſent under Slavery to
States, profeſſing Chriſtianity and enjoying the Benefits of ſuperior intellectual Cultivation, become gradually free Servants under voluntary Contract to the permanent Benefit of the Planters, and to the
Recovery of the Honour, in this inſtance ſo long obſcured, of public
Humanity and national Juſtice.*

" where

* P. 383 " where the fpontaneous * acknowledgment of the Client
" can alone be the adequate, alone the fatisfactory re-
" ward †

Par 3.

Delivery in Law.

Menetone v
Alnawei.
Mic. 15 G III
3 Burr. Manf
1592

" The following Cafe illuftrates a point of fome impor-
" tance, which will foon require to be more diftinctly in-
" veftigated

" On *Affumpfit* for *Work* and *Labour done*, and *Materials*
" provided in repairing the Defendant's *fhip*.

" The fhip being damaged was obliged to put back, and
" was to have gone out of the *Dock* on a *Sunday* The
" Dock was the Shipwright's own · but the Owner had
" agreed to pay him 5*l* for the Ufe of it In the mean
" time, on the day precedent to that when fhe was to have
" failed, only about three Hours work being wanted to
" complete the *Repairs*, a Fire broke out in an adjacent
" Brewhoufe, which communicated to the *Dock*, and the
" fhip was *burnt*

" And as the Dock became *quoad hoc* the Owner of the
" Ship's by the Hire, the Court was of opinion, on all
" the circumftances of the Cafe, that the Action was well
" brought

" In treating of Bailments, fimilar Confiderations will be
" hereafter to be noticed "

SECTION II

GENERAL OBSERVATIONS *concerning* ASSUMPSIT

Condition performed.

Stil 46t

One brings an *Affumpfit* for twenty Pounds, and gives in
Evidence a Promife that if two would furrender their Right,
he would pay them twenty Pounds a-piece, and that they
did furrender their Right. this is good Evidence to maintain
the Declaration for though the Promife is laid *abfolutely* in
the Declaration, and the Promife in Proof is upon Condition, yet when that Condition is *performed*, the Duty becomes *abfolute*, and fo is a good Proof upon this Declaration.

† Multa honeftè accipi poffunt quæ tamen honeftè peti non
poffunt
Noluerint rem tantam pretio vilefcere.

" Formerly

Rent.

" Formerly it was holden that *Affumpfit* would lie for L N P 138.
" *Rent* on an *exprefs*, but not on the *implied* Promife.
" But now, where the Agreement is not by Deed, the 11 G II 19.
" Landlord may bring an Action on the Cafe for *Ufe* and § 14
" *Occupation*, to recover a reafonable fatisfaction, and if in
" Evidence on the Trial of fuch Action, any parol Demife
" or Agreement not by Deed fhall appear, whereby a cer-
" tain Rent was referved, the Plaintiff fhall not therefore
" be non-fuited, but may make ufe thereof as Evidence of
" the *Quantum* of the Damages to be recovered

" In Cafe for *Ufe* and *Occupation* of an Houfe by Per- Lewisand Wal-
" miffion of the Plaintiff, the Defendant pleaded that the lace Hil 25.
" Plaintiff *nil habuit in Tenementis* and upon *Demurrer*, the G ll K B.
" Court held it not a good Plea, for if the Plaintiff, had
" an *equitable* Title or *no Title* at all, yet if the Defendant
' have enjoyed by Permiffion of the Plaintiff, it is fuffici-
" ent and it is not neceffary for the Plaintiff to fay it is his
" Houfe any more than in *Affumpfit* for Goods fold to fay
" they were the Goods of the Plaintiff "

Par 3.

Promife difcharged or continued.

A Promife to marry *B* within three Months, and after Hill v Chaplin.
there is another Promife to marry her within a Fortnight: Pafch 1658
this does not difcharge the firft Promife but if it had been B R
a Promife to marry her within half a year, it would have
difcharged the firft Promife, for by taking a later Promife
of longer time, the Parties muft be fuppofed to intend a
difcharge of the former, otherwife the latter Promife could
have no manner of Intent

Difference between fpecial and implied Affumpfit

" There is this" characteriftic Difference between an *Affumpfit* in Deed and an *Affumpfit* in Law in the *Affumpfit* in
Deed, where the Contracts are mutual, and either fide declares for Nonperformance, there he muft fet forth the very
Contract, and if he miftakes in Quantities or fums he fails,
becaufe his Injury is in the Nonperformance of the very
Contract alleged in the Declaration, and if he does not fhew
fuch

such a Contract, he does not entitle himself to a Recompence of the Breach of it.

Dyer, 210
Al. 28
Styl 62
Cro Eliz. 292.
2 Sid. 236
Com Rep 373

But where he brings his Action for an *Assumpsit* in Law, if he shews part of the Goods delivered, or part of the Money lent, it is good because on every several Delivery of Goods, or Receipt of Money, *the Law implies a several* Contract for Restitution and there the Gist of the Injury is, not whether such a particular Contract is broken, but whether the Goods were delivered, or Money paid to the Defendant; and the Quantity of the Goods or the sum is no farther material than to increase or lessen the Damages.

V supra, 377

" And therefore, where there is a special Agreement, by " which something is comprized in the Contract which the " Law would not imply of course from the general Nature " of the Transaction and the common Principle of good " Faith essential to all Contracts," in every " such" *Assumpsit* " this distinguishing" and substantial part of the Promise must be laid in the Declaration: as if a Man be to deliver Goods according to a sample, " under specific Terms " of private Contract between the parties, the party who " means to assist on this Undertaking" must lay it so in the

Maidstone Ass
1700

* P. 386

* Declaration: for the Courts of Justice must go according to the *Allegata et Probata*, and it is not enough that a good Contract should be proved, if it be not alleged " And " this is founded on that *universal Logic*, which must pervade every rational system of Jurisprudence; for of this " it is a necessary Principle, that you cannot comprehend " in the *Conclusion* more than is contained in the *Premises* " Now the *Premises* are the *Pleadings*, and the *Issue* taken " on them; Evidence therefore of Matter not comprized " in these will not maintain the *Issue* for it goes beyond " the Premises on which the legal Conclusion is to be found-" ed " And " therefore," if the Contract be proved otherwise than as alleged, that is not good Evidence to maintain the Declaration for then it cannot be supposed the same Contract with the Contract alleged, and the party therefore must fail in the Proof of that *Assumpsit*

Turner's Case
Hil Aff 1701
ir Sussex per
Tract.

" Thus," an *Assumpsit* for fifteen Quarters of Malt, Evidence of fourteen or fifteen Quarters of Malt and the Plaintiff nonsuited, because not the same Promise but an Obligation to deliver twenty Bales of Wool or twenty Pounds,—upon Non-payment by the Obligor, the Obligee may sue on either.

Par 5.

Variance, where fatal or otherwise.

Action on a Promise that the Defendant would not fue the Plaintiff, and Evidence " that an Action was com-
" menced and the Defendant promifed, on certain confider-
" ation," that he would *forbear* to fue him on that Action,
" Queftion, whether this fhall b-" allowed to maintain the
Declaration. becaufe the forbearing to fue fupports the
fuit began, " and the Promife * not to fue, as laid in the
" Declaration, feems to relate to an Action impending,
' and not yet commenced How, 1, it appears to be
" good, becaufe an Action having been commenced is a
' Matter within the Knowledge of the party fued on this
" Promife, being his own Act, and therefore no furprize
" on him by the manner of declaring on the Promife and
' the material Point is the fame, that he who fues on the
" breach of this engagement fhould be free from legal Mo-
" leftation on the Matter *P 387'

If a Man affumes to pay fo much money for Hops, if
delivered well packed, picked, dried, and bagged, this is
good Evidence on a *general Affumpfit* becaufe fo they ought
to be whether " fpecially" contracted for or not, for the
party ought to make them merchantable Goods and fee
them well delivered without any fpecial Provifion in the
Contract, though there were no more than a general Sale
of the Commodity ; " and the undertaking fpecially to do
' what he was under a general antecedent Obligation of
" doing, makes no Variation as to the Right of fuing on
" the general implied Contract

" But where the Contract turns on a fpecific Agreement L. N P 145.
" between the Parties, there it muft be ftrictly laid and
" proved accordingly

* " Thus if an Agreement be to deliver *merchandizable* *P 388.
" Corn, Proof of an Agreement to deliver good Corn of 1 Raym 735.
" the *fecond fort* is not good

" So where the Agreement declared upon was to fell the At Salop, 1744.
" Plaintiff all his *merchandizable* fkins, and the Agreement
" produced by the Plaintiff, and figned by the Defendant,
" was fo, yet the Agreement of the fame Date, entered in
" the Defendant's Book, being to fell all his merchandizable
" *Calves* fkins, the Plaintiff was nonfuited

" But fome Cafes where, in reality, there may be deem-
" ed no Variance, feem to have been decided rather on
" temporary than fettled Principles, and have been there-

L. N P qua
fupra, 145

"fore juʰly difcriminated from Authorities on which to
"rely as ʾrecedents.

"Such ʾere ʾheʾe in relation to *South Sea* Contracts

D of Rutland.
v Hodgſon
P 1 G 1 re
Raym. Ch J

"The Plaintiff declared upon a Promiſe to pay ſo much
"Money ʾpon the Plaintʾff's transferring ſo much *South Sea*
"Stock: at the Trial, the Note produced appeared to be to
"pay on a Tranſfer to the Defendant or his Order yet this
"was holden to be a Variance, and the Plaintiff nonſuited."

Payne and
Paxex.

*P 389.

S.r 74

Churchill v
Wilkins. T R
Mic. 27 G III.

"The Contract declared on was, to deliver ſtock the
"22d of *Auguſt* the Contract in *Evidence* on the * Trial,
"by entry in the Broker's Books, was a Contract for *open-*
"*ing* It was notorious that the Books were to open
"on the 22d, and the Broker ſwore he took the 22d of
"*Auguſt* and *opening* to be *convertible* Terms. However,
"this was then taken to be a fatal Variance

"In an Action upon a *ſpecial Agreement* to buy all the Tallow
"which the Defendant ſhould have to diſpoſe of, at 4s per ſtone.

"The Agreement proved was, that the Plaintiff ſhould
"give 4s. per ſtone, and if he gave any other perſon more,
"he was to give the ſame to the Defendant

"*Eyre*, Baron, before whom this was tried, held this a
"Variance from the Declaration, and nonſuited the Plain-
"tiff, and upon Cauſe ſhewn, the *Nonſuit* was confirmed

C-a EL 79

"Though the Promiſe alleged be proved, yet if it appear
"to be made on a different Conſideration than mentioned
"in the Plaintiff's Declaration, it is not ſufficient or if it
"was made on the Conſideration alleged and ſomething
"elſe beſide

C o Ja 127

"Where in an *Aſſumpſit* two Conſiderations are alleged.
"the one good and ſufficient, the other idle and vain, if
"that which is good be proved, it ſufficeth"

* P. 390.

Godb 151

* In an *Aſſumpſt* the Plaintiff declares, that the Defendant, in Conſideration of Marriage, aſſumed to do ſuch a
Thing, upon *Ner aſſumpſt* the Plaintiff proves a Promiſe, in
Conſideration of Marriage, to do three ſeveral Things of
which two were performed, and the third left undone,
for which he brought this Action

To this the Objection was taken that the Contract proved
was ſubſtantially different from the Contract alleged, for to
do three ſeveral things, and to do one thing, are not the
ſame, but ſubſtantially different, and the Exception was
allowed, and the difference taken, between a verbal Contract and a Deed for if the Contract had been by Deed,
the Plaintiff might have declared for Non-performance of
one only becauſe it appears by the *Profert*, that the Contract alleged, and the Contract proved, are exactly the
ſame; and therefore a Complaint for the Non-performance
of

of one only will be well enough, but on a verbal Contract, you muſt prove the individual Contract you ſet forth in your Declaration for if a Latitude were allowed that Contracts might be taken to be the ſame that ſubſtantially differ, no man by the Allegation could prepare any Defence; for " in" the great Variety of Tranſactions that are among Mankind, ſeveral Contracts might have a reſemblance one to another: and " therefore" men ought to be put to prove the ſame individual Contract

* " But in an Action of *Aſſumpſt* againſt a common Carrier   * P 391.
" for not ſafely carrying the Goods of the Plaintiffs *Con*   Moore und
" *ſignors*, which he undertook to carry for a ceitan hire   other v Wil-
" and reward, to be paid by the Plaintiffs, it was proved   ſon 659 T R/
" that the *Conſignee* had agreed with the Plaintiffs to pay   E 27 G III.
" the Carriage, and it was therefore urged that the Evidence
" did not maintain the Declaration The Judge who tried
" the Cauſe being of that opinion the Plaintiff was *non-*
" *ſuited* On a Motion for a new Trial, the Judge candidly
" took notice, that on conſidering the Queſtion, he found
" he had miſtaken the point of Law for that the (private)
' Agreement between the Vendor and the Vendee could
" not prejudice the (public) Right and Obligation between
" the *Carrier* and the Vendor, the latter being in Law liable
" to the former for the hire †

T i t. II.

Consideration

" A mere voluntary Contract will not raiſe a Conſider-   Hob 115
" ation ſufficient to maintain an *Aſſumpſit* but if ſuch   Cro. J 181
" Courteſy were moved by requeſt of the Plaintiff, that
" gives an *Aſſumpſit* and therefore, if the Plaintiff declare,
" that whereas the Defendant had differences with ſuch a
" Perſon, who threatened him with an Action, and the De-
" fendant requeſted him to endeavour a Compromiſe, where-
" by a good Underſtanding * might be reſtored, and the ex-   * P. 392.
" pences of the Law avoided; thereupon the Plaintiff did
" do his endeavour, in riding, &c for the furtherance of
' the ſaid Deſire of the Defendant, who, in *conſideration of*
" *the premiſes*, did promiſe to pay the Plaintiff 10 l. it will
" be ſufficient, though the Plaintiff prove no riding, if he
" prove any other effectual endeavour according to the Re-
" queſt · and if the Conſideration were future, namely, that

† *Res inter alios acta alteri nocere (vel præter Jus et æquum pro-
deſſe) non debet.*
Actus privati Juri publico non intercedunt.

" on

" on a promife of 10 l from the Defendant, the Plaintiff
" would endeavour, (in which cafe the Plaintiff muft lay his
" endeavour fpecially) and the Defendant would not deny
" the Promife but the Endeavour, he muft traverfe the
" Endeavour in the general, and not the Riding in the
" fpecial.

" And this leads to a Diftinction between Promifes upon a
" Confideration executed and executory.

Par 2.

CONSIDERATION executed and executory.

" In Cafe of a Confideration executed, the Defendant
" cannot traverfe the Confideration by itfelf, becaufe it is
" incorporated with the Promife, and if it were not then
" acte, it is nudum pactum But if it be executory, the
" Plaintiff cannot bring his Action till the Confideration
" performed and if in Truth the Promife were made, and
" the Confideration not performed, the Defendant muft tra-
" verfe the Performance, and not the Promife, becaufe
" they are diftinct in Fact

* " Where the Action is brought upon mutual Promifes,
" it is neceffary to fhew that they were both made at the
" fame time, or elfe it will be nudum Factum and though
" the Promifes be mutual, yet if one Thing be in Confider-
" ation of another, a performance is neceffary to be aver-
" red, unlefs a certain day be appointed for it.

Salk 22
† P 393
Hob 88.

Par 3

LEADING CASE, explaining the Nature of a CONDITION in
Law

Peeters v Pel-
ter.

On *Affumpfit* the Plaintiff declared, that the 27th of
June, 1712, at *Hoddefden*, the Plaintiff bought of the Defendant, and the Defendant bargained and fold to the Plaintiff *one hundred Quarters* of as good Barley as one *William
Ford's* was to be delivered to the Plaintiff at *Hoddefden*, between Harveft and *Candlemas* in the fame Year, where the
plaintiff fhould appoint, after the Rate of fixteen fhillings
per Quarter, to be paid by the Plaintiff to the Defendant,
whereof the Plaintiff paid to the Defendant two fhillings
and fixpence in hand, and agreed to pay the Refidue at the
times of the Delivery, according to the Quantity of the
fame at every time of Delivery, and according to the Rate
aforefaid that the Defendant, after the faid Bargain, in
Confideration of the Premifes, *affumed* that he would deliver

ger to the Plaintiff the faid Barley fo bargained and fold,
according to the Bargain

On *Non affumpfit* the Jury found four Pounds Damages,
fubject to the Determination of the Lord Chief Juftice
Parker, on a Cafe agreed between the Parties, which in fubftance is this:

* The Defendant, on *Saturday*, the laft of *January*, (Can- * P. 394.
dlemas Day being the *Monday* following) in the Year 1712,
and not before, delivered to the Plaintiff's Ufe, at Mr
Plumer's Malt-houfe at *Hoddefden*, (where the Plaintiff appointed the Barley to be delivered) a Quantity of Barley,
which was fent for *twenty Quarters*, but when the fame was
meafured by *Ford*'s bufhel, it was found to be but nineteen
Quarters and a half according to that meafure

That the Plaintiff, at the time, paid to the Defendant's
fervant, who brought the Barley, *ten Pounds*, and no more;
for although he had the Money, not only which the faid
twenty Quarters of Barley, but likewife the one hundred
Quarters came to, according to the fame Agreement, ready
by him in his Houfe, yet, becaufe the Barley did not hold
out in meafure, he paid only *ten* Pounds, and did not pay
the other fix Pounds at that time, but afterwards paid it to
the Defendant before the Action brought

That the Price of *Barley*, between the time of the Contract and the Delivery of the faid twenty Quarters, rofe
about—&c

" And " if, upon thefe Facts proved, the Plaintiff upon
this Declaration, hath good Caufe of Action, or not, was
referred to Determination

In confidering of this Matter, two Queftions " were "
ftated

FIRST, whether the Plaintiff has a Right to the *Refidue*
of the one hundred Quarters of Barley, having * not paid * P 395.
the full Price for the nineteen *Quarters* and a half within the
time prefixed, but only TEN Pounds towards it

SECONDLY, *whether the Defendant can take any advantage
if this Non-performance upon the Iffue of* NON-ASSUMPSIT?

" And it was argued —

As to the *firft* Point, whether the Plaintiff has a Right to
the Refidue of the one hundred Quarters of Barley, having
not paid the full Price for the nineteen Quarters and a half
within the time prefixed, but only ten Pounds towards it,

" That " here are to be laid down two or three Rules,
which have been " applied " in adjudging feveral " Quef-
" tions of " Law in the Books: and then this Cafe compared with thofe Rules.

" That "

7 Co 9.10,&c.
Ld Raymond,
665, 6.
Styl 186
2 Mod 33, 4
2 Mod. 62.

"That" the firft Rule is, where there are feveral Promifes mutually *executory* and independent of each other, that there the Promifes are Confiderations each of the other, and the Plaintiff may bring his Action for Breach of the Defendant's Promife, even though his Counterpromife be alike broken · becaufe in fuch Cafe the Counterpromife, and the Remedy upon it, is the Confideration of the Defen 'ant's Agreement, and not the Plaintiff's performance of his Promife: according * to *Juftinian's* Rule in the Civil Law, that " *he + who hath in Action for the Recovery of a Thing is deemed virtua* l *y to have the Thing itfelf*," and upon this reafon, concerning mutual Promifes, there are feveral Cafes refolved in the Books

* P. 396.

Hob. 88, 106
Roll. Rep 135,
336

"That" the *fecond* Rule laid down in the Books touching thefe mutual Promifes is,

That where there are any Words " ufed" in any Promife, Covenant, or Agreement, that do not import a *Condition,* they are never conftrued to be *conditional,* " unlefs" elfe the part, would be without all manner of Remedy without fuch Conftruction

Hob 41
Ow 54

This " is" laid down in *Hobart,* in the Cafe of *Cowp* and *Andrews* , and in *Owen,* and in feveral other Books

And it is in itfelf a Rule founded in the greateft Reafon for where Words in themfelves do not exprefs a Condition, the Law will not frame any Conftruction to make them conditional, unlefs fuch Implication be abfolutely neceffary, and it cannot be abfolutely neceffary where the Parties have another Remedy.

If an Annuity be granted *pro Confilio impen'o, vel impendendo,* there the word *pro* is conftrued to be a Condition , becaufe the Party has no other Remedy for the Counfel than by ftopping the Annuity

* P. 397.

* And if an Action be brought upon the common Covenant for quiet Enjoyment in a Leafe, that the Leffee fhall quietly enjoy,' paving the Rent and performing the Covenants ; there though the word *(paying)* would make a Condition, if the party were without Remedy, yet it is not conftrued to be conditional in this Covenant, but the *Defendant* is left to his Remedy upon the Refervation of the Rent and Covenants in the Leafe

2 Sd 280
2 K.b 23
2 lod 3, 5
Roll Abr. 15

And fo it was refolved in the Cafe of *Allen* and *Babington,* and in the Cafe of *Hay* and *Bickerftaff*

So is the Cafe in *Rolle's Abridgement.* There were Articles of Agreement made by *A* in behalf of *B* and *C* and a Covenant that *B* for the Confideration aforefaid in the

+ *Qu. an rner habet ad rem recuperandam, rem habere viactur*

Deed

Deed expreſſed, ſhall convey certain Lands to *C* in Fee;
and *C* covenants, on his part, " FOR the ſaid Conſidera-
" tions," to pay *B* one hundred Pounds· here though
" FOR" would make a *Condition* n the Caſe of an Annuity,
yet ſays the Book, that notwithſtanding *B* doth not aſſure
the Lands to *C* yet *C* is bound to pay the Money, and to
take his Remedy againſt *A* on his Covenant

The ſame Law is laid down in the Caſe of *Nicho's* and
Rainsbrede There *Nichols* brought an *Aſſumpſit*, in Conſideration that he *promiſed* to deliver to the Defendant, to his
own Uſe, a Cow, the Defendant *promiſed* to pay him fifty
ſhillings · adjudged that the Plaintiff nee not aver the Delivery of the Cow, becauſe it is Promiſe for Promiſe

* But, " THIRDLY," if the Defendant's Promiſe do
ariſe on the *Condition* of ſome Act to be done and performed, and not on a *Promiſe* to do and perform ſomething,
there the Act muſt be firſt *executed*, and averred to be performed, before the Defendant's Promiſe can ariſe. for the
Performance is here the Conſideration, and not a Counter-
promiſe.

So is the Caſe, *Rolle's Reports*. In Conſideration of *ten*
Pounds, I promiſe to deliver to you all the Books of the
Law .—it is good without alleging the payment of it ; for
the other may have an Action for it: but if it be, that in
conſideration that you *will* pay (in the future Tenſe) to me
ten Pounds, ✝ I will deliver to you all the Books of the Law,
it is not good without alledging the Payment of the ten
Pounds he muſt aver the Thing to be done. becauſe, ſays
the Book, there is no Remedy on this Promiſe, ſince it does
not ariſe until the Money is paid , for the party does not promiſe to deliver the Books till after payment of the Money.

So is the Caſe of *Hobart* —If I promiſe, in Conſideration
of a Man ſerving me a Year, that I will pay him *ten Pounds*,
there the ſervice ought to be actually performed before he
ſhall bring his Action for the Money, becauſe the Promiſe
for the ten Pounds ariſes * not from the Promiſe to ſerve,
but from the actual ſervice.

So *Brocas's* Caſe —The Lord of the Manor covenanted
with his Copyholder to aſſure to him and to his Heirs the
Freehold and Inheritance of his Copyhold · and the ſaid
Copyholder, in Conſideration of the ſame performed, covenanted to pay ſuch a ſum the Court held that the Copyholder was not tied to pay the ſaid ſum before the Aſſur-

Margin notes:
Hob 88 cited
in Lutw 250
I d Raym 665.
and ſee Salk
171, 2
* *Thorpe* v
Thorpe, agree-
ably to the Di-
ſtinction in the
next Page
* P. 398.

125, 336.

Hob, 106
7 Co 10 b.
See Vin Abr
8, 9
5 Vin 57 pl 1
* P. 399.

3 Leon 219

✝ *It does not ſeem too much to aſſert, that about the Reign of* Elizabeth, *ten Pounds would approach nearer to the Purchaſe of a complete*
Engliſh *Law Library than* 1500l. *at preſent.*

ance made and the Covenant performed; but if the Words had been in *Confideration of the faid Covenants* TO BE *performed*, then he is bound to pay the Money prefently; and to have his Remedy over by Covenant.

In all thefe Cafes the *Confideration* of fuch Promifes is not the *Counterpromife* or *Agreement*, but the *Performance:* but where the *Confideration* is merely a *Promife* or Agreement to do fomething, there the firft Promife arifes before fuch Agreement on the Plaintiff's part is performed, or fulfilled

Now, to compare this Cafe to the precedent Rules

FIRST, There are no Words that are conditional · for the Premife is not expreffed in any conditional Terms, that if he be paid for the Delivery of the firft Barley, he fhall deliver the reft:

But the Words of the Bargain are altogether abfolute · for they fet forth, that the Plaintiff bought of * the Defendant, and the Defendant bargained and fold to the Plaintiff one hundred Quarters of Barley, according to the Rate of fixteen fhillings per Quarter for every Quarter, to be paid by the Plaintiff to the Defendant; and that the Confideration of this Bargain was the Payment of two fhillings and fixpence in hand, which was the only Act *executed* · and the Act *executory* was the Agreement to pay the Refidue at the Times of the Delivery of the Barley, according to the Quantity of the Barley at every time delivered, and according to the Rate to be paid

Now in this executory Act there is nothing laid that is antecedently to be performed before the firft Promife is to rife · fince the firft Promife doth import a complete Bargain and Sale of the one hundred Quarters, and fuch Promife is not to arife upon any *precedent Condition*, or Act to be firft performed or done by the Plaintiff

And if there be " not " Words in the Bargain, which import a Condition, and the Counterpromife is in its own Nature executory, the Law will not raife any Condition upon any implication whatfoever, but leave the Parties to their mutual Remedies

The rather in this Cafe, becaufe if the whole had been delivered at once, then plainly there had been nothing conditional in the Bargain and if the Defendant provided himfelf that there fhould be feveral ⸗ Deliveries, and does not actually provide, by an exprefs Condition, that if the Mony be not paid for what he hath delivered at once, he fha'l not go on to deliver, the Law cannot create fuch a Condition by Implication , fince the Promife, on the Plaintiff's Part, is totally executory, and there is no Act executed

* P. 400

⸗ P 401

executed or ſtipulated to be performed, before the Promiſe ariſes.

And if there were any ſuch Act *executed* that was neceſſary as a *precedent* Condition to the raiſing of the Promiſe on which the Plaintiff declares, it would be an Objection to the Declaration for not averring ſuch precedent Condition to be performed.

And for this there is the Caſe of *Betteſworth* and *Campion.* Yelv 133, ‡ The Plaintiff, as Executor to his Father, declares there was a Communication and Agreement that the Defendant ſhould have all the Iron made at ſuch a Furnace, paying after the Rate of forty ſhillings *per* Ton; upon which the Teſtator did *aſſume* to the Defendant, that he ſhould have all the Iron made in that Furnace, in Conſideration whereof the Defendant promiſed to pay the Teſtator according to the Rate aforeſaid —and ſhews, that the Defendant had ſo many Tons, which amounted to ſo much Money: and it was objected, in Arreſt of Judgment, that the Plaintiff had not ſhewn that the Conſideration was performed on his part, and that the Defendant had *all* * the Iron made at the Fur- * P. 402, nace, which was the Conſideration that induced the Defendant to make his Promiſe. but it was anſwered, and reſolved by the Court, that the Conſideration, on the part of the Plaintiff, was, *not* that the Defendant ſhould have all the Iron as an Act *executed*, but that the Teſtator *promiſed* that the Defendant ſhould have all the Iron: ſo that the Conſideration on each part was the *mutual Promiſe*, the one to the other, for which there is a mutual Remedy.

So here, that which induces the Defendant's Promiſe to deliver the one hundred Quarters of Barley is *not the actual Payment* of any ſum more than the two ſhillings and ſix pence mentioned in the Declaration.

But it is the promiſe of paying the Reſidue which is undertaking for an Act *executory*, and ſo expreſſed in the future Tenſe that it ſhould be paid on the Delivery of each Quantity of Barley, wherefore it is the *Promiſe* to pay, and not the actual Payment, that makes here the Conſideration

The SECOND Queſtion is, whether the Defendant can take advantage of this upon the Iſſue of *Non aſſumpſit*

And for this my Lord *Hobart* is expreſsly to the contrary Hob 106 There the Conſideration was, that if a Man * ſerved me a Cro Eliz 250. Year, I ſhould pay him ten Pounds there my Lord *Hobart* (14) ſays that if the ſervice was not done, and yet the Promiſe, * P 403. " as in the Declaration," the Defendant muſt not traverſe Roll Rep 43. the *Promiſe*, but he muſt traverſe the *Performance* of the (16) 401,(29). ſervice, (11). Roll Rep 391, service; becaufe they are diftinct in Fact, though they muft concur to the barring of the Action

And here the true Difference feems to be between an *Affumbfit* in *Deed* and an *Affumbfit* in *Law* · for an *Affumpfit* in Law, in Confideration of Money received, creates, from the natural Juftice, a Promife of Payment. here " there- " fore' the actual Payment, or fatisfaction, or a Releafe, or any other Matter that excufes Payment, may be given in Evidence on *Non affumpfit*

For when the natural Juftice for Repayment of the Money ceafes, there the Law no longer creates a Promife; and therefore thofe Matters that go by way of Excufe, are proper *Evidence* upon *Non affumpfit* · becaufe there is really no Promife when the Defendant can fhew there is no Juftice to pay the Money

But where the Promife arifes by *Act of the Parties*, and the Defendant would fhew any thing for an Excufe for Non performance, there he muft fhew it to the Court by proper *Pleading* · becaufe it confeffes the * Being of fuch Promife, or that fuch Promife was actually made by the Parties, and avoids it by fhewing fome *fpecial Matter* or reafon for not performing it

* P. 404.

2 Cid 236
Mod 210
3U 29

This Diftinction was taken in the Cafe of *Bedford* and *Clarke*, and in the Cafe of *Fitz* and *Freeftone*.

It was argued by the Defendant, that fuch Bargains are made for ready Money: and if the Plaintiff promifes to deliver fuch Goods, and the Defendant promifes to pay for them; in common Underftanding, if the Goods are ten- dered, and the party has not the Money, this fhall excufe and for this they quoted 17 *E* IV fol 1 where an Action of Trefpafs was brought by the Plaintiff againft the Defen- dant for breaking his Clofe, and taking his Corn: and " the " Plea of Juftification was," that a long time before the Trefpafs fuppofed, the Plaintiff and Defendant bargained at fuch a Place in *London*, that the Defendant fhould go to a Place where the Oats were, and fee them, and if they pleafed him when he faw them, that then he fhould take them, paying the Plaintiff three fhillings and four pence an Acre one with the other.

That the Defendant went to fee them, and was content with the Bargain, and for that Reafon took the Corn, which is the fame Trefpafs

* P 405

* Remcke,
Div. 1

* It was there objected that this Plea was not good, be- caufe he had not paid the Money according to the Bargain; and it would be mifchievous, if, upon fuch Communication, a Man fhould take another Man's property before the Mo- ney is paid and *Littleton* there put a Cafe, that if a Man

fhould

should come to a Draper, and there demand of him how much, he will have for such a Piece of Cloth, and he says so much, upon which the other says he will give him so much for the Cloth, but does not give him the Money, if he takes the Cloth, the Draper may maintain an Action of Trespass So *Choke* put a Case, that if a Man should ask how much he should give for my Horse at *Smithfield*, and I say, so much, if the other does not pay the Money immediately, I may sell the Horse to whomsoever I please for otherwise I should be compelled to keep my Horse against my own Contract until such time as the Man should pay it, which was certainly against the Intention of the Parties in their Agreement. and *Littleton* said, that in all such *forehanded* Bargains, there was a *Condition implied* in Law, that it should be delivered upon payment, and that if Payment did not follow, the whole Contract should be void

Fulb. ut sup 6. *Noy'e Max* *P 87. Ch 42.*

And it was argued in this Case, that common Usage implied such a Contract where the Goods were to be delivered for ready Money and that if the * Money was not paid, I should not be obliged to part with my property

* P. 406.

PARKER, Chief Justice, " in the principal Case," resolved, That the Non-performance of such a Bargain might be properly given in Evidence upon a *Non assumpsit* · for now *Non assumpsit* is held to be the general Issue in this Action, though they formerly held the contrary

But as to the Bargain itself, he said that the Defendant having delivered nineteen Quarters and an half without ready Money, he had dispensed with the Condition as to that Quantity for though he might have chosen whether he would deliver it until paid; yet when he did deliver it upon Credit, and without the ready Money paid down, it was a dispensing with the Condition as to that Quantity

" But", then there was no reason that he should not go on with the Delivery of the Residue according to his Contract for suppose a Condition should go along with it, as it is " argued" for the Defendant, that upon every Delivery a ready Payment should be made, yet if the Defendant has dispensed with the Condition as to the Quantity delivered, by letting the Plaintiff have it without prompt payment, that will be no reason why he should not go on to make the Delivery of the Residue according to his Bargain for if * the Argument be good, that the Law implies a Condition, upon the Delivery of every Quantity, that there should be prompt Payment made by the Plaintiff, yet it will not raise a farther Condition, that if he deliver the first Quantity upon Credit, he should not go on to make a

* P 407.

Delivery

Delivery of the reſt for ready Money, which here the Deſ fendant has not done

And it " is" by no means to be admitted, that if the Defenoant delivered part upon Credit, which was his own Folly, that it ſhould excuſe him for delivering the reſt for ready Money according to his Promiſe

Par 4.

Promiſe in CONSIDERATION of ASSETS good to maintain an ASSUMPSIT againſt an Executor.

Atkins & Lx
v P'l
E. 5 G III
B R
Cowp 284
H 1 22 G III
Pawle & L.
v Snider.
Cowp 289.

" That ASSETS came to his hands is a good Conſideration " for the promiſe of an Executor to pay whereon to ground " an Aſſumpſit

" But if the party be charged generally, as in his own " right, and not ſpecially as Executor, and the promiſe " appear to have been made by him as Executor, in conſ- " deration of Aſſets, the Judgment can only be of the Goods " of the Teſtator "

* P. 408.

* SECTION III.

NON ASSUMPSIT infra SEX ANNOS.

We now come to the Iſſue of Non aſſumpſit infra ſex Annos, " that he did not undertake within ſix Years."

TIT. II.

This Iſſue is founded on the Statute 21 Ja c 16 and lies in all Actions on the Caſe· and the reaſon of the Statute is, becauſe the Debt muſt be ſuppoſed to be paid, if the Action be not brought within that Compaſs " and it is " for the Intereſt of the public, as well as of Individuals, " to defend againſt latent Claims where the remoteneſs of " the Evidence might otherwiſe intercept a ſatisfactory De- " fence upon the Merits " for Witneſſes may die or change their Abode, ſo that it may be a very hard thing to prove the payment of the Debt and the Law Wager is avoided by Aſſumpſit. for if a Man were, in caſe of ſimple Con- tract, charged with a Debt he would avoid it by Law Wager: but this charges a perſon with the damage for not performing that promiſe on which he depended, which being a charge that ſuppoſes Deceit and Injury, there was no Law Wager allowed.

This Iſſue does not lie on any Aſſumpſit between Merchant and Merchant for they may have occaſion to truſt one an- other

other much longer, and therefore thefe perfons are excepted by the Statute " but how far this Exception extends
" will hereafter be noticed "

* This Iffue is pleaded either by way of Negative to the * P 409.
Declaration, and then it is pleaded that the Defendant
cometh and defendeth the Force and Injury when " and
' where he ought to do," and faith that he did not take on
himfelf at any time within fix Years before the day of the
fuing out of the original Writ, and for this he putteth himfelf on the Country

Or elfe they may plead it by way of Bar, and then it is
—and faith that the aforefaid Plaintiff the Action aforefaid
hereof againft him ought not to have, becaufe he faith that
he did not undertake, &c and this he is ready to verify.

And the Reafon why either way of pleading is allowed,
is, becaufe that it is a direct Negative to the Plaintiff's Declaration _which is the Gift of the Action and therefore it
may properly conclude to the Iffue, there being a direct
Negative contrary to the Plaintiff's Affirmation, and becaufe it exhibits a Statute Law to the Court in Difcharge of
the Plaintiff's Demand, it may be pleaded in Bar

On the Iffue of Non affumpfit infra fex Annos, the Defendant proves a Debt of nine Pounds ten Years ago, and an
Acknowledgment of the Debt within fix Years, and an offer to pay five Pounds for the * whole the Plaintiff was * P 410.
nonfuit for the Acknowledgment of the Debt is no more
than he does by his Plea but there muft be a new Promife
of the Debt within fix Years to make the Action hold, and
here the Promife or Offer to pay five Pounds, gives no Action for the nine Pounds

But the Confeffion of the Debt within the time is Evidence
of a new Promife (though not of itfelf a new Promife, if
found by a fpecial Verdict) for that may be Evidence of a
new Promife to a Jury, which, when fpecially found to the
Court, will not amount to a Promife in exprefs Words

" And now a very flight acknowledgment is held fufficient
" to authorize a finding againft the Defendant on this Iffue;
" and this agreeably to the fenfe and fpirit of the Statute,
" which is not for preventing Debts clearly proved from
" being paid on account of the length of time they have
" been due, but to eftablifh a fecurity againft fraudulent
" Demands, when Vouchers perhaps are loft, or Witneffes
" to a payment made without written proof are deceafed,
" and to guard againft furprize upon Executors or other
" Reprefentatives, by bringing forward Claims obfcure and
" ambiguous by the remotenefs of the Period to which
                                                        " they

" they are referred :—to be a fhield of *Innocence*, not a fcreen
" of *Evofion*

* P 411.
L N P 149
2 Vertr 151
Heyl rg and
Hafting
£.ls MSS.

Salk 29
S C. Car.n
471
1 Ravm 471

Owen-ncWol-
ley, Scl45,
1751

L N P 49

~ P _r c.

Yen, In..

(..' B. R

*" If the Defendant plead *Non affumpfit infra fex Annos*,
" it is fufficient for the Plaintiff to prove a *Promife* to pay
" within fix Years, without any other *Confideration* for the
" Plea admits a Caufe of Action before fix Years. And if
" the Defendant fay, *Prove it due, and I will pay it*, fuch
" a Promife, with a Proof of the Debt, is fufficient but,
" as hath been intimated above, a bare acknowledgement
" of the Debt, or of Delivery of Goods within fix Years,
" is not in itfelf a new Promife, though it is *Evidence of*
" *a Promife* a fimilar Obfervation will be applied to
" TROVER

" In an Action by an Executor for Money had and re
" ceived to the Ufe of his Teftatrix, where upon this Iffu-
" the Defendant was proved to have faid, I acknowledge
" the Receipt of the Money, but the Teftator gave it to
" me Mr. Baron *Chve* directed the Jury to find for the
" Defendant for the Qualification of the Acknowledge
" ment was fuch as to negative, inftead of admitting a Pro
" mife to pay

" In *Affumpfit* on a promiffory Note, the Defendant plead
" e A n affumpft infra I x Annes and it appeared on the
" Trial that the Defendant was furety in a Note for 7 s
" and that I Years were elapfed fince the Note was given
" but had not a Demand within fix Years, the Defendan
" fay, You know I had not any of the Money myfelf,
" but I am willing to pay half of it The Judge was of
            a lile Affizes, that this Promife took it out of
        t c. but the Jury found for the Defendant on a
            n for a new Trial, the Court clearly held that the
        Judge as right, that this Promife was fufficient and
        granted a new Trial †

                                        " In

2 P - k, -
  c
: r cn le
1 1 c o' ,
w 1- S ^ Ill
P 1 n 2t .
Vol II E
I 1d 176.

† This feems to be *Yea* (Sir *W*) v *Fouraker*.

In alufion o w ha been precedently quoted from a late
Work of eminence it will not be difpleafing to attend to the re
marks of a very acute and difcriminative Writer.

*Se times civil Laws, for ufeful Purpofes, require a ceremony or
form, e a cabure that is t anting, their decrees run contrary to the
uhel tenor of Juftice, but ere who takes advantage of fuch chicanes
is not commonly regar ed as an Honeft Man.*

*Thus the interest of fo te require that Contracts be fulfilled, and
to re is not a more material article of natural or civil juftice But
the Cr ff er of a trifling circumf ance will often, by law, invalidate
a Contract, in foro humano, but not in foro confcientiæ, as di-
vines exprefs themfelves. In thefe Cafes the Magiftrate is fuppofed*
                                                        only

" In an *Indebitatus assumpsit*, on a promise to pay *on De-*
" *mand*, the Defendant pleaded *Non assumpsit infra sex Annos* : Ca. K B 444.
" the Plaintiff demurred, for that the Plea should have been,
" that there had been *no Demand* within six Years after De-
" mand But the Court held that an *Indebitatus assumpsit*
" shews a Debt due at the time of the Promise, and there-
" fore the Plea is good · but if the Promise had been of a
" collateral Thing, which would create no Debt till Demand,
" it might be otherwise. In such Case the Plea is that which
" shall next be mentioned

Tit. III.

Actio non accrevit infra sex Annos.

" This is the proper Plea where the *Cause of Action* is dif-
" *tinct* from the Promise · thus on *Assumpsit* in consideration
" that the Plaintiff, at the request of the Defendant, would
" receive *A* and *B* as his *Lodgers*, and diet them, whereup-
" on the Defendant was charged with Promise to pay—The
" Defendant pleaded, *Non assumpsit infra sex Annos* · and on
" Demurrer * it was holden to be no Plea ; for it is not mate-   * P. 413.
" rial when the Promise was made, if the *Cause of Action*
" arose within six Years ; therefore the Plea ought to have
" been, that the Action accrued not within six Years.

Tit. IV.

On Action on an Account current, *Effect of this Plea of* Non
assumpsit infra sex Annos

" The Defendants were Executors of the Executor of   Cotes v Harris
" *W W* and in an Action of *Assumpsit* pleaded *Non af-*   &al Guildhall
" *sumpsit infra sex Annos* . the Plaintiff replied, that on the   Tr 29 & 30
" third of *June*, 28 G II he sued out a Bill of *Middlesex*   G II.
" against the Defendants . and that the *Testator*, in his Life-

rly to withdraw his power of enforcing *the right , not to have* alter-
ed the right
Here the general reasoning meets the subject under consideration · in another place the argument applies directly to the
subject itself
  It is highly requisite that prescription or long possession should con-   Sect on III
stitute property but what number of days, or months, or years, shall be   P 1 p 263
sufficient for that purpose, it is impossible for reason alone to deter-
mine Civil Laws here supply the place of the natural Code and
assign different terms for prescription according to the different Uti-
lities proposed by the Legislator Bills of Exchange and promissory
Notes, by the Laws of most Countries, prescribe sooner than Bonds and
Mortgages, and Contracts of a more formal Nature.
                                                              " time,

" time, promifed to pay the Demand within fix Years be-
" fore the Bill of *Middlefex* fued. On this two points were
* P. 414 " debated; the * firft, whether on an Account current, of
" which part was *within fix Years*, fuch part drew the whole
" out of the Statute? *Dennifon* Juftice was of opinion that
" the Statute was a Bar to all *Items* of the Account beyond
" the fix Years

" Another Queftion on this Cafe was, whether it came
" within the Defcription of *Merchants Accounts* fo as to be
" excepted from the Statute

" *Dennifon* held this Claufe to relate only to mutual Ac-
" counts and reciprocal Demands between one perfon and
" another in commercial Dealing but that fimply a Demand
" of *A* againft *B* in the common Way of Bufinefs, as of a
" Tradefman againft a Cuftomer, could not be called a *Mer-*
" *chant's Accounts.*

Tit. V.

Executors

" If an Fxecutor take out proper Procefs within a Year
" after the Death of his Teftator, if the fix Years were not
" lapfed before the Death of the Teftator, though they be
" lapfed within that Year, yet it will be fufficient, under the
" Equity of *Section* the *fourth*, to take it out of the Statute †
* P 415
Green Cafe
hi 5 A B R
Salk M5S ‡ " If an Fxecutor bring *Affumpfit* on a Promife made
' to his *Teftator*, and the Defendant plead that he made no
" Promife *to the Teftator* within fix Years, if Iffue be joined
" *thereon*, a Promife to the *Executor* within fix Years will not
" maintain the *Iffue*

SECTION IV.

Of Bailment

" The Confideration of Actions founded on *Bailment*
" properly has place here as fometimes the *general*, fome-
" times the fpecial *Affumpfit* relates to them. fometimes the
" Cafe refulting from them refts in CONTRACT, as the *pre-*
" *ceding*, and fometimes it is founded on TORT, as the *fub-*
" *fequent* Clafs of Actions.

† On 1 ke Principles a Debt gone by Statute is fufficient confideration for a promife (as in Bankrupt's *Certificate*) fo that it
fhall not be *nudum Pactum* as on a Devife to pay *Debts*, the b-
nefit fhall extend to creditors otherwife barred by the Statute of
Limitations.

" I. *Mandate,*

"We will obferve on *Bailments* under the following Divi-
"fion, purfuant to the Analyfis:

  " 1. *Mandate,*
  " 2 *Loan of Hire,*
  " 3 *Loan of Ufe,*
  " 4 *Pledge,*
  " 5 *Depofit.*

Tit. I.

" 1. Mandate, or *gratuitous Commiffion.*   L B 52—52,

" A gratuitous Commiffion, or *Mandate*, in the fenfe of
" the *Roman Law*, is one of the fimpleft, *and at the fame   * P. 416,
" time one of the moft unfrequent, in the Order of Bail-
" ments, being where a perfon undertakes to perform an
" Act for another, without reward or an antecedent Ob-
" ligation

" This was the Ground of the Cafe, in which the Lord
" Chief Juftice Holt took occafion to confider the feveral
" *fpecies* of *Bailment*

" In that Cafe, *Cogges* v. *Bernard*, of which a very ela-   1 Ld Rayn.,
" borate and interefting Report is preferved, the Facts   909
" were thefe   Tr. 2 A,

" The Plaintiff declared, that whereas *Bernard*, the
" Defendant, had, on the *tenth* of *November*, 13 *W.* III
" at, &c undertaken fafely and fecurely to take up feveral
" hogfheads of Brandy then in a certain Cellar in D and
" fafely and fecurely to lay them down again in a certain
" other Cellar in *Water lane*, the Defendant and his Servants
" and Agents *negligently and improvidently* put them down into
" the faid other Cellar, whereby, *through Defect of Care*
" of him, the Defendant, his fervants and Agents, one of
" the Cafks was ftaved, and a great Quantity of Brandy,
" *videlicet*, fo many Gallons, fpilt

" After *Not Guilty* pleaded, and a Verdict for the Plaintiff,
" there was a Motion in Arreft of Judgement and the Cafe,
" however familiar in the *Roman* Law, being deemed new
" in the *Englifh*, it was argued *feriatim* by the whole Court.

* " The ftrefs of the Objection was, that the Defendant   * P. 417,
" was neither laid to be *a common Porter*, nor that he was to
' have any *Reward* for his labour

" Holt, Chief Juftice, after entering into the Diftinc-   Vin III 27.
" tions and Principles of the feveral forts of *Bailments*, pro-   § 684.
" nounced the Bailee, in this Cafe exercifing a *gratuitous*   Br. Act III 100,
" *Commiffion* for the benefit of the Plaintiff, to be liable for   2 H VII 11.
" the Damage occafioned by his neglect and mifconduct: 919, 20.
" for that the Neglect is a *Deceit* to the *Bailor*, and a breach
" of *truft* is a fufficient caufe of action and for that it is

Vol. I.   U   " not

" not *rudum pactum*, the *undertaking* itself, to which the Plain-
" tiff gave faith, being a sufficient Consideration

L. B. 52.
' And the neglect, for which the *Mandatary* is answera-
" ble, is according to the *degree* of skill and diligence which
" the Business he hath undertaken requireth

L B 567
" And for *Non f-asance*, by which Damage accrueth, a
" Mandatary may be chargeable equally as for Mis-feasance
" Yet he is not liable in the same extent as if he contracted
" for a reward · for then he may not retract without consent
" of the party who hath retained him, but in a *gratuitous*
" *Commission*, if he withdraw his offered Assistance *before any*
" Damage incurred, and give notice that he cannot perform
" the Work, no Action at Law is maintainable to enforce
*P 418   " him to the performance

L B 59, 60
Ld.Raym ,10   *· it is justly observed, that however perhaps *suppos'd*
" new, the Case of *Bernard* was not new in reality · and of
" this *Pollexfen* was well aware, who cites the Writ in the Re-
" gister, of the *Pipe of Wine*, and of the *Cure of the Horse*,
" as Authorities *in point*, with this remark, that in a Writ,
" as in a Declaration, no circumstance *necessary* to found the
" Action may be omitted and farther the Writ and Declara-
" tion in *Rastel* for *negligently* and *improvidently* raising a
" Qualset in oge, all without consideration alleged.
' The observation of the learned and judicious Author
' of the excellent *Digest* now cited, and of which we shall
" avail ourselves throughout this Title of the Work, appears
" perfectly well founded, that there was no necessity for a
" *special* understaking to deliver safely and securely, in order

13 H VI
" to have made the Defendant liable in *Bernard*'s Case that
' indeed the Contract lying *in feasance*, this Condition was
" implied in the Nature of it and that in the Case already
" cited in the Year Books, for *negligently* keeping the Plain-
" tiffs sheep, whereby they were *drowned*, neither reward
" nor *special* undertaking are stated
" There may also be a *gratuitous Commission* or *mandatory*
" Bailment of mere Custody

Tit II

2 Loan of Hire, or Location.

L B 75
" The *locati*, *Conductio* of the *Roman* Jurists, or *Loan of*
' *Hire* of our *English* Lawyers, is one of the most common
' of all Bailments, being of daily Utility in the general in-
" tercourse of Life   It is *threefold* ·
Hire, 1 Of Things.
  2 Of Industry *concerning* Things.
   1 *Workmanship*,
   2 *Carriage*

" By

* " By the LOAN of THINGS the *Hirer* gains a *transient* * P 419.
L B 86
" property in the thing hired, the Lender an absolute one in
" the stipend or hire this consequently, not like the pre-
" cedent, is *onerous* to the Bailee, and *profitable* singly to the
" *Bailor*, but it is mutually advantageous to both a distinc-
" tive circumstance not to be overlooked in determining the
" *degree* of care incumbent upon the *Hirer*

   " This hath been expressed in Terms grammatically *super-*
" *lative* but GRAMMAR does not give Law to LOGIC
" the found Construction must be derived not from Words
" merely, but Things from Reason, Analogy, and from con-
" fiftent Authorities.

   " Therefore when JUSTINIAN describes this care as that of l 3 25; 5.
Bract 62 b
Ld Raym 916,
" the DILIGENTISSIMUS *Paterfamilias*, when BRACTON,
' as usual, adopts the expression of *Justinian*, when HOIT
" considers (incidentally) the Hirer as bound to the UTMOST
" Diligence, when a modern Publication demands of him L N P 72.
" *all* IMAGINABLE Care these strong Terms will restrict
' themselves, from the Nature of the subject, to a general
" import of *such* Care as men of *common prudence* exert to-
" wards their *own* property he is answerable therefore for
" *theft*, if suffered by *carelessness*, but not for *robbery*, unless
" incurred by *gross* or wilful neglect And he is answerable
" no farther than as to those particulars which the Owner
' hath not committed to the Care of another not, confe- L B 86,7.
" quently for the horses, if the Owner of a *hired* Carriage
" fend his own Poftillion

   + " And it is upon this Limitation of an Excuse for Acci- * P 420.
Tr per Pais.
399
" dents, which the reasonable Care of the Party, had the
" property been absolutely his own, could not be expected
" to prevent, that *on*" a Promise to restore an Horse hired Lefley's Cafe,
cited in Mu-
traver's Cafe,
1652 B R.
" for a Journey, if the Defendant give in Evidence that the
Horfe died in the Journey, without the Rider's fault, the
Obligation of his Promise is avoided in as much as it becomes impossible by the Act of God + without any fault of
U 2
the

+ I here transcribe the admirable Reflections of the Author of
the Law of Bailments though few Readers, studious of under-
standing the Analogies of Laws and Reason, will be without the
Tract, such is the strength of Judgment and Accuracy of Diftinction manifefted in that Work, recommended by an Elegance of
Arrangement, and illustrated by a Felicity of Style, which not
more adapts itself to the Flow of Fancy and the Embellishments
of Fiction than to the precision of Law and the dignity of moral
Science

   Although the ACT *of* GOD, *which the Ancients too call* Θεοσίαν,
and vim divinum, *be an expression which long Habit has rendered
familiar to us, yet perhaps on that very Account it might be more
proper, as well as more decent, to substitute in its place* inevitable
Accident.

the Defendant . and no man's promise fhall be fuppofed to
" extend to Impoffibilities ; " for what is not within his
" power by fair and probable Intendment," is not the fubject of any Man's " implied" Promife , " though it may be
" of a Warranty.

Par. 2

HIRE of INDUSTRY concerning THINGS

" In civilized Life *Induftry* in almoft every inftance confers
" a manifold Value on the fubjects of its Exertion, beyond
" their Utility or imaginary Eftimation as grofs Materials'
" and at the fame time, as many Articles can be wrought
" only in a certain place to their deftined Perfection, or as a
" preference to a particular Artifan governs the Employer,
" this Induftry of *Manufacture* would not anfwer its Intention,
" and indeed could be very imperfectly exerted without the
" fecond branch of Labour, that of *Conveyance* But in
" order of Time and dignity of Relation, that of Work-
" marfhip hath an evident Precedency

*P 421
L 8 91, 2

* " Where Things are bailed, that they may be *wrought*
" to a certain Form and Purpofe for a *Reward*, the *Bailee*
" is not only bound to the *workmanly performance*, but to
" *ordinary* Care for the *prefervation* of the thing committed
" to him And this without an exprefs Contract for a *Price*,
" or a *fpecial* Undertaking for their fafe Cuftody fince, on
" the one hand, the delivery of Articles to a Perfon who
" profeffes to work for profit by his Trade is an implied en
" gagement to pay the cuftomary and reafonable Price, and
" on the other hand, the acceptance of materials to be wrought
" is equally an implied undertaking that they fhall be fafe
" ly kept as well as properly manufactured for the Ufe of the
" Owner.

Accident Religion and Reafon, which can never be at variance
without certain Injury to one of them, affure us that not a Guft of

See the Preface
o Hawkes-
worth s C l
I 3 1 of V3
&c.

Wind blows, nor a flafh of Lightning gleams, without the know
ledge and guidance of a fuperintending Mind But this Doctrine
lofes its grace, and fublimity by a technical application of it, and
1 , 1 fome inftance border even upon profanenefs, and Law, which
is a practical fcience, cannot ufe Terms too popular and perfpicuous.

Before, however, we leave the Train of Obfervations fuggefted
by this, in itfelf awful, though too familiarized mode of expref
fion, it will be pleafing to advert to the Language of that glori

†CLEANTHIS

ous Fragment which thus, in a philofophic Hymn † of almoft un
equalled Excellence, celebrates the univerfal Energy of the
Supreme

Οὐδ- τι λιλνεται Έωγον επι χθ-ς σε δι χκ Δαιμον
Ολ. και αιθ ριον δαιον Πολον.

" A perfon

" A perſon may indeed, without any farther concern re- L. B 96, 7.
" lating to them, have the mere *keeping* of Goods for
" *Hire*: and this *Cuſtody* engages him to ſuch Care as the
" *Nature* of its *Object*, joined with the Conſideration of the
" *Reward* ſtipulated for his *attention* and *vigilance*, import

" One ſpecies of *Depoſitaries* for *Hire* is indeed under
" ſtricter Obligations from the views of *public Policy*, in
" regard to their employment· and this is the *Inn-keeper*,
" * who is *neceſſarily* as ſuch a general Depoſitary of the * P. 422.
" Goods of Travellers reſorting to his Houſe, and ſhall
" not, while he hath 100m, excuſe himſelf on a *refuſal* to
" take charge of them, or that, notwithſtanding his *Dili-*
" *gence* to prevent it, the Goods have been *deſtroyed*, *da-*
" *maged*, or *ſtolen* by any perſon whatever

" And this upon Principles exactly analogous to the Caſe
" hereafter to be conſidered of a *common Carrier*, and with
" ſimilar Limitations, where the Force is *irreſiſtible* and re-
" *medileſs*.

" But the *Innkeeper* may diſcharge himſelf from this Bendl 18 pl.2.
" *primâ facie* Liability, if" in an Action on the Caſe brought Dy 158 b
" againſt him for ſuffering the Goods of the Plaintiff to be Ander 29.
taken out of his Houſe, and *Not Guilty* pleaded, he give in pl 69
Evidence that he told the Plaintiff that his Houſe was full, R Abr. 3.
and that he could not lodge him " and prove the Truth of
" the Facts according to ſuch Notice," and that notwithſtanding the Plaintiff went and lodged in his Houſe for
this *Evidence* falſifies the Declaration " by" proving that
there was no Injury done to the Plaintiff as Gueſt to the
Defendant

Par 3

Hire of Carriage

" A *private* Carrier for Hire is anſwerable for that ge-
" neral good Faith which implies that he ſhall carefully
" convey the Goods entruſted to him, ſo as to *deſerve* the
" recompence for which he hath undertaken to carry them.
" The Degree of Care muſt be proportioned to the Nature
" of the Goods when he is appriſed of them that would
" be *groſs Negligence* with reſpect to *Glaſs*, *China*, or a *Pic-*
" *ture*, which would be ſufficient care of leſs damageable
" Articles Travelling by Night, or through unfrequented
" Roads, with a ſum of Money, might incur reſponſibility·
" though with Goods not likely to be ſtolen or injured in
" conſequence of being thus conveyed, the Caſe would not
" have been ſo.

Par.

* *Par* 4.

Of *a common or* public *Carrier*

L B 103, &c   " The common Carrier is anfwerable for much more
" fo far, that nothing fhort of inevitable and remedilefs
" Lofs, as by *Tempeft*, or by public *Infurgents*, can exempt
" him

1 R. Abr 2 nl.   " This ftrong univerfal Liability is believed to have been
Woodl ef and   " eftablifhed when the *fecurity* of *Trade* and *Commerce* be-
Gerus H1   " came a grand object of Attention in the Reign of Queen
36 Eliz B R.   " *Elizabeth*
L B 103, 4

     " It cannot (which has been well obferved) be the re-
" ward of Hire upon which this peculiar Liability depends
1 Inf. 89, a.   " for though fo much ftrefs has been laid on this circum-
" ftance by Lord *Coke*, it would in itfelf oblige only to or-
" dinary Care the true Ground muft be derived from the
" extent and peculiarity of this *public* employment, the dan-
" ger of combinations, and the great importance to the
" Community of a certain Refponfibility.

Forward r   " Accordingly in a very recent inftance, an Action on
ard   " the Cafe was brought againft a *common Carrier* for not
   G I'I   " fafely carrying and delivering the Plantff's Goods It
   R 27   " was tried at the *Dorchefter* Summer Affizes, before Mr
" Baron *Perryn* when the Jury found a Verdict for the
" Plaintiff, fubject to the Opinion of the Court on a Cafe
" referved, which was this
     " That the Defendant was a *common* Carrier from *London*
" to *Shaftefbury* That on *Thurfday* the 14th of *October*,
" 1784, the Plaintiff delivered to him on *Weyhill* twelve
' pockets of Hops to be carried by him to *Andover*, and
* P 424   " to be by him forwarded to * *Shaftefbury*, by his public
" Road Waggon, which travels from *London* through *Ando-*
" *ver* to *Shaftefbury* That by the courfe of travelling,
" fuch Waggon was not to leave *Andover* till the *Saturday*
" Evening following That in the Night of the following
' Day, after the Delivery of the Hops, a FIRE broke out
' in a booth, at the diftance of about 100 yards from the
" booth in which the Defendant had depofited the Hops,
" which burnt for fome time with inextinguifhable violence,
" and during that time communicated itfelf to the faid
" Booth, in which the Defendant had depofited the Hops
" and entirely confumed them, *without any actual Neglrgence*
" *in the Defendant* That the Fire was NO r occafioned by
" Lightning

P 33   " Lord MANSFIELD, after ftating the Cafe, thus deli-
" vered the opinion of the Court.

                             " The

" The Queſtion is, whether the common Carrier is liable
" in *this* Caſe of *Fire?* In all the Caſes for a hundred years
" back, it is moſt clear that there are Events for which the
" Carrier is liable *independent of his Contract* But there is
" a farther degree of Reſponſibility by the Cuſtom of the
" Realm; that is, by the COMMON LAW, a *Carrier* is in
" the Nature of an INSURER It is laid down that he is
" liable for every Accident, except *by the* ACT *of* GOD, or
" *of the King's Enemies* Now, what is the ACT of GOD?   * P. 425.
" I conſider it to mean ſomething in oppoſition to the * Act
" of Man for" otherwiſe " every thing is the Act of God,
" it happens by his permiſſion or his appointment To pre-
" vent litigation, confuſion, and the neceſſity of going
" into circumſtances impoſſible to be unravelled, *the Law*
" *preſumes* againſt the *Carrier* , unleſs he ſhews it was done
" by the King's Enemies, or by ſuch Act as could not
" happen by the intervention of Man, as Storms, Lightning,
" and Tempeſt

' If an armed force comes to rob the Carrier of his
" Goods" (ſo they be not Invaders or Rebels) " he is liable·
" and a reaſon is given in the Books, which is a bad one ;
" that he ought to have a ſufficient force to repel it that
' would be impoſſible in ſome Caſes, as for inſtance, in
" the riots in the year 1780 The true reaſon is, for fear
" it may give room to colluſion,--that the Maſter may con-
' trive to be robbed on purpoſe, and ſhare the ſpoil

" In this Caſe, it does not appear but that the Fire aroſe
" from the Act of ſome Man or other It certainly did
" ariſe from ſome Act of Man for it is expreſsly ſtated not
" to have happened by Lightning The Carrier, therefore,
" in this Caſe, is liable : in as much as he is liable for in-
" evitable accident.

" Judgment was accordingly for the Plaintiff   * P 426.

† " And ſo early as the Reign of *Elizabeth* the Law thus L B 106, 7.
" far ſettled, the inference was obvious and neceſſary, that Hob c 30
" the circumſtance of *water carriage* no way eſſentially af- 2 Cro 330
                                                             Rich and Knee-
" fecting the Caſe, an *hoyman* muſt be equally liable   land
                                                             12 Mod 480
" It was, however, ſtill contended that neither the Au- 1 Str 128
" thority of Precedents, nor the juſt Extent of the Prin- Palm 548
" ciple, would apply to the Maſter of a SHIP This at-   W Jo 159.
" tempt to diſtinguiſh the reſponſibility in the Caſe of a ſhip Vide alſo
" from that annexed to an *hoy* or *barge*, after ſolemn Argu- Vale v Hall
                                                             Mic 24 G II.
" ment both of Civilians and common Lawers, before one B R
" of the greateſt men of his own or any Period,† was, as 1 Wilſ 281
" might naturally have been foreſeen, completely unſucceſsful. † Mors and
                                                             Slew
                                                             1 Ventr 100
                                                             2,8
                                                   Par   Raym 220
                                                             Ld Raym.92

Par. 5.

LETTERS *sent by the* GENERAL POST.

L. B. 109—12.
" There remains one Species of *Bailment* of *Carriage* of
" amazing comprehensiveness with regard to its objects. †
" of constant use and neceffity, and connected with the moft
" important interefts public and private, the *conveyance* of
" LETTERS under the Eftablifhment of the POST OFFICE.

12 Car. II. c 35
" A *private* Poft-mafter was fubject to the fame liability
" as another Carrier but reafons not originally fo much of

Carth 487
E. 11 W III.
† *Lane* and
Catem.
S C
5 Mod. 455 6
and Ld. Raym
646
" Revenue, as of fuppofed State Expediency, having an-
" nulled the liberty of employing a *private* Poft where the
" *public* could be employed, a Cafe came to be debated,
" whether the Poft-mafter of the public Office was anfwer-
" able for a *Lofs* circumftanced as it there was.

❋ P. 427.
❋ " The Plaintiff brought this Action againft the De-
" fendants as *General Poft-mafters* and on a fpecial Verdict,
" they were ftated to have been in the Exercife of that
" Office at the time of the Plaintiff's fending *Exchequer*
" *Bills* to the Value of 300*l* in a Letter directed to a Per-
" fon in *Worcefter*, and delivered to the Defendants at their
" Office in *Lombard Street* · and that this Letter with the
" Bills was *not* conveyed to *Worcefter*, but *loft* by the negli-
" gence of the Defendants and their fervants

" For the Plaintiff it was contended, that the Statute,
" when it took away the liberty of fending Letters, and va-
" luable Articles inclofed in them, by the particular Pofts
" previoufly fubfifting, could not be fuppofed to fubject the
" individual to the hazard of a Lofs incurred under a public
" Mode of Conveyance, which he was not at liberty either
" to regulate or decline that the *falary* of the Defendants
" arifes out of the Revenue created by the Poftage of Let-
" ters, and that the Revenue itfelf is a fecondary Object of
" the Act

" On the other fide, the *fmallnefs* of the Poftage was ar-
" gued as a proof that it was no *premium* for *rifque* · the
" indefinite refponfibility it would infer, if the Poft-mafters
" fhould be anfwerable for all employed under them by Sea
" and Land · that the fecurity was not given from the
" Under-officers to the Defendants, but to the Crown that
" *Exchequer Bills* were equivalent to Money, and therefore
" not meant to be protected by the Act but, unlefs *fpeci-*
" *ally* accepted by the Poft-mafters, muft abide the hazard
" at the Peril of the fender.

† *By a late calculation it appears that the* weekly average *of*
Letters *fent from the* GENERAL POST OFFICE *in* LONDON *is more
than* 100,000*l.*

" Three

* " Three of the Judges, HOLT diffentient, were for the * **P. 428.**
" Defendant. The Cafe, with his Reafons, and thofe of
" the Majority of the Bench, is very concifely but excel- Salk. 17.
" lently reported in *Salkeld*

" Afterwards the Queftion of the Liability of the Gene- † *Whitfield v.*
" ral *Poft-mafters* came to a folemn Inveftigation in the fol- Lord *Le De-*
" lowing Cafe . *fpencer et al.*
                                                              E 18 G III.
" In CASE, the Declaration confifted of three Counts. Cowp. 755.
" The *firft* fet forth the Statute of ANNE for eftablifhing
" one general POST OFFICE through the Kingdom, and
" that one *Poftmafter-general* fhould be appointed by Letters
" Patent under the Great Seal who and his deputy and de-
" puties, and *no other Perfon*, fhould have the receiving, &c.
" of all Letters That by virtue of the faid Act, one
" General Poft-Office was erected, and a Poft eftablifhed
" between the city of *London* and the Town of *Lewes*, in
" the County of *Suffex* . and that the *Defendants* were ac-
" cordingly appointed to the Office of *Poftmafter-general*,
" TO HAVE AND TO HOLD the fame, with all powers, &c.
" during the King's pleafure, referving always to his Ma-
" jefty all *Duties* and Sums of Money payable for the
" *Poftage* of Letters and that the King, by the faid Let-
" ters Patent, of fpecial grace and mere motion, granted
" to the Defendants the falary of 2000*l per Annum*, PAY-
" ABLE OUT OF THE REVENUE AFORESAID that the
" Defendants were accordingly poffeffed of the faid Office :
" and they holding and exercifing the faid Office, the
" Plaintiff, on the 24th of *September*, 1774, being poffeffed
" of a Bank Note for * 100*l* inclofed it in a Letter, feal- * **P. 429.**
" ed and directed to one *John Moxham*, at *Lymington*, in
" the County of *Hants*. That the Letter was carried from
" *Lewes* to *London*, and there entrufted to the care of the *De-*
" *fendants*, in order to be by them fent and delivered as direct-
" ed that neverthelefs they, not regarding the Duty of their
" Office, but wholly neglecting the fame, did not deliver, or
" caufe to be delivered, the faid Bank Note fo inclofed by
" reafon of which neglect the faid Bank Note was wholly
" loft out of the faid Letter.

" The *fecond* Count ftated a Lofs, by *negligence* of the
" Defendants, through the *theft* of RICHARD MICHEL,
" *fervant of the Defendants, and a Letter-forter, who converted*
" *it to his own Ufe*

" The *third* charged generally, that by *negligence* of the
" *Defendants*, the Note was *ftolen*

" The Jury found a SPECIAL VERDICT (after *acquitting*
" the *Defendants* on the *firft* and *third* Counts,) fetting forth
" the eftablifhment of the Poft Office under the Statute in
" the beginning of the prefent Reign for carrying the Re-
" venues of the Poft Office to the aggregate Fund ; the ap-
                                              " pointment

"pointment of the *Defendants* POSTMASTERS, as in the
* P. 430. "Declaration; * their power to appoint deputies, fubfti-
"tutes, *forters,* &c and to fufpend, &c at difcretion and
"to take fecurity in the Name and to the *Ufe* of the Crown,
"and to fettle *falaries,* to be paid by the Receiver-general

"The Jury find farther the falary of 2000*l per Annum*
"granted to the *Defendants,* payable by the Receiver general

"And that the faid Letters exprefs that the *Defendants*
"fhall not be *chargeable* for the *Revenue,* or for the *Officers*
"by them appointed, fave *only for their own voluntary de-*
"*faults* and *mifeazances*

"They find the *Defendants* in the *exercife* of their faid
"Office and the *appointment* of *Richard Michel* as a *forter*
"under them. and the *fecurity* taken of him to the King's
"*Ufe.* His *Oath* not to delay or embezzle, his employ-
"ment, his receipt of the falary, the fending of the BANK
"NOTE, as alleged in the Declaration, the delivery of it
"at the GENERAL POST OFFICE, in order to be *forted* and
"conveyed to *Lymington,* and its coming into the hands of
"*Richard Michel,* as *forter,* and being by him felonioufly fe
"creted and *ftolen,* and that he was thereupon tried, con
"victed, and executed

"The Cafe was twice argued, and Lord MANSFIELD de
"livered the Opinion of the COURT

* P 431. *"His Lordfhip faid, that the Cafe was to be confidered
"*Firft,* as it ftood in 1699, before the Determination of
"*Lane* v *Cotton.*

"And then, as it ftood fubfequent to that Cafe,

"That the POST OFFICE, as ftated in Argument, was
"firft erected by *Cromwell* during the Ufurpation, and af-
"terwards regulated more fully by the Statute of *Charles.*

"That there never had been any Action brought, either
"on the ordinance or the ftatute, prior to the Cafe of *Lane*
"and the Mode of Action in that was the fame as in the pre
"fent That by the *Form* of Action, which was the fame
"in both, no demand appears to have been intended on the
"*Fund* · for this is a Form adapted to a demand on the Poft-
"MASTER *perfonally*

"That it appears indeed, both from the Terms and from
"the practice, that the Fund is not left anfwerable under the
"ftatute, nor was originally fo defigned to be The whole
"is *appropriated* and no item of a Lofs was ever charged as
"coming in under the *appropriation*

"And in this Action clearly, the charge not applying to
* P. 432. "the Fund, the Ground is, as in the Cafe of "*Lane* and
"*Cotton,* that the *Poftmafter* is liable for his *Hire* But what-
"ever was argued at the *Bar,* Lord HOLT, in that Cafe,
"does not extend the Liability fo far as that Principle would
"carry

" carry it ; which muſt apply to Loſſes wherever incurred ᐧ **Ld Raym:**
" for he takes a difference between a Letter *loſt in the Office* **650, 653.**
" by a ſervant employed by the *Poſtmaſter*, and a Loſs *on the*
" *Road*, or by *robbery* after the Mail has been ſent *out of*
" the Office

" That Lord HOLT compares a POSTMASTER to a *common*
" *Carrier*, or Maſter of a *Ship* taking goods on board for
" *freight* but that the compariſon appears not to hold : for
" that the *Poſtmaſter* has no *hire*, enters into no *contract*, car-
" ries on no merchandize or *commerce* that his Office is a
" branch of the *Revenue*, and of *Police*, created by Act of
' Parliament

" That the ſecurity is given to the *Crown* ᐧ that they take
" the oaths taken by all public officers , that they are charge-
' able with *capital felony* under circumſtances which in a *com-*
" *mon Carrier* or other perſon would be puniſhed only as a   **§ 5.**
" *breach of truſt* That the Caſe is remaikable, in which the
" *Poſtmaſter* is made liable it being for *not finding poſt-horſes*
' and there too in a Caſe where it is ſcarcely poſſible he'
" ſhould be *perſonally* in fault, his liability is very particularly
" reſtricted

 ᐧ " That an Action on the Caſe would have lain againſt **∗ P. 433.**
" the *Poſtmaſter*, or any of his ſervants, *ſorter* or others,
" for a *perſonal* neglect in their ſeveral departments, by which
" a Loſs was occaſioned to the Plaintiff. but not ſo for mere
" *conſtructive* Negligence

" That the *ſalary* is only for the trouble of executing an
" Office concerning the *Revenue* and *Police*, and by no means
" either a *premium* of *inſurance*, or a conſideration implying
" reſponſibility for Loſs happening by default of others than
' the party charged

" That the POSTMASTER, therefore, is like other officers,
" the *Lords Commiſſioners of the Treaſury*, of *Cuſtoms* and
" *Exciſe*, the *Auditors* of the *Exchequer*, who were never
" thought to be thus reſponſible for the negligence or miſ-
" conduct of the inferior officers

" That thus upon Principles it ſtood in 1699, when a ſolemn
" Judgment was given, that *an Action on the Caſe would not lie*
" *againſt the POSTMASTER for a Loſs in the Office by the negli-*
" *gence or crime of his ſervant* That the Nation underſtood
" it to be a Judgment, the Bar had ſo underſtood it ;
" the Parliament and popular Uſage had ſo received it , and
" therefore it made no difference if the *Writ of Error*
" was ſtopped by paying the Money, as had been ſuggeſted.
" So, ＊ many times had the mail been *robbed*, yet no Action
" ever brought. Merchants dividing their Bills, and ſending   **∗. P 434.**
" them by different Poſts, was an expedient which argued they
" did not look to a Remedy againſt the Office

" That

" That if there could have been any previous doubt, the
" solemn Decision in the Cafe of *Lane* and *Cotton* put the
" Queftion beyond difpute

" That therefore the whole Bench was clearly of opinion
" that the Action would not lie

Par 6.

SPECIAL ACCEPTANCE *in the Cafe of a* common Carrier

" A common Carrier may fpecially accept and to a certain
" Extent, compatible with the Nature of his Employ, *Evi*
" *dence* that he has fo accepted will difcharge him

L B 1c6.

" And therefore" in an Action for fafe Carriage, if no
Price be fet, it fhall be intended for the common Price, " if
" no Diftinction as to the Value or Nature of the Goods be
" proved, it fhall be taken generally ," but if a fpecial Agreement be fet out to carry for 4s per hundred, it muft be
proved , and " if a *fpecial Acceptance* be pleaded, it muft be
" proved alfo "

" And this *fpecial* Acceptance, which fhall difcharge, will
" admit of other proof than abfolutely a direct perfonal No
" tice to the party individually

Burr Manuf.
2298
E. 9 G III

" In *Gibbon* v *Paynton and another*, the *Defendant* was
" charged, as *Coachman* of the *Birmingham Stage*, for 100l
" in Money, fent by his Coach and *loft* It was fent hid in
" hay in an old Nail Bag The Bag and the Hay arrived
" fafe, but not the Money

※ P. 435.

※ " It was proved that the *Coachman* had inferted an *Adver*
" *tifement* in the *Birmingham* Paper, with a *Nota bene,* that
" the Coachman would not be anfwerable for *Money,* or Jew-
" els, or other valuable Goods, unlefs he had *Notice* that
" it was Money, or Jewels, or other valuable Goods, that
" were delivered to him to be carried He alfo proved dif-
" tribution of *Hand-bills* to the fame effect

" It was proved to be a Matter of Notoriety in that Coun-
" try, that the Price of carrying Money was three pence in
" the pound, which is 1 ¼ *per Cent*

" The *Plaintiff,* it appeared on the *Evidence,* was a Dealer
" in *Birmingham,* and had frequently fent Goods from thence.
" It was proved that he had been ufed for an Year and an
" half to read the *Newspaper* in *which* this Advertifement
" was publifhed , though it could not be proved that he ever
" actually read that individual Paper wherein it was
" inferted

" It was farther proved, by a Letter of the Plaintiff, that
" he knew the Courfe of this Trade, that Money was not
" carried from that Place to *London* at the ordinary Price of
" the Carriage of other Goods.

" The

" The Jury found for the Defendant.

" On the Motion for a *new Trial* the Counsel for the *P 436.
" Plaintiff denied the Facts proved to amount to Evidence
" of a special Acceptance

" They contended that a *Carrier* is liable, though he did
" not know it was *Money*, and cited the Cafe in *Alleyne* and
" *Ventris*, and in *Carthew* · together with that in *Strange*,
" where the Lord *Chief Juflice* KING held, that if a Box
" be delivered generally to a Carrier, he is answerable, Titchburne
" though not told there was Money in it · otherwise if he v White
" asks, and is answered in the negative, or accepts *conditionally*, Str 145.
" provided there be no Money.

" On the other fide, they argued on the *Fraud* of the
" *Plaintiff* and on the *Advertisement*

" Lord MANSFIELD observed on the greater *Responsibility*
" of a common Carrier for Hire than that of a mere
" Bailee   And said,

" This Action is brought against a *common Carrier*   His
" *Warranty* and *Insurance* is in respect of the *Reward* he is
" to receive · and the Reward ought to be proportionable
" to the Rifque   If he makes a greater Warranty and In-
" furance, he will take greater Care, use more Caution, and
" be at the Expence of more Guards and other Methods of
" Security: and * therefore ought, in Reason and Justice, to * P. 437.
" have a greater Reward   Consequently, if the Owner of
" the Goods has been guilty of a *Fraud* upon the Carrier,
" such Fraud ought to excuse the carrier

" That as to the Cases cited from *Alleyne* and *Ventris*, in
' the former, the Judge allowed the Jury might consider
the Fraud in the *Damages*, in the other, whatever might
" be thought of the reafons on which the Carrier was held
' liable, it was allowed, that with all the other Facts of the
" Cafe remaining, the Carrier would have been excused
" if he had faid, that he dared not take charge of it, *if* it
" contained *Money*

" That the Cafe in *Carthew* was determined upon *true* Carth 485.
' Principles   There, two Bags were delivered to the Car- Sir Joseph
" rier fealed up   The fervant of the Plaintiff told the De- other, v
" fendant's *Book-keeper* it was 200 *l* and defired a Receipt Morrice
" for the Money   the Book-keeper gave a Receipt purport-
" ing accordingly, and promising to deliver them to *T*
" *Davis* at *Exeter*, on fuch a day, he paying 10 *per Cent* for
" *Carriage* and *Rifque*

" The Carrier being robbed on *Hounflow Heath* in the *Night*
" *time*, paid 200 *l* to *Davis* agreeably to his Undertaking.

" The Plaintifs in their Action declared for 450 *l* and
" proved that full fum to have been in the Bags at the time
" they were delivered to the Carrier as 200 *l*

" The

* P. 438.   * " The *Chief Justice* was of opinion that the *Carrier* wa,
" anfwerable for no more than the 200 *l* which he had alrea-
" dy paid his *particular Undertaking* and the *Reward* extend-
" ing no farther than to that fum : and the Defendant had a
" Verdict accordingly

" And in an Action againft the fame Carrier, in a Cafe
" fimilarly circumftanced, there was the like Direction and
" the like Verdict

" That in the principal Cafe the *Fraud* is manifeft and
" the *Advertifement, Hand bill, Price* of *Carriage* of *Money*
" from *Birmingham,* weie, together with the Letters of the
" Plaintiff, circumftances of *Prefumption* of *Acceptance* proper
" to be left to the Jury and that, on the whole of this
" Cafe, the Plaintiff ought not to recover and in this the
" other Juftices, *Tates, Afoot,* and *Willes,* concurred, of
" whom the two former gave their reafons

Tit III.

L. B. 64, 74.   " We are now to treat briefly of the LOAN of USE · and
" this is *lending* fomething *gratuitoufly,* which is to be *fpeci-*
" *cally* returned this being beneficial *only* to the *borrower,* re-
" quires *extraordinary Care.*

Tit IV.

" We are to confider next that Species of BAILMENT
" which is termed a PLEDGE

Par 2.

" A PLEDGE, or PAWN, is an engaging of Goods by way
" of fecurity for the payment of a Debt

L. B. 75, 9   " This confequently is a *Bailment* of mutual Convenience
" and the PAWNEE is anfwerable for *ordinary* Neglect of
" which the Pledge being *fecretly* taken from him by *Theft*
" is *prefumptive* Evidence but for *robbery* he is not refponfi-
" ble, if it be fo loft. unlefs fpecial circumftances appear of
" his wantonly expofing the Pledge, as Jewels, for inftance,
L. B. 70, 81, 2 " to the hazard of being thus forcibly taken from him the
* P. 439.   " Author of the Effay to which we have had fuch · conft.nt
" recourfe upon this fubject hath clearly fhewn the Doctrine
" of Lord *Coke* on this head to be neither confiftent with the
" nature of the fubject, nor with prior opinions and that
" the fubfequent ores have not adopted it.

Tit

Tit V.

" We are led now to the laſt Claſs of *Bailments*, which is
" that by DEPOSIT and the principles on which this ſpe-
" cies of implied contract is ſtated by Sir *William Jones* ap-
" pear to be perfectly diſtinct and ſatisfactory ; though the
" old Caſes and Obſervations of great Lawyers upon them
" were in no ſmall degree confuſed.

Par 2.

" A DEPOSIT is a Bailment of Goods to be kept for the L. B. 117.
" *Bailor*, without recompence

" As this is ſimply advantageous to the *Bailor*, and neither L. B. 36, 52.
" beneficial to the Bailee as the bailment of *Uſe*, of *hire*, or
" of *pledge*, nor implies ſkill as the *commiſſion* of *employment*,
" the Bailee is anſwerable only for *good Faith*, in which is
" included the avoiding of groſs Neglect. unleſs by volun-
" tary application, or by ſpecial Agreement, be either impli- L. B. 47, 8.
" edly or expreſsly obliges himſelf farther

" On the whole, it appears that a *Bailee* of *Uſe* is reſpon- L. B. 120, 1.
" ſible for *ſlight Neglect*, a *Mandatary* of *employ* is anſwera-
" ble for the *ſkill* and *care* preſumed in the Nature of the ſub-
" ject, an *Hirer*, *Pawnee*, *Workman* for Hire, and one who
" undertakes *cuſtody* or *conveyance* for reward, are anſwerable
" for Loſs by *ordinary* Neglect · a *Depoſitary* is liable in gene-
" ral for *groſs Negligence* only The Caſe of *Inkeepers*, and
" the much ſtronger one of *Carriers*, depend upon the par-
" ticular Nature of their reſpective Buſineſs ; which is re-
" ſtricted by public Policy from the temptation of colluſive
" practices difficult to be detected, and is therefore ſubject to
" a peculiar Liability "

END *of the* FIRST VOLUME.

Lightning Source UK Ltd.
Milton Keynes UK
UKHW020610120320
360196UK00008B/158